Rethinking *Missio Dei* among Evangelical Churches in an Eastern European Orthodox Context

Vladimir Ubeivolc

MONOGRAPHS

© 2016 by Vladimir Ubeivolc

Published 2016 by Langham Monographs
An imprint of Langham Publishing
www.langhampublishing.org

Langham Publishing and its imprints are a ministry of Langham Partnership

Langham Partnership
PO Box 296, Carlisle, Cumbria CA3 9WZ, UK
www.langham.org

ISBNs:
978-1-78368-104-4 Print
978-1-78368-127-3 Mobi
978-1-78368-126-6 ePub
978-1-78368-128-0 PDF

Vladimir Ubeivolc has asserted his right under the Copyright, Designs and Patents Act, 1988 to be identified as the Author of this work.

All rights reserved. No part of this publication may be reproduced, stored in a retrieval system or transmitted, in any form or by any means, electronic, mechanical, photocopying, recording or otherwise, without the prior written permission of the publisher or the Copyright Licensing Agency.

Unless otherwise indicated, scripture quotations are taken from the New American Standard Bible®, Copyright © 1960, 1962, 1963, 1968, 1971, 1972, 1973, 1975, 1977, 1995 by The Lockman Foundation, Used by permission.

British Library Cataloguing in Publication Data
A catalogue record for this book is available from the British Library

ISBN: 978-1-78368-104-4

Cover & Book Design: projectluz.com

Langham Partnership actively supports theological dialogue and a scholar's right to publish but does not necessarily endorse the views and opinions set forth, and works referenced within this publication or guarantee its technical and grammatical correctness. Langham Partnership does not accept any responsibility or liability to persons or property as a consequence of the reading, use or interpretation of its published content.

Dr Ubeivolc's book is an excellent introduction to mission theology and practice in the Eastern European Post-Soviet setting. Based on solid academic reflections and expert knowledge of the evangelistic practices of Christian churches encountering each other in mission, the book offers invaluable insights into the missiological conceptualizations and paradigms of mission engagement in a culturally Orthodox context. Grounded in the particular context of mission encounters in Moldova and in the erudite use of the overarching concept of *missio Dei*, the author explores resources of, and argues persuasively for, a holistic ecumenical cooperation in common gospel-witness to the transforming presence of God in the contemporary social and spiritual realities of life. I commend this richly textured work to academics and scholars-practitioners seeking to understand mission in times of momentous transition in Eastern Europe.

Parush R. Parushev
Senior Research Fellow, International Baptist Theological Study Centre,
Amsterdam, Netherlands

The concept of *missio Dei* has not been well known in the context of the former Soviet Union. Vladimir Ubeivolc has presented it here not only as a key concept for mission, but also as a central point at which the evangelical and orthodox dialogue can take place. As mission has often been a divisive issue between the different traditions, this research is a turning point and marks out a better way of understanding and appreciating each other in light of the mission of God. Opening this book, the reader will appreciate the perspective offered and the ground proposed for continuing what mission is and church in mission needs to be.

Peter Penner
Director of Advanced Studies, Professor for Mission and New Testament,
Haus Edelweiss Campus, TCM International Institute

Contents

Abstract ix

Acknowledgments xi

Abbreviations xv

Introduction 1
    Purpose and Motivations of the Current Dissertation 2
    Situation in Moldova 3
    Situation in the Union of Evangelical Christian Baptist Churches 5
    Definition of the Basic Conceptual Apparatus 7
        Missio Dei 7
        Evangelical Churches 7
        Eastern European Orthodox Context 8
    Overview of the Presented Dissertation 9
    Expected Results 11

Part 1 The Evangelical Churches in an Orthodox Context
Moldova 13

Chapter 1 15
The Birth and Development of Evangelical Churches in Moldavian Orthodox Context
    The Emergence of Christianity in the Territory of Moldova 16
        The Emergence of Orthodoxy in the Territory of Moldova 16
        The Emergence of the First Non-Orthodox Groups 18
        Communities of *Molokans* 18
        Mennonite Communities 19
        Evangelical Communities 22
        Baptist Communities 23
        General Overview and Conclusions 26
    The Growth of Evangelical Churches in Moldova in the Period
    (1918–1944) 28
        Self-identification of Moldavian Evangelical Baptists 28
        New Challenges 32
    The Growth of Evangelical Churches in the Soviet Period
    (1944–1991) 36
        Evangelical Churches in Stalin's Time 36

  Evangelical Churches in Khrushchev's Time 39
  Evangelical Churches in Brezhnev's Time...................41
  Evangelical Churches in Gorbachev's Time 44
 Conclusions..44

Chapter 2 47
Mission of Evangelical Churches in Moldova from the End of the Twentieth to the First Decade of the Twenty-First Century
 Religious Situation after Collapse of the USSR Block 48
 Evangelistic Crusades and Church Growth in
  Independent Moldova 55
 Theological Reflections in the ECB Union.........................73
 Conclusions..75

Chapter 3 77
Contemporary Relationships between Evangelicals and the Orthodox Church
 The Orthodox Church in Moldova in the Early 21st Century............77
 Proselytism and Foundations for Conflict between
  Evangelicals and the Orthodox Church 82
   Overview of the Moldavian Situation 82
   Theological and Ideological Foundations for Conflict 85
   Canonical Territory and the Ecumenical Movement 91
   "Aggressive" Evangelism..97
 Evangelical-Orthodox Dialogue in Moldova in the
  Early 21st Century 102
 Conclusions..108

Part 2 Missiological Paradigms and Their Connections with Churches in Moldova.. 111

Chapter 4 113
How "Mission" is Perceived by Evangelical Theologians
 Managerial Missiology 113
 Post-Imperial Missiology..121
 An Anabaptist Missiology 130
 Conclusions..138

Chapter 5 141
How "Mission" is Perceived by Orthodox Theologians
 The Foundation and Content of Orthodox Mission........142
 Kenosis as an Incarnated Method of Orthodox Mission ...153
 Theosis as the Final Goal of Orthodox Mission 159

  Conclusions 166

Chapter 6 169
 How "Mission" is Perceived in Ecumenical Circles
  Missio Dei as an Ecumenical Paradigm 169
  The Content of *Missio Dei* 177
  The Goal of *Missio Dei* 187
  Conclusions 192

Part 3 Perspectives for the Mission of Evangelical Churches in Moldova 195

Chapter 7 197
 The Trinitarian Foundation for Mission
  Mission of the Father 197
  Mission of the Son 208
  Mission of the Spirit 217
  Conclusions 222

Chapter 8 225
 Analytical and Synthetic Evaluation of the Missiological Paradigms
  Distinctions and Similarities in Different Missiologies 225
   Orthodox Missiology *vis-à-vis* the Church Growth Movement 226
   Orthodox Missiology *vis-à-vis* the Lausanne Movement 227
   Orthodox Missiology *vis-à-vis* the Anabaptist Movement 231
   Orthodox Missiology *vis-à-vis* the Ecumenical Movement 233
   Comparative Analysis of All Paradigms 239
   Mission of the Orthodox Church *vis-à-vis* the Mission of ECB in Moldova 241
  Mission of the Church – Synthetic Dynamics for the Whole Church 245
  Conclusions 254

Chapter 9 255
 Holistic and Cooperative Approach in Mission
  Biblical, Theological and Practical Aspects for Holistic Mission in Moldova 256
   Social Responsibility and Social Action 256
   Prophetic Presence 260
   The Relationship between the Prophet and Social Problems in the Bible 262
   Prophets and Social Activity Nowadays 263
   Evangelism or Witness? 268

  Mission as Dialogue and Common Witness.....................................273
    Common Witness in Soviet Time 273
    Common Witness in Contemporary Neighboring Countries...276
    General Situation in Ecumenical Circles..................................279
    New Paradigm for Evangelical Churches in Moldova from a
    Missio Dei Perspective..283
  Conclusions...291

Conclusion... 293

Bibliography... 301
  Primary Sources 301
  Books and Monographs 303
  Articles, Essays and Component Parts within Books 308
  Theses and Dissertations 318
  Electronic Sources...319
  Interviews 319
  Web Sources 320

Abstract

The main purpose of this research is to discover what God is doing among and through evangelical Christians in Moldova. The vast majority of the Moldavian population affiliate themselves with the Orthodox Church. The country is full of Christian symbols, people are aware of the name of Jesus Christ, and almost every settlement of the country has a visible Orthodox presence in church building and priest. At the same time, Moldavian Evangelical Christian Baptists (ECB) are very active in doing mission by church planting and preaching the gospel. The union of ECB from Moldova experienced significant church growth in the 1990s. The beginning of the twenty-first century shows very different results – decreasing numbers of church members and new believers. Many churches show signs of frustration and apathy, while applying the same missionary methods they were using ten to fifteen years ago. This dissertation tries to evaluate the missionary approaches in Moldova, and in harmony with that, to shape a missionary paradigm for evangelical churches.

The proposed dissertation consists of an introduction, three main parts and a conclusion. The first part describes the Evangelical churches in a Moldavian Orthodox context, talking about the birth and development of the Evangelical churches in Moldova, evaluating the mission of the Evangelical churches in Moldova during the last twenty years of Moldavian independency, and observing contemporary relations between Evangelicals and Orthodox communities in Moldova. The first part is primarily descriptive.

The second part helps to understand the current situation in Moldova, observing and evaluating the missiological paradigms, which are relevant to this country, such as Church Growth Movement, Lausanne Movement and Anabaptist Movement. It is important to understand the Orthodox view of mission, which is the dominant paradigm in the context of Eastern Europe. To fulfill the objective task of the evaluation of mission approaches, this part presents the ecumenical paradigm for mission, which is known as *missio Dei*. This *missio Dei* concept tries to reconcile Orthodox and Evangelical missiological perspectives, to build a bridge between them and to create a platform for further dialogue. The methodology is analytic.

The third part is synthetic in methodology. This part is about perspectives for the mission of Evangelical churches in Moldova, addressing evaluations of missionary paradigms that were proposed in the previous part. It suggests a theological and biblical foundation for Moldavian churches and points to a new missionary paradigm for Eastern European Evangelical churches from the *missio Dei* perspective.

Acknowledgments

This is one of the hardest tasks in a dissertation – to pay tribute to all the people who invested their time, support, money and souls during my studies. At the same time, this is a blessed task, because in writing acknowledgments, I was put into a situation where I spent a lot of time thinking about these people, praying for them and remembering them.

During the years of writing I was blessed by many people whom I knew before, and who believed in me and influenced me to continue after my masters level studies and who encouraged me to doctoral level work. I also met a lot of people whom I didn't know before and they were a gift from God for me.

First of all I want to mention my father Ilia and especially my mother Nadejda, who are very simple people without higher education, but they are faithful to Christ following him in their daily lives. Because of their example, when I became a Christian I saw that a relationship with God was not just following rituals, but was a reality. When I evaluate my life, I can say that their following of Christ in daily life was an example for me.

Then I want to mention people who were not involved in my PhD studies, but who showed me the beauty of studies and the value of knowledge: they were my first teachers and instructors in my first theological institution – Fiodor Mocan, Semion Placinta, Valentina Belchiug and Dr Loreen Itterman. They played a key role in my spiritual formation and becoming a minister in the Evangelical church.

It is impossible not to mention my teachers who inculcated in me the skills of critical thinking and the beginning of analysis: Professor Dr Valerii Karpunin and Alexander Negrov from St Petersburg Christian University.

Closer to the first step in my PhD studies, the first person who influenced me was Dr Wesley Brown, who came to Chisinau to teach there and asked me, "Would you like to continue your education at IBTS at doctoral program?" In those days for me it was like a joke, like a dream, because I never thought that it might be possible. The second person who convinced me to make this step was Dr Peter Penner, who in those day was one of the course leaders at IBTS. We knew each other from St Petersburg and he was the one who helped me a lot in honing and sharpening my ideas and concentrating me on the particular area of interest. He was also my first supervisor at IBTS. I am sincerely thankful to him for his knowledge, open heart and the great impact he has had in my life.

Next step was to share this vision with colleagues from College of Theology and Education in Chisinau, where I worked as dean of the Christian Education Department. I was astonished that the administration of CTE immediately supported this idea and tried to do the best they could for my studies. I would like to mention the names of Dr Mihai Malancea (Academic dean), Serghey Namesnic (rector), Nina Teplitskaya, Serghey Germanov, Pavel Poperecnii, Victor Ormanji and others who supported me during these years. I should mention my student Denis Shuparski who helped me with the data collections.

A special word of recognition to my colleague from CTE, Dumitru Sevastian, with whom I started my studies at IBTS. Thanks for all the years of mutual support and encouragement. He was a helper who every time when he saw me asked, "How are doing with your dissertation?"

There is another team in Moldova, whom I want to thank for their part in my studies – NGO Beginning of Life, where I served as a president for the last 3 years, and where I learned what it means to do holistic mission in practice. Together with them we applied a number of ideas, which I got from my research. They showed me in daily ministry that mission is much more than I imagined before. A few of them were a special blessing for me, because they were people with whom I shared all ideas and insights which I realized from the books and research. I want to mention particularly Natalia Clapaniuc, Peter Litnevski, Roman Citac, Elia Kapakli, Benjamin Sazonov, but special word of thanks to Sergey Mikhailov, who was my student in the past, and then became my first "examiner," asking hard questions about my conclusions and presuppositions. His questions helped me to shape my ideas more clearly.

Of course, there were people with whom I met only once, or I met them occasionally, but they were very open for conversations and discussions about my dissertation: Dr Bradley Nassif, Scott Archer, Steve Babbit, Dr Dennis Leggett, Dr Lauran Bethel, Sven-Gunar Liden and a few others.

A big portion of my dissertation is focused on the ecumenical dialogue, and I am very thankful to God for providing me a great opportunity to be a part of an ecumenical roundtable in Moldova – Moldavian Christian AID – which is focused on helping people in need. There are a few people who showed me that religious tolerance is not an unreachable ideal, but a living reality. We worked with them very hard – it was not easy – but we did it with Orthodox priests Frs. Ion Solonaru, Octavian Moshin, Pavel Valuta and Vasilii Ciobanu. A great blessing was to work with a chairman of this organization, Lilia Bulat, and also with a representative from the Moldavian Lutheran Church, Natalia Mozer.

I am very thankful to the leadership of the Evangelical Baptist Union from Moldova, to the former bishop Valeri Ghiletchi and current bishop Ion Miron, who helped me to understand better the vision and mission of Baptists churches in Moldova and to see their strengths and weaknesses.

It is impossible to overestimate the role of the IBTS community during my studies. It has created such an academic environment where I was accepted with my questions, struggles and insights. It was a blessing and pleasure to listen to presentations of my colleagues during the doctoral colloquia and to present different parts of my dissertation for their critical review. Words of recognition are directed to Dr Jim Pervis, Dr Tim Noble, Dr Andrew Kirk, Doc Dr Ivana Noble, Dr Keith Jones, Dr Greg Nichols, Dr Darell Jackson, Dr Hannes Wiher, Dr Valentin Kozhuharov (my second supervisor) and others. Special acknowledgments are to Dr Ian Randall, who helped me with the structure of this dissertation and to Nancy Lovely, who with great patience, care and love corrected my English grammar.

I want to mention two organizations whose support was crucial for my studies: the Overseas Council International supported me at the first stage of my research and Langham Partnership Program (John Stott Ministries) financially supported my studies for the last years. Colleagues such as Dr Ian Shaw and Dr Elaine Vaden showed not only academic interest in my studies but they were very interested in my ministry and family as well.

Dr Parush Parushev played a key role in my studies, being not just my first supervisor, but also the catalyst who encouraged me when my hands became weak. There were a few periods when I was so depressed by difficult situations in my life that I was ready to give up and to stop my research and writing. Dr Parushev used all his persuasion to convince me to go forward, to continue and to complete my work.

Finally, I would like to pay tribute to Yulia and Ana Ubeivolc, my wife and my daughter, who are the greatest blessing in my life. I am most grateful to them for their patience. But the word "patience" doesn't describe our relationship and what they did for me. Even the words "encouragement," "influence" and "support" are not strong enough to describe their role in my studies. They believed in me, they trusted me and they were sure that my PhD studies were not in vain – that I will use all my knowledge, all my skills which I received during my research for the work of the kingdom.

Abbreviations

AUCECB	All-Union Council of the Evangelical Christian-Baptists
BM	Bessarabian Metropolis
BWA	Baptist World Alliance
CEC	Conference of European Churches
CGM	Church Growth Movement
CIS	Commonwealth of Independent States
CPRM	Communist Party of Republic of Moldova
CTE	College of Theology and Education
EAAA	Euro-Asian Accrediting Association
EBF	European Baptist Federation
ECB	Evangelical Christian Baptist
IBTS	International Baptist Theological Seminary
MCA	Moldavian Christian AID
MELC	Moldavian Evangelical Lutheran Church
MM	Moldavian Metropolis
MPP	Moldavian Partnership Program
P.E.A.C.E. Plan	1- Promote reconciliation; 2- Equip servant leaders; 3- Assist the poor; 4- Care for the sick; 5- Educate the next generation, in terms of liquidation of illiteracy.
ROC	Russian Orthodox Church
SBC	Southern Baptist Convention
UCECBM	Union of Churches of Evangelical Christian Baptists of Moldova

UNAIDS	United Nation Program on HIV and AIDS
UCCEFP	Union of Churches of the Christians by Evangelical Faith-Pentecostals
USSR	Union of Soviet Socialistic Republics
WCC	World Council of Churches

Introduction

To rethink something means that there has been a particular experience or a piece of knowledge which should be evaluated and may be changed. Sometimes rethinking is the result of frustration or apathy. People realize that something is not working and something should be done to change the inauspicious environment. Not every rethinking is followed by change. Sometimes rethinking brings positive results and people understand that they are on the right track – that their methods are effective and they are satisfied.

To rethink God's mission *(missio Dei)* means to become closer to achieving God's purposes. People, churches, and nations cannot foresee God's plans or be in control of God's actions. The church can only discover what God is doing, consider its own calling and join God's mission. The church's responsibility is always to be attentive not only to God's written Word (which has the highest standing among Eastern European Evangelicals), but to hear God's voice from other sources – nature, society and personal revelation.

To hear God's voice is not enough. It is also very important to be involved in God's work, God's mission and God's actions. To rethink God's mission among Evangelical churches in Moldova means to re-discover what God is doing among Evangelical churches in an Orthodox country saturated with Christian symbols, where almost all people have heard the name of Jesus Christ and with long history of Christian presence, and to discover the role of Evangelicals in such a country.

Purpose and Motivations of the Current Dissertation

The main purpose of this research is to discover what God is doing among evangelical Christians in Moldova, and in harmony with that, to shape a missionary paradigm for Evangelical churches, which will have a biblical foundation, relevant to contemporary society and will be done in unity with other Christians.

A few of the most important questions which I pursued were: Who are the Orthodox people? Are they the same Christians as Evangelicals but with just another style of worship? Or are they nominal cultural Christians, representatives of a dead church? Are they Christians, but weak, with a lot of pagan rituals and traditions? The first motivation is my family situation. I was born during the Soviet time, but was baptized as an infant in the Orthodox Church because my father wanted to do that. Two years later my mother was converted and baptized in an evangelical Baptist church, and from that time two worlds were represented in one family. Almost all the relatives from father's side were Orthodox, and almost all the relatives from mother's side were Baptists. It was not easy to make any faith decision in such circumstances.

The second motivation was connected with ministry in the Evangelical Church in independent Moldova. I met a number of people, who from their spoken words, believed in Jesus Christ, but they did not want to be betrayers of their Orthodox faith, even if they disagreed with it in many points. Many times in the past I tried to convince such people to leave the "wrong" church and join an Evangelical one. Every time I did this I felt that something was wrong in what I was saying, but I could not understand what it was that was wrong.

The third motivation appeared when I became a pastor in an evangelical Baptist church and instructor in a theological institution. Works of the church Fathers and contemporary Orthodox theologians amazed me with their deep search for God, their understanding of grace, and the role of Jesus Christ. I discovered that there are a lot of myths and prejudices about Orthodoxy among Evangelicals. Doing mission in Moldova, I have faced a lot of cases of real compassion from Orthodox people to those who are poor and oppressed, and at the same time I have seen a lot of examples of neutral positions from evangelical circles towards needy people. I found those attitudes and actions not only on the level of individuals, but also on the high level of leaders.

The last motivation was connected with frustration, which was shown by the leaders of the Evangelical Baptist Union regarding the effectiveness of its mission. A few times the declaration was made that "we are no longer effective."[1] Church growth stopped at the end of the 1990s, and bishops and pastors did not know what to do. Evangelical Baptists discovered that their mission approach should be rethought, but at that time they did not know how and when. Because of all these reasons, I received the vision to rethink mission approaches in Moldova from an academic point of view – to revise them and to shape a new paradigm from the *missio Dei* perspective.[2]

Situation in Moldova

The history of evangelical Christianity in Moldova is only about 200 years long. During this time, Moldova became a part of Romania seven times, as well as part of the Russian Empire. It was a battleground in four terrible wars, survived a civil war, and was a land where migrants from Germany settled and at the same time served as a place of exile for political prisoners from Tsarist Russia. There was a time when its boundaries extended to the Black Sea and the Romanian Carpathians, and after that, narrowed to the territory between the rivers Prut and Dniester (today's borders). German migrants, Bulgarians and Gagauz, Russians and Ukrainians all settled in this territory. Chisinau was known as one of the cities most favorable to the settlement of Jews. In the past, there were also wandering gypsy tribes in Moldova.

---

1. Such declarations were made regularly by the bishops Valeri Ghiletchi and Ion Miron at the pastoral conferences, beginning from 2003. All these conferences were organized as evaluation meetings for the previous years, where bishops presented reports, which were based on the reports that the main office got from the local churches. I attended all conferences from 2003 until 2010, and every time the declaration about the inefficiency of mission work was made.

2. The *missio Dei* concept plays the key role in this dissertation, and a detailed evaluation will be done in chapters 6 and 7.

The territory, whose population has never exceeded 4.5 million inhabitants, was the most densely populated republic of the USSR.[3] Moldova has become the poorest country in Europe and more than 50 percent of the labor force has left the country in the last fifteen years to find work abroad, most of them illegally.[4] Because of that, more than 30 percent of the nation's children are social orphans (parents leave their children with extended family, in orphanages, or with neighbors for years at a time to work abroad).[5] More than 100,000 people are victims of human trafficking.[6] UNAIDS suggests that up to 69,000 individuals are living with HIV/AIDS in Moldova.[7]

The vast majority of the population refers to itself today as belonging to the Orthodox Church,[8] despite the fact that Moldova has the greatest number of Evangelical Christian Baptists in Europe, considering the size of the population throughout the country. Approximately 700 missionaries, members of the Union of Evangelical Christian Baptists as well as of the Union of Christians of Evangelical Faith, moved out of Moldova between 1991 and 2006.[9] For the 1,200 settlements in the country, there are about 500[10] churches and groups of Evangelical Christian Baptists. At the same time, there are about 1,500 Orthodox parish churches.

From my point of view, the actual political and social situation in Moldova should be a part of the mission agenda for every Christian church in the country. Moldova has faced so many challenges for so many years

---

3. http://www.worldofmoldova.com/en/moldova-general-information/people-of-moldova (Accessed 8 September 2011).

4. http://pan.md/paper/Obshiestvo/Velikoe-pereselenie-moldavan-blago-ili-zlo (Accessed 13 August 2011).

5. http://www.investigatii.md/index.php?art=494 (Accessed 13 August 2011).

6. http://www.angelcoalition.org/drupal/content/torgovlya-lyudmi (Accessed 13 August 2011).

7. http://data.unaids.org/pub/GlobalReport/2006/2006_GR_ANN1R-T_en.pdf (Accessed 13 August 2011).

8. About 96% of the population identified themselves as Orthodox in the last census. http://www.worldofmoldova.com/en/moldova-general-information/people-of-moldova (Accessed 08 September 2011).

9. Statistics provided by the Christian mission, "Vozrojdenie", cited according to the speech of Viktor Hamm at the missionary conference in Chisinau, 2006.

10. http://ebf.org/member-unions/member-info.php?country=29 (Accessed 08 September 2011).

causing people to feel hopeless. They are tired from the lack of stability; many of them don't see any future for themselves and for their children. Because of that, people leave the country. Evangelical churches haven't articulated their social position towards resolving the situation. Instead Evangelicals continue to be concerned about church growth and "winning souls." There is no clear understanding about social participation of the church – is it a part of the church's mission or not? There are a lot of good examples of social projects among Evangelical churches, but most of them do not work with each other, and local congregations are not aware about other groups who do similar projects in the country. All networks happen by accident, based on personal relations between leaders, instead of being intentional.

There is no mission platform, which could play a catalyst role for the local churches. Mission approaches are defined many times by the foreign partners, but not by deep theological analysis. From my understanding, *missio Dei* could play such a role, because it is based on the integral understanding of mission. It touches many aspects of social life, has a deep theological foundation, and can give an answer for Moldavian churches in self-identification of their mission focus. This study aims to determine the role of Evangelical churches and their mission in a country with a dominant Orthodox population and serious social problems.

Situation in the Union of Evangelical Christian Baptist Churches

The Evangelical Churches in Moldova represent very disparate groups; some of them involved in joint activities, others operating independently. In the territory of Moldova, according to official statistical data, the most numerous evangelical unions are the Union of Churches of Evangelical Christian Baptists (238 churches)[11] and the Union of Churches of the

---

11. All these statistics used 2006 data provided by the State Service for Cults of the Government of the Republic of Moldova. In fact, official statistics are very different from the unions' statistics, as a large number of churches function without being registered. For example, the Union of Churches of Evangelical Christian Baptists counted for the same time period, about 500 churches (http://old.baptist.org.ru/index.php/sub/hotprayline_articles/69/). Many churches in the countryside gather in private homes, prayer houses registered as individual property. Nowadays, most churches (except for the Council of

Evangelical Faith Christians-Pentecostals (27 churches).[12] There are also the independent associations ECB (3 churches) and the Council of ECB churches (no data). It is interesting to note that after the collapse of the USSR, in Moldova there was a unification of all the Pentecostal churches into one union. This is a rather unique association; there were no other Pentecostals or Baptists who united in one structural body in the former USSR. There is a union of Independent Charismatic Churches (18 churches), Independent Bible Churches (3 churches), and also the less numerous but socially active Moldovan Evangelical Lutheran Church (7 churches).[13] There is also a community of Presbyterians and several communities of Messianic Jews and the Salvation Army. In order to better elucidate the matter I would like to focus on those churches and unions that are either numerous or maintain an active dialogue with the Orthodox churches. Subsequently, I will refer only to the Moldovan Evangelical Lutheran Church as the most active in the dialogue, and to the Union of Churches of Evangelical Christian Baptists as well as to the Union of Churches of the Christians by Evangelical Faith (Pentecostals) as the most numerous, and therefore influential, evangelical associations in the country.

One of the main questions for the Moldavian Evangelicals is: "What is the role of Evangelicals in a country with so many social issues and unresolved problems?" "Does the Evangelical presence change something in the country?" "Are there any connections between church growth and changes in society?" I will work on a possible response to these questions and will try to find a link between the questions themselves.

Churches) do not register, not because this is prohibited by the Scripture but because they simply try to avoid bureaucratic delays.

12. The vast majority of Pentecostal churches are activated as branches of larger and older churches, so they do not even seek registration. The Union of Churches of Evangelical Christian Baptists and The Union of Churches of the Christians by Evangelical Faith -Pentecostals are almost equal in the number of churches constituting them. The CECB Union has about 21,000 members, and the Pentecostal Union – about 20,000.

13. In fact there are only two actively functioning Lutheran communities – one in Chisinau, the other in Tiraspol.

Definition of the Basic Conceptual Apparatus
Missio Dei
The phrase "*missio Dei*" consists of two Latin terms. The first term *missio* is a Latin translation of the Greek word *apostellō* and has the meaning "I send." The English language has received its word "mission" from this Latin term *missio*. The second term *Dei* is the Latin translation of the Greek word *Theos*, which in English means "God." So, *missio Dei* means "God's mission." "In Protestant missiological discussion especially since the 1950s, often in the English form 'the mission of God'."[14]

In early church times, Irenaeus and Tertullian touched upon the question of sending the Son from God. Later Athanasius and the Cappadocian fathers developed the concept of sending the Son from the Father, and the Holy Spirit from the Father through the Son. But originally this concept was used by Augustine in Western discussions of the Trinity for the "*sentness of God (the Son)*" by the Father (John 3:17; 5:30; 11:42; 17:18).[15]

Evangelical Churches
When we talk about Evangelicals in Eastern Europe, we need to have in mind that the meaning of this word is used differently, for instance, in Germany and the USA. It is different even from Romania, where *Cristini dupa Evangelia* [Christians according to gospel] are closer to Russian *Molokans*.

When we use the term "Eastern European Evangelical" we think less about denominations or doctrines, but about the local church from a comprehensive perspective: style of worship, style of leadership, forms of discipline, etc. As L. Androviene and P. Parushev have written: "This is about church as congregation."[16] Taking into consideration that our first target country is Moldova, the question becomes easier, because there are only two

---

14. J. McIntosh, "Missio Dei" in *Evangelical Dictionary of World Mission*, ed. A. S. Moreau, H. A. Netland, C. E. van Engen, and D. Burnett (Grand Rapids: Baker; Carlisle: Paternoster, 2000), 631.

15. Ibid.

16. L. Androviene and P. Parushev, "'Tserkov', gosudarstvo I objestvo: o slojnosti uchastia postsovetskih evangeliskih hristian v jizni obshchestva" [Church, State and Culture: On the Complexities of Post-Soviet Evangelical Social Involvement], *Bogoslovskie razmishlenia* [Theological Reflections] 3 (2004): 182. For the historical development of evangelical communities in Eastern Europe, see Parush Parushev and Toivo Pilli, "Protestantism in

denominations, which are correlated to these criteria: Evangelical Christian Baptists and Christians by Evangelical Faith (Pentecostals). Pentecostals in Moldova are united in one structure under the umbrella of one union, but Baptists have more separations – union of the churches of ECBM, association of autonomous churches of ECBM, independent non-registered ECB, a few others who came out from the UCECBM, and established smaller associations or unions. Nevertheless, my main focus will be concentrated on the Union of Churches of Evangelical Christian Baptists. I was converted to Christ and baptized in one of the new churches, which is a part of this union, and was ordained there and for many years was a pastor in the same church and an instructor at the College of Theology and Education, which is affiliated with the same denomination. From time to time I will also address Pentecostals from Moldova, but only with one task – to compare methods, figures and strategies. I will not try to suggest my conclusions for Pentecostals, because I have been very limited in gathering resources from this union.

Eastern European Orthodox Context

When we talk about the Eastern European orthodox context from Moldavian point of view, we have in mind first of all Moldova's closest neighbors – Romania, Ukraine and Russia. We need to underline that even if Ukraine is closer than Russia, the Russian Orthodox influence is much stronger in Moldova than the Ukrainian. One of the reasons for that is religious – a vast majority of Moldavian and Ukrainian Orthodox churches function under the Moscow Patriarchate. Of course, not all Orthodox churches submit themselves to Moscow, and in both countries there have been splits and separations. I will evaluate the Moldavian split in chapter 3. However, for 200 years Chisinau was influenced by Russia and was under Russian control.

There are many more cultural connections with Romania, because the official language in Moldova is the same as in Romania – contemporary Moldova and part of today's Romania using the name of Moldova were parts of one country in the past. There are a lot of cultural common events

---

Eastern Europe to the Present Day," in *The Blackwell's Companion to Protestantism*, ed. Alister E. McGrath and Darren C. Marks (Oxford: Blackwell, 2004), 155–160.

today between these two countries. Romania has the same very influential Orthodox Church as Russia and the role of the church is very important in society.

At the same time, I can say that the situation in Bulgaria is very similar to Moldova and from time to time I will address the Bulgarian experience. The results of this thesis could be interesting also for Belorussia, Georgia and Armenia and to some extent in the Balkans.

Overview of the Presented Dissertation

The proposed dissertation consists of an introduction, three main parts and a conclusion. Each part contains three chapters, therefore there are nine chapters.

The first part describes the Evangelical churches in a Moldavian Orthodox context. The first chapter of this section talks about the birth and development of the Evangelical churches in Moldova, taking into consideration the general history of the country, connecting church history with the political situation around and in Moldova variously, when Moldova was a part of the Russian Empire, then a part of Romania and later a part of the USSR. During the last one hundred years Moldova moved from Russia to Romania, and back and forth, five times. Of course these moves affected both the Orthodox and Evangelical churches. The second chapter attempts to evaluate the mission of the Evangelical churches in Moldova during the last twenty years (years of Moldavian independency). Mission in Moldova is correlated with that in other post-Soviet countries, especially when we talk about the 1990s, right after the collapse of the Soviet Union. I see many more differences today, than I did from ten years ago. I observe evangelistic campaigns, which have been organized with support from some missionary agencies from the West, and their influence on Moldavian churches. I study almost all periodicals from 1991 until 2008 in UCECBM, looking for the values which were proclaimed and applied among Moldavian ECB. The third chapter is dedicated to contemporary relations between Evangelicals and Orthodox in Moldova. From the very beginning we need to look on the very complicated situation within the Orthodox Church, which is divided into two parts. This chapter tries to analyze the reasons for such a split and look on the role of Evangelicals in that situation. Later some space will be committed to the accusations concerning proselytism and the role of canonical territory in that. A platform for social actions was established, and information about this dialogue will be given. The first part is more descriptive with elements of analytical apparatus. This descriptive part is very important to understand the actual situation in Moldova and its neighboring countries.

The second part tries to help the reader understand the current situation in Moldova, observing and evaluating the missiological paradigms which are relevant to this country. Chapter 4 looks through three Evangelical approaches: the Church Growth Movement, the Lausanne Movement and the Anabaptist approach. The reason is to find real roots for the actual situation in Moldova and to discover the most influential bodies for Moldavian Evangelicals. Chapter 5 describes the Orthodox view of mission which is accepted in Eastern Europe. The main focus is directed to Romanian and Russian theologians and church leaders. It makes an attempt to understand the content and final goal of Orthodox mission. Chapter 6 finally shows the ecumenical paradigm for mission, which is known as *missio Dei*. This *missio Dei* concept tries to reconcile Orthodox and Evangelical believers, to build a bridge between them, to create a platform for further dialogue. When a church talks about its mission, it can always be rejected by other churches because they see it as competition. At the same time, when the conversation is about God's mission, it could humble people, churches and denominations. This chapter also makes an effort to study the content and goal of *missio Dei*.

The third part is more synthetic than the previous, which was more analytic. This part is about perspectives for the mission of Evangelical churches in Moldova. It studies the Trinitarian foundation for mission, trying to define the mission of God the Father, God the Son and God the Holy Spirit. Chapter 8 addresses the analytic and synthetic evaluations of missionary paradigms, which were proposed in chapters 4 to 6. It compares them with each other and also prepares for the last chapter through study of the mission of the church as a synthetic dynamic, where every denomination sees itself as a part of the Whole Church. As a result chapter 9 flows from the preceding arguments. This chapter suggests a theological and biblical foundation for Moldavian churches, and this message has been "translated" from ecumenical language to the local evangelical way of speaking, which could be relevant to other Eastern European churches. It proposes mission as dialogue and common witness in a spirit of peace. Also it suggests a new missionary paradigm for Eastern European Evangelical churches from the *missio Dei* prospect.

I expect this dissertation will bring some results and fruits for Eastern Europe in general, and for Moldavian Baptists in particular. I understand that it will not resolve all the problems, and perhaps will never be applied in its full content, but I hope that at least some of the ideas explained in this dissertation will produce results.

Expected Results

When human beings do something, they expect that it will bring results, that it will make at least some differences. I want to list some of the expectations I have for this research.

First, I expect that the *missio Dei* concept will be evaluated by Moldavian churches and that Moldavian Evangelicals will see that a holistic approach could create some positive results not only within their churches, but also in society and among Christians who are representatives of different traditions.

Second, I expect that this work will show the relevancy of actual missionary paradigms in Moldova and that a newly shifted missionary approach will be created.

Third, I expect that this research will shape a foundation for mission, which could at the same time be both biblical and understandable for contemporary society.

Part 1

The Evangelical Churches in an Orthodox Context in Moldova

Talking about contemporary mission of Evangelical churches in Moldova, we need to be very attentive to their roots, comparing different opinions about the appearance of Evangelicals in Eastern Europe and at the same time taking into consideration that Evangelicals came to this country when the majority of the population ranked themselves with a very old tradition of Orthodoxy.

Moldova, as was mentioned in the introduction, during its history was under influence from the West, East and South. Russians, Turks, Romanians, and Germans influenced not only the political world of Moldova, but also its religious life. We will never understand the relevancy of the evangelical movement in this country if we neglect its connections with Mennonites and Lutherans, Russian Baptists, Romanian Baptists and, of course, the Orthodox Church.

The goal of the first part of this dissertation is to emphasize the intersections between these movements and their influence on the modern Moldavian society and church life. I will compare the general history of the country with church history. This piece of dissertation should depict the reality of the Christian world in Moldova, outline the crisis of identity for Evangelicals and evaluate the effectiveness of their mission approaches. Without this part I cannot talk about "rethinking" *missio Dei*, because this part helps us to make a first step of rethinking – to begin to think about the weaknesses and strengths of the evangelical mission in an orthodox context.

CHAPTER 1

The Birth and Development of Evangelical Churches in Moldavian Orthodox Context

This chapter examines the emergence of evangelical Christianity in the territory of Moldova in its historical and religious context. All the historians researching this subject matter in Moldova stressed the lack of archival documents and original resources.[1] Thus, I will refer to accessible Russian, Ukrainian and Romanian sources, which may shed light on what happened in Moldova. Each time I will have to tear down the subjectivist thinking of the authors, each of whom observed the history of Moldova from the perspective of Kiev, Moscow or Bucharest.

Therefore, to objectively understand the mission of Evangelical churches in Moldova, to rethink *missio Dei* among Evangelicals in Moldova, I need to explore the emergence of Christianity in this area, the appearance of the first Evangelical communities, and their development in Moldova as part of Tsarist Russia. I will then switch over to the sources that can bring light about Evangelical churches in Moldova in the period of *România Mare*

---

1. This is evidenced by I. Bondareva, who wrote a research work on the history of the church in Moldova for a MTh degree at IBTS; by V. Bulgac, who wrote his doctoral dissertation at the Moldova State Pedagogical University on the history of baptism in Moldova; by O. Mocan, who engaged in research for her book on the history of the women's movement within the Union of Evangelical Christian Baptists; by V. Shemchishin, who wrote a thesis for the Doctor of Ministry Degree on the history of Evangelical Christian Baptists in southern Bessarabia and some others. The lack of archival documents is due to the fact that every time the territory of Moldova was aligned to Romania, or to Russia, many archival documents were either destroyed or transferred to other archives in Bucharest, Iasi, Odessa, Kherson and other cities.

from 1918 until 1944. This chapter will end with an analysis of the history of Evangelical churches in the Soviet period.

The Emergence of Christianity in the Territory of Moldova

The Emergence of Orthodoxy in the Territory of Moldova

The first Christians settled in the territory of Moldova in the second and third centuries AD. These were Roman soldiers and colonists. When the Emperor Constantine declared full freedom of religion and Christianity became the state religion, the whole territory of Dacia came under the religious jurisdiction of the bishopric of Tomis (nowadays Constanta). When the Roman Empire collapsed under the onslaught of the barbarians in AD 476, all those lands were taken under the protection of Constantinople. By that time, all the territory of Dacia had already been Latinized under the influence of Rome, and even before the Middle Ages the Christians of Moldova were very close to Rome even though all official contact between the Pope and the Patriarch of that time had already been suspended. At the same time, church organization and beliefs tied the Moldavian church to Greek Byzantium.

In 1401, the Moldavian Prince Alexandru cel Bun sought from Constantinople an independent Metropolitan Church with three bishoprics. The Metropolitan itself was initially located in Suceava and later was moved to Iasi. Thus, when Constantinople succumbed to the onslaught of the Turks in 1453, Moldova had already formed a well-organized church structure with its own centers, internal culture and interfaith relations. The center of world Orthodoxy was then transferred to Moscow. A new stage of relations began between Moldova and Russia. Slavic culture and language entered Moldavian culture, while at the same time Moldova gave the Russian Orthodox Church one of its best representatives – Petru Movila, who became known in Kiev as Petro Mohyla. He became the Metropolitan Bishop of Kiev and opened the first university there.

After the fall of Constantinople, theological thinking continued to develop in Moscow and Kiev, although the church was going through difficult periods. After the reign of Peter I, a major crisis began to emerge in the Russian Orthodox Church, because the Great Russian emperor had done everything possible in order to make the church one of the levers of the state apparatus. After the abolition of patriarchal rule and the establishment of the Synod of the Church (following the example of the Senate) the priority in decision making focused on the public interest.

After the Russian-Turkish War of 1812, Bessarabia (the eastern part of Moldova) was annexed by Russia. In Chisinau, under the jurisdiction of the ROC, an episcopate was opened. From 1856 to 1878 a part of Bessarabia was united with Moldova from the right bank of Prut River and Walachia during the unification into one state – Romania. After the Russian-Turkish war it again became part of the Russian Empire. Charles King in his fundamental book on Moldavian history notes that "Russian Bessarabia was frequently characterized as the Siberia of the west, a place about which Pushkin, exiled there from 1820 to 1823, was unequivocal: "Accursed town of Kishinev," he wrote, "to abuse you the tongue will grow tired.""[2]

This did not affect the process of *Slavyanisation* of the region, which actively began in 1812. "Indigenous Moldavian culture was relegated to the countryside, with the urban centres dominated by Russians, Jews, and russified Moldavians."[3]

For one hundred years the Orthodox Church in Moldova was under the jurisdiction of Moscow, while in those same years, the Orthodox Churches of Wallachia, Western Moldova and later Romania were under the authority of the Ecumenical Patriarch. The Patriarch of Constantinople recognised the autocephaly of the Romanian church only in 1885, although the first Romanian Patriarch was elected in 1925. Nicolas Dima sees this period as an era of "Romanian renaissance."[4] During these years, Moldova (Bessarabia) was part of the Russian Empire, thus, the wave of the flourishing of Romania side affected it. As for the ROC this century was not the most prominent in its history.

---

2. Charles King, *The Moldovans: Romania, Russia, and the Politics of Culture* (Stanford University: Hoover Institution Press, 2000), 23.

3. Ibid., 26.

4. N. Dima, "Politics and Religion in Moldova," *The Mankind Quarterly* 34, no. 3 (1994): 182.

The history of the Church in Moldova is inseparable from the history of the state. The lack of stability influenced the outlook of the inhabitants of the country, its leadership and the church leaders. The ideals one generation aspired to were criticised by the next one. There was no opportunity to increase the cultural and intellectual potential of the people by transmitting accumulated knowledge from one generation to another. "Literacy among the Bessarabian population remained low, just over 15.6 percent by 1897; for ethnic Moldovans the figure was only 6 percent."[5]

This short study of the emergence of the Orthodox Church in Moldova will help us understand the current split within Moldavian Orthodoxy and the role to be played by the Evangelical church.

The Emergence of the First Non-Orthodox Groups

The first Russian "protestants" began to appear in the Middle Ages from among Orthodox believers: *The Strigolniki* (14th–15th century), the so-called whips (17th–18th centuries), Judaizers (18th century), and jumpers (19th century). Later, the movement within Orthodoxy resulted in *Dukhobors* and *Molokans*, who rejected the official Orthodox obedience to authority, recognized the Holy Scriptures as the sole source of revelation (*Molokans*), and the prophecy of the Holy Spirit (*Dukhobors*), and rejected prayers before the icons and church liturgy. V. Popov said that people's faith in Russia for the most part was mystical and superstitious or extremely rationalist.[6]

In the nineteenth century there were several parallel centers of emergence of Evangelical communities in the territory of the Russian Empire, a part of which was then Moldova.

Communities of *Molokans*

The communities of *Molokans* revised their traditions under the influence of the Scriptures, which appeared in accessible language. Molokans gathered together in a very simple location. Particular emphasis was placed on their collective singing and their singing of the psalms of David is especially

---

5. King, The Moldovans, 23.

6. V. Popov, "Evangel'skie hristiane-pashkovcy. Voznikonovenie i duhovno-prosvetitel'skoe sluzhenie" [Evangelical Christians-Pashkovtsy. The Emergence and the Spiritual and Educational Ministry], Bogomyslie [Theological Thinking] 7 (1998): 135.

famous. Communities were run by the council of elders. The Molokans had a reputation of being honest and decent people.[7] Originally, Molokans recognized baptism and communion only as spiritual symbols and did not actually practice them. But in the late 1840s and early 1850s the "so-called wet Molokans [appeared] who recognized the necessity to execute God's rule about baptism by faith and Holy Communion."[8] Molokans gave life to many leaders of the Evangelical and Baptist movements in the Russian Empire – Nikita Voronin, Dey Mazaev, Vasily Pavlov, Ivan Prokhanov and others. In addition, there were cases when whole groups of Molokans moved to Baptist communities.[9] The conversion to baptism was sometimes spontaneous, but Baptists regarded Molokans strategically as a field for their primary activity.[10]

It was Molokans who started the first Evangelical communities in Bessarabia. In 1806, in Bessarabia, there were several Molokan communities.[11] They were related to the Molokans from Ukraine and Russia.

Mennonite Communities

Since the times of Catherine II, Mennonite/Lutheran Communities of German settlers populated the southern lands of Ukraine. To a greater extent, they were concentrated in the Odessa district, although there were also such settlements in other parts of Ukraine. In the territory of Bessarabia, the first migrants settled between the years 1814 and 1827.[12] Alexander II invited settlers from Germany and Switzerland to this area, exempting them from taxes, promising freedom of religion and giving them a certain freedom in self-government of their settlements. Vadim Bulgac, researcher of the history of the Moldavian Evangelical movement, remarks that about

---

7. S. Lieven, *Duhovnoe probuzhdenie v Rossii* [*Spiritual awakening in Russia*] (Light in the East, 1990), 10.

8. A. Sinichkin, "I oni poshli . . ." [And they went . . .] *Missioner* [The Missionary] 1 (2004): 30.

9. S. Lieven, Duhovnoe probuzhdenie v Rossii, 100.

10. V. Popov, *Stopy blagovestnika: zhizn' i trudy V.G. Pavlova* [The Footprints of an Evangelist: the Life and Works of V. G. Pavlov] (St. Petersburg: Biblija dlja vseh, 1996), 17. V. Bulgac, "Apariţia Mişcării Baptiste în Besarabia (1812-1890)" [The Appearance in Bessarabia of the Baptist Movement (1812–1890)], *Pulse of Ministry* 5 (2002): 7.

11. Bulgac, "Apariţia Mişcării Baptiste," 6–7.

12. V. Lubachshenco, *Istoria Protestantismu v Ukraine* [The History of Protestantism in Ukraine] (L'viv: Prosvita, 1995), 186.

25,000 Lutheran migrants from Germany and 5,000 Mennonites from Switzerland occupied the southern part of Bessarabia, mostly in the counties of Cetatea Alba (Belgorod-Dnestrovsk) and Ismail, as well as in the Cahul region.[13] They served as a second source of infiltration of Protestant and Evangelical ideas in the territory of Bessarabia.

The colonists led a quiet life and did not preach among the local population. It is worth noting that this was forbidden by the authorities.

Religious activity may be observed among Lutherans in Bessarabia significantly earlier than in the rest of the empire. Between 1824 and 1839, Bessarabia was visited by the German pastor I. Bonekemper who not only aroused the German communities, but also developed the first missionary activity among the peoples inhabiting Bessarabia. In 1839 he moved to Romania to work with German settlers there and his ideas continue to live among Bessarabian people.

By the middle of the nineteenth century the way of life of the colonists began to attract the attention of the native population of the Russian Empire. The tsarist authorities named this as the first cause of the growth of the *Shtundizm*, who according to Sergei Zhuk, drew first on Anabaptist theology and the Pietist religious practices of Western Protestantism, and then, during the 1870s, on the German Baptists.[14]

Two other causes were named: the missionary activity of all the *Shtundists*, from executives to children, as well as support from abroad.[15] V. Popov adds one more cause – evangelical Christianity began to develop as a counterweight to the nihilistic ideas in society.[16] On the basis of archival documents it is possible to mention another reason, which has parallels with the one stated hereinabove by Prokhanov towards the Orthodox Church. According to the report of the police officer of the village Dubovoj Log of the Vylevsk parish, one of the causes of the mass conversion to *Shtundizm* was the exactions imposed on people by the priesthood. Also, he notes that

---

13. Bulgac, "Apariţia Mişcării Baptiste," 7.

14. S. Zhuk, *Russia's Lost Reformation: Peasants, Millennialism, and Radical Sects in Southern Russia and Ukraine, 1830-1917* (Washington: Woodrow Wilson Center Press; Baltimore and London: The John Hopkins University Press, 2004), 178.

15. Y. Reshetnikov, "Istorija Evangel'sko-baptistskogo dvizhenija v Ukraine" [History of the Evangelical Baptist Movement in Ukraine], *Bogomyslie* 6 (1997): 212–214.

16. Popov, "Evangel'skie hristiane-pashkovcy," 133.

the *Shtundists* refused to renounce their faith and were ready to give their lives for it.[17] I would like to add one more thing, which we read "between the lines." V. Lubachshenco gives the figures from the Ukrainian archives, which show that many Mennonites were very wealthy people. Some of them were millionaires. They were philanthropists who invested a lot of money in educational and agricultural programs. She considers that one of the reasons why Ukraine became a well-developed European region at the end of the nineteenth and the beginning of the twentieth centuries is because of the Ukrainian-German Mennonites.[18] Traditionally Mennonites are connected with peasant styles of life, but they influenced not only their neighbors in the villages, but also all of society. This argument adds something new to the well-known Anabaptist style of witness, which we will discuss deeper in chapter 4.

Gradually, the local inhabitants started to attend the German religious meetings, although many of them did not renounce Orthodoxy – the majority of them were even attending worship in the local Orthodox churches. In their spare time they gathered to study the Bible. Many of them were called *Shtunda*. Official Orthodoxy, with the consent of the authorities, banned such meetings, and thus Shtundists separated from Orthodoxy and their communities became independent without a structural relationship with other Christian groups. In some cases, the ushers required the local priests to admonish *Shtundists* to turn back to Orthodoxy, and in case the admonition was unsuccessful to invite the district Orthodox missionary, who played a very important apologetic role. Regardless of the results of the admonition, it was necessary to write to the authorities and attach a list of names of all the *Shtundists*.[19] An important record was found in the archive of the CGIAU of the Kamenetz-Podolsk office, which imposed certain penalties on the parish priests, because they did not inform authorities

---

17. Regional State Archive of Zhytomyr region, f.1 inv. 22 E 1336, sheet 40, the first letter, on CD *Evangelical Movement in Russia*, 3.0.

18. Lubachshenco, *Istoria Protestantismu v Ukraine*, 193.

19. *State Archive of Odesa Oblast*, F.37 inv.1 D 3797, p. 2–3, on CD *History of the Evangelical Movement in Eurasia*, 3.0. It is important to note that this document refers to 1896 and an indication is given to restore order in the *Shtundist* community of the village Trudomirovki of the Tiraspol County.

in time about the *Shtundists* meeting in their parish.[20] J. C. Pollock considers "the blind anger of the priests having killed any hope that *Stundism* would become a reformation within the Orthodox Church."[21]

V. Lubachshenco adduces proofs, that until the mid 1870s *Shtundists* visited Orthodox churches, received the Lord's Supper from priests, confessed their sins, fasted according to the Orthodox canons and prayed before icons in their homes (including such authorities of this movement such as Ivan Riaboshapka and Mikhail Ratushnii).[22]

In 1869, the *Shtundists* were visited by the German Baptist Johann Gerhard Onken, who tried to convince them to convert to baptism. He also ordained the first pastors for the *Shtundist* communities. "By the 80s of the nineteenth century there were the first attempts to unite into a union of churches. However, those efforts failed."[23]

Evangelical Communities

An Evangelical community emerged in Saint Petersburg after the ministry of Lord Radstock in 1874. Sharyl Corrado writes that Radstock and his successor, the retired colonel Vasilii Pashkov, emphasized the individual's relationship to Christ, rather than doctrine or denominational politics.[24] Gregory Nichols makes his affirmation even stronger: "Over time, Pashkovite cell groups lost contact with the established churches and developed into independent house churches, distinct from other evangelical groups. They did not want to become Baptists because of the heavy Oncken-type leadership and restrictive doctrines."[25]

---

20. CGIAU of the Kamenetz-Podolsk office, *Podolsk Spiritual Consistory*, fund 315, inv. I Volume I; units.9808, l.52, on CD *Evangelical movement in Eurasia*, 3.0.

21. J. C. Pollock, *The Faith of the Russian Evangelicals* (New York; Toronto: McGraw-Hill Book Company, 1964), 64.

22. Lubachshenco, *Istoria Protestantismu v Ukraine*, 225–226.

23. W. Sawatsky, *Evangelicheskoe dvizhenie v SSSR posle Vtoroj mirovoj vojny* [Evangelical Movement in the Soviet Union after the Second World War] (Moscow: ITS-Garant, 1995), 33.

24. S. Corrado, "The Gospel in Society: Pashkovite Social Outreach in Late Imperial Russia," in *Eastern European Baptist History: New Perspectives*, ed. S. Corrado and T. Pilli (Prague: International Baptist Theological Seminary, 2007), 53.

25. G. L. Nichols, "Ivan Kargel and the Pietistic Community of the Late Imperial Russia," in *Eastern European Baptist History: New Perspectives*, ed. S. Corrado and T. Pilli (Prague: International Baptist Theological Seminary, 2007), 85.

Among Radstock's followers the most notable were Princess Liven, Earl Korf and Colonel Pashkov. Pashkov later became the leader of this movement and in his honor, for some time, the whole movement was called *Pashkovite*. He opened the door of his large house for meetings. *Pashkovites* recognized baptisms officiated in the Orthodox Church, rejected ordination, and were active in social[26] and educational activities.

There is a not-very-well-known fact, that an Evangelical church was planted in Bessarabia in 1912. Albert W. Wardin draws attention to the fact that a Russian congregation was formed in Cetatea Alba (Akkerman, today in Ukraine),[27] but the influence of this community was so small, that I cannot find any direct relations between Pashkovite and Prokhanov with Moldavian churches. At the same time their role in the evangelical movement in Russia was incomparably larger. For further readings on the evangelical movement in the Russian Empire and Soviet Union I call attention to Sh. Corrado[28], S. Lieven[29], V. Popov[30], Gr. Nichols[31], W. Sawatsky[32], I. Prokhanov[33] and others.

Baptist Communities

The official date of the emergence of the Baptist movement in the Russian Empire is considered to be 20 August 1867. It was when Nikita Voronim was baptized by full immersion. He was baptized by Kalfeyt Martin, a German who came from Lithuania. This kind of baptism took place in Tiflis, and from there spread throughout the empire, although it is worth noting that for about fifteen years Caucasus was the main place of the

---

26. They worked with orphans, elders, homeless people, prostitutes, etc.

27. A. W. Wardin, *Baptists around the World: A Comprehensive Handbook* (Nashville: Broadman & Holman, 1995), 227.

28. Corrado, "The Gospel in Society," 58.

29. Lieven, *Duhovnoe probuzhdenie v Rossii*, 45–52.

30. V. Popov, *I. S. Prohanov: stranicy zhizni* [I. S. Prokhanov: Pages of Life] (St Petersburg: Biblija dlja vseh, 1996), 63.

31. Nichols, "Ivan Kargel," 85.

32. Sawatsky, *Evangelicheskoe dvizhenie v SSSR*, 33.

33. I. Prokhanov, *V kotle Rossii. Avtobiografija Ivana Stepanovicha Prohanova s izlozheniem glavnyh faktov dvizhenija Evangel'skih hristian v Rossii* [In the copper of Russia. Autobiography of Ivan Stepanovich Prokhanov outlining the main facts of the movement of the Evangelical Christians in Russia] (Chicago: World Fellowship of Slavic Evangelical Christians, 1992), 20.

Baptist movement. "German Baptists started the first Baptist work in Bessarabia in Turtino in 1876 with the baptism of nine believers. In 1879 a congregation was formed which became independent in 1907 from its mother church in Ukraine. In the same year the three German Baptist churches, then in Bessarabia, formed an association."[34]

One of the well-known Baptist activists, Pavlov, moved to Odessa where for a time he served as a pastor. At the time Pavlov was living in Odessa, Andrei Ivanov, the leader of a group of activists who were studying the Scriptures in Chisinau, realized the necessity to convert from being a Molokan to being a Baptist. His mother (also a Molokan activist), trying to help her son to find the right way, came from Chisinau to Odessa seeking advice from Pavlov. Meeting Pavlov there she realized that her son had never strayed from the gospel path. In 1907, Pavlov himself visited Chisinau, encouraged Ivanov and inspired him for the foundation of the Baptist church. At the same time, in parallel, another group was emerging. A retired soldier of the tsarist army, Hizhnyakov, began independently studying the Bible, and later invited other soldiers to the study. At the end of 1907, Ivanov and Hizhnyakov's groups united into one and in 1908[35] went to Odessa to be baptized. In the same year, Ivanov went to St Petersburg and entered the Union of Baptist Churches of Russia. In 1909, Andrei Ivanov was appointed as a pastor and was responsible for the work in Bessarabia. By 1914 this church had about fifty members.[36]

In addition, in Chisinau, there was a community of Messianic Jews under the leadership of Joseph Rabinovich, who from the beginning cooperated closely with Ivanov-Hizhnyakov's Baptist community.[37] Later, when

---

34. Wardin, *Baptists Around the World*, 227.

35. A. Mitskevich refers Ivanov's baptism to 1910. I. Ivanov, "Iz istorii evangel'sko-baptistskogo dvijenia. Vospominania o vozniknovenii dela Gospodnego v Moldavii" [From the History of Evangelical-baptist Movement. Memoirs about Birth of Lord's Deeds in Moldavia], *Bratskii Vestnik* 2 (1955): 53.

36. *Istorija EHB v SSSR* [History of Evangelical Christians Baptists in the USSR] (Moscow: AUCECB Publishing House, 1989), CD-ROM, *Evangelical Movement in Eurasia*, 2.0, Chapter 9.

37. Bulgac, "Apariția Mișcării Baptiste," 38.

the leadership of the Jewish community was transmitted to Leo Averbukh, there was a merger with the already established Baptist church.[38]

V. Bulgac related that in 1918, in Bessarabia, there were officially registered 75,000 Lutherans and Neo-Lutherans (*Shtundists*), but there were not more than 65,000 ethnic Germans among them. The nature of the remaining 10,000 was not found out, as Moldovian archives available today do not provide any data on this subject.[39]

It is interesting to note that Vasily Pavlov, one of the most eminent pastors of the Russian Union of Baptist Churches, was expelled from the country and received an invitation to be a pastor in Romania, in Tulcea, where a lot of Russians and Bulgarians lived at that time.[40]

Parallel to the Baptist movement in Russia, a Baptist movement was born in Romania. "The Baptists in Romania can be traced back to two distinct sources, independent of each other, although starting at about the same time, fifty years ago [1860s] . . . (1) German craftsmen immigrants; (2) brethren from Russia, who had been exiled from their own homes for their fidelity to Jesus Christ and their adherence to Baptist principles."[41]

C. T. Byford names some of them: "Ivanoff of Baku; Kostromin of Nicolaiev; Pavloff of Odessa; Kuchnireff of Kieff, and others."[42] Indeed they were people, who settled in Tulcea. It appears that the conversation is about different people, but Pavloff is the same Pavlov, whom I mentioned earlier. There is just a different spelling of Russian names, which was

---

38. I. Bondareva, *Investigate and Give a Critical Account of Baptist Origins and Early Development in Moldova*, (CD-ROM, *Evangelical Movement in Eurasia*, 2.0).

39. Bulgac, "Apariția Mișcării Baptiste," 38.

40. Popov, *I. S. Prohanov: stranicy zhizni*, 71–74.

41. C. T. Byford, "The Movement in Russia: Appendix Work Among Non-Russian Slavonic Peoples and the Balkan Races Generally," in *The Baptist Movement in the Continent of Europe: A Contribution to Modern History*, ed. J. H. Rushbrooke (London: The Carrey Press; The Kingsgate Press, 1915), 95. Ot. Bunaciu in his paper "Romanian Baptists and Mission in the Twentieth Century" in *Baptists and Mission. Papers From the Fourth International Conference on Baptist Studies*, ed. I. M. Randall and A. R. Cross (Milton Keynes: Paternoster, 2007), says that the first Baptist church in Bucharest was started in 1856 by a carpenter, Karl Johann Scharschmidt, who had been baptized by Oncken and who came to Bucharest with his trade. The first official recognition of the Baptist church in Bucharest took place in 1865 when the magistrate of the city gave permission to the German Baptist church (as it was called) to keep its own marriage register.

42. Byford, "The Movement in Russia," 97.

changed from 1915, when Byford wrote his paper, until today. But "the first Romanian-speaking church met in Bucharest on 29 December 1912."[43]

There are some observations which should be noted. When we compare four different origins of the evangelical movement, we will see that "Baptists, not *Stundists*, became a symbol of Russian sectarianism."[44] Further, "despite decades of anti-religious propaganda, 'Evangelical Christian' as a definition did not become a negative term, whereas the word 'Baptist' clearly came from foreign roots and was frightening for its oddity and incomprehensibility."[45] At the same time Pobedonostsev persecuted all non-Orthodox Russian-speaking groups; they were put into prison or expelled from the country. Nevertheless, the image of the Evangelicals was much better than the image of the Baptists. I believe that there were two reasons: (1) Evangelicals did not cut their relations with the Orthodox Church, they did not re-baptize people, even Prokhanov[46] developed relations with the priests and hierarchs; (2) Evangelicals were very involved in society with their social "projects." They felt this responsibility towards poor and marginalized people; they served them and answered their needs. Furthermore, Baptists were adversarial to the Orthodox Church.

The same conclusions can be made studying Mennonite origins. The first Brethren churches were German, later many Ukrainians joined them. As I mentioned, the Mennonite movement was also socially oriented, maybe in a different way as Pashkovites, but they were "salt of the earth," witnessing first of all with their deeds, and then, with words. Mennonites were known in Russian Empire as a sect, and the label Mennonite was never a symbol of a sectarian movement in Russian-Ukranian-Moldavian lands.

General Overview and Conclusions

From 1880 to 1905 there were serious problems concerning the freedom of activity of non-Orthodox denominations. K. P. Pobedonostsev was

---

43. O. Bunaciu, "Romanian Baptists and Mission," 92.

44. A. Negrov and T. Nikol'skaia, "Baptists as a Symbol of Sectarianism in Soviet and Post-Soviet Russia" in *Eastern European Baptist History: New Perspectives*, ed. S. Corrado and T. Pilli (Prague: International Baptist Theological Seminary, 2007), 134.

45. Ibid., 136.

46. Ivan Prokhanov began to re-baptize people, who saw the need for re-baptism. But Redstok and Pashkovite did not use the practice of re-baptizing.

appointed as Ober-Procurator of the Holy Synod. He was the initiator of practically of all the discriminatory laws in those years. Alexander III and Nicholas II shared Pobedonostsev's fervor. On his initiative, the so-called "missionary institute" was created, where all the missionaries sought to identify the active leaders of the Protestant-Christian movement in Russia from all sects and report them to the authorities. One of the methods of these missionaries was the organization of religious debate. In most cases, the Evangelical preacher who took part in the debate was soon arrested and deported.[47]

In 1903, there was relief from the persecution of non-Orthodox believers. In 1905, the first revolution occurred in Russia, which changed the situation even more. In 1910 new regulations came out, seeking to limit the activity of the local communities, and in some cases these regulations succeeded, especially in small rural communities, because the law permitted the communities to be activated only if there were twenty-five baptized adult citizens of the Russian Empire. In 1914 persecutions began in Bessarabia. Hijniakov and Groshevik were put into prison for fifteen days; the rest of the congregation began to gather underground.[48]

After the beginning of the First World War, the situation worsened. The whole country was at war. A part of the country was occupied, while there were rumors that all Evangelical Christians were unreliable and dangerous people working for the West.[49] Nevertheless, Baptists positioned themselves as patriots, and during World War I they were involved in social activity. Lubashchenco notes that they, together with the Evangelical Christians, established a charitable foundation "Merciful Samaritan," which gathered money among their churches for organizing field hospitals and free distribution of spiritual literature among soldiers.[50]

The situation in Bessarabia shows that there was a lot of fruit from such ministries. A. Mitskevich says that after World War I many soldiers

---

47. Prokhanov, *V kotle Rossii*, 20.

48. Mickievich, "Iz istorii evangel'sko-baptistskogo dvijenia. Vospominania o vozniknovenii dela Gospodnego v Moldavii" [From the history of evangelical-baptist movement. Memoirs about birth of Lord's deeds in Moldavia], *Bratskii Vestnik* 2 (1955): 53.

49. Popov, *I. S. Prohanov: stranicy zhizni*, 66.

50. Lubachshenco, *Istoria Protestantismu v Ukraine*, 243–244.

from different battle fronts came back to their villages, who had came to belief in Christ during the war, because of the testimonies of other soldiers (Evangelicals and Baptists) and because of the reading of spiritual literature.[51] They established small groups for Bible reading and prayer in their locations, and all of them were separated from each other.

In January 1918, Bessarabia came out of Russia and in November of the same year, became a part of Romania. Due to this, Moldovian churches escaped the persecution and repression which was experienced by the churches in Russia and Ukraine. The destiny of the Evangelical churches in Moldova is seen differently in Romania.

This historical overview of the origin of the Evangelical movement in the territory of Moldova within the Russian Empire shows us the origins of the first Evangelical churches. Thus, having studied the emergence of the Evangelical communities, I continue into the analysis of the growth of the Evangelical movement in the territory of Moldova, when it was a part of *România Mare* (Greater Romania).

The Growth of Evangelical Churches in Moldova in the Period (1918–1944)

Self-identification of Moldavian Evangelical Baptists

The Bessarabian Evangelical-Baptist Church experienced huge growth during those years. In this context, it is necessary to mention the political and social changes in Bessarabia of those times.

In October 1917 the socialist revolution occurred. Battles were taking place not only on the front, but in almost every locality of the empire. Wrangel, Kolchak, Denikin, the Czech divisions, were far away in Siberia, fighting first on the side of the White Army. At the same time, there were Petlura and Makhno's armed groups and a huge number of other disparate bands raiding the nearby villages and towns. The Bolsheviks obviously were not strong enough to withstand all internal and external enemies. Lenin gave the right of self-determination to Finland, a part of Poland, Galicia, as well as to Bessarabia.

---

51. Ivanov, "Iz istorii evangel'sko-baptistskogo," 53.

The Birth and Development of Evangelical Churches

On 2 December 1917 in Chisinau the established Council of the Country (*Sfatul Țsarii*) proclaimed the Moldavian Democratic Republic within Russia.⁵² On 24 January 1918, under influence from Romania, Bessarabia declared its independence from Russia as the Moldavian Democratic Republic. Soon after, Bessarabian unionists began to insist on the union of Bessarabia with Romania. The Moldovan Parliament voted against the union, but within a few months Pantelimon Halippa, being at the head of the unionist movement, convinced the assembly to vote for the union. At the same time, Romanian troops entered Chisinau.⁵³ Bessarabia did not have its own regular army, so everything worked out with no fighting. It must be noted that the Romanians did not open fire. This was explained by the fact that Bessarabia needed assistance in confronting local Bolsheviks, as well as the expansionist mood of certain Ukrainian waves. The Bessarabia Bolshevik force was not large, and its influence was very limited.

In March 1918, the unification of Bessarabia and Romania was proclaimed, and in November 1918 in Chisinau, the Parliament was dissolved and prominent unionists were invited to Bucharest. Sovereign Moldova existed for about six months. It should be noted that not only the current territory of the Republic of Moldova but also Bukovina (today part of Chernovtsi region) and Southern Bessarabia – Akkerman, *Kilia, and Ismail* (which belong nowadays to Ukraine) adhered to Romania.

Soldiers were returning to the country and finding it in those conditions. In the 1920s all Bessarabian Evangelical Christians and Baptists formed the Union of Evangelical Christians-Baptists,⁵⁴ which was mostly

---

52. King, *The Moldovans*, 33.
53. Ibid.
54. The last senior presbyter in Moldova of the USSR period wrote: "Even before the war, when Moldova was under Romanian rule, the Evangelical Christians-Baptists of Moldova had their confraternity, which was called the Bessarabia Union of Evangelical Christians-Baptists. At the same time, Romania had its own Baptist Union. The Bessarabia Union was functioning independently. The first congress of the Moldavian fraternity was in 1927. After the war, the Moldavian confraternity merged with the All-Union Council of Evangelical Christians-Baptists. However, the Moldavian confraternity kept the specifics of life and activity of the Bessarabian union." In K. S. Sedletski, "Otchiotnii doklad episkopa soiuza tserkvei evangeliskih khristian-baptistov Moldovi K. S. Sedletskogo 26-mu siezdu moldavskogo bratstva" [Final Report of the Bishop of the Union of the Evangelical

Russian speaking, although in many villages there were believers gathering and reading the Bible in Romanian.

The year of 1920 is known as a year of new movements. The "Lord's Army movement began in the early 1920s, initially as a campaigning force concerned about the morally degenerate state of Romanian society."[55] Further, the "Lord's Army continues to regard itself as an Orthodox movement within the Orthodox Church, although it has 'evangelical' characteristics and many of its members enjoy good relations with non-Orthodox evangelicals."[56]

In the same year of 1920 another event occurred and had an impact on the life of the Evangelical Christian Baptist Churches of Moldova which has lasted until the present day. In London within the Baptist World Union there was a meeting of the largest Baptist missionary agencies of the world. The meeting was attended by US representatives (Southern as well as Northern Baptists), Germans, Canadians, Swedish and some other countries' representatives. England and Scotland were represented by separate delegations. One of the objectives of the meeting was the distribution of human and financial resources so as to most effectively use them and not interfere with each other. All the big agencies took responsibility for a particular region of the world. The Southern Baptist Convention was responsible for Romania, Ukraine and the southern regions of Russia.[57] Moldova, or Bessarabia, is not mentioned, probably because that year it was already part of Romania.

Also at the same meeting agencies tackled the issue of the needs of Central and Eastern European churches. Interestingly, among the recommendations concerning human and financial resources there were others related to the creation and development of: educational institutions – recommendation 2, publication of specialised literature – recommendation 3, construction of buildings – recommendation 4, the reaction to

---

Christian Baptist Churches to the 26th Congress of Moldavian Brotherhood], *Bratskii Vestnik* 4 (1992): 88.

55. P. Walters, *World Christianity. Eastern Europe* (Monrovia, CA: Missions Advanced Research & Communication Center, MARC, 1988), 259.

56. Ibid.

57. Minutes of Executive Committee, and Other Representative Baptists, held at the Baptist Church House, Southhampton Row, London, from 19 to 23 July 1920, 18–19.

the economic problems faced by the church – recommendation 5c, and the support to persecuted churches in Romania – recommendation 5h.[58] Support to others at that time concerned all aspects of the church's life. It is interesting to mention the fact that there were references to Romania. R. T. McConnell was very critical towards the speeches pronounced at the meeting by the Southern Baptist Convention representatives: "Not only did Southern Baptists see themselves as uniquely called to witness to the world, but because of their theological certainty, they felt that they alone were qualified for the task."[59] Further, citing Everett Gill, he says: "By sending missionaries to Europe, the Foreign Mission Board of the Southern Baptist Convention proclaimed, not incidentally, the South's superiority over decadent European culture and Baptist superiority over the 'historic churches' of Europe."[60] I will come back to that point in chapters 4, 8 and 9.

In Bessarabia during the inter-war period, it is worth noting that people were illiterate. People from Bessarabia had been largely Slavonized for about one hundred years. Fifty percent of the population of Chisinau were Jews, and about 25 percent were Ukrainians and Russians. More than half of the Orthodox churches conducted liturgy in Russian – few could read in Romanian. The percentage of illiterates in Bessarabia was the largest in the times of the *România Mare* – 61.4 percent compared to the neighboring Bucovina which had 34.2 percent.[61]

The following information was collected in the village Moldavanka of the Falesti district. Believers began to get together there in 1928 in the house of Harlampy Frasinyuk. It happened that he was absent from the village for two months and he was the only literate person from the group

---

58. Ibid., 15–18.

59. R. T. McConnell, "Indigenous Baptists and Foreign Missionaries: Baptist Communities in Romania, Hungary, and Yugoslavia 1872–1980," (A dissertation submitted as partial fulfillment of the requirements for the degree of Doctor of Philosophy in the Department of History, University of South California, 1996), 38.

60. Ibid., 62.

61. S. P. Ramet, *Nihil Obstat: Religion, Politics, and Social Change in East-Central Europe and Russia* (Durham: Duke University Press, 1998), 182.

of believers. In his absence group members were forced to invite a non-believer to read the Gospel to them so that they were able to pray.[62]

It was in those years that sayings such as "Father – Russian, Mother – Russian, but Ivan – Moldovan" appeared. There were cases until 1940 when street signs in Russian could be seen in Chisinau.[63] Nevertheless, the Romanian government had taken all measures to train a new staff of teachers, to educate a new generation of pro-Romanian Bessarabia intellectuals and to raise the average level of literacy.

New Challenges

During this time, in the territory of Bessarabia, there were associations that were independent from central authority. "Churches were quite independent in pursuing their own pattern of worship, prayers, church structure, doctrinal positions (anthropology, salvation)."[64] An example of such an association is the Union of Evangelical Christians-Baptists, who in 1930 began to publish their own journal "The Light of Life" mainly in Russian.[65] For a few years believers lived in relative peace. Talking about Bessarabia, Philip Walters underlines: "Since 1929, all organized mission and charitable activity has been banned, and evangelism has therefore become the responsibility of the local church, and, above all, of the individual Christian. The witness through word and example of each Christian has assumed the greatest importance. In these circumstances evangelism is generally not targeted at particular groups, but at neighbors and work-mates."[66]

Churches grew and multiplied. "In spite of poverty and persecution, the Baptist cause among Ukrainians and Romanians grew rapidly and included adherents from Jews, Bulgarians, and Gagauz. The growth from 254 members in 1918 in two churches to 18,000 in 347 churches by 1942 was almost unprecedented."[67]

---

62. "Poseshchenie obshchin Moldavskoi SSR starshim presviterom bratom F.R. Astahovim" [Senior Presbyter F. R. Astahov Visits Congregations in Moldavian SSR], *Bratskii Vestnik* 6 (1956): 54.

63. From the memories of the father of the author of this work.

64. Bunaciu, "Romanian Baptists and Mission," 96.

65. Wardin, *Baptists Around the World*, 227.

66. Walters, *World Christianity*, 94. This approach we see as a result of a serious Mennonite presence in the Moldavian territory.

67. Wardin, *Baptists Around the World*, 228.

The Birth and Development of Evangelical Churches 33

Already in 1920 in Romania "the Baptists were forbidden to hold services or to conduct burials. Later there was a period of comparative freedom from 1928–1937, but the next seven years were a time of fierce repression."[68] The same author remarks that between December 1938 and April 1939 and from 1942–1944 all Baptist churches were closed.[69] Tandy McConnell adduces the following figures: "By 1935, 50 churches had been closed in Bessarabia where Baptists were enjoying substantial growth. Most of the harassment consisted of petty bureaucratic regulations. Baptist school children were compelled to attend religion classes taught by Orthodox priests and punished if they refused to attend mass; many governmental jobs were open only to members of the Orthodox Church, and churches could be closed for engaging in any form of 'proselytism' or for criticizing the Orthodox Church in any way."[70]

Evangelical believers were facing some difficulties. "The order led to the persecution of many Baptist believers especially in the regions of Bucovina, Bessarabia and Moldova. Many were tried and sent to jail and some were executed and thrown in the river Dniester."[71]

Of course, these persecutions cannot be compared to Stalin's repressions and the almost complete destruction of the institute of the church in the 1930s in Russia. In Bucharest, albeit with many restrictions, there was a Baptist Theological Seminary. Ivan T. Slobodchikov graduated from the 4-year program in theology (between 1933 and 1937) at that seminary.[72] For many years during the Soviet era he worked first as a senior presbyter in Moldova, as assistant of the senior presbyter, then as presbyter of the Chisinau Evangelical Christian Baptist Church, known today as the "Bethel."

---

68. T. Beeson, *Discretion and Valour: Religious Conditions in Russia and Eastern Europe* (London: Collins, Fontana Books, 1974), 304.
69. Ibid., 305.
70. McConnell, *Indigenous Baptists*, 95.
71. Bunaciu, "Romanian Baptists and Mission," 98.
72. Mickievich, "Iz istorii evangel'sko-baptistskogo," 55.

It should be noted that Romanian gendarmes often mistreated[73] believers, beating[74] them and sentencing them to short-term imprisonment. There was a short period of time when all the churches of the non-Orthodox Christians were closed. However, Romania has always aspired to equal participation in the European Community and reacted very quickly to the arrival of the President of the Baptist World Alliance Rushbrooke, and to the appeal of the BWA addressed to the League of Nations. Churches opened, and Evangelical Christians-Baptists began to witness even more energetically.

Many churches had the opportunity to either buy[75] or build[76] houses of worship. Small groups in many villages were getting together in the leaders' houses.[77]

In 1940, the signing of the Ribbentrop–Molotov pact led to the carving-up of parts of Eastern Europe. Ultimately Stalin gave Romania forty-eight hours to withdraw from Bessarabia. After that, the Soviet troops entered Chisinau.[78] The creation of the Moldavian Soviet Socialist Republic with its capital in Chisinau was soon announced. In the short period of time until June 1941 Moldova did not experience the cruelty of the Soviet power although the hand of Moscow was trying to "quickly restore an order." One of the first acts Stalin carried out was to allow all Germans inhabiting these lands to go to their historic homeland. That year, many Germans who did

---

73. *Bratskii Vestnik* 6 (1956), 55.

74. D. I. Ponomarchiuk, "Starshii presviter VSEHB po Moldavskoi SSR brat D. I. Ponomarchiuk soobshchaet" [Senior Presbyter AUCECB in Moldavian SSR brother D. I. Ponomarchiuk reports], *Bratskii Vestnik* 4 (1957): 77.

75. The Baptist church from Pirlitsa village bought a church building in 1945. From "Poseshchenie obshchin Moldavskoi SSR," 51.

76. In Chisinau, in 1925, a house of worship was built with 500 seats in Ivanov, "Iz istorii evangel'sko-baptistskogo," 57.

77. My grandfather at one time was a presbyter of the Evangelical Baptist Church in the village of Maksymovka, 15 km from Chisinau. The entire village consisted of Ukrainians, previously deported from the Chernovtsi region. According to the memoirs of my mother (born in 1935), the meetings took place in their own home. It happened that up to thirty people were coming to the meeting.

78. The author's archive contains photographs of the parade of 1940, which was organized by the Soviet troops on the central square of Chisinau. It is unprecedented that among the guests of honor of the parade there were officers in the form of SS and SD. The German officers have confirmed by their presence, that everything that was happening was a part of an overall plan.

not want to live in the Soviet Union, went to Germany. When the borders were closed, almost all the remaining Germans were deported to Siberia and Central Asia; that is as far as possible from the border.[79] This had an immediate impact on the number of churches and believers in Moldova. Many churches became empty. In addition, the Soviet government was recruiting soldiers for the Red Army, and many young people, including believers, were drafted into the army.

In June 1941, Germany, without a declaration of war, began to bomb the Ukraine and Belarussia. Romania was one of the few European powers of that time that voluntarily took the side of Nazi Germany. To some extent, this saved Moldova. The entire territory of Bessarabia as well as the southern regions of the Ukraine up to Nikolaev were under the control of the Romanian army.

All these instances bring once again into light the heterogeneity of Moldavian society. Because of Romanian and Russian influences, Bessarabian society has been suffering from this dichotomy. A special role was played by the ECB Church, which from 1920 until today has been able to maintain tolerance towards people of other nationalities. Though during the Soviet regime there was a dominance of the Russian language on the Moldavians, and nowadays there is a reverse tendency, most of the leaders of the Baptist Union speak Romanian as their first language and very often seek for Russian translation during the official meetings. At the same time there were (and there are) churches in Moldova practicing two types of language use.

Consciously or unconsciously, the ECB Church of Moldova has always been a place where the rights of everybody were respected. It has served as a peacekeeper in these complex inter-ethnic relations. Even if in the time period between the two world wars it could not make these calls at the societal level, it coped very well with this on an everyday level. "One of the characteristics of the Moldavian Baptist churches was their passion to help

---

79. I. Bondareva-Zuehlke, "Separation or Co-operation? Moldavian Baptists (1940–1965)," in *Counter-Cultural Communities. Baptistic Life in Twentieth-Century Europe*, ed. K. G. Jones and I. M. Randall (London: Paternoster, 2008), 71.

others, thus supporting an atmosphere of fellowship and building bridges to their fellow countrymen. Baptists had nursing homes, for example."[80]

The Growth of Evangelical Churches in the Soviet Period (1944–1991)

Evangelical Churches in Stalin's Time

As a result of the Iasi-Chisinau operation in 1944, Soviet troops entered Moldova and after long battles seized the capital. A large part of Chisinau city was destroyed and communications were damaged. Almost immediately the liberation of the Moldavian Soviet Socialist Republic from the fascist invaders was proclaimed. The end of war brought hope. People were looking to the future awaiting a new, easier life.

Believers had similar hopes. In 1944 in Moscow, Evangelical Christians and Baptists associated into a union, which was later named the AUCECB. In 1945 the majority of Pentecostal churches joined the union. Walter Zawatsky considers that there was something unnatural about evangelical Christians, Baptists, Mennonites[81] and Pentecostals working together in the AUCECB, as if their historically distinct polities and emphases were secondary.[82]

The Bessarabia Union of Evangelical Christians-Baptists became part of AUCECB. Although for the rest of its history it had its own peculiarities, "the Moldavian Baptists had similar experiences as Baptists in many other newly formed Soviet Republics after World War II."[83] Immediately after the war, Ivan Slobodchikov was appointed as leader[84] of the AUCECB in the Moldavian SSR.

But the years 1946–1947 brought various new challenges.

---

80. Ibid., 73.

81. Mennonites joined the AUCECB in 1967.

82. W. Sawatsky, "The Re-Positioning of Evangelical Christians-Baptists and Sister Church Union Between 1980 and 2005," in *Eastern European Baptist History: New Perspectives*, ed. S. Corrado and T. Pilli (Prague: International Baptist Theological Seminary, 2007), 191.

83. Bondareva-Zuehlke, "Separation or Co-operation?", 63.

84. The term which was used by the public services had also been used for a while in churches but it did not settle down and after several years it was replaced by the term "senior presbyter" of the country (province, region, etc.).

The Birth and Development of Evangelical Churches

First, Bessarabia experienced severe famine. Besides the fact that those years were not especially fertile, the Soviet government was taking out the so-called "surplus," which in practice was almost a complete expropriation in favor of the Soviet regime. Nowadays, this phenomenon is well known (especially in Ukraine) as the *Holodomor*. Hundreds of thousands of people in Moldova died from hunger in just two years.

Second, there was a "cleansing" of the inhabitants of Moldavia[85]. "In 1949 the eviction of 'undesirable elements' was carried out under the code name 'Operation South,' and in 1951 'sectarian elements' were expelled from Moldavia."[86] All the *kulaks*, rich peasants, and shopkeepers had been identified and many of them were deported to camps in Siberia. As many Christians conducted their affairs properly, weren't drunkards, and worked a lot, they were in possession of large plots of land before the war. Accordingly, many of them fell into the category of *kulaks* and were either deported forever to Central Asia with their families or sent to Siberia to detention camps.

Third, believers were not tolerated for a long time, and in 1949 another wave of persecutions began. Thus, the expected life of freedom and relief never came. In spite of this, the *Bratsky Vestnik* journal articles are full of optimism, positive attitude and faith in a brighter future. It should be noted that this was typical for the whole of the periodical press in the USSR.

There were visibly fewer churches in Moldova ("in 1933 the Bessarabia Baptist Union had 238 churches. In 1940, the Moldavian Evangelical Christian-Baptists had only 108 churches, and in 1949 the authorities registered only 83"[87]), however, the same situation prevailed throughout the Soviet Union. Many died on the front, many were repressed, the German communities were almost deserted, and many died of starvation. The ECB Union of Moldova suffered losses due to the fact that southern Bessarabia was given to Ukraine, and with it, about 2,000 adult members of churches[88] joined the Evangelical Christian Baptist Union of Ukraine.

---

85. The original name of the country is Moldova, but Soviet government called it Moldavia.

86. Bondareva-Zuehlke, "Separation or Co-operation?", 67.

87. Ibid., 64.

88. Ibid., 79–80.

But in 1946 growth of churches and many baptisms were again recorded.[89] I. Slobodchikov says that in 1948 there were 3,788 members of Evangelical Christians-Baptists Churches in Moldova.[90]

The mission of the church was to survive. The only form of ministry was holding general meetings. Meetings at the homes of believers, evangelism and social activities were prohibited by law. Education was provided by the state. Personal witness and invitations to meetings were the only forms of evangelism in those years. "In the Soviet Union, Baptists became known as those who took care of each other. This became a powerful message in the socialist society that theoretically offered the best social care in the world, but practically was able to do very little. But Baptists still had to learn how to address issues of social work in the wider society."[91]

In 1948, the AUCECB dismissed I. Slobodchikov from the position of senior presbyter, and appointed Frol Astakhov, who had been regional presbyter in Siberia, in his place. It is surprising that the dismissal of a pastor of national importance was held without consultation with the churches. Michael Bourdeax names this style "the communist style of leadership."[92] That was the practice in those years. One explanation for this lies in the fact that in the statute, which was adopted in 1944, the concept of "election" or "congress" was not even envisaged. The AUCECB authorities ran the Union with full rights and without new elections. From the perspective of today's democratic model, it seems a little far-fetched, but the Soviet people at that time took it for granted because it was the only model that had been accepted. In the case of Moldova things were different, as before World War II congresses were held and senior presbyters were elected in due form. There were various reasons for the replacement of Slobodchikov

---

89. I. Ivanov, "Po obshchinam Moldavii" [On the Moldavian Congregations], *Bratskii Vestnik* 5 (1946): 35.

90. I. M. Orlov, "Otchiot starshego presvitera I. T. Slobodchikova" [Report of the Senior Presbyter I. T. Slobodchikov], *Bratskii Vestnik* 3 (1948): 66–67.

91. T. Pilli, "Baptist Identities in Eastern Europe," in *Baptist Identities. International Studies from Seventeenth to the Twentieth Century*, ed. I. M. Randall, T. Pilli, and A. Cross (Milton Keynes: Paternoster, 2006), 103.

92. M. Bourdeaux, "Religious Liberty in Soviet Union: Baptists in the Early Days of Protest (1960–1966)," in *Eastern European Baptist History: New Perspectives*, ed. S. Corrado and T. Pilli (Prague: International Baptist Theological Seminary, 2007), 126.

with Astakhov, and one of them was that Slobodchikov was not able to negotiate with the authorities.[93]

It was during those years that the practice of holding prayer meetings appeared. There was an acute shortage of Bibles and religious literature. In many churches there was one Bible for the whole community. People needed the Word of God. Frequent visits to houses of worship were the only form of support for the people's faith, the raising of community spirit, and I would add, the controlling of discipline.

Even among preachers there were many in those years who did not have their own Bible,[94] and therefore had no opportunity to prepare for sermons. Then the practice of preaching without preparation appeared and was then called "where the Lord will open." The Bible was on the pulpit, the preacher went up to it, not even knowing what he would read and talk about. He opened the Bible at some page read out the first passage he saw and preached. Typically, the sermon consisted of a narration of the passage. The ability to link together some of the passages from different books of the Bible and introduce some life stories related to the subject was seen as skillful preaching. It sounds strange nowadays but in those days it was the only opportunity for people to listen to biblical texts.

Evangelical Churches in Khrushchev's Time

Khrushchev's coming to power was also seen with hope. The cult of personality associated with Stalin was condemned; a "thaw" began. Quite interesting is the fact that in 1957 the senior presbyter of Moldova was changed. In place of Astakhov, the AUCECB authorities appointed Dmitry Ponomarchuk, former leader of the Christians of Evangelical Faith (Pentecostals) of Ukraine.[95] Even more interesting is the reason for this

---

93. Bondareva-Zuehlke, "Separation or Co-operation?," 87.

94. From the memories of Olga and Mikhail Mocan, Ivan Boiarskii, Elena Rimskaia and many other evangelicals of the third generation.

95. Belonging to Pentecostals in the past immediately reflected on the reports that D. Ponomarchuk sent to the AUCECB leadership, and which are printed in the Confraternity Herald. As an example, we can look through issues of 1957 No. 4 p. 78–79 – meetings with representatives of Pentecostal churches who wished to join the AUCECB were held, 1958 No. 5–6, p. 28 – it is mentioned that about 300 members of Pentecostal churches joined the AUCECB; 1959 No. 2, p. 8 – there is a great emphasis on the fact that a lot of Pentecostal believers continued to join the AUCECB.

change. Moldavian presbyters wrote a collective letter to the AUCECB with complaints against Astakhov asking for them to replace him with somebody else.[96] In Stalin's time it would have been impossible to write such a letter. Khrushchev's pluralism was warmly received in churches.

Everyone was waiting for change and when change arrived, they came. But the changes were not for the better. The authorities realized that faith could not be eradicated by force. Cruel repression ended, but was replaced by more sophisticated methods. A special department was created to monitor the activities of sectarians – the Council for the Affairs of Religious Cults, which worked very closely with the AUCECB.

Surely, this was not an isolated case of cooperation between the authorities and the AUCECB leadership. Thinking critically in this case, we must always remember the period in which these events happened. Despite the fact that before the war the crucial repressions literally scattered the church, I believe people were hoping that once the union would be registered, things would change for the better. Many did not see the authorities as the enemy anymore and perhaps this was the aim of the secret services and of the commissioners for Religious Affairs.

In 1959, the famous circular prohibiting any religious activities outside the church building entered into force; presenting a list of all members of the church was required as well as discussing candidates for baptism with the authorities. A ban on children under eighteen years of age attending meetings, restrictions on the baptism of young people under thirty years, a ban on musical activities (except for the chorus) and many others, were imposed. Such bans did not intimidate the church. Immediately after the government circular was produced there followed the "Letter of Instruction" of the AUCECB leadership, which was written in the spirit of that circular. In this "Letter" there were examples from the Bible cited and a spiritual explanation. Such measures led to changes in the meetings, which were held, and cut for a long time the desire to find new forms of liturgy.

I must mention the fact that the consequences of those decisions are being felt in many churches to this day. "A dichotomy developed in Baptist life: the world became sharply divided into two spheres – a public sphere

---

96. Bondareva-Zuehlke, "Separation or Co-operation?", 88.

and a private sphere. Partly because of atheistic pressures, religion was pushed into the private sphere of life. In some regions, there was also the strong influence of Pietism."[97]

The letter of instruction and the measures undertaken to implement it led to the separation of the Union into the so-called "registered" and "unregistered" churches, which became known as *Initsiativniki*. In Chisinau, the religious services were carried out by one of the most prominent *Initsiativnik* of All-Union significance – Michael Horev. His name was often mentioned together with the names of Vince, and Kruchkov.[98] The unity that was so painstakingly acquired was lost. Taking into consideration the current situation in the churches of the initiative group, it is difficult to disagree with the statement: "Radicals opened the door to sectarianism and 'Christian' extremism."[99]

There continue to be contradictions between the two associations until today, and in Moldova communion between the two groups has not yet been restored.

Evangelical Churches in Brezhnev's Time

Brezhnev's times were indeed a temporary relief for the church. The church's "thaw" began only during that period of time. "It seems that the religious situation in Brezhnev's period of Soviet history was relatively good; indeed it could be compared with the 1920s when the majority of Evangelical Christians enjoyed even more liberties than in Tsarist Russia."[100] Although this statement can be attributed to the USSR as a whole, in different republics there were different attitudes towards believers, and the local authorities gave specific authorizations or prohibitions to one or another activity. Ph. Walters gives an example: "In the 1970s the Baptist church in Moldavia had received permission to print 8,000 Bibles and 8,000 hymn books in Moldavian."[101]

---

97. Pilli, "Baptist Identities in Eastern Europe," 102.
98. Bourdeaux, "Religious Liberty in Soviet Union," 120.
99. C. Prokhorov, "The State and the Baptist Churches in the USSR (1960–1980)," in *Counter-Cultural Communities: Baptistic Life in Twentieth-Century Europe*, ed. K. G. Jones and I. M. Randall (Milton Keynes; Colorado Springs: Paternoster, 2008), 53.
100. Ibid., 49.
101. Walters, *World Christianity*, 101.

The AUCECB obtained not only relief but also the opportunity to develop international contacts, participate in various forums and to engage in different kinds of ecumenical organizations, although this trend had begun to appear even since Khrushchev's time. In different years the AUCECB took part in BWA, EBF, WCC, CEC and other associations. The Secretary-General of the AUCECB, A. Karev, reported to the Congress in 1969: "The value of the present-day ecumenical movement rests also in that it brings to the world practical Christianity which bends over humanity's numerous wounds and seeks ways to heal them."[102] But Walter Zawatsky sees that all these activities were negotiated more from a pragmatic stance than deliberate theological commitment to unity.[103] It is difficult to disagree with him especially considering the fact that almost all newly formed alliances of the ECB after the Soviet collapse withdrew from the World Council of Churches, some from the Baptist World Alliance, and even from the European Baptist Federation.

In the journal *Bratsky Vestnik* in the 1950s there were such articles as "Christians for World Peace." In the 1960s this kind of article was part of the column "Voice for Peace" and no issue of the journal was published without articles on the subject. K. Jones considers that "Russian Baptists found this involvement [Peace Conferences] in the call for peace a way of keeping a tolerable relationship with the Soviet government. It held a possibility of relating in some way to the outside world."[104] This is the only activity of the so-called public or social sphere, which was permitted to the church.[105] "The churches were legally prevented from becoming involved

---

102. "Report of the AUCECB General Secretary, A.V. Karev to the All-Union Congress of Evangelical Christians-Baptists, 1969" in *Proceedings of the All-Union Congress of Evangelical Christians-Baptists, 1969*, 35.

103. Sawatsky, "The Re-Positioning," 193.

104. K. G. Jones, "The European Baptist Federation. A Case Study in European Baptist Interdependency 1950–2006" (Thesis is submitted for the degree of Doctor of Philosophy, 2007), 267.

105. A case is known when in Mikhailovka village, Singerei district, Baptist church members were instructed by Senior Presbyter, Frol Astakhov' not to continue collecting "freewill offerings for the needs of the poor and orphans" – Bondareva-Zuehlke, "Separation or Co-operation?", 73.

in charitable or social welfare activities because, in theory, a socialist state is fully competent in these areas."[106]

It is worth noting that in Brezhnev's era, as well as regular columns there were also "Christian's Solidarity," "Theological Essays," "History of the Church," and "Reports from Everywhere." At least one third of each volume was occupied with articles on peacemaking and unity. The AUCECB authorities were calling for unity, not only with the unregistered ECB churches, but also with the Anglicans, Orthodox, and with all the Protestant denominations.[107]

Particular attention was paid to the relationship between the leadership of the ECB and Orthodox churches. "Friendly relations have been established between the AUCECB and the Russian Orthodox Church. Brotherly contacts are set, exchange of Christian literature takes place, and mutual visits and conversations are practiced."[108]

Antagonism, rejection and attacks were things of the past. The Soviet government gave equal rights to Evangelical and Orthodox believers and this fact had an impact on the nature of their relationships. At the same congress, A.V. Karev said: "We must all know, and thank God, that there are many Orthodox believers and Catholics with a truly Christian heart, with whom we can have truly Christian relations."[109]

The mission of AUCECB churches focused on social peacekeeping, maintaining unity[110] and spiritual growth[111] of the church achieved by

---

106. Walters, *World Christianity*, 105–106.

107. *Bratsky Vestnik*, 1959, no. 2; 1960, no. 5–6; 1961, no. 1; 1961, no. 4; 1962, no. 3; 1962, no. 4; 1962, no. 5-6; 1965, no. 1; 1965, no. 2; 1966, no. 5; 1967, no. 1; 1967, no. 6; 1968, no. 4; 1968, no. 5; 1976, no. 2; 1977, no. 2 and many others.

108. Ibid.

109. "Report of the AUCECB General Secretary, A.V. Karev to the All-Union Congress of Evangelical Christians-Baptists, 1969," 35.

110. All of the Councils (1963, 1966, 1969, 1974 and 1979) spent significant time discussing the theme of separation and seeking ways to build unity, mentions K. Prokhorov, "The State and the Baptist Churches," 43.

111. Russian Baptist community disciplines historically included: corporate adherence to evangelical faith in God; regular church attendance 2–3 times a week; studying the Bible; faithfulness to one's spouse; a modest appearance manifested by a simple haircut, inexpensive clothes and a lack of adornment; total abstention from alcohol and tobacco; and active assistance in any church needs, writes Prokhorov, "The State and the Baptist Churches," 44–45.

church meetings: "services [common gatherings] take central place in the spiritual work."[112]

In 1973, the Moldovan ECB Union provided Malanchuk with his pension (on request) and elected as senior presbyter K. Sedletsky,[113] who held the office until 1992.

Evangelical Churches in Gorbachev's Time

Gorbachev's era brought freedom of expression as well as *freedom of belief*. Probably the date that divides one era from another is 1988, the year of celebrating the Millennium of Christianity in Russia, which was actively joined by the AUCECB. For the first time preaching was heard in stadiums, theaters, and even in public places on the street.

In the short period of *Perestroika* there was significant growth of the Moldavian churches. More than one hundred people were baptized in the central church "Bethel" in 1990. Many more were baptized in other churches.

Conclusions

Taking account of the information above, we can draw some conclusions for the first chapter.

1) During the last two hundred years, Moldova was a part of Russia and Romania and because of that was under the influence of the Russian Orthodox Church and the Romanian Orthodox Church.
2) The emergence of the Evangelical movement in the territory of the Empire did not have only a single source and cannot be associated with a particular name or even a confession.
3) Evangelicals survived a lot of persecution during the entire period of time.
4) Evangelicals were very active in their mission. Mennonites evangelized through their lifestyle and in some cases by their social involvement in education and charitable acts. Baptists and

---

112. *Evangelical Christian-Baptist in the USSR* (in Russian and English languages), (Izdanie Vsesoiuznogo Soveta Evangei'skih hristian baptistov, Moskva, 1979), 15.

113. *Bratskii Vestnik* 5 (1973): 76.

Shtundists mostly saw their calling in evangelism and spiritual growth.

5) The churches of Bessarabia, in contrast to the churches of the Russian Empire, united relatively painlessly in one union, which was a continuation of tolerance laid down by Ivanov, Khizhnyakov and Averbukh. Churches united to make their ministry effective, and that resulted in a huge amount of growth.

6) The main form of missionary activity during the Soviet time was personal witness and invitations to meetings, where the Word of God was preached. For various reasons, evangelical churches in Bessarabia were not involved in social activities.

The AUCECB was involved very actively in ecumenical forums, and also in dialogue with the Russian Orthodox Church. ПрослушатьНалатинице

CHAPTER 2

Mission of Evangelical Churches in Moldova from the End of the Twentieth to the First Decade of the Twenty-First Century

In the previous chapter, I reviewed the roots of the Evangelical movement in Moldavian territory, paying attention not only to original documents, but also trying to foresee the relations between the history of the church and general history. I tried to show the history of Evangelical churches from a missiological perspective, taking into consideration different approaches which were used by various Evangelical groups. I pointed out the difference in mission methods between Baptists and Mennonites, where Baptists were more involved in personal evangelism, discipleship and spiritual growth, while Mennonites emphasized personal witness as the main method for sharing the gospel in Tsarist Russia. During the Soviet period, personal witness remained the only mission approach used by Evangelicals (united in one union) and it was the only way permitted by authorities.

It was mentioned that Evangelical Baptists were active in their dialogue with the Russian Orthodox Church during the Soviet times.

Now I will proceed to an overview of the religious situation in Moldova, and then I will look at the evangelistic crusades in Moldova. I will examine the mission of Evangelical Baptist churches in Moldova, learning from the official declarations of the bishops, published articles in magazines and newspapers, and theological reflections of the main theological body for Evangelical Baptists in Moldova – the College of Theology and Education.

I will show how narrative descriptions of Moldavian churches show their values in mission, and how these values are connected with the *missio Dei*.

Religious Situation after Collapse of the USSR Block

The UCECBM and the UCCEFPM represent a very diverse association of churches. They differ on the grounds of their theological positions, as well as forms of worship, structure, social activity and willingness to enter dialogue. After the collapse of the Soviet Union all the churches were busy for a certain period of time with self-identification, restructuring within independent states, carrying out mass campaigns, actions, building new churches etc. Mihail Nevolin, talking about the situation in Russia in his article "The Theological, Structural and Social Self-identification of Russian Protestants," emphasizes three most important areas in which the Protestants must identify themselves, and they are reflected in the title of his article. Moreover, the author notes that even at the turn of the millennium, our churches were not yet self-identified.[1] A certain union might include churches that adhere to different doctrines, have different structures and weak social activity. Nevolin is concerned that the Protestant denominations could fail to present themselves as a cohesive community as they have not yet agreed on a unique form and belief. Further, he suggests laying down a code of belief, church structure, form of carrying out divine services, and social doctrine of the church, believing that this would make it possible to consolidate the Protestant churches.[2]

I disagree with M. Nevolin in this matter. I have had the occasion to attend pastoral conferences and congresses in Moldova where similar proposals were articulated. The UCECBM has even established a committee to formulate such a provision under the leadership of one of the leading Baptist apologists of Moldova, Alexandru Girbu. He acknowledged that drawing up such a document would probably lead to a lot of controversy

---

1. M. Nevolin, "The Theological, Structural and Social Self-identification of Russian Protestants," http://www.kbogu.ru/?3-5-21

2. Ibid.

within the union.³ Since the collapse of the Soviet Union, churches have become so different and have experienced many influences both from outside and from inside. This is why it is so difficult to bring together almost 500 communities and make them agree on matters of dogma and ecclesiastical unity. The leadership of the ECB Union of Moldova has decided to give churches the opportunity to develop along their chosen paths, and find ways to unite on the basis of free association and general agreement. Thus, the conclusion is that churches should not wait to unite to be able to represent their creed or to enter a dialogue with other churches. The results of the research done in this field between the years of 2000 and 2001 by the Ukrainian sociologist Elena Nazarkina support this idea. Her study was on the social image of the Evangelical communities in the Donetsk region (Ukraine).⁴

According to her research, about a third of the church members of the four different surveyed denominations (the Churches of Evangelical Christian Baptists, Evangelical Christian Churches, Charismatic Churches and the Churches of Christ), have during their lifetime changed from one evangelical church to another. Only 33 percent of them did this because of changing residence. Others changed church because of doctrinal disagreements with the leadership of the church, being offered a specific ministry in another church, because of conflicts, etc. Nevertheless, "fluidity facilitates the search for a more favorable psycho-emotional climate. As a result, these communities are that social organism that performs significant socializing activities in society," considers E. Nazarkina.⁵ People, as well as churches are trying to identify themselves, the passage occurring both from one community to another one within a denomination, and also between denominations. This process continues till nowadays, and in spite of this, there is a great deal of high social activity conducted by churches, although, churches in Ukraine are experiencing the same identity crisis as churches in Russia. It may happen that the search for identity will lead the

---

3. A. Girbu to author, November 2005.

4. The Donetsk region was chosen for the reason that it has the largest concentration of evangelical communities throughout Ukraine, http://www.religio.ru/relisoc/97.phpl

5. E. Nazarkina, "The Social Image of the Protestant Communities in Modern Ukraine," http://www.religio.ru/relisoc/97.phpl

church to an introspective analysis to such an extent that it could forget what the main purpose of this analysis was: to make themselves known by society and other denominations. Despite the fact that there are different views and structures within the Orthodox Church, we are still talking about the Orthodox Church as a single entity and see the Lutheran Church as an entity, even if there is no harmonization either in one or the other of these denominations.

In this case, it would be relevant to quote the Patriarch of the Russian Orthodox Church: "The Russian Orthodox Church of Moscow Patriarchate has a high opinion of the Lutheran Church, which adopted a conservative position, and exists in Russia under different jurisdictions."[6] We see that the difference in structure does not represent for the ROC an impediment to dialogue with the Lutherans, who presently have a close relationship with the Orthodox Church in the territory of the CIS. Although, the same Kirill declares:

> The Orthodox Church does not set any taboos in the cooperation with the evangelical churches . . . The Russian Orthodox Church of Moscow Patriarchate is ready to collaborate with the Protestant churches for the consolidation of the civil society, but this does not mean that all the critical issues and problems will find their immediate solution. There is a long history of relationship between Orthodoxy and Evangelical Christian Baptists, lasting since the Soviet era. Orthodox Churches hold regular round table discussions with Baptists on social and socio-political issues and disagreements arise only in relationships with the Pentecostals.[7]

There has never been an easy relationship between the Evangelical churches and the Russian Orthodox Church of Moscow Patriarchate. The 1990s presented many examples of mutual accusations and insults. There have been attempts of incitement to physical extermination of pastors of the Baptist churches by some priests of the Orthodox Church (in Moldova several cases were registered of the destruction of printed material

---

6. http://portal-credo.ru/site/?act=news&id=38090&cf accessed 15 November 2005.
7. Ibid.

spread by Evangelical churches and damage to the prayer houses).[8] Similar violent acts have been carried out in Russia too. The organization called "International Religious Freedom Watch" believes that the persecution of Baptists from Lyubuchansk, Moscow, and the silence of most of the international organizations on this issue, threatens the religious freedom of all the believers in Russia.[9]

At the same time, many Evangelical preachers sit in judgment against the Orthodox Church, deriding its traditions, comparing them with pagan ones.[10] There is no doubt that often such statements and actions are caused by a lack of awareness concerning the tenets and beliefs both of individual believers and churches in general. In the same study, E. Nazarkina considers the relationship between members of the Evangelical churches and the Orthodox Church. One of the questions was: "What spiritual gift can the Orthodox believers get in their church?" Forty-four percent of respondents were undecided on this issue. Twenty-one percent responded that the Orthodox Church is a wrong one, invented by people, and leading people nowhere. Thirty-five percent of respondents said that some of the spiritual gifts might be given to Orthodox, while specifying that these should be true believers.[11] There are serious prejudices showing the negative attitude of many Evangelical believers towards Orthodoxy. It can be assumed that such an opinion is made up of personal experience, and also due to errors

---

8. Particularly active in collecting such information is the Division of Intercession of the International Council of Evangelical Christians-Baptists, which recorded many such cases while limiting these to occurances in Moldova. Just to cite a few: the beating of the Baptist preachers by an Orthodox priest in the village Ishnovets, Criuleni District on July 5, 2004, in the village Semeny, Ungheni District, repeated attacks on prayer houses in the village of Rocky Dubasari district, circulation of leaflets in the village of Roshkany village Anenii-Noi District, http://iucecb.com/news/20050114-1705 accessed 14 January 2005.

9. http://portal-credo.ru/site/?act=news&id=33660&type=view accessed 24 May 2005.

10. I have repeatedly heard such preaching in different churches, not only in Moldova, but also in Ukraine and Russia. Prayers before the icons are compared with idolatry, and priests are presented as uneducated people. In some families, there were cases of refusal to attend the weddings of their children only because they married an Orthodox believer. I know many cases when believers who married an Orthodox were excluded from the evangelical communities, with the words: "What fellowship to light with *darkness*? What concord to *Christ* with *Belial*?"

11. E. Nazarkina, "The Social Image."

committed by certain believers or even ordained priests, which are then projected onto the church as a whole.

It is useless to deny the fact that such a state of affairs exists and that the negative attitude towards people of other confessions has some reasonable grounds. It is notable that attempts to start a dialogue, or proceed to joint actions, are seen by many pastors as attempts to look good in the eyes of the "Big Church."[12] The end of the twentieth century is marked not only by large-scale evangelistic campaigns, but also by interfaith struggle on the one hand, and interfaith cooperation on the other.

At the moment, the issue of the relationship between the Evangelical and Orthodox churches is also one of the most controversial. The secretary of the Department for External Church Relations of the Moscow Patriarchate, Mikhail Dudko, referring to Russia's Protestants, offered to support the legalization of agreements on social partnership between churches and government at the highest level. In response in 2005, the former chairman of the Russian Union of Evangelical Christian Baptists, Y. K. Sipko said, "The equality of the religious associations in contemporary Russia is determined by their size . . . this is insanity and a violation of the principle of equality since the agency concluded agreements only with the Russian Orthodox Church of the Moscow Patriarchate . . . You say, 'Try and sign agreements with the government.' We have tried, but they made it clear – 'every cricket should know its own hearth.'"[13]

Undoubtedly, such rough remarks towards the State are in some way justified and followed ineffective experiences of uncooperation with governmental structures. There is evidence that attempts at cooperation in the social sphere are taken as "religious dialogue," and activity of the Evangelical churches in this direction is taken as public proselytizing.

---

12. There was a case within the Union of the Evangelical Christian Baptists of Russia when at a local level pastors carried out joint actions with the orthodox, after which the media published the results with attached photos. Some of my colleagues from well-known organizations in Russia, structurally related to the ECB, pronounced themselves in a hostile way on such actions and articles, bringing forward the following arguments: "How would it be able to evangelize the orthodox, if our brothers are photographed with them?" and "Is it for this that our fathers suffered?" It is important to note that here are presented the views of educated young leaders presently holding key positions in large organizations.

13. http://portal-credo.ru/site/?act=news&id=34722&cf accessed 19 July 2005.

The Director of the Social Assistance Center, "Feel the Force of the Change," Yuri Ananiev, talking about the social project which was implemented in the Arkhangelsk region by the Union of Evangelical Christians-Baptists, the Russian Union of Christians of Evangelical Faith (Pentecostals), the Russian Evangelical Church and the Seventh-day Adventist Church, wondered why Bishop Tikhon of the Arkhangelsk diocese of the Russian Orthodox Church, having been invited to participate jointly in this action, changed soon from a passive observer into the initiator of an aggressive campaign against the participating churches. Ananiev himself declared that he wished a dialogue, not a confrontation.[14]

In this case, it should be noted that the same sharp remarks towards the State indirectly hurt the Orthodox Church too. Despite the fact that there has been little cooperation, there has been some positive experiences. In 2005, in Russia, the project "Time to Live"[15] was initiated by Evangelical believers, which was aimed at young people and supported at the highest level, up to governors and ministers. The project, by means of concerts, festivals, and Social Issues Documentary Film contests, showed the perspective of combating and preventing such social problems as drug addiction, AIDS and others. In another interview in 2004, Y. Sipko said:

> I am very pleased with the results of the inter-religious dialogue. All the participants unanimously decided to make such meetings regular. We concluded that we need to consult together on matters of relationship with the government, social service, military service and alternative civilian service. In all the discussions there was an atmosphere of closeness, which is present in the Christian world, but about which we often forget in the turmoil of life. It was obvious for everybody that the Orthodox with all their might and the less numerous Baptists, need each other. We have one Lord and one future. Of course, such meetings help to reduce inter-religious tensions.[16]

---

14. http://portal-credo.ru/site/index.php?act=news&id=33673&type=view accessed 24 May 2005.

15. http://www.time-to-live.ru

16. *Nezavisimaya gazeta, Religions* 12 May 2004, no. 8.

I referred to two different quotation made by K. Sipko and they contradict one another. He was very positive in 2004, but his remark in 2005 was very negative. I am not sure about the grounds of this changed attitude, but it shows that the reality of inter-denominational dialogue is very controversial. It looks like that there is no common agreement or common policy even in one ECB Russian union.

In Ukraine and Moldova, Evangelical Christians have founded charities and non-governmental organizations in order to prevent many social problems and have held lectures in schools and summer camps. Many such organizations are registered with the Minister of Justice and have no declared evangelistic purposes. I would suppose that many cooperation projects with the government were unsuccessful because most Evangelical churches do not have clearly defined differences between their evangelistic and social activities. Frequently, the social activities transmit an implicit evangelistic message. The second part of this research work will consider in detail all the concepts of Evangelical mission and will compare them with those existing in Moldova. Nevertheless, it should be noted that evangelistic efforts[17] alert both the state and the Orthodox Church, which in such cases, accuse Evangelical churches of attempts at proselytism and knowing the background of the Evangelical churches, I could say with certainty that these accusations are not groundless. At the same time, by the means of an approach dominated by mutual respect, the situation could change radically. The studies conducted by Oleg Gavrish in Ukraine have shown that in that country the heads of the most numerous churches are ready not only for open dialogue but also for joint cooperation.[18]

---

17. In this context, I am not talking about the violation of the commandment of Jesus Christ to spread the good news to the ends of the earth. I am talking about the so-called "aggressive evangelism" from which many communities of evangelical Christians became known to the whole society. These are attempts to impose the evangelical view of salvation, while condemning all other possible interpretations within the Christian tradition. This is the so-called "evangelism of condemnation," which does not spread the good news, but preaches the torment of hell and death. This is "evangelism from the opposite," which condemns the Orthodox Church and sees their own church as the only panacea.

18. O. Gavrish, "Ukrainskoe hristianstvo: bol'she obwego, chem razlichnogo" [Ukrainian Christianity: More Alike than Different]', *Zerkalo nedeli* [The Mirror of the week] 32, 24 August 2002. The author presents interviews with Bishop Mitrophan, the business manager of the Ukrainian Orthodox Church, Archbishop Igor of the autocephalous Ukrainian Orthodox Church, Bishop Dmitri of the Ukrainian Orthodox Church of the

The third part of this research work will also focus on the relationship between evangelism and social action from the perspective of *missio Dei*, which was developed in the middle of the twentieth century by Protestant theologians, mostly European, within the World Council of Churches, part of whom are both Russian and Romanian Orthodox churches. At this stage, the study should enlighten the current situation, stressing the main existing problems and the common points between the Evangelical and Orthodox churches.

Evangelistic Crusades and Church Growth in Independent Moldova

As already mentioned, *Perestroika* and the collapse of the USSR offered the churches of Moldova wide opportunities for evangelism as well as for social activities. In 1992, Karl Sedletsky surrendered his powers as senior presbyter of Moldova. He was replaced by Viktor Loginov[19] who, two years later, suggested Victor Popovici be appointed to the same position, which was approved by the Congress. Since then, the senior presbyter of Moldova has become known as the Bishop of the Union of Evangelical Christian Baptists of Moldova.

The 1990s in Moldova (as in many other former Soviet republics) were marked by new unknown phenomena: rampant criminality, unemployment, an increasing number of poverty-stricken and destitute people in the country, the spread of drug use, an increasing number of abortions and teenage pregnancies. Against this background, there was a visible thirst for accepting the gospel. Speaking about those times, Fiodor Mocan (the founder of one of the new churches in Chisinau and of the first Bible

---

Kiev Patriarchate, Father Victor Makkovski of the Ukrainian Roman Catholic Church, Archpriest Olexa Petrov of the Ukrainian Greek Catholic Church, Bishop Vyacheslav Gorpinchuk of the Ukrainian Lutheran Church, Vitaly Tkachuk of the *All-Ukrainian Union of Churches of Evangelical Christian Baptists*, Vladimir Franchuk of the Union of Christians of Evangelical Faith – Pentecostals, Anatoly Kalyuzhny from the Council of Independent Evangelical Churches of Ukraine, Vasily Davidyuk of the Association of Missionary Churches of Evangelical Christians of Ukraine and Anatoly Gavrilyuk of the Association of Independent Charismatic Churches of Ukraine of the Full Gospel. All of them, in one voice, assert that unity is a biblical principle and all of them are ready for cooperation and mutual acceptance.

19. http://www.bethel.md/view_post.php?id=25 accessed 2 September 2010.

College in Moldova) said, "We did not do anything special for the evangelization of the city. We were just walking in the streets inviting people to come to worship services, and people were coming. They were coming ready to accept Christ. The churches were growing. A good example is our church 'The Light to the World' which grew from twenty people attending it in 1994 grew to 170 people in 1999."[20]

Some Western evangelists such as Luis Palau, the Billy Graham Evangelistic Association, Campus Crusade for Christ and others also took advantage of the new opportunities. Evangelistic campaigns were held in tents, stadiums, concert halls, streets and squares.[21] I was personally involved in most such events held in Chisinau, from 1993 until 1996. All these were happening against the backdrop of yet another phenomenon – migration. Hundreds and later, thousands, of members of Evangelical churches took the opportunity to move to the USA permanently. In addition, ethnic Germans began to move to Germany and the Jews to the USA, Germany and Israel. "[In 1991 alone], 60 members of the Chisinau 'Bethel' church left abroad for various reasons, and in 1992, more than 120."[22] There were over 10,000 adult baptized members of the Union of Evangelical Christian Baptists who moved abroad during the years after the proclamation of independence of the Republic of Moldova."[23]

Nevertheless, the number of church members grew from 10,000 in 1990 up to 20,000 in 2000.[24] "Baptists were engaged in church planting and active evangelism."[25] Though, in the early 1990s, the idea of founding new churches was not just new, but even unacceptable. The former Bishop of the Union of Evangelical Christian Baptists, Victor Popovici said: "When the Southern Baptist Convention representatives first came to our country and, having studied our situation said that we still needed at least twenty Baptist churches in Chisinau, we were outraged. We did not understand at

---

20. F. Mocan interview given to the author 16 August 2010.
21. T. Pilli, "Baptist History in Moldova," in *A Dictionary of European Baptist Life and Thought*, ed. J. H. Briggs (Milton Keynes; Colorado Springs: Paternoster, 2009), 337.
22. http://www.bethel.md/view_post.php?id=25 accessed 2 September 2010.
23. Pilli, "Baptist History in Moldova," 337.
24. Ibid.
25. Ibid.

that time the reason of planting lots of churches. Our guests had to make a lot of efforts to convince us. We are thankful to them for this."[26]

Yet in 1995, in the first post-Soviet Moldovian Baptist Journal, was written: "God blessed the Republic of Moldova with awakening, and in comparison with the 70s there are three times more churches."[27] Only in Chisinau, the number of churches increased from two in 1990 to eight in 1995 and to twenty-one in 2007.[28] Churches appeared in nearly every small district and suburb of the capital.

It is worth mentioning that, in the 1920s, when Bessarabia was part of Romania, the Moldovan Union of Evangelical Christian Baptists experienced almost exactly the same phenomenon of church growth. During a period of twenty years, the number of churches increased to 250.[29] In 1929, at the congress devoted to the tenth anniversary of evangelism in Moldova, it was said: "The times when we, the Evangelical Christian-Baptists, were considered a miserable sect, has passed."[30] As noted above, the Tsarist Russia times were times of persecution, and this is why church growth had been hampered. Once relative freedom was achieved, the church began to actively engage in evangelistic activities, to establish new communities, and as a result to grow rapidly. Moldova went through almost the same seventy years later. I assume that the people of Moldova are relatively open to the gospel.

There is also another element to which I would like to draw attention – the official language of the Union of Evangelical Christian Baptists was Russian, even when Bessarabia was part of Romania. The official magazine of the union "The Light of Life" was published in Russian in those years and only since 1930 were some pages in Romanian added. The churches were multinational, and this was noted in different publications: "During the worship service people were praying in different languages – Romanian, Russian, Bulgarian, Hebrew, German, Ukrainian, and

---

26. V. Popovici, "Report at the Congress of the Union of Evangelical Christian Baptists of Moldova," Chisinau, Moldova, August, 2002.

27. *The Light of Life* no. 1 (May–June 1995), 3.

28. V. Ghiletchi, "Annual Report of the Bishop of the UECBCM," Chisinau, March 2008.

29. *The Light of Life* no. 6–7 (1930): 17.

30. *The Light of Life* no. 5 (1929): 10.

Gagauz."[31] Periodically, sermons were preached in Hebrew for the edification of those present at the meeting of the Jews.[32] The 1990s echoed the events of the 1920's. The working language of the congresses was Russian, although sermons were also delivered in Romanian, and prayers were heard in Ukrainian, Gagauz and Bulgarian languages despite the fact that the official language in that period was Romanian (Moldavian). This small observation allows us to identify another trait of the Evangelical movement in Moldova – the times of church growth and awakening were not related to the growth of nationalism or national identity in the churches. On the contrary, there was a growing tolerance and respect towards the representatives of different nationalities.

Tolerance and indulgence were manifested in the care for outcasts. In 1931, under the Chisinau churches, an asylum for elderly women and widows,[33] and a house of mercy,[34] were built. In the 1990s, the Evangelical Christian Baptist Churches were involved in charitable activities aimed at children with disabilities,[35] launching service projects for drug addicts,[36] helping the orphans,[37] the poor and the sick,[38] and conducting ministries for deaf people.[39] It is important to note that these charitable projects and activities were not carried out just because they were mentioned in the documents or the statements of the Union. More often, they were a spontaneous movement.

In 1998, the main strategy of the Evangelical Christian Baptist Union was to plant Evangelical Christian Baptist Churches in every locality of the country. In Moldova, there are about 1,200 settlements, and at that time there were about 300 churches. The Congress attendants accepted the strategy according to which, in the next 3 years, every church should plant

---

31. Ibid.
32. *The Light of Life* no. 6–7 (1930): 17.
33. *The Light of Life* no. 11 (1931): 11.
34. Ibid.
35. *The Light of Life* no. 1 (1996).
36. *The Light of Life* no. 6 (1996).
37. Ibid.
38. *The Light of Life* no. 1 (1997).
39. *The Light of Life* no. 1 (1995).

a new church, and thus by the end of 2000, the target would be achieved.[40] The vision and the strategy were developed with the assistance and support of the International Mission Board of the Southern Baptist Convention. The Evangelical Christian Baptist Union of Moldova was involved every three years in a strategic partnership with the association of SBC churches of some state. At each Congress, the representatives of the convention delivered sermons and lectures motivating the pastors to plant new churches. Even so, there were pastors and representatives of the Union authorities who did not share that vision. In 2003, Valery Ghiletchi at the annual pastoral conference said that it was better to have one strong church than two weak ones.[41] This assertion was based on the fact that according to statistics the number of new churches and groups for several years had actually increased by almost half, while the number of members of those churches remained unchanged. Thus, churches needed more and more preachers and pastors, as often a pastor or a missionary was working in 2–3 places. Given the fact that pastors are rarely rewarded financially for their church activity this meant that they had to have an additional job as well as church responsibilities. Church growth stopped. It could be seen in two areas: (1) reduction of the number of newly planted churches; and (2) stagnation of the number of the members of the denomination.

I have studied all the periodicals published by the Evangelical Christian Baptist Union of Moldova from its foundation to the year 2008 to be able to make a more complete presentation of the situation that was created at this time. I can distinguish several periods in the publishing activity of the Evangelical Christian Baptists in Moldova. The first period is the period of time up to World War II, when Bessarabia was part of Romania. In 1929 the magazine "The Light of Life" was founded and was issued until 1941 when the editor-in-chief was shot by the Soviet authorities. The second period is between 1995 and 1997 when the magazine continued to be issued under the same name. It was decided at a union leadership meeting that the magazine contain the same headings as when it was founded[42] although,

---

40. V. Popovici, "Report at the ECB Congress," July 1998.

41. V. Ghiletchi, *Report of the Bishop of the UECBCM at the annual pastoral conference*, March 2003.

42. *The Light of Life* no. 1 (May–June 1995), 1.

in practice, the magazine differed from what it was before. New headings appeared and some old ones disappeared. During those years, the magazine was written in Russian and translated into Romanian and was published in two languages. The third period began in 1998 when the funding of the magazine was reduced, circulation decreased, frequency of publication was reduced, and in 2000–2001 it was printed on a copy machine, at home, by the editor-in-chief, Alla Alexeeva. In early 2001, the magazine ceased its existence. The fourth period began in 2003 when a new publication "The Word of Truth" was issued. The form was changed from a magazine to a newspaper. Since then, the newspaper has been published once a month.[43] I needed all of this data to make objective conclusions for the present research work. This is why I studied the magazine issues from 1929 to 1931, all the magazines issued in the second period, and all the newspapers of the last period from 2003 to 2008. Thus, conclusions based on almost complete data have a firm foundation.

In this case, I appeal to the so-called "Biography as Theology" approach, proposed by James McClendon, Jr. One of the basic postulates of this approach is the idea that on the basis of moral, behavioral and communal practices one can judge the persistent and strongly held beliefs (or convictions) of a person, community or denomination. As McClendon said: "One way in which theologians may do better work is through a certain attention to other people's lives. A key to these biographies is the dominant or controlling images which may be found in the lives of which they speak."[44] In other words, beliefs influence our everyday life as a whole and in particular matters. The same statement can be interpreted in reverse order – our behavioral patterns point out our convictions, which define our daily life. Thus, based on the biography of a person, one's attitude and behavior can judge one's convictions.

Applying this concept to our case, I can make more or less reasonable conclusions about the strongly held beliefs or convictions of the ECBCM on the basis of a detailed study of the above-mentioned periodicals. The

---

43. The data on the history of the magazine are based on an interview with the editor-in-chief Alla Alexeeva, the 2nd of September 2010.

44. J. Wm. McClendon, Jr., *Biography as Theology: How Life Stories Can Remake Today's Theology* (Eugene: Wipf and Stock Publishers, 2002), 69.

church's life, its practices, and its experiences are reflected in the pages of the religious newspapers and journals. On this basis, we can deduce the main objective or the mission of Evangelical Christian Baptist churches.

Thus, having accomplished a detailed study of the above-mentioned issues of the magazine "The Light of Life" and of the newspaper "The Word of Truth," I observed that all the articles and the notes can be divided into four clearly defined groups according to the subject they treated. The first group: articles and notes related to the edification and spiritual growth of believers. This category includes sermons as well as articles about the history of the church, creationism, stories of God's help, appeals to God, and articles on pastoral care. The second group includes informative articles and notes on the life of the churches. Here, there are two subgroups: (a) the life of the churches in Moldova. Most of the articles in this category are about ordinations in churches, the launching of new prayer houses, seminars and conferences, decisions of the union authorities, announcements of pastors' appointments at the regional or national level; (b) the life of believers abroad such as international meetings and symposiums, the life of the Baptist World Alliance and the European Baptist Federation, important events of friendly unions from Romania and the CIS countries as well as articles about the persecution of believers. The third group: articles and notes about evangelism and missions. It also should be noted that the term "mission" is used only in the sense of "evangelism," which means conducting evangelistic campaigns, opening new churches, benedictions for missionaries going abroad.[45] The fourth group is comprised of articles and notes on social projects and the involvement of churches in the needs of society and charity events. The results of the study of periodicals are summarized in the following table:

---

45. Exceptions are the cases when the term 'mission' is a substitute or abbreviation for the term 'missionary organization.'

	1 Edification and spiritual growth	2A Life of the churches in Moldova	2B Life of believers abroad	3 Evangelism and missions	4 Social projects	Total
The Light of Life, 1995–1997	71	129	22	23	12	
The Light of Life, 2000	43	88	36	41	12	
The Word of Truth, 2003	83	50	22	26	3	
The Word of Truth, 2004	82	35	18	11	3	
The Word of Truth, 2005	109	77	24	32	7	
The Word of Truth, 2006	116	106	15	25	17	
The Word of Truth, 2007	89	99	25	14	11	
The Word of Truth, 2008	74	57	24	5	11	
TOTAL	667	641	186	177	76	1747
Percentage	38.18%	36.69%	10.65%	10.13%	4.35%	

In all the issues studied there was just one note on the relationship between Evangelical and Orthodox believers, relating a case of aggressive behavior of priests raising people against the Evangelical Christian Baptists.[46]

I counted the number of all the articles, including small-size notes, and divided them into four categories, based on the subject matter and the content of the article, and finally, calculated the percentage correlation between each group of articles and the total number of articles. If I include articles from group 2A and 2B in the same category, which is quite logical,

---

46. P. Mikhalchuk, "Aggravation of Relations," *The Light of Life* no. 3 (2000): 41–42.

then there are the following ratios: the articles and notes on church life constitute over 47 percent of the total number of articles; edification articles slightly over 38 percent, articles on evangelism a little over 10 percent and articles on the social projects of the church constitute almost 4.5 percent. Considering that the articles and notes on edification are ultimately still focused on the internal life of the church, these constitute more than 85 percent of the total number of articles, while articles on the social projects of churches is hardly ever mentioned.

Can we claim that the study is objective, impartial, and does not reflect the views of the editors-in-chief or executive editors? First, note that the editors-in-chief of the publications were the Bishops Victor Loghinov, Viktor Popovici and Valery Ghiletchi. They played a key role in determining the strategy and vision of the Union of churches during the period under study. I admit that some of the articles may have passed by without their attention, but they always coordinated the headings and the main content of the magazine.

Second, in 2003 a group of professors of the Prague International Baptist Theological Seminary carried out a study of the major issues faced by some countries in Eastern Europe and Central Asia, including Moldova. I am citing onwards some conclusions made by the Prague team: "According to its importance for the ECB churches in Moldova, the involvement of churches in the life of the society is ranked 8th after such issues as the education of leaders, spiritual life, lifestyle issues, unity within the church, unity within the local churches, Calvinist-Arminian debate and doctrine of salvation."[47]

This demonstrates once again that the issues concerning internal church life came first. The issue of the Calvinist-Arminian debate was more important than the issue of the involvement of churches in society. To the question "How do Baptists intend to change the existent society?" the following answers were given – "by prayers for people and society, personal evangelism, church events, helping the needy people and by involvement

---

47. R. Grams and P. Parushev, "Baptists in Moldova," in *Towards an Understanding of European Baptist Identity: Listening to the Churches in Armenia, Bulgaria, Central Asia, Moldova, North Caucasus, Omsk and Poland: Mapping a Baptistic Identity,* ed. Grams, R. and P. Parushev (Prague: International Baptist Theological Seminary, 2006), 128.

in electing the government, politics and civil protest."[48] In other words, the purely social events were almost ignored. They distinguished as most important the church practices of prayer and evangelism. It is interesting that help to needy people was mentioned while the question concerned the whole society. It is a quite controversial viewpoint that we can change society by helping needy people, while at the same time social participation was practically rejected as a means of changing society by the Baptists. The Baptist respondents claimed not having the opportunity to participate in social, political, or governmental activities.

An interesting fact is that predominantly young church leaders participated in the survey (only 12 percent of the respondents were more than thirty years old), and yet "Baptists were seen to be separatists while also speaking prophetically to culture."[49]

I personally assisted the IBTS team in conducting this survey, and it is justified to assert that the respondents were not just youth from the churches, but most of them were magistracy students in a theological educational institution. It seems that if a similar poll was conducted among regular church members or among the representatives of the older generation who make up a significant part in the Union, the percentage of those willing to get involved in public life would be even smaller. Thus, the results of the survey confirm the conclusions I have made after studying the periodicals issued by the UCEBCM.

Third, I propose to examine the strategy of the Union, which was adopted at a pastoral conference in March 2008. The strategy was presented by the leaders of the Union and was adopted as a guide to action for the next four years. Hereafter, I render the concise text of the strategy:

The strategy of the ECEBCM follows some main directions:

1) The preaching of the gospel

   The preaching of the gospel is the most important task of the church. And first of all, by preaching we mean evangelism. We invite everyone to join the following goal – every

---

48. Ibid., 130–131.
49. Ibid., 133.

believer should lead to Christ one person a year. We suggest some evangelization methods:

- Personal evangelism (from heart to heart);
- Christian festivals (in stadiums, cultural centers);
- Evangelistic Christian movies (for example, the project "Hope Exists");
- Evangelistic worship in local churches;
- Evangelism through social projects (social canteens, caring for the elderly, etc.);
- Evangelism through building friendly relationships (friendly visits, meetings over a cup of tea, etc.);
- Once a year, to carry out a week-long community evangelistic campaign;
- Evangelism through sport (Taekwondo, football, basketball, volleyball, "fun starts," etc.);
- English language teaching (English for a New Life);
- Evangelism through launching computer courses.

A survey was conducted, which showed the following results – church members prefer personal evangelism for several reasons: (1) it is a very simple method, (2) it does not require financial investments, (3) it is efficient, (4) it can be used by each member of the church.

2) Spiritual growth

There are several factors which contribute to the spiritual growth:

- The study of the Word of God;
- The Holy Spirit working in us;
- The involvement in ministry of every member of the local churches according to their spiritual gifts;
- The instruction of new leaders.

Spiritual growth produces changes in people who in their turn change the world – we grow quantitatively. To achieve this goal the following methods are suggested:

- Inductive Bible study;
- Age group Bible study, collective Bible study;
- Group Bible study, family Bible study;
- General church seminars and conferences;

3) Leader formation and instruction courses

Leaders should be formed not only in theological schools, but also in churches. For the achievement of this goal, we suggest the following methods:

- Bible study with the new leaders;
- Joint prayers with the new leaders;
- Personal example;
- Pastoral counseling;
- Communication between instructors and disciples;
- Delegation of responsibilities;
- Teamwork.

4) Mission and new churches planting

The missionary church is the church which loves God passionately, which has compassion for the lost world, and which sends missionaries and supports them financially. We suggest every local church be involved in local, national and international missions. Local mission is aimed at the village or the city where the church is located. National mission is aimed at other settlements in Moldova. International mission means evangelization outside the country.

We should be involved in missions for the following reasons:

- God has called us to go;
- This is a biblical example and it is very efficient;
- God has a plan for you and for the people living in the locality which is the aim of your mission. Therefore, he guarantees his presence in your life and in your ministry.
- Moldavians are ready to carry out missions in difficult life circumstances.

We suggest each church plant a new church in the next four years.

5) Donations and financial support

The way we donate money for the church's needs determines the level of our spiritual development.

- It is necessary to organize seminars on financial donations in all churches.
- It is necessary to teach the church to pay the tithe. The tithe is a New Testament teaching.
- Pastors should receive financial support from local churches.
- It is necessary to promote financial transparency within the church. To this end, the pastor of the church must present a financial report every 4 months, and provide monthly reports to the church council.
- We inspire the church to worship through weekly financial donations.

6) Reaching the new generation

Suggestions concerning the young people who have not yet accepted Christ in their life:

- Provide Christian camps.
- Lauch computer courses.
- Reach young people through sport.
- Teach the English language.

Suggestions regarding the young people who have already accepted Christ in their life:

Young people feel distant from the church. There is even the phrase: "The youth and the church." Young people go their own way; the church does the same. In order to help young people become involved in the life of the local church, it is necessary:

- To organize Sunday schools within each church.
- To investigate the Word of God.

- To give young people the opportunity to take the lead.
- As pastors, to open our hearts to young people.
- To plant in young people the missionary spirit.
- To teach them live such a life as to be able to feel part of the local church.

7) Christian unity

It is possible to achieve unity among Christians by:

(A) Organizing monthly meetings of pastors at the district level. It has been already proved that these meetings:

- Motivate for a more active service;
- Create opportunities for greater cooperation with each other;
- Pastors may pray for each other, and together for each church member;
- Develop a system of visits and interactions between Moldavian churches;
- Give the possibility to develop and evaluate the collective missionary work at the national or international levels.

(B) Defining the context in which we live:

- Lack of interest and passivity of Christians;
- Lack of vision of some churches;
- Lack of self-sacrifice and devotion;
- Non-governmental organizations acquire more importance and priority than the local church;
- There is an increased interest in material well being, while the interest in mission and consecration decreases;
- International mission is viewed of greater interest than the local mission.

(C) The secret of our success in unity lies in our sacrifice.

- It is based on love;
- This implies self-rejection;
- This implies good will towards others;

- This implies responsibility;
- This implies perseverance and tenacity;
- This implies expectation of changes.[50]

I am going to draw some conclusions based on the strategy adopted in 2008. The main goal is evangelism, which is called herein "the preaching of the gospel." It is also interesting that the fourth task above relates to the same goal – the mission and new church planting – but for some reason it is placed in a separate paragraph, probably due to its strategic importance. The first half of the second task also relates to evangelism, but in this case, with an emphasis on the younger generation. Further, the tasks aim at the internal life of the church – the second task (spiritual growth), the third task (instruction of new leaders), the fifth task (financial donations in the churches), the second half of the sixth task (spiritual growth of young people) and the seventh task (unity of Christians). With regard to social participation[51] of the church, then, there is only one reference – the fifth point of the first task, – and once again, it is mentioned in the context of evangelism. The appropriateness of social projects in the context of evangelism is considered in the fourth chapter of this research work. At the moment, I will just mention the presence of this task. Task 6 points 2, 3 and 4, talk about English classes, computer courses and sports activities. It looks like a kind of social participation, but in practice, English classes in the ECB union in Moldova are based on a special curriculum, which is known as "English for a new life" where students learn English using one of the English translations of Bible. The program was issued for computers classes.

About sport's activities, I need to mention that the most well-known program in Moldova is based on Inductive Method for Bible studies, which

---

50. "Strategy of the Evangelical Baptist Union of Moldova," proposed by General Secretary Ion Miron, March 2008 at the UCECBM Congress.

51. Chapters 4 and 6 will talk a lot about the role of social participation in Church's mission, and chapter 9 will bring the detailed definitions for such concepts as social participation, social responsibility and social action. Though, it is important to give a short and simple definition for social participation from my point of view in this chapter. Social participation is an active position towards society, including social help and support of needy people, as well as public articulation Church's position on the main social, economic and political problems in the country. It could have a deep theological foundation or not. The main question is if Church serves outside of the Church's "walls."

is promoted by Taekwando federation. Each training session is divided into two parts, with the first part devoted to physical exercise and the second part to a Bible study. It is important to mention that these three programs were shaped and promoted by the same movement under the leadership of Vasile Filat, one of the pastors in ECB church in Chisinau. All of them were very effective in terms of evangelism and bringing new people to know Christ. I would like to mention that these social projects serve only as a tool for evangelism and in chapter 4 I will revise the theological foundation for such approach.

I counted the number of recommendations given in the Union's strategy. There were forty-five different reasons, recommendations and tips offered to strengthen local churches, and sixteen different kinds of activities were suggested for conducting evangelistic activities, including the call for every church to plant a new one, although this appeal is not highlighted in the text as a separate point. With regard to the recommendations concerning social participation, then, there are only four points on this subject (which refers once again to evangelism).

I also would like to remark that the task related to the unity of Christians clearly expresses the position which reflects the importance of the unity of Evangelical Christian Baptists, members of the same union, but there were no references about the union with the representatives of other confessions. Nevertheless, in 1990, the first interdenominational organization – the International Bible Society – was founded in Moldova. "The meeting was attended by the representatives of the United Bible Societies from England, New Zealand and the United States, the representatives of the Union of Evangelical Christian Baptist churches of Moldova, headed by the Bishop K. S. Sedletsky, the representatives of the Seventh Day Adventist Church, Christians of Evangelical Faith (Pentecostal), the representatives of independent Evangelical Christian Baptist churches, the representatives of the Orthodox Church headed by the Metropolitan Vladimir, and representatives of independent Pentecostal churches."[52]

Besides, since 2003, the leaders of the Union have been involved in the organization of a "Round Table" under the patronage of the World

---

52. http://www.bethel.md/view_post.php?id=26 Accessed 2 September 2010.

Council of Churches (I will give more details on this subject in the third chapter of this work). Baptists have cooperated closely with the representatives of Pentecostal churches regarding evangelism. The year 2000 was a particularly significant one in this direction, which is clearly reflected in the Evangelical Christian Baptist periodicals. During just one year, forty-six articles and notes regarding motivating believers to evangelism, as well as reports on evangelistic activities carried out, were published. These were mostly campaigns conducted with the participation of the Billy Graham and Campus Crusade for Christ Associations. Both campaigns were carried out by the Evangelical Christian Baptist Union together with Pentecostals. It seems that the development of fraternal relations with the representatives of other churches did not constitute a strategic objective of the church in those years. It is worth mentioning that, in the above examples, the initiative of cooperation always came from the Western partners. But at the time of the adoption of the strategy the union with representatives of different confessions was not a main task.

In 2009 and 2010 the only campaign on a national level in the history of modern Moldova was carried out through the initiative of local churches. It was the Festival of the Family, which was held for two consecutive years in the central square of the capital by the Evangelical Christian Baptist Churches, Christians of Evangelical Faith, Seventh-Day Adventists, independent Evangelical Christian Baptist Churches, Bible and Charismatic churches. Further, I am going to consider some other objectives set by the union in its strategy. The task concerning the internal organization of the local churches is given twice as much attention as evangelistic mission. This is the third argument, which confirms my hypothesis about the importance of internal church life and the spiritual growth of believers as a primary concern of the church, despite the statement that evangelism is the first priority. Here are some further figures. In 2005, the newspaper "The Word of Truth" published thirty-two articles on evangelism. In 2006, there were twenty-five such articles, in 2007 there were fourteen, and in 2008 only five. Almost all of them were written by the same author, Vasile Filat, who is actively involving in evangelistic and social work in Moldova, heading several organizations and informal movements. Thus, there was not even so much as one article on evangelism in two of the issues of this newspaper, and the articles that did appear were all written by the same author.

What is the explanation for such a sharp decline in interest in this topic? Oleg Turlac assumes that "in the twenty-first century the religious climate in Moldova has changed. The 1990s, when many people were willing to fill the existing religious vacuum are over. With the strengthening of the influence of the Orthodox Church in Moldova on culture, politics and social life, Christianity has ceased to be perceived as an innovation which resulted in a sharp decline in interest in the evangelical churches."[53]

I agree that on the one hand, there was a decline in public interest in Evangelical churches, but does this mean there should be a decline in the interest of Evangelical churches in people? Probably the emphasis has been refocused from the achievement of external objectives to the solution of internal church issues. Although the changes in the format of the newspaper led to a smaller number of articles issued in general, the percentage of articles on the life of the church or edification did not decrease, but in some cases even increased (articles about the life of believers abroad). This is also confirmed by the data on ECB church membership. In 2005, there were 20,826 church members within the union. In 2006, 936 people were baptized and at the end of the year there were 20,667 church members (taking into account that some people died, moved abroad and others were excommunicated from the churches). In 2007, 670 people were baptized and the general membership by the end of the year decreased to 20,391 people. These figures demonstrate the inefficiency of the applied methods.

I think that the strategy adopted in 2008 reacted neither to changes in society nor those happening within the churches themselves. Churches isolated themselves from society, from its needs. Even friendship with unbelievers was regarded as an evangelistic task (task 1, point 6 of the strategy), and the spiritual growth of Christians should inevitably lead to the quantitative growth of churches (task 2, point 4 of the strategy). The fourth chapter of this book intends to examine the causes of the situation created in Moldova. In chapter 9, I am going to suggest a new paradigm in redefining the boundaries of the church and will show some possible ways

---

53. http://www.bethel.md/view_post.php?id=26 Accessed 2 September 2010.

to overcome the current crisis. Nevertheless, it seems that the aim of the ECBM mission is the local church, the criterion of measurement is the growth of the local church, and the starting point is also the local church. Looking ahead, I define this approach as the ekklesio-centric approach. At the end of the chapter, I will make a preliminary conclusion that the approach which was efficient in the 1990s is inefficient nowadays.

Theological Reflections in the ECB Union

Previously, I have identified the core values and the essence of the mission of the Union of Evangelical Christian Baptists of Moldova, based on official declarations at national conferences and congresses and in the periodicals reflecting the life of the union. Besides that identification, it is necessary to outline the development of theological thought within evangelical churches in Moldova. In 1995, the College of Theology and Education was established under the UCECBM with the purpose of training Christian men and women to serve in local churches and spreading a Christian witness throughout Eastern Europe and Central Asia. The college was founded by the merger of the Bible institute *Sfânta Treime* and the municipal Bible college *Harul*.[54] Since 1999, the CTE has been offering four accredited programs: Theology, Mission, Social Work, and Christian Education. In 2000, the first issue of "Pulse of Ministry," a magazine for Christian ministers, was published by the College of Theology and Education. It seeks to provide spiritual nourishment for pastors who dedicate their lives to bringing people to the Kingdom of God and to helping young people discover the noblest mission. The magazine publishes articles from the fields of theology and missiology, as well as counseling and Christian ethics, aiming to help Christians strengthen their faith in a world overflowing with false teachings.[55]

Given that one of the college programs aims at training social workers, it is expected that the magazine will develop a holistic approach to ministry, to the mission of the church in the world. To determine the point of

---

54. N. Teplitskaya, "Istorija teologo-pedagogicheskogo kolledzha" [History of the College of Theology and Education], *Pulse of Ministry* no. 7 (2003): 5.

55. M. Malancha, "From the Editor," *Pulse of Ministry* no. 1 (2000): 2.

reference of the magazine, I have conducted research work based on the study of fifteen issues of the magazine published between 2000 and 2009. As a result, I have come to the following conclusions: In the fifteen issues I have studied there are 213 articles and essays which can be organized into the following categories: (1) internal life of the church – sermons, church ethics, pastoral counseling, homiletics; (2) theology – the study of the Old and New Testament, articles on historical and systematic theology, church history; (3) mission – missiology, evangelism, mission to Muslims; (4) other – articles on the culture of speech, student essays, poetry, quotations, encyclopedia entries, etc.; (5) theological education – college advertising, EAAA activity, theological education in other countries; (6) social service, church and society; (7) Christian pedagogy and psychology. The following chart reveals the number of articles and the percentage of treated subjects.

Category	Number of articles	%
Sermons, Church Life, Church Ethics, Pastoral Care and Counseling, Homiletics	70	32.9%
Old and New Testament Studies, Theology, Apologetics, Church History	41	19.2%
Missiology, Evangelism, Mission to Muslims	35	16.5%
Other	25	11.7%
Theological Education	22	10.3%
Social Responsibility, Church and Society	17	8%
Christian Education, Psychology	3	1.4%

It is obvious that the category "Internal Life of the Church" occupies a leading position. Even if the correlation between quantity and percentage is not as significant as in the case of the UCECBM periodicals, the subject is tackled in a third of all the written articles. Almost one-fifth of the articles refer to theological research and a little over 16 percent refer to articles on mission. In fact, I was expecting different results thinking that the magazine authors (who are mostly college professors) would emphasize some different issues. Thus, I have to admit that the outcome of the research did not meet my expectations. I was very surprised to find out that the articles included in the "Other" category are ranked higher than those related to the social participation of the church.

In my opinion, it looks as if there is an evident lack of interest from the UCECBM as well as the CTE representatives in developing a holistic approach to church service. It would be better to pay more attention to the social projects launched on theological bases and to work out a development strategy. Moreover, the leadership of the CTE is inclined to ignore the social responsibility of the church, categorizing it as "women's projects,"[56] while preaching and internal church activities are viewed as "fulfillment of highest calling."[57]

In addition, the imbalance in the ratio of articles based on the name of the college, which means theology and pedagogy studies, should be noted. Whereas, on the basis of the published articles, one could have the impression that the college forms primarily preachers and pastors which, in essence, is the reality. It also should be clear that we do not pursue the goal of diminishing the importance of the mission of the college. I only highlight the discrepancy between the name of the institution, its particular departments and programs and the outlook the students and teachers acquire through the magazine articles.

The conducted research confirmed the data obtained on the basis of the previous research on Evangelical churches in Moldova, even if in a little different light. Nevertheless, it can be concluded that the mission carried out by the CTE is also ecclesiocentric.

Conclusions

On the basis of realized studies, I can confirm the following conclusions:
1) Evangelical churches in the CIS countries (including Moldova) have lost their identity, which was formed during the Soviet times, and have not created one common identity, even for churches that are part of the same denomination.
2) Many Evangelical churches in Moldova have had a negative

---

56. S. Namesnic (CTE rector) to the author, 14 December 2010.
57. Ibid.

experience of cooperation with the Orthodox Church.

3) The leadership of the Evangelical churches in Ukraine and Russia shows its readiness for dialogue, which, first, could be expressed by the willingness of society and the Orthodox Church to hear the voice of the Evangelical churches, as the voice of Orthodoxy is already known and familiar to Evangelicals.
4) One of the main impediments to this dialogue was the "aggressive" evangelism of the Evangelical churches, which alarmed the Orthodox; therefore, the Evangelical Christians should reconsider their evangelistic and social programs if they want to be heard.
5) The main goal for the UCECBM according to their official declaration is proclaiming the gospel, but according to our studies, it is the spiritual growth of church members.
6) A holistic approach in the life of the Union and theological reflections is not seen.
7) The mission of the UCECBM could be defined as ecclesiocentric.

The next chapter will show contemporary relations between Evangelicals and the Orthodox Church – how they were established and the current situation.

CHAPTER 3

Contemporary Relationships between Evangelicals and the Orthodox Church

The previous chapters presented a historical overview and analysis of the origin and development of the Evangelical churches in Moldova, and also a critical evaluation of the missionary movement of the Evangelical churches in the country. It was realized that the mission approach of the UCECBM is ecclesiocentric, and that there are a lot of different methods on the local level which are not united in one system or network.

The next step requires consideration of the actual relationship between Evangelical and Orthodox churches. To find out what God is doing in an "Orthodox country" by means of the Evangelical churches and what the mission of these churches is, it is necessary to consider what these two churches have in common and possible ways of interaction. In this chapter, a brief historical note on the development of the conflict between the Russian and the Romanian Orthodox Church over the Orthodox Church in Moldova is given. Also presented is the willingness of the Evangelical churches to cooperate against the background of similar attempts in Russia and Ukraine, as well as an attempt to comprehend the emergence and the first years of activity of the World Council of Churches in Moldova.

The Orthodox Church in Moldova in the Early 21st Century

After so much attention has been paid to Evangelical churches, it would be worth paying attention to the Orthodox Church in Moldova and the dynamics of the relationship between the Russian and Romanian Orthodox

Churches after the collapse of the Soviet Union. I will refer to the original sources of the two Orthodox churches and will give a cursory review of the existing conflict, because it is impossible to speak about the Evangelical-Orthodox dialogue without paying attention to the fact that there is a difficult dialogue among the Orthodox themselves in the country.

The twenty-first century has on one hand brought an improvement in the relationship between the Evangelical churches and the Orthodox Church in Moldova; but it has also brought a split within the Orthodox Church into two jurisdictions – the Moldavian Metropolitan under the Moscow Patriarchate and the Bessarabian Metropolitan under the Romanian Patriarchate. In fact, this separation occurred as early as in 1992, when a delegation headed by the bishop of Balti, Petru Paduraru and the archpriest Petru Buburuz went from Chisinau to Bucharest to seek the permission of the Holy Synod of the Romanian Orthodox Church to incorporate the Metropolitan Church of Bessarabia into the Romanian Orthodox Church. It is worth noting the political climate in the period when the movement was started. In 1991, Moldova was proclaimed an independent state; the Parliament condemned the signing of the Molotov-Ribbentrop agreement on the division of Europe and proclaimed unity with the Romanian people.[1] Naturally, this concerned the churches as well. Between 1918 and 1940, the Orthodox Church of Moldova was under the jurisdiction of the Romanian Patriarchate. In the Soviet period the Moldavian Church was placed under the authority of the Moscow Patriarchate. Thus, many agreed that to restore historical justice, the Moscow Patriarchate should recognize the territory of Bessarabia as the canonical territory of the Romanian Church. But this did not happen. This was what prompted some of the priesthood to appeal directly to Bucharest. On 20 December 1992, the Holy Synod of the Romanian Orthodox Church recognized the reinstatement of the BM within the Romanian Orthodox Church and gave the BM the same rights as those of the Metropolitan of Walachia, Transylvania, Moldova, Oltenia and Banat. In 1995, the Metropolitan of Bessarabia, Petru, was raised to

---

1. This doesn't mean the reunification of Moldova and Romania, but the spiritual and cultural unity of the Romanian people, living in two separate states – Romania and the Republic of Moldova – although there were strong voices in favor of the reunification of the two states during those years.

the rank of exarchate, with jurisdiction over the Romanian Orthodox communities of the ex-Soviet bloc and the Moldavian Diaspora worldwide.

The delegation returned to Chisinau, requiring the government of the Republic of Moldova to register the BM. The government refused to comply with the request. Since that time there has been real tension within the Moldavian Orthodox Church. In 2002, after years of legal hurdles against the government of Moldova and a final decision by the European Court on Human Rights, the Orthodox Church of Bessarabia received official registration. At the end of 2007, there were about 250 parishes under the jurisdiction of the BM and nearly 1,200 under the MM. The registration of the BM did not stop the disputes and disagreements between the two patriarchates, but on the contrary – nowadays they have reached a new level, as official registration gives the BM the right to be recognized as successor of the BM existing in the territory of the Republic of Moldova until 1940, and accordingly to claim all property that was in the possession of the BM those years – and these are hundreds of church buildings, monasteries, land, etc. Bucharest suggests Moscow should renounce its rights to this property and leave under its jurisdiction only those churches which are attended by ethnic Russians and where worship is held in Russian.[2] The Romanian Church leaders say that the church remains the strongest means of ideological influence and pro-Russian attitude in the territory of Moldova.

It is necessary to recognize that Russia's influence in the Republic of Moldova is still substantial although it is very difficult to determine what kind of role the church plays in this case. Many factors must be taken into account including economic,[3] cultural,[4] historical,[5] social,[6] and others. It

---

2. A. Maximilian, "Causes of the Conflict between the Metropolitan of Moldova and the Metropolitan of Bessarabia" at http://www.mitropoliabasarabiei.ro/cauzele_conflictului.html Accessed 8 February 2008.

3. According to the International Organization for Migration, about 70% of economic emigrants are working in Russia.

4. Cable television networks broadcast about 70 TV channels to Moldova in the Russian language and only 8 from Romania.

5. The 45 years of Soviet government when Moldova was a part of a single space with Russia being the leading power, left a deep imprint especially on the older generation.

6. A lot of inter-ethnic marriages were concluded during the time of the USSR, and nowadays many Moldavian families have relatives in Russia.

is possible that the church is also one of the tools for maintaining Russian influence. Bessarabia was a part of Romania between 1918 and 1940, but from 1945 until 1991 Moldova was a part of the USSR and over the years, new relationships have been built. Over the past 200 years, almost every generation of Moldovans has experienced a change of course two or three times – from Romania to Russia, and vice versa. Since 1991, Moldova has been an independent state, but unfortunately it has not yet acquired independent thinking, and this refers both to politicians and many church authorities. Nicolas Dima observes: "According to Orthodox Tradition, the church organization accommodates itself to the political organization of the nation that it serves. The strength of this tradition was that it led to the formation of national churches. The weakness was that the church abdicated to a large degree its rights, and it subordinated itself to the leaders and authorities it served."[7]

Another weak point is the unstable political situation in Eastern Europe; some national boundaries have disappeared and others have appeared instead. A future-oriented society is ready to accept such kinds of changes. The globalized world requires a different attitude to the doctrine of canonical territory.

What is the position of the MM of the Russian Orthodox Church under the Moscow Patriarchate? To date, the MM does not recognize the legitimate registration of the BM. The official sources of the MM continue to call it "the so-called Metropolitan Church of Bessarabia."[8] It is clear that the MM feels more confident, being aware of its number of parishes, priests and parishioners, and therefore does not have to stand on the defensive. As well the MM attacks the BM openly. It is worth mentioning that some priests are trying to manipulate the Metropolitan's leadership. In 2007, it was known that several churches from the Cahul district which were under the canonical jurisdiction of the MM, passed under the jurisdiction of the BM.

The BM, being the younger of the Orthodox groups in contemporary Moldova and less numerous, and wanting to maintain its status, enters into

---

7. Dima, "Politics and Religion in Moldova," 178.
8. http://www.mitropolia.md/index_news_rus.htm accessed 8 February 2008.

polemics, arguments and attacks. In all its documents, the Metropolitan Petru is called exclusively "His Eminence," while the Metropolitan Vladimir is written as Nikolai Kantaryan, often with the remark "a retired colonel."

What is also interesting is the fact that the MM spreads rumors about the merger of the two Metropolitans into one autocephalous church by the authority of the Ecumenical Patriarch,[9] although within the same Moldovan Metropolitan there are voices against the autocephalous. Ignatii Venediktov, a proponent of the merger with the Russian Orthodox Church, believes that the MM is weak and not able to function efficiently, either at the level of an autocephaly, or even at the level of a diocese. He considers that the leadership of the MM must develop a strategy to halt the gradual destruction of the nation.[10] This strategy consists, from his point of view, only in a union with the Orthodox Church, which has only grown stronger since the merger with the Russian Orthodox Church Abroad. In his article I, Venediktov clearly shows his pro-Russian sympathy, but we should agree with at least one point – the church should not only be a priest for its people, but also a prophet speaking about its problems.

The representatives of the Metropolitan Church of Bessarabia deny a possible merger to form an autocephaly, arguing that the 34th Apostolic canon states that in the territory of one nation there can be only one autocephalous Orthodox Church.[11] In this case, it is not enough to use just religious polemics. Does the Moldavian nation exist as an ethnic group or are the Moldavians from the Prut-Dniester region Romanians? The Pro-Romanian politicians and cultural figures insist upon the second variant; the supporters of the independence of Moldova, on the first. Under the patronage of Ex-President Voronin, a Romanian-Moldavian dictionary was issued. Moldavians were recognized as an independent ethnic group resulting from the mixing of the two peoples – the Vlachs and the Slavs. The

---

9. His Pre-Eminence Marchel, the Bishop of Balti and Falesti was speaking openly about this perspective.

10. I. Venediktov, "The Reunification of the Russian Orthodox Church and the Moldovan Christians" at http://www.mdn.md/ru/ortodoxal.php?rubr=3144 accessed 22 July 2007.

11. http://www.mitropoliabasarabiei.ro/dreptul_canonic.html accessed 08 February 2008. The Canonic law of the existence of the Metropolitan Church of Bessarabia, as part of the Romanian Patriarchy, on the territory between the Prut and Nistru.

present research does not have, as an objective finding, a solution to all the historical or linguistic issues that have emerged in the Moldavian territory. We just have to accept as fact the existence of some highly contentious issues concerning the identity of the Orthodox Church in Moldova depending on existing political views.

What should be the position of the Evangelical churches in this situation? One of the variants would be to remain neutral and even "take advantage" of this conflict, presenting it to the people in a negative light. Another variant would be to assume the role of a conciliator. Even if it may sound unbelievable for Moldova that a few evangelical alliances can reconcile the two large Orthodox churches, we can at least express this idea.

Proselytism and Foundations for Conflict between Evangelicals and the Orthodox Church

Overview of the Moldavian Situation

Talking about the difficulties faced by the Orthodox Church in Moldova, it is impossible to focus only on the internal issues related to the relationship between the Russian and the Romanian Orthodox Churches. There is quite serious tension between the Orthodox and Evangelical churches. Leaders of the denominations have distanced themselves from each other. Although it is widely believed that after the legalization of the Romanian Orthodox Church in Moldova, tension between the Orthodox and Evangelicals eased, I agree with Valery Ghiletchi that the easing of tension is primarily associated with changes in the legislation of the Republic of Moldova with regard to the freedom of religion.[12] The article of the constitution regarding proselytism has been revised. Now it gives a clearer definition of the concept of "proselytism" or rather "nonviolent proselytism," which means the use of violence or abuse of authority to change someone's religious affiliation. In the "Law on Cults and its Constituent Parts" of 11 May 2007 the notion of "excessive proselytism" was introduced which means actions aimed at converting another person or group of people to

---

12. Interview with the Bishop of the Union of Evangelical Christian Baptist Churches of Moldova Valery Ghiletchi, http://mdn.md/ru/index.php?view=viewarticle&article id=944 accessed 25 November 2004.

another faith by violence, abuse of authority, blackmail, malicious intent, threats, coercion, use of religious hatred, deceit, psychological manipulation or different procedures for sublimation.[13] Thus, "no one under the law can accuse us of proselytising,"[14] and, nevertheless, "the Orthodox Church often accuses us that we are practicing religious proselytism."[15] To confirm his words, V. Ghiletchi gives examples of pressure from Orthodox priests consisting in bans on funerals, community registration prohibition, prohibition of prayer house construction and discrimination against children in schools.[16]

The conflict exists, and in this case, the state of affairs dissatisfies the majority of churches as well as the minority communities and groups. Unfortunately, in Moldova not a single round table on the topic has been organized which would be attended by the heads of churches. Most of the dialogues were conducted at the level of public society, students, foreign partners, and social agencies.

In order to get closer to solving this problem, it is necessary to define the terminology. What is meant by the term "proselytism"? Is this phenomenon seen by the representatives of different churches in one light, or does it take on a different tone in various settings? Is it possible to find a compromise on this issue in the foreseeable future? "The original meaning of the term 'proselytism' was positive,"[17] considers Lawrence A. Uzzell, speaking of times when Christianity began to spread in the Roman Empire and when barbarians, converted to Christianity. "I have argued that far in the history of the Christian church the two words evangelism and proselytism have not been carefully nuanced and differentiated, and that these two words have been seen as synonyms due to some particular historical

---

13. Article 4, paragraph 4. Quoted after "Proselytizing and Religious Freedom in Moldova," http://kultam.net/rus/Ukraine/Science/ExpertOpinions/article-28 accessed 16 March 2009.

14. Interview with the Bishop of the Union of Evangelical Christian Baptist Churches of Moldova Valery Ghiletchi, http://mdn.md/ru/index.php?view=viewarticle&articleid=944 accessed 25 November 2004.

15. Ibid.

16. Ibid.

17. L. A. Uzzell, "Don't Call It Proselytism," *First Things* (October 2004): 14.

developments."[18] Later the teaching about canonical territory came, which will be studied below, and the transfer from church to church has since been perceived differently. Darrell Jackson says: "The term 'proselytism' came to have negative connotations with the Enlightenment, where it was identified with fanaticism and intolerance."[19]

The formal definition of the term proselytism was given by a working group within the WCC: "promise of economic or social advantages."[20] Jacques Matthey, WCC officer and missiologist, gives a wider explanation: "The encouragement of Christians who belong to a church to change their denominational allegiance, through ways and means that contradict the spirit of Christian love, violate the freedom of the human person and diminish trust in the Christian witness of the church."[21]

Mark Elliot, talking about Russian Evangelicals said: "Sad to say, Russian Evangelical attitudes typically are negative toward Orthodox and vice versa. In the mid-1980s the same previously cited survey documented Protestant dismissal of Orthodoxy as 'a dead church' with 'drunkards' for priests."[22]

Unfortunately, such an attitude was characteristic not only of the mid-1980s but actually continues to this day. Churches see each other as rivals competing with one another rather than as partners carrying out one and the same mission. "Any competitive or parallel mission is fraught with threats to the unity of the church and fraternal relations among Christian churches."[23]

---

18. M. T. Thangaraj, "Evangelism sans Proselytism: A Possibility?" in *Sharing the Book: Religious Perspectives on the Rights and Wrongs of Proselytism*, ed. J. Witte and R. C. Martin (New York: Orbis Books, 1999), 340.

19. Darrell Jackson, "Proselytism in a Central and Eastern European Perspective," *Journal of European Baptist Studies* 8, no. 2 (January 2008): 19.

20. "Communicating the Message: Common Witness/Evangelism/Proselytism (point III. Proselytism) Group Report," *International Review of Mission* 90, no. 358 (2001): 357.

21. J. Matthey, "Evangelism, Still the Enduring Test of Our Ecumenical – and Missionary Calling," *International Review of Mission* 96, no. 382 (July/October 2007): 356.

22. M. Elliot, "Orthodox Relations in the Post-Soviet Era," article presented at a conference on Evangelicals in Mission within CIS, IBTS, Prague (February 2003).

23. Kirill, Metropolitan of Smolensk and Kaliningrad, "Gospel and Culture" (text speech presented at World Council of Churches Conference on World Mission and Evangelism, November 1996, Bahia, Brazil) in *Proselytism and Orthodoxy in Russia: the*

"In Orthodox theology the only true mission is a mission that serves unity. This is a truth that is eternally validated in the person of Christ, that is, through the incarnation of the Word and his unity with the Father in the triune Godhead."[24] Patriarch Kirill confirms the existence of bilateral relations with various Protestant denominations in Russia, noting that the factor of theological conservatism of many churches only promotes mutual dialogue,[25] highlighting the relationship between Orthodox and Evangelical Christians-Baptists, existing since the Soviet period.[26] "In Russia Orthodox and Evangelicals have great difficulty agreeing on a single definition for proselytism – stemming from conflicting understandings of what constitutes a believer. Evangelicals assume a personal, conscious commitment to Christ alone as Savior, lived out in worship and life. In contrast, if a Russian has been baptized as an infant, even if faith is dormant or nonexistent, Orthodox consider an evangelical witness to that person to be proselytizing."[27]

The fact that the problems faced by believers in their daily lives in an attempt to establish relationships between different faiths cannot be ignored – they have deep historical and theological roots. I do not pretend to examine objectively all the theological differences between Evangelical and Orthodox believers, but will only touch on some of them which are closely related to the issue of proselytism.

Theological and Ideological Foundations for Conflict

There are substantial grounds to begin such a dialogue, not only in ecumenical circles, but also among the basic documents of the Russian Orthodox Church. "The church status of those separated is not defined.

New War for Souls, ed. J. Witte and M. Bourdeaux (New York: Orbis Books, Maryknoll, 1999), 74.

24. V. Guroian, "Evangelism and Mission in the Orthodox Tradition," in *Sharing the Book: Religious Perspectives on the Rights and Wrongs of Proselytism*, ed. J. Witte and R. C. Martin (New York: Orbis Books, 1999), 239.

25. http://portal-credo.ru/site/?act=news&id=38090&cf accessed 15 November 2005.

26. Ibid.

27. M. Elliott and A. Deyneka, "Protestant Missionaries in the Former Soviet Union," in *Proselytism and Orthodoxy in Russia: The New War for Souls*, ed. J. Witte and M. Bourdeaux (Maryknoll, NY: Orbis Books, 1999), 214.

In a divided Christendom there are some common points uniting it: the Word of God, the faith in Christ as Lord and Savior in flesh (1 John 1, 1–2; 4, 2, 9), and sincere piety."[28] "Orthodox and Evangelical Christians both hold a similar, if not identical, high regard for Scripture."[29] In other words, there is something that unites different churches, and the third part of this work will show it in detail. "Evangelicals and Orthodox have much more in common theologically than either has in common with modern mainline Protestantism, whether Reformed or Lutheran."[30]

Below I examine two groups of theological and ideological backgrounds, which play key roles in identifying issues related to proselytism. The first group includes issues on the doctrine of salvation and the church. I have included them in one group, which seems illogical for members of the Evangelical community, because of their inseparable connection to Orthodoxy. To maintain a productive dialogue, not only the ability to express a position is necessary, but also the ability to listen. In this case, I try to interpret the doctrine of salvation held by Evangelical churches, taking into account the Orthodox doctrine of salvation, and thus methodologically (but not theologically) choosing the path of Orthodoxy.

The second group of questions is related to ideological aspects: the view of a person and society. I will touch on issues of cultural anthropology and sociology in order to determine whether it is appropriate to talk about human rights in the selection of church affiliation.

Soteriology and Ecclesiology

The first step is to determine the soteriological and ecclesiological issues. After all, most of the church's actions in matters of evangelism stem from a desire to spread the message of salvation through Jesus Christ. I agree with Jacques Matthey that, "the issue of proselytism will only be resolved through in-depth discussion on the nature of salvation and of the church."[31]

---

28. Basic principles related to the attitude of the Russian Orthodox Church towards the Non-Orthodox, article 1.16, http://www.patriarchia.ru/db/text/418840.html accessed 26 August 2010.
29. Elliott and Deyneka, "Protestant Missionaries," 210.
30. Ibid.
31. Matthey, "Evangelism," 363.

On the one hand, according to Orthodox belief, salvation is possible only in the church (meaning the Orthodox Church); on the other, God's grace is present in the communities that have broken away, although their life of grace is damaged in some way.

The Protestant formula of *sola fide* is not perceived as the only means of salvation. The grace of God, descending through the sacrament of baptism binds people to the church, and contributes to their salvation. Many Evangelicals believe that the secularization of Christians happens due to this and the number of so-called nominal Christians increases, and as a result, Evangelicals are becoming more active. "In some countries where nominal Christianity appears to be the norm rather than an exception many of these baptized are hostile towards 'the mother church' and have little idea of the true gospel."[32] Furthermore, "the Christian is responsible for evangelizing those who do not follow Jesus Christ, even those who claim the name Christian, but who are truly non-authentic."[33]

Evangelical Christians believe that faith in the sacrifice of Jesus Christ and personal repentance before God, bring to human beings forgiveness of sins, peace with God, and thus, eternal life (salvation). This means that people may be aware of the message of salvation just being evangelized by the spoken word.[34] The role of the church is not to bring salvation but to make people aware of salvation and the grace of God acts independently of visible sacraments. Salvation depends entirely on the human response to God's call.[35] Salvation outside the church is not only possible, but it is achieved outside the church. A God-saved person goes to church in the view of Evangelicals; in the case of Orthodox teaching, the saving grace acts through the church, both at the individual and collegiate level. "Contrary to Western individualism . . . Orthodox Christianity holds up concepts of history and tradition that are supported by stories of national conversion .

---

32. C. Stalnaker, "Proselytism or Evangelism?" *ERT* 26, no. 4 (2002): 338.

33. Ibid., 350.

34. Jacques Matthey, in his article, "Evangelism," 363, explores the beliefs of Pentecostals. The same is stated by Pentecostals and Evangelical Christians Baptists of Moldova.

35. We are not entering the debate between the followers of the Calvinist and Arminian doctrines of salvation. We are not talking about predestination, but only about a reaction to God's call, regardless of the ratio in this case of human will and the will of God.

.. Evangelization is about conversion, but not just the conversion of individuals. The Slavs were converted by Saints Cyril and Methodius, not just individuals, but as a whole people converted."[36]

Ion Bria, talking on the topic of salvation outside the church, gives a biblical example well known in Orthodox circles, when the disciples wanted to turn back the person preaching Christ's name, but walking alone. Jesus prohibited them to do so.[37] Naturally, a parallel between the Orthodox Church and the disciples is drawn and another one between a believer walking alone and all other believers in Jesus Christ. This means that, exceptions are possible, but they only prove the rule.

At the same time the Orthodox Church cannot recognize equality between denominations. Those fallen away from the church cannot turn back while being in the conditions in which they are without changing those conditions. The existing dogmatic differences should be overcome, not simply bypassed. This means that the way to unity is through repentance, conversion and renovation.[38]

In the near future we are unlikely to witness a mass repentance of Evangelicals and Protestants, standing on the threshold of Orthodox churches. At the same time, Evangelical Christians in Eastern Europe expect Orthodoxy to accept them, if not as equal partners, then at least as partners. To elucidate this and other issues, I will turn to a study of anthropological and sociological components of the issue of proselytism.

Anthropology and Sociology

In addition to doctrinal differences between the two traditions it is necessary to draw attention to the so-called "human factor," which is not less important than the theological one. Most people do not have the opportunity to delve into the historical and theological roots of the conflict. Many of them participate in the life of a church for very different reasons – family traditions, a sense of acceptance and love, a response to their emotional,

---

36. Guroian, "Evangelism and Mission," 240.

37. I. Bria, *The Liturgy after the Liturgy: Mission and Witness from an Orthodox Perspective* (Geneva: WCC Publications, 1996), 77.

38. Basic principles related to the attitude of the Russian Orthodox Church towards Non-Orthodox, article 2.7, http://www.patriarchia.ru/db/text/418840.html accessed 26 August 2010.

physical, cognitive needs, etc. All of these factors are related to the anthropological and social aspects of the issue of proselytism. Naturally, I will address the issue of human rights in its narrow aspect of "right of choosing" the church, as well as draw attention to the role of postmodernism in relations between churches.

So, one of the greatest differences between Eastern and Western churches is individualism vs collectivism, which in the church community is called "collegiality." Harold Berman is skeptical of such a concept as "religious pluralism" in the Eastern countries in which there is a principle of unity and not that of democratic individualism.[39] The Baptist missiologist Darrell Jackson confirms this: "Vision of the Russian Orthodox Church is collectivist and heteronomous (in contrast to autonomous). It is holistic, mystical, and arises from a profound reflection on incarnation and the indivisibility of the body of Christ."[40]

Mark Elliot and Anita Deyneka, trying to find a consensus, write: "Orthodox should recognize that religious pluralism is unavoidable in a free society and that a renewal of state-enforced Orthodox privilege would only sap its spiritual vitality. Evangelical ministries, for their part, ought to pay a great deal more attention to legitimate Russian sensitivities through substantially improved missionary orientation and through a sober appreciation of their own cultural limitations."[41]

Nowadays it is quite difficult to determine where the border is between individualism and unity, and to what extent one people tend to make decisions through democratic votes, or another to follow the historical tradition. It is also difficult to make this difference from person to person. It is even harder to answer the question – what about those who fall out of common standards of one or another society? How much attention should we pay to human rights in self-determination? Protestants declare proudly:

---

39. H. J. Berman, "Freedom of Religion in Russia: An Amicus Brief for the Defendant," in *Proselytism and Orthodoxy in Russia: The New War for Souls*, ed. J. Witte and M. Bourdeaux (Maryknoll: Orbis Books, 1999), 279.
40. Jackson, "Proselytism," 25.
41. Elliot and Deyneka, "Protestant Missionaries," 220.

"The idea of conversion led to the development of the human rights."[42] If any individual decides to transfer from one church to another, it is entirely his or her prerogative. Besides, the more such decisions will be made, the more human rights will develop in each country.

Among the Orthodox community, there are some serious concerns about the promotion of human rights closely related to postmodern deconstruction. These fears spring from the vivid example of the secularization of some Western countries that went along the path of liberalization, democratization and individualization. But at the same time, Ion Bria understood that the church had to respond somehow to the postmodern worldview. He says that Orthodoxy cannot ignore the complexity of the new era of postmodernity.[43]

Bria also was concerned about the modern approach of the missionary movement, namely that the fact that the evangelical witness is perceived as completely different brings new symbols alien to this culture, and the youth, detached from their roots, accept them but they still remain alien elements to the given culture.[44] Evangelical churches, by virtue of their greater flexibility, somehow are more responsive to changes in culture, and consequently become more appealing to today's youth. Thinking about the heterogeneity of a particular culture, we cannot ignore the fact of the existence of a globalized youth culture under the influence of the West. It is impossible to combat this phenomenon and it is pointless. Churches that want to remain relevant in modern society must reconsider their methods and approaches, including in matters of transferring from church to church. Unfortunately, these questions are often raised only by churches that are in the minority.[45]

---

42. D. K. Hainsworth, "Deciding for God: The Right to Convert in Protestant Perspectives," in *Sharing the Book: Religious Perspectives on the Rights and Wrongs of Proselytism*, ed. J. Witte and R. C. Martin (New York: Orbis Books, 1999), 201.

43. I. Bria, "Evangelism, Proselytism, and Religious Freedom in Romania: an Orthodox Point of View," *Journal of Ecumenical Studies* 36, no. 1–2 (Winter-Spring, 1999), 179.

44. Bria, *The Liturgy*, 50.

45. Jackson, "Proselytism," 34.

Minorities seek tolerance; majorities have to figure out how their principles shape the whole.[46] So, if the anthropological issues, which are seen as solvable, theological issues with some reservations, are discussable, then the issue of canonical territory requires a lot more attention because of its complexity and ambiguity.

As Rik Torfs mentioned: "Even if evangelical missionaries from the United States try to convert poor people in Siberia by promising them attractive scholarships for an American university, nothing can be done. No crime can be proven, granting scholarships differs from illegal bribery. The only way to adequately tackle the proselytism problem lies in the conclusion of agreements between religious groups themselves."[47]

Canonical Territory and the Ecumenical Movement

I need to deal with one of the most controversial issues of orthodox teaching – the role of canonical territory in resolving the issue of proselytism and in the ecumenical dialogue. This is a particularly difficult issue from the perspective of missiology in the modern world.

The first step is to trace the history of the issue – where and when this question was formulated, what were its premises and how it developed. Thus, "the term 'canonical' refers to the canons of the church councils, the rules of Canon Law. Although the term 'canonical territory' has only recently been used to assign a particular area to a particular church, the contents of that term are, according to the facts, deeply rooted in church tradition."[48] "Constantine changed, the Imperial Church Organization reinforced the territorial principle: the secular administrative structures (dioceses) served as a model for the organization of the church. Already soon afterwards, the emergence of heretical trends and schismatic groups made it necessary to enact the territorial principle in Canon Law. Thus, canon

---

46. Hainsworth, "Deciding for God," 206.

47. R. Torfs, "Experiences of Western Democracies in Dealing with the Legal Position of Churches and Religious Communities" in *Legal Position of Churches and Religious Communities in South-Eastern Europe*, ed. S. Devetak, L. Kalcina, and M. Polzer (Maribor: ISCOMET; Ljubljana: IDSE; Vienna: OSI, 2004), 21.

48. J. Oeldemann, "The Concept of Canonical Territory in the Russian Orthodox Church" in *Religion and the Conceptual Boundary in Central and Eastern Europe: Encounters of Faith*, ed. T. S. Bremer (New York: Palgrave Macmillan, 2008), 230.

8 of the First Council of Nicaea (325) states that in one city there should only be one bishop."[49]

In some orthodox circles the view is popular that the apostle Paul testifies that each of the apostles proclaimed the good news of Christ's truth in his place, within particular geographic points, and nobody went beyond his "right." In modern terms, "the apostolic rule" means the canonical territory of this or that bishop who has the apostolic continuity through ordination.[50] There is a New Testament justification for the belief that among the apostles there was a certain distribution of forces: the Apostle Paul calls himself "the apostle of the Gentiles" (Rom 11:13; 2 Tim 1:11). Also, in Galatians 2:9, Paul mentions the agreement between himself, the Apostle Peter and Barnabas, according to which Paul was to preach among the uncircumcised, while Peter and Barnabas were among the circumcised. But did this agreement have a theological ground, was it strictly fulfilled and what kind of measures were undertaken to make the agreement possible?

The same Apostle Paul in his first epistle to the Corinthians is angry with the behavior of the Corinthians who were calling him apostle or teacher (1 Cor 3:6). He calls such debates spiritual infancy (1 Cor 3:3–4), assuming that all the ministers were doing only what God wanted them to do regardless of the territory allocated to the sermon. All ministers belong to the church, regardless of their location, since further, he cites Peter (1 Cor 3:22), who was also called "our apostle" by the Corinthians. It is hardly necessary to search premises for evidence of the canonical territory teachings in Scripture. It is obvious that it happened in the era of Constantine at the Council of Nicaea.

A new interpretation of the concept of canonical territory appeared immediately after the Reformation, when, after a 30-year war the Peace of Augsburg in 1555 brought peace between Catholics and Lutherans with the establishment of *cuius regio eius religio* (the religion of the ruler is the religion of the state) – a principle that supported nationalism, the rise of the European nation-state. "Under the 1555 Peace of Augsburg, religious

---

49. Ibid., 230.

50. Ioann, Archbishop of Belgorod and Stariy Oskol, "Ecclesiological and Canonical Foundations of Orthodox Mission" (ET from Russian by Olga Vorobyeva), *International Review of Mission* 90, no. 358 (July 1990): 278.

freedom for individual subjects thus extended only to the right to migrate to a region where their particular religion was protected."⁵¹ Further "in the same time, it follows a very natural consequence – 'people had a right to exodus from the rule of earthly lords for the sake of faith' – it was the result of Luther's impact."⁵²

In this case, the motive clearly serves the political aspect. Europe was tired of wars. Especially after the conversion to Lutheranism of a significant number of princes and kings it became clear that victory in those wars was impossible. Again, the political map of Europe of the sixteenth century was taken as a model. Although that division had nothing to do with Orthodoxy, which in those years was quite puzzled with other problems, it touched the Protestants. Anabaptism was a movement of ordinary people and none of the rulers joined it. Thus, the Anabaptists were persecuted throughout Europe by both Catholics and Protestants. This way, the predecessors of Baptists and Evangelicals remained without their own land.

Based on the foregoing, the lack of any boundaries for the mission of the Baptists is explainable and understandable, because never in history have they associated themselves with any land. They were driven from everywhere, but they adapted themselves as best they could wherever they went. For a century it was a movement which had no institutional forms. Even later, when the Baptist Church received official recognition from the authorities, they saw themselves as a movement without borders: Judson, Taylor, Carey, Oncken, and many others spread the gospel throughout the world.

Nowadays, "the term 'canonical territory' is used most frequently by the representatives of the Moscow Patriarchate."⁵³ There is a constant escalation of the issue and an increasing tension within the WCC. "*Russian* and *Orthodox* are taken as synonyms by conservative churchmen and nationalists."⁵⁴ "The Moscow Patriarchate makes clear that today the Russian Orthodox Church considers even those areas to be part of its

---

51. Hainsworth, "Deciding for God," 205.
52. Ibid.
53. Oeldemann, "Concept of Canonical Territory," 230.
54. M. Elliot, "Evangelism and Proselytism in Russia: Synonyms or Antonyms?," *International Bulletin of Missionary Research* 25, no. 2 (April 2001), 74 (italics from original).

canonical territory which had only been annexed to the Soviet Union under Stalin at the end of the Second World War with exception of Georgia and Armenia."⁵⁵

There again, such a statement is made to justify that the models used are not the historical or doctrinal positions, but the political structure of the state at a specific time given that every time a question was raised about canonical territories, the church sought help from the state and its structure. In this context, it is interesting that for twenty years after the collapse of the Soviet Union a single step towards the independence of the Orthodox churches of Ukraine, Moldova, Belarussia and other former Soviet republics has not been taken. This attitude of Moscow has caused many divisions within the church: several independent patriarchates were founded (e.g. Ukraine). In Moldova this led to tensions with the brotherly Romanian Orthodox Church, as mentioned in chapter 2 of the work and below in this chapter.

The teaching of canonical territory generates controversy not only between the Orthodox Church and other churches, but also within Orthodoxy itself. I would like to designate some other contradictions that follow from this situation.

Following the logic of the teaching of canonical territory, all the traditional Christian churches outside the Orthodox countries having their own bishop, have the same rights on their lands as the Orthodox Church on its own. Thus, the appearance of Orthodox churches and Orthodox missionaries in other countries appears to be controversial. Pavel Evdokimov lists the countries where Orthodox missions were carried out: peoples of Siberia, the Altai, the Far East, the Far North and Alaska, China, Korea, Japan and Finland. In addition, there are Orthodox jurisdictions in London, the USA, Turkey and Australia.⁵⁶ While there were fewer problems with peoples of Siberia and the Far East, the Orthodox missionaries in Finland (Lutheran country), England and Australia faced a lot of difficulties. On the one hand, this can be explained by the fact that there, Orthodoxy preaches to ethnic Russian, Serbian, Greek (and other Orthodox peoples). On the

---

55. Oeldemann, "Concept of Canonical Territory," 232.

56. P. Evdokimov, *Pravoslavie [Orthodoxy]* (Moscow: Biblical Theological Institute of St. Apostole Andrew, 2002), 238–241.

other hand this creates a precedent to explain that in addition to canonical territory it is necessary to talk about the "canonical peoples," that is creating the foundation for the national church: "a Church for the Russians" or "a Church for the Romanians."

It is interesting to cite Mark Elliot on this question: "At what extent was justified the presence of the mission of Cyril and Methodius in Moravia, while there were Catholic missionaries at that time?"[57]

In this context it is appropriate to ask a contemporary question: "Do the Orthodox bishops ask permission to preach from the Lutheran, Baptist and Presbyterian bishops when coming to other countries?" Hardly. Rather, they receive an invitation from the Orthodox bishops from those countries. The same happens in the case of Baptist preachers coming from the West to the Baptist Eastern European churches. If the teachings of canonical territory are rigidly followed, it is difficult not to agree with Lawrence Uzzell: "With demographic mixing such demarcations inexorably come to be drawn along ethnic rather than geographical lines. In effect, today's Moscow Patriarchate is arguing if you are an ethnic Pole living in Russia you should be Roman Catholic, if you are an Uzbek you should be Muslim, and so on – contradicting the New Testament teaching (Gal 3:28) that in Christ 'there is neither Jew nor Greek.'"[58]

I think that if the Orthodox Church continues to insist on the universal application of this provision, then the universal church will have to face new threats and risks. In particular, I am talking about the emergence of ecclesiological exclusivism (as it was called by Johannes Oeldemann), when the church can be used to achieve nationalist goals.[59]

The second great danger is the suspension of ecumenical dialogue. A striking example is the case of conflict escalation in Romania, when the Romanian Orthodox Church has insisted on being given the status of "national" church. Naturally, this caused a reaction from other churches, especially when considering the fact that for about three years there were negotiations within the approved commission, which included representatives from many churches, including the Orthodox. The Orthodox required

---

57. Elliot, "Evangelism and Proselytism," 74.
58. Uzzell, "Don't Call It Proselytism," 15.
59. Oeldemann, "Concept of Canonical Territory," 235.

including the article at the last moment, when the documents were to be submitted to the government and the parliament. There were diverse reactions to this. For example, the German Lutheran church announced Sibiu a missionary field, although it is one of the centers of Orthodox life in Romania. Churches, which until now have been open to ecumenical dialogue (in particular this applies to the Lutheran and Reformed churches), do not see further opportunities for collaboration and are ready for open confrontation. Pentecostals said they also had the right to be called a national church because they have communities in almost every village in Romania.[60]

The statements about exclusive rights to any territory only on the basis of historical argument can convince few people nowadays. The dialogue initiated between the churches is in the early stage. The peace between the churches is extremely fragile, and in some places it has not yet been established. Therefore we need to be sensitive and attentive with our statements and suggestions.

Probably the above arguments by the Orthodox Church would have been more convincing if the Orthodox Church itself would show an example of unity and recognition of the "right of the bishop." Even Ion Bria recognized that today conciliarity, especially at the global level, has shown signs of brokenness and weakness.[61]

It means that canons are not inviolable. "It is not clear whether the canons of the ancient church can be transferred to the present situation without any problem."[62] Hence, they also depend on the political situation and, consequently, today's changing geopolitical situation should also cause a revision of decisions relating not only to the relations between the various Orthodox churches, but also to the relations of Orthodoxy with other churches. The WCC concern seems to be quite justified: "When members

---

60. E. A. Pope, "Ecumenism, Religious Freedom, and The 'National Church' Controversy in Romania," *Journal of Ecumenical Studies* 36, no. 1–2 (Winter-Spring, 1999), 194–198.

61. Bria, *The Liturgy*, 75.

62. Oeldemann, "Concept of Canonical Territory," 231.

of one Christian community fail or refuse to listen to the memory of another, the danger of proselytism increases."[63]

"Mission that is 'successful' but reinforces divisions and increases conflicts between Christians and churches is an unfaithful mission. A search for unity that neglects evangelism is similarly unfaithful to God's purpose."[64] In this context there is hope due to the fact that to date the patriarch of the Russian Orthodox Church is the former head of the department for external church relations, who stated the following: "There are no taboos for the Orthodox clergy to cooperate with the evangelical churches."[65]

It is necessary to admit that it is unlikely that the principle of canonical territory will be changed formally, just as it is unlikely that Evangelical Christians will return massively in the bosom of the Orthodox Church as noted above. But modern Orthodoxy is able to soften its position, especially given the huge number of internal and external conflicts, which created the existing situation. Evangelical churches should make exactly the same step in the direction of the Orthodox. Evangelicals should listen to the voice of Orthodoxy: "The Orthodox refuse to become a *terra missionis* of the Western churches."[66] I will directly tackle this particular aspect – the form of evangelism, which is especially annoying to the Orthodox clergy – "aggressive" evangelism.

"Aggressive" Evangelism

It is "aggressive" evangelism which generates most complaints from the Orthodox towards Evangelical churches. Given all the ambiguity of the issue of canonical territory, I will proceed to analyses of different forms of evangelism characteristic for Eastern Europe.

First, I must define the terminology. What do I mean by the concepts of "evangelism" and "aggressive evangelism"? I will present several definitions of evangelism that will help to find the margin between evangelism and proselytism. M. Thomas Thangaraj gives his definition of evangelism: "I define evangelism as the task of sharing the good news of Jesus the Christ,

---

63. "Communicating the Message," 356.
64. Matthey, "Evangelism," 367.
65. http://portal-credo.ru/site/?act=news&id=38090&cf accessed 15 November 2005.
66. Bria, *The Liturgy*, 71.

inviting people to a personal commitment to Christ and consequently to join the church."[67] Jacques Matthey expands this definition: "Evangelism – the proclamation of the good news accompanied by an invitation to turn away from false absolutes (whether religious or not) and to turn to the living God, to follow Jesus Christ as one's only Savior and Lord, to join the community of his church and to live a life under the prompting of the Holy Spirit and taking its ethics of the kingdom of God as one's guide."[68]

The formal definition of the WCC is as follows: "To evangelize means to pray, to preach, to teach, to baptize, to found churches, to ordain, celebrate, proclaim, and to dedicate ourselves to living and working for the fulfillment of God's saving plan among people everywhere."[69]

The definition of M. Thomas Thangaraj and Jacques Matthey are more ecclesiocentric from my point of view, while the official definition of the WCC is more theocentric and holistic. Interestingly, Petros Vassiliadis, an Orthodox theologian and teacher in Thessalonica does not see the introduction of this concept as biblically justified: "From the words mission, conversion, evangelism or evangelization, Christianization, witness and martyria only the last two have been widely adopted in 'ecumenical' circles as the more appropriate for a genuine and authentic Christian mission."[70]

In his view, the term "evangelism" is closely related to sectarian activities that are contrary to the gospel.[71] Many associate evangelism with colonization because of the terminology as well as the methods used. "This work is not Christian mission [talking about Western missions], it is spiritual colonialism. The urgent task therefore is to get rid of colonial practices and develop a new attitude to mission – or rather, to return to the apostolic and early church understanding of mission not as enslaving or bribing people but rather as liberating and bringing them into the light of Christ's truth."[72]

This is not only the opinion of the Orthodox patriarch:

---

67. Elliot, "Evangelism and Proselytism," 336.
68. Matthey, "Evangelism," 355.
69. "Communicating the Message," 354.
70. P. Vassiliadis, "Mission and Proselytism: An Orthodox Understanding," *International Review of Mission* 85, no. 337 (1996): 259.
71. Ibid., 263.
72. Metropolitan Kirill of Smolensk and Kaliningrad, "Gospel and Culture," 75.

Hymns, writings and speeches use militaristic imagery that promotes the idea of mission as coercion and expansion in subtle and hidden ways. Moreover, the host of books published in recent years with regard to increasing membership in the churches all over the world has given way to a reductionist view of evangelism as membership drive. For example, the writings of mission thinkers such as Donald McGavran have made church growth the measuring rod for the effectiveness of the evangelistic task of the church.[73]

According to the Russian Orthodox Church, Catholics, Protestants, and cults are expanding their ranks in the former Soviet Union by bribing them with material goods.[74]

Orthodox Christians do not agree either with the methods used by the Western Evangelical missionaries, or with the way they are perceived:

In most cases the intention (for foreign missionaries) was not to preach Christ and the gospel, but to tear our faithful away from their traditional churches and recruit them into their own communities.[75]

A second factor, besides "expansion," that has contributed to the conflation of *evangelism* and *proselytism* is the perception that the primary task of the church is to work toward the *conversion of heathens*.[76]

The Working Group of the WCC is quite clear on this point: "Since most societies on the planet have already heard the gospel message in some form, the introduction of a new faith tradition into a particular geographic region often leads directly to conflict rather than cooperation, to interconfessional rivalry rather than healthy competition."[77]

---

73. Thangaraj, "Evangelism *sans* Proselytism," 339.
74. Elliot, "Evangelism and Proselytism," 73.
75. Metropolitan Kirill, "Gospel and Culture," 73.
76. Thangaraj, "Evangelism *sans* Proselytism," 339.
77. "Communicating the Message," 356.

Such methods of suppression of local Christians, which have been mentioned above, should not be admissible in evangelism, the goal of which still remains the reconciliation of human beings with God, and not separation of people and churches. Despite the fact that "evangelicals believe they have an obligation to witness to nominal believers as well as to non-believers,"[78] "the sharing of the good news ought to be done in a spirit of vulnerability and humility. Cruciform responsibility points to the Christian act of responsibility that is chastened by the vision of the cross as God's expressing of God's responsibility in vulnerability and suffering."[79] "When evangelism is shaped by the idea of cruciform responsibility, one understands the issue of growth very differently. We are called to invite people to join the Christian community, yet it cannot be done in any other way than the way of vulnerability and humility."[80]

Proceeding from the above, tension is rising not only because of direct action, but also because of attitude. "The difference between evangelism and proselytism is that proselytizer boldly presents his religious institution or organization, whereas the evangelist faithfully presents the gospel as defined by the Word of God."[81] "True evangelism is not aimed at bringing the nations to our religious 'enclosure', but to 'let' the Holy Spirit use both us and those to whom we bear witness to bring about the kingdom of God. This means that in the church's mission, priority should definitely be given not to 'quantity' conversions, but to the 'quality' and exclusiveness of the kingdom of God."[82]

Unfortunately, there is a negative reaction towards Western Evangelical missionaries not only from the Orthodox, but also from local Evangelical ministers. For example, in the CIS there is a well-known open letter, signed by Peter Lunichkin, Pavel Pogodin, Semyon Borodin, Andrei Bondarenko, Vasily Davidyuk and others, addressed to all the Western missionary organizations, asking them not to impose their plans on our countries but to listen to the vision of the local people. Two arguments are presented: no

---

78. Elliott and Deyneka, "Protestant Missionaries," 213.
79. Thangaraj, "Evangelism *sans* Proselytism," 344.
80. Ibid.
81. Stalnaker, "Proselytism or Evangelism?", 348.
82. Vassiliadis, "Mission and Proselytism," 265.

missionary organizations have coordinated with each other's plans, and all of them put those plans on the shoulders of local churches, and churches do not have the necessary infrastructure to implement them. The second reason is that the local organizations cannot compete with Western ones, and for this reason the mission of local churches is stagnated.[83]

This assertion seems to be echoed by: "The priests of the ROC are not ready to enter into competition with Western missionaries who have been trained accordingly."[84] Thus, the problem of aggressive evangelism affects the representatives of different churches. Perhaps we can assume that there is a crisis of relationship not so much between the Orthodox Church and the Evangelical Church, as between the Western churches and the churches of the CIS countries. As noted by the Working Group of the WCC, the effectiveness of mission shall be determined not by "autonomous and self-sustaining churches, as their founders and supporters judge their work to have been successful, even if the *missio Dei* may in fact have been poorly served."[85]

To achieve this we need to see evangelism in the light of a proposed theology of mission, and such evangelism can only be aimed at the holistic liberation of peoples. As M. Thangaraj says, such a form of evangelism may or may not lead people to join the church.[86] "The tendency to reduce mission to involvement in the field of social work, accompanied by acts of worship and programmes of Christian education, is still dominant in many traditional churches . . . I do not see how it is possible to claim that the church is participating in God's mission if sharing the good news with those outside the walls of the church is ruled out."[87]

As a result changes will occur in three dimensions: (1) personal transformation; (2) societal transformation; (3) ecological transformation.[88] "When such a theological move is taken, one comes to define the mission of the church as 'the working out of its commitment to cruciform

---

83. Elliott and Deyneka, "Protestant Missionaries," 209.
84. Berman, "Freedom of Religion," 279.
85. "Communicating the Message," 355.
86. Thangaraj, "Evangelism *sans* Proselytism," 346.
87. Matthey, "Evangelism," 356.
88. Thangaraj, "Evangelism *sans* Proselytism," 348–349.

responsibility, liberative solidarity, and eschatological mutuality.'"[89] "Those who are serious about Christian mission should work not only to develop their own specialized code of ethics but to name and shame its violators. That would make it easier to retire the hopelessly inflated term 'proselytism' to the linguistic museum where it belongs."[90]

Evangelical-Orthodox Dialogue in Moldova in the Early 21st Century

I have presented above an overview of the current situation in the Orthodox and Evangelical churches in Moldova, comparing and evaluating it from the perspective of the neighboring countries, Romania, Ukraine and Russia, and basing this overview on their experience and positions. Subsequently, I will explore the relationship between the Evangelical churches and the Orthodox Church in Moldova and will examine the dynamics of these relationships, especially given the negative experience of mutual accusations and confrontations, which have already been mentioned.

Until 2003, in the territory of Moldova, the International Bible Society was the only example resulting from inter-religious cooperation.

At the beginning of the twenty-first century the World Council of Churches developed its vision of cooperation and partnership between churches, and made an assessment visit to Moldova. In 2002, the WCC made the first visit of this kind, and did not find any common ground between different churches. Miroslav Matrenczyk, coordinator of the Eastern European office of the WCC wrote in his report: "The main findings of the Moldova first study visit, May 15–20, 2002, demonstrated there were no existing inter-church mechanisms or structures for regular contacts and cooperation among churches in Moldova. Moldavian churches and partners remained relatively isolated from international partnership but there was willingness and readiness of all the visited church leaders for inter-church cooperation on the social and developmental levels."[91]

---

89. Ibid., 343.

90. Uzzell, "Don't Call It Proselytism," 16.

91. M. Matrenczyk, "WCC Moldova Partnership Program: Report on Activities for 2003–2004," 7.

It should be understood that when Matrenczyk talked about the lack of inter-church and international cooperation, he referred first of all to cooperation within the WCC, and especially cooperation with the Orthodox Church. The Evangelical churches have conducted some very successful projects in cooperation with each other as well as in collaboration with Western partners. During this first visit to Moldova, he visited the leaders of all the major denominations of Moldova, and indeed, all of them expressed their willingness to cooperate, especially in social projects. A year later, the first treaties of cooperation with the heads of the denominations were signed except with the leaders of the Pentecostal Union, who expressed unwillingness for such dialogue and partnership. As it turned out later, neither the leadership of the Pentecostal Union nor the Orthodox Church, were ready for dialogue.[92]

In October 2003, the Moldavian Partnership Program within the territory of Moldova was created, which was intended to consolidate the efforts of various churches to tackle social problems. An overall objective was declared: "To assist 'people in need' through churches and related organizations. Specific objectives were pronounced: (1) To "equip" churches and related organizations to fulfill their mission in social and development fields (mainly through increasing their capacities for future sustainability); (2) To help churches and related organizations in the development of project initiatives in priority sectors. In accordance with previous consultations with local partners, Moldova Partnership Pilot Programme (2003–2004) was founded on four pillars:

- Social protection – starting with care for elderly;
- Unemployment reduction – starting with development of accessible credit schemes and job creation (likely to include

---

92. I have conducted two interviews on this topic: the first, with the coordinator of the partnership program in Moldova, Lilia Bulat, who correlates with the Moldovan Metropolitan under the Russian Orthodox Church of the Moscow Patriarchate. Being asked about cooperation with the churches of evangelical Christians she replied that, "They did not agree, and we did not insist, as between the Orthodox Church and the Pentecostal, there are serious discrepancies on matters of faith. I did not want to worsen the situation and gaining the Pentecostals, to lose the Orthodox . . . I think that the WCC would also agree." The second interview was also conducted in 2006 with the MPP Project manager, Tudor Lungu, who himself is a member of the Pentecostal church. He said that the Pentecostal pastors, being invited to cooperation, replied that it was not appropriate for them to enter into such a relationship at that stage.

the agro-processing plants, the small enterprise sector and service sector);
- Capacity building – starting with development of management skills for projects and small businesses (but also stimulating the voluntary associations and cooperation among farmers and the restructuring of the agro-processing plants);
- Information and Advocacy – starting with anti-trafficking in women's initiatives."[93]

The first meetings were organized and there was training for representatives of all the interested churches. The Metropolitan Church of Moldova, the Metropolitan Church of Bessarabia and the Evangelical Lutheran Church of Moldova were the first to take part in these projects. In 2004, a representative of the Evangelical Baptist Union joined the program. The Catholic Church of Moldova participated in various seminars and training sessions, but did not participate in working meetings and the distribution of funds. The first international partners were the WCC, Conference of European Churches, HEKS/Switzerland, Church of Sweden, ICCO/Netherlands, Catholic Relief Service/USA (partly only) and AIDROM.[94]

The partnership began, and many saw it as the beginning of a future round table. There was hope that cooperation in the social sphere would bring churches together and give them grounds for further cooperation and subjects for round tables.[95] The first three years of the MPP were very difficult and tense. G. Russu, the representative of the Baptist Union in the MPP at that time, said that almost every meeting was tense and often ended in conflict.[96] The platform had been established for dialogue, but turned merely into a place for the distribution of grants.[97] Given the difficult relationship between the two Orthodox churches, conflicts sometimes ended with insults.[98]

---

93. Matrenczyk, "WCC Moldova Partnership Program," 7–8.
94. Ibid.
95. M. Matrenczyk to the author, June 2010.
96. G. Russu to the author, February 2006.
97. N. Affermann (official representative from Diakonisches Werk, German partner of WCC in Moldova) to the author, December 2007.
98. G. Russu to the author, February 2006.

G. Russu, in the end, decided to suspend his activities as a member of the board of the organization. Long before he finally decided, he stopped attending the meetings and participating in discussions.[99] The years of opposition and difficulty in building interfaith relations influenced his decision. At some point, it even seemed the partnership might end, but, fortunately, an adequate solution was found. It was proposed to replace two people who were creating conflict situations,[100] and thus, the meeting moved from confrontation to a constructive dialogue.

In 2006, the Bishop of the UCECBM invited me to represent the Union in the council. The position of the UCECBM was clearly defined – only partnership at the level of distribution of grants in the social sphere. Many pastors of the Union of Evangelical Christian Baptists, in general, are against such cooperation, thus "our presence must be very strictly regulated."[101] The dialogue itself has no potential prospect.[102] Moreover, the Union of Evangelical Christian Baptists is not only unprepared for a dialogue, but it seems, also, that the dialogue could lead to a split within the Union. Therefore, to preserve unity within the Baptist denomination, it was decided not to start a dialogue with another denomination. Naturally, the question arises about the ethical side – would the Western organizations/partners be ready to cooperate in the future, if they knew the position of the board members?

In 2007, the MPP was transformed into Moldovan Christian AID from its previous informal platform. It is now a non-governmental organization aiming to jointly participate in the implementation of social projects. The founding meeting was attended by representatives of five churches: the Moldovan Orthodox Church (Russian Patriarchate), the Bessarabian Orthodox Church (Romanian Patriarchate), the Union of Churches of Evangelical Christian Baptists, the Catholic Church in Moldova, and the Moldovan Evangelical Lutheran Church. In the course of the discussion there were revealed some structural and strategic divergences. The normal functioning of any organization involves activities in accordance with the

---

99. Ibid.
100. L. Bulat (coordinator of the MPP) to the author, May 2007.
101. V. Ghiletchi to the author, December, 2006.
102. Ibid.

law. The Moldovan Legislation supposes two ways of registering activities similar to those carried out by MCA: (1) as a non-governmental organization; (2) as a public foundation. The registration as a foundation assumes that churches have to be the founders of the foundation, or more precisely the heads of churches, and the current council would become a leading body of the organization. The registration as a NGO implies that the current council could be the founders. The governing body of the foundation would consist of one representative from each denomination, the governing body of the organization supposes the representation by quota, in other words, the less numerous Lutheran church cannot have the same number of representatives as the larger Orthodox one.

The idea of registering as a foundation has been warmly supported by the Orthodox Church of Bessarabia, which, having six times less parishes in the country than the Moldavian Orthodox Church, is very active in social activities presented in a common platform, and developing them in all directions. Thus, equal representation in the governing body would give equal rights to decide on the allocation of grants. In this case, the Metropolitan Petru was ready to sign the founding document along with other hierarchs.

The Lutheran Church was also ready to sign the founding document, but it happened that the MELC was actively cooperating with the MM ROC. Perhaps, this is the only interfaith project, which was implemented from the beginning of the existence of the platform until December 2007. Thus, despite the fact that the MELC had the opportunity for equal participation in the new organization, it chose the perspective of a public organization. Throughout the meeting, the representative of the MELC often repeated the argument: "The MM ROC is the largest church, and we must reckon with this fact."

The Catholic Church immediately expressed its position that they would not participate officially in any activities of the foundation or the organization. They are ready to cooperate, to participate in some selected projects, but not at the official level. It is worth mentioning that at this meeting, the representative of the Catholic Church had an equal voice. The Catholic Church supported the Metropolitan Church of Bessarabia, wishing everyone to have equal rights.

The Moldavian Orthodox Church stated that the Metropolitan Vladimir would not sign the founding documents along with the representatives of other confessions. This is the first reason why they are for a NGO. The second one is the unfair distribution of votes taking in consideration the different size of the churches.

The Union of Churches of Evangelical Christian Baptists was the last one to express its position. The right to vote was given only to five people – one representative from each church – therefore the decision depended on the Evangelical Christian Baptist vote. The Union of Churches of Evangelical Christian Baptists pronounced itself in favor of the registration as a NGO, as previously a meeting had been held with the bishop, who refused to sign the founding document.[103]

Thus, it was decided to register as NGO (association). Sometime later, the Metropolitan Church of Bessarabia decided to withdraw from the organization where its rights could be abridged. As a result, today in Moldova the MCA has three church founders: the MM, the MELC and the UCECBM. The Council has the following composition: one representative from the MELC, one from the UCECBM, three from the MM of the ROC of the MP, and one Executive Director who belongs to the MM. The Moldovan Metropolitan has an overwhelming majority. It is an interesting fact that the Romanian Orthodox Church is more active in the ecumenical movement in the world than the Russian, while in Moldova, due to certain political reasons, the representatives of the Romanian church found themselves out of the movement.

It is also worth noting that the cooperation is restricted to social action. Neither the MM nor the ECB are ready for a round table. Only the MELC is prepared for the next step.

Among the joint social actions it is worth mentioning the National Day of Prayer for the victims of human trafficking, which was joined by two other participating churches besides the founding churches. On 2 December 2007, in all the churches of Moldova of these five confessions, sermons were heard on the biblical view on human trafficking and prayers for the victims of this kind of trade. A collection of sermons on this

---

103. V. Ghiletchi to the author, December 2006.

subject (consisting of four booklets – the sermons of each confession were printed separately – and all four booklets were distributed to all the communities and parishes in Moldova) was published with the support of the International Organization for Migration. The Catholic Church abstained from participating in the writing and publication of the sermons.

There are developing relations between some priests of the Orthodox Church and the pastors of the Evangelical Christian Baptist Church on a personal and communitarian level. At the same time, the leaders of all the denominations have never participated in joint prayers and dialogue in Moldova (as happened at the inauguration of the Ukrainian President Viktor Yushchenko in 2005). Often criticisms can be heard in the address of the leadership of churches, mentioning that all the attempts to carry out joint actions have been implemented only at the initiative of the authorities. The example of Ukraine demonstrates contrary evidence. If the inauguration of common prayer was initiated by the presidential administration, then 100 days after the inauguration of Viktor Yushchenko, the five leaders of churches gathered again to pray, but on their own initiative[104] – stated the Religious Information Service of Ukraine.

Conclusions

This third chapter is an analysis of current relations between the Evangelical and Orthodox churches in the territory of the Republic of Moldova; it has given the positions, views and experience of both Orthodox and Evangelical personalities from Romania, Ukraine and Russia. I examined the dynamics of the conflict between the Russian and Romanian Orthodox Churches in Moldova, as it is impossible to talk about a dialogue between the Evangelical and Orthodox churches without mentioning the difference in approaches of the various Orthodox churches. The final point of the chapter showed the history of the WCC in Moldova, the first years of its existence and possible ways for further functioning.

On the basis of the performed research, I draw the following conclusions:
1) The presence of two Orthodox Metropolitan churches in such a small country as Moldova, heating up the spiritual atmosphere,

---

104. http://www.risu.org.ua/rus/news/article%3b5337/ accessed 4 May 2005.

has made additional tensions in the country among Orthodox believers. At the same time, the tensions between Orthodox and Evangelical believers have decreased. Both Orthodox churches are ready to lend a sympathetic ear to Evangelical churches. The Evangelical churches are responsible for expressing an opinion on this matter. Based on the principles of Jesus Christ of the unity of the church, the Evangelical churches have to call the Orthodox to peace and harmony.

2) The Evangelical church should reconsider its evangelistic and social vision based on the principles of interaction with Orthodox churches. Social projects should not play the role of pre-evangelism or "hidden" evangelism, and evangelistic approaches should not contain elements of "aggressive" evangelism and proselytism.

3) There was a polarization within the Orthodox, as well as within Evangelical churches in regard to joint cooperation, dialogue and mission. The first attempt as well as the second has both supporters of cooperation and dialogue, and advocates of the "true" faith, which cannot be "diluted" by means of relationships with other churches. The issue of cooperation and dialogue should be further explored, however attempts to force cooperation could lead to disastrous results. This is why it is necessary to conduct further monitoring of public opinion to find tense situations, while studying and modeling the positive experience of joint discussions and joint actions.

4) Cooperation between Evangelical and Orthodox churches has already been initiated. The beginning was difficult, but there is an open platform for interaction.

5) The leadership of large Evangelical denominations (ECB and CEF) is quite reticent at the possible prospect of cooperation, as many pastors openly express their negative views on the subject. The desire to maintain peace within their own denomination is greater than the desire to find common ground with the Orthodox Church. The less numerous MELC is ready for open dialogue and cooperation.

6) On a personal and communitarian level, joint projects and dialogues are being carried out and new relationships are being built. It is necessary to support such initiatives at all levels.

The first part of this work shows the historical and current tensions between the Orthodox and Evangelicals in Moldova. The second part will give us a theological and missiological explanation of such a situation, and will help to evaluate the reality for further dialogue or changing paradigms.

Part 2

Missiological Paradigms and Their Connections with Churches in Moldova

The first part of the research revealed the emergence and the growth of the Orthodox Church in the territory of the Republic of Moldova, its split into two jurisdictions at the end of the twentieth century, and its potential prospects for future development. Also, there was presented a brief historical overview of the roots of Evangelical communities in Moldova and their development at the time of the Russian Empire, *România Mare*, Soviet Union and Independent Moldova. In addition, the work has drawn attention to the main campaigns for the evangelization of Moldova, as well as to the social involvement of the evangelical communities. Besides, the beginning of the twenty-first century is marked by the first attempts at dialogue and joint actions of Orthodox and Evangelical churches. An attempt was made in this research to reflect critically the origins of the round table and the appeal of the World Council of Churches to interaction in the development of joint social projects.

As a result of the work conducted for this dissertation, a number of conclusions were drawn, as well as preliminary recommendations, which gave possible ways of future cooperation. In the current difficult situation, rather careful and adequate dialogue steps should be undertaken. The church authorities are not ready for an exchange of ideas and thus, there is no direct interaction between them.

There are weighty reasons for an isolation of this kind among which the theology of mission plays a key role. The research work makes an attempt to identify the missiological concepts having an effect on the functioning of the Evangelical churches. The difficulty consists in the fact that, unlike the Orthodox Church, the Evangelical churches of Moldova do not have a clearly defined missiological position. Although, at the same time, it is impossible to assert that mission is merely carried out spontaneously and chaotically. The fourth chapter of the research work pays attention to the missiological approaches familiar in evangelical circles and makes an attempt to identify the degree of influence of various theories on the mission of Evangelical churches of Moldova at the beginning of the twenty-first century.

The fifth chapter of the research work is dedicated to the study of Orthodox missiology, as well as to the analysis of its key standpoints, which slow down interaction and cooperation.

The sixth chapter concludes the second part of the research work with an analysis of the birth and development of the concept of *missio Dei*, its goal and contents. The concept was born in ecumenical circles and we will see how WCC theologians and missiologists could be of benefit to the mission of Evangelical churches in Moldova. On the basis of the results of part 2 I will construct a new paradigm for Moldavian Evangelicals and trying to find common points with the Orthodox Church in Moldova.

CHAPTER 4

How "Mission" is Perceived by Evangelical Theologians

During the entire twentieth century, Evangelical churches were particularly active in launching domestic as well as foreign missions. The twentieth century is also called the century of mission. It was not the century of pointless and desperate attempts. The twentieth century can be called not only the century of missions, but also the century of missiology. Moreover, it is worth noting that this phenomenon affected both historic churches and entirely new movements. Since the middle of this previous century there were particular debates and arguments between WCC representatives and Evangelical missiologists.

What is the definition of mission? What is the relationship between the church and mission? How are the roles of God and church distributed in missionary theory and practice? What is the essence of mission? Are there any degrees of priority between evangelism and social responsibility?

I will try to answer these and other questions in this chapter, focusing on three missiological paradigms originated and developed in evangelical circles: managerial missiology, post-imperial missiology, and Anabaptist missiology.[1]

Managerial Missiology

S. Escobar attributed to this paradigm a movement which became known as the Church Growth Movement. Donald A. McGavran wrote the book

---

1. This classification may be found in S. Escobar, *The New Global Mission: The Gospel from Everywhere to Everyone* (Downers Grove: InterVarsity, 2003).

The Bridges of God in 1955 and is considered by right to be the founder of this movement. Among his colleagues, followers and disciples there are such outstanding and well-known missiologists such as Arthur Glasser, Peter Wagner, Van Engen and others. Perhaps Rick Warren achieved the best practical implementation of this missiological paradigm, declaring that, for him, McGavran's approach constituted the starting point in the establishment of a new church model.[2]

It all started when McGavran, asking himself if the money invested justified the received results, introduced into the theory of mission, elements of sociology and statistical analysis. In his first and fundamental work on this subject, he repeatedly raised the issue of the effectiveness of the fund's investment in church mission. Being born in India and having spent many years there as a missionary, he took as an example for a comparative analysis the so-called missionary stations, where, as a rule, there are not only churches, but also schools and hospitals, farms, and sometimes even colleges. There are a lot of people working there. Frequently, churches and denominations, considering these stations the only possibility to help people in Third World countries, have been supporting them financially for decades.

McGavran thought about the number of souls won for Christ at these stations and found out that for years and decades in many places nothing changed – the number of church members remained the same, there was no awakening, the missionary stations were administered by foreign missionaries, and the necessary conditions to transfer responsibilities there to local ministers were not created.[3] However, he did not suggest closing the missionary stations, but only making them outposts for the growing people movement.[4] McGavran's innovation lay in the fact that he offered two absolutely new approaches: (1) to refocus the mission from involvement in society's needs onto evangelism and the organization of new churches, "back of our Christian thinking today lies the growing conviction that

---

2. R. Warren, *The Purpose Driven Church: Growth Without Compromising Your Message & Vision* (Grand Rapids: Zondervan, 1995), 29.

3. D. McGavran, *The Bridges of God: A Study in the Strategy of Missions* (New York: Friendship Press, 1955), 143–149.

4. Ibid., 157.

church growth is a central and continuing business of Christian mission. God expects church growth. We are about our Father's business when we study its crucial issues in these days;"[5] (2) to found new churches on a homogeneous basis, "recognizing homogeneous units and claiming them for Christ emphasizing the biblical goal of discipling the tribes,"[6] transferring all the responsibility as soon as possible to local leaders.

McGavran believed that the local congregation is considered to be the starting and, at the same time, the ultimate point of mission. From local churches people can move towards other territories or groups of people. Matthew 28:19–20 is seen not only as the main but almost the only mandate of the church. *Making disciples* of *all the nations* – this is the main goal of all the Christians on earth.[7]

He was convinced that a missionary, starting a new church, should use all the known principles for a demographic study of the community, using sociology and anthropology as tools,[8] determining and focusing only on the target audience, experiencing, thus, rapid success and church growth. From his writings I can see that by using the "tools," church leaders and missionaries can manage church growth. It means that local congregations "should" grow; if pastors and missionaries will take into consideration a demographic study of their communities, the growth will be natural as the result of right methods. Understanding the cultures, using their language and type of mentality, will bring results. When he spoke about "results," he had in mind the number of people who dedicated their lives to Christ. This is the reason, why his approach was called "managerial."

Having noticed the difference between Eastern and Western thinking, he came to the conclusion that in the East, decisions are often taken corporately and not individually.[9] Living in tribes, castes, races or social classes, people have much in common facing difficulty together or rejoicing together, and often social groups of this kind have a headman or a leader

---

5. D. McGavran, *Church Growth and Christian Mission* (New York: Harper & Row, 1965), 10.
6. Ibid., 73.
7. McGavran, *The Bridges of God*, 126–140.
8. McGavran, *Church Growth*, 80.
9. McGavran, *The Bridges of God*, 8–12.

whose opinion is respected. McGavran proposed to evangelize the group beginning with these key people. "Most necessary, enough individuals and groups of that most winnable people must be converted in a short enough time and a small enough area so that each Christian comes into the church with some of his kindred."[10] This approach should bring not only individuals, but nations to Christ.

Beginning with the 1960s, McGavran had to engage in a dialogue with the more powerful and influential World Council of Churches. He warned the Christian community about the discrepancy between their understanding of mission and the Bible. Appealing repeatedly to the definitions given by H. R. Niebuhr and J. C. Hoekendijk, who believed that mission is any action happening outside the walls of the church, McGavran always returned to the origins of the WCC, or to be more exact of the *International Missionary Council,* which later merged with the World Council of Churches. Initially, the missionary movement was eager to achieve just one goal – to take the gospel of Jesus Christ to every nation, every tribe and individual. Having formulated the concept of *missio Dei*, the WCC articulated theological justification for a new missionary paradigm, although McGavran's school considered that this was capitulation to the world. "In time, the major implications of this reconceptualization of *missio Dei* began to filter down to the churches. In all too many circles they came as heady wine. There was no longer any reason for the church to confront the world with a message whose first word was 'Repent!' There was no essential difference between Christians and non-Christians."[11]

Later the emphasis shifted to social participation and presence evangelism. This was what he turned against, believing it a distortion of biblical truth.[12] He introduced a new term – "sub-Christian" – using it for those Christians who were shifting the focus of their mission from proclaiming the gospel and church growth, to good deeds. McGavran aimed at two groups of people at the same time: (1) those who do not consider Jesus

---

10. Ibid., 129.

11. A. F. Glasser and D. McGavran, *Contemporary Theologies of Mission* (Grand Rapids: Baker, 1983), 93.

12. McGavran, *Church Growth*, 238, and Glasser and McGavran, *Contemporary Theologies of Mission*, 21.

Christ the only way of salvation, and simply engaged in philanthropy with a Christian bias; (2) those who believe in the exclusiveness of Christ's sacrifice, but saw their primary mission in peacekeeping or other good deeds, shifting the preaching of the gospel to the background.[13] Further and even tougher: "Some switch to philanthropy has negative theological roots. When men cease to believe in the uniqueness of Christ, they often defend themselves by ardent compensatory humanitarianism. The conservative branches of the Christian church like to believe that these theological roots – this lukewarmness of belief, yet reluctance to face the flinty reality of eternity without God – account for the reinterpretation of mission."[14]

His appeal for over thirty years remained unchanged – the church must wisely use human and financial resources and no longer donate money for programs that are the responsibility of state and public organizations. All the funds allocated to mission must go to creating new churches and making disciples. McGavran's disciple Robert C. Guy wrote: "In a real sense, therefore, every true theology is a theology of redemption and of church growth."[15]

Every newly founded church should be able not only to continue to grow, not just to be self-sufficient, and not only be self-governing. Wagner suggests a new formulation of old ideas: "The description we will attempt goes beyond the self-supporting, self-governing, and self-propagating categories . . . Mature churches can take care of themselves, they are churches for others, and they are relevant to their cultural situation."[16]

Earlier, McGavran said that Christian mission resembles a pendulum, which swings from liberal to conservative theology and from social gospel to evangelism and proclamation of the gospel of good news.[17] In his view, Christianity was tired of the general and vague concepts of the WCC, and the pendulum had swung in the direction of the organization of new churches. Making a summary of all his works, McGavran concluded: "Christians

---

13. McGavran, *Church Growth*, 19.

14. Ibid.

15. R. C. Guy, *Theological Foundations in Church Growth and Christian Mission* (New York: Harper & Row, 1965), 43.

16. C. P. Wagner, *Frontiers in Missionary Strategy* (Chicago: Moody Press, 1971), 163–169.

17. McGavran, *Church Growth*, 9.

are necessarily concerned with at least four great tasks: (1) evangelizing the world; (2) worshiping God; (3) translating, expounding, and teaching the Bible; and (4) applying biblical truth so that God's will be done on earth as it is in heaven."[18] Further, "the purpose of Christian mission is not to bring about peace, mercy, and justice (1 John 3:1). It is to lead God's lost sons and daughters back to him. Then the former will follow."[19]

Thus, it was proposed to withdraw social responsibility from the field of mission and transfer it to the field of ethics. It should be noted that, if we take mission seriously, we notice that it is based on Commandments, and particularly, imperatives. The mission suggests what we should do, while modern ethics avoids imperatives, as well as the main question of the ethics, which is, "why." Ethics helps to define what is good and what is evil, and sets down compulsory standards of behavior. Transferring social responsibility from the field of mission to the ethical one, we thus define it as optional. Arguing over all the tasks that lie before the church or individual Christians, McGavran suggested not to call them mission, but to select other words such as "task," "ministry," "responsibility" or other terms, believing that otherwise we lose the essence of mission.[20] Only evangelism may be called mission in the fullest sense of the word.

In his latest work, McGavran expressed his joy that in the late 1980s, the activity of the WCC began to decline and the missiologists of this branch of Christianity gave up: "It rejoices that justice is beginning to roll down like the waters and that a mighty stream of righteousness is beginning to be felt in many parts of the world."[21]

Rick Warren, impressed by the ideas of the Church Growth Movement, took the same texts as targets for his church[22] that were previously proposed

---

18. D. McGavran, *Momentous Decisions in Missions Today* (Grand Rapids: Baker, 1984), 11–13.

19. Ibid., 14.

20. Ibid., 142.

21. D. McGavran, *Effective Evangelism: A Theology Mandate* (Phillipsburg: Presbyterian and Reformed Company, 1988), 103.

22. Wagner, *Frontiers in Missionary Strategy*, 27.

by Peter Wagner,[23] but on their basis, he came to somewhat different conclusions. In his book *Purpose Driven Church* Warren proposed five objectives the church should achieve: (1) Celebrate God's presence in worship; (2) Communicate God's Word through evangelism; (3) Incorporate God's family into fellowship; (4) Educate God's people through discipleship; (5) Demonstrate God's love through service,[24] among which evangelism is but one part. Ten years later, in 2005, he called Christianity to join his P.E.A.C.E. Plan, which reflected the following ideas: (1) Promote reconciliation; (2) Equip servant leaders; (3) Assist the poor; (4) Care for the sick; (5) Educate the next generation, in terms of liquidation of illiteracy.[25]

A few decades ago similar ideas were put forward by WCC missiologists and were fiercely criticized by Warren's predecessors:

> Our definition of mission does not narrowly confine mission to verbal announcement of the gospel. It accepts the practice of the last 150 years that a great variety of activities may be used to communicate the gospel across linguistic and cultural barriers to those who have yet to believe: education, literacy programs, agriculture, medicine, presence, dialogue, proclamation, social action. All these are mission when their purpose is so to witness to Christ that men and women may know him, love him, believe him, be found in him, become members of his church, and create in the segments of society they control, a social order more agreeable to God.[26]

Moreover, Warren's new goals are not based on Bible verses, but on a profound concern about the world's needs. Arthur Glasser considered the reasons why in less than 50 years the emphasis has shifted in world mission. He made a historical review of the WCC, starting with the Student

---

23. It is interesting that Wagner, unlike McGavran is more likely to use the terminology that was common those days in the discussions with the WCC. He was one of the first evangelical missiologists who introduced a Trinitarian foundation to justify the mission. Although, to be more exact, it should be noted that all the three Persons of the Trinity in the end have the same mission – evangelism, church growth and making disciples. Wagner, *Frontiers in Missionary Strategy*, 19–25.

24. Warren, *Purpose Driven Church*, 103–107.

25. http://thepeaceplan.com accessed 22 March 2011.

26. Glasser and McGavran, *Contemporary Theologies of Mission*, 27.

Volunteer Movement, when all the dreams and plans were related to the evangelization of the whole world within one *generation*. Glasser determined some reasons for these changes, among which I will mention two: "Two world wars had ruthlessly demonstrated the moral bankruptcy of the West . . . Second, the peoples being evangelized were beginning to acquire a new awareness of their national identity and pride."[27]

Often this was happening by means of the most brutal methods. The example of Rwanda is relevant; until 1915, only a small percentage of people identified themselves as Christians there. For eighty years, about 90 percent of Rwanda's population belonged to Christian churches; herewith, the genocide of 1994 could surpass even Hitler's Germany in the speed of killing people. Eight hundred thousand Tutsis were killed in one hundred days![28] This is more than 10 percent of Rwanda's population.[29] At the same time, the average life expectancy was forty-eight years,[30] due especially to the spread of AIDS. In Rwanda, according to official statistics, about 3 percent of the people are HIV-positive.[31] This proves that evangelization and Christianization of the country are not always a panacea for evil. Of course, in such circumstances it is natural to ask – what has changed in the country? How can we evaluate the growth of churches, in a case when the national, ethnic and social statuses remain people's task number one? This was what made Rick Warren include Rwanda in the P.E.A.C.E. Plan, as one of the neediest countries. Can we say that the example of Rwanda is an exception to the rule and a missionary oversight?

The April 2009 events in Moldova have shown that there are also other countries facing difficult times. When in central Chisinau there were protests against the then ruling regime of the Communist Party, Romanian-speaking young Christians participated actively in the riots, while many of Russian-speaking Evangelical believers supported the CPRM.

---

27. Ibid., 85.
28. http://www.genocide.ru/lib/genocides/rwanda.htm accessed 22 March 2011.
29. http://ostranah.ru/rwanda accessed 22 March 2011.
30. Ibid.
31. http://www.unaids.org/ru/KnowledgeCentre/Resources/FeatureStories/archive/2009/20090826_EXD_Rwanda.asp accessed 15 September 2009.

Warren himself says about his plan: "Each P.E.A.C.E. trip is a comprehensive strategy, which attacks all five problems because they are entwined. NGOs have historically had a tendency to specialize in just one problem area and governments have historically tended to ignore the spiritual dimension, but churches are uniquely called to care about all of the problems."[32]

It seems that the pendulum has reversed direction again.

Post-Imperial Missiology

McGavran's school, developed mainly from the 1970s to the 1990s, being very categorical, worried many theologians and missiologists. Historically, the church has been involved in social issues,[33] has tried to respond adequately and in specific historical stages has even been the flagship of social, socio-economic and even political changes. It seemed illogical to abandon the existing theological and biblical understandings of social service, not to take account of the accumulated historical experience, and merely to open new churches. Missiological thinking was seeking ways for its realization and application.

After the merger of the IMC with the WCC in 1961, Evangelical missiologists felt a certain emptiness; a vacuum was created due to the lack of space for communication. But the presence of so many skilled professionals led unavoidably to the creation of such a space.

In 1966, with the financial support of the Billy Graham Association, a forum was held in Berlin on the development of Evangelical missiological thought – "the Congress addressed itself to some social problems under its section dealing with One Race."[34]

---

32. http://www.thepeaceplan.com/ accessed 15 September 2009

33. V. Samuel and C. Sugden, "Evangelism and Social Responsibility – A Biblical Study on Priorities" in *In Word and Deed: Evangelism and Social Responsibility*, ed. B. Nicholls and Lausanne Committee for World Evangelization and the World Evangelical Fellowship (Grand Rapids: Eerdmans, 1985), 191.

34. T. Adeyemo, "A Critical Evaluation of Contemporary Perspectives" in *In Word and Deed: Evangelism and Social Responsibility*, ed. B. Nicholls and Lausanne Committee for World Evangelization and the World Evangelical Fellowship (Grand Rapids: Eerdmans, 1985), 44.

This meeting was followed by a series of consultations that led to the convening in the city of Lausanne, Switzerland, of the World Congress in 1974. It was attended by about 2,300 delegates from 150 countries[35]. It is impossible today to overestimate the role of this meeting. It served as an impulse for the development of missiology as an academic discipline, as well as for the practical orientation of the church. Working groups were created. They met with some regularity and issued new documents, articles and books. The purpose of the Lausanne Movement was stated publicly as: "To further the evangelization of the world by building bridges of understanding and cooperation among Christian leaders everywhere to mobilize the whole church to proclaim the whole gospel to the whole world."[36]

In 1989, a second World Congress of Lausanne II was held in Manila, which was attended by about 4,300 delegates from 173 countries[37]. The third congress gathered 4,000 delegates from 198 countries in Cape Town in 2010[38].

One of the main shifts in Evangelical missiology was the rethinking of mission in Trinitarian terms.[39] We see how ecumenical debates influenced Evangelical missiologists for some new steps. From my perspective, the Trinitarian theology of mission made an inestimable effect for Evangelical circles. First of all, it gave a common language to Evangelicals and the WCC. Second, it returned the church to a more holistic theological understanding of the Bible. Third, it is full of the desire to understand God's image, God's mission and God's calling. John Stott was one of those who initiated this rethinking in the Lausanne Movement.[40] Fourth, it is very close to the main goal of this work in that it gives us an additional chance

---

35. http://www.lausanne.org/en/gatherings/lausanne-1974.html accessed 30 January 2012.

36. *The Lausanne Story* (Lausanne Committee for World Evangelization), 16.

37. http://www.lausanne.org/en/gatherings/manila-1989.html accessed 30 January 2012.

38. http://www.lausanne.org/en/gatherings/cape-town-2010.html accessed 30 January 2012.

39. Lausanne Committee for World Evangelism, *Evangelism and Social Responsibility, An Evangelical Commitment*, 2 (c) (Wheaton: Lausanne Committee for World Evangelism, World Evangelical Fellowship, 1982), 15.

40. J. Stott, *Evangelical Truth: A Personal Plea for Unity, Integrity and Faithfulness* (Carlisle: Langham Global Library, 2013), 10–11.

for Evangelical-Orthodox dialogue. Orthodox theologians have always been extremely deep and relevant in describing the relationship between the three persons of God. Orthodox Trinitarian theology draws attention to the beauty of Trinity; it makes a solid foundation for the building of society, family and personhood according to the same beauty. I talk more about Orthodox Trinitarian theology in chapter 5; for now, I will just underline the future possibility for dialogue on this foundation.

The Lausanne Movement brought together a pleiad of missiologists and theologians from five continents. Many of them came from the former colonies. The appearance of the Lausanne Movement was in the same years when many countries in Africa, South America and Asia received their independence. They became equal players among other countries in the United Nations and other international bodies on the very high level. Their voices became heard among politicians. The Lausanne Movement gave them an opportunity to become partners in theological and missiological discussions. The old "imperial" paradigm was changed to a new "post-imperial" paradigm.

The key role in creating a field for discussion and collaboration was played by John Stott. I cannot say, however, that all the movement seemed monolithic and all missiologists worked within the same school. In the article, entitled "The Lausanne Story" it is written: "Here it is helpful to distinguish between the Lausanne Movement and the 'Ecumenical Movement.' The Ecumenical Movement seeks to bring Christians and churches together with a minimum of few denominational distinctives for the purpose of unity. The Lausanne Movement allows Christians and churches to maintain their denominational distinctives, while bringing them together for the singular purpose of world evangelization. Thus Lausanne draws people from many different denominations."[41]

I cannot agree with the assertion that the WCC drew together churches with minimal differences, but one of the advantages of the Lausanne Movement consists in the diversity of approaches and opinions.

One of the key issues is that the role of social responsibility in the mission of the church and God's mission has always been on the agenda of the

---

41. Lausanne Committee for World Evangelization, *The Lausanne Story*.

Lausanne Movement. One of the serious reasons that pushed Evangelical missiologists to rethink their missiology was a great change of the map of the world in the 1960s:

> The shackles of political and ecclesiastical colonialism were finally shaken off and there was an almost euphoric conviction that all would now go well and that, in due time, The Third World would catch up with the West, both socio-politically and ecclesiastically. In this atmosphere, evangelism in the sense of winning individual converts to Christ and the church became less and less of a priority. The church's task was, rather the *missio Dei*, increasingly understood in terms of the church's involvement in the world.[42]

Samuel Escobar supported this idea: "The rediscovery of holistic mission among evangelicals in the 1960s was occasioned by the experience of churches whose evangelistic work took place in countries or social classes going through painful processes of social transformation."[43]

In the 1970s, the situation changed, or rather the attitude to the situation changed. In most cases the world did not see the expected results from political changes. David Bosch considered that new watchword in the 1970s was no longer *development*, but rather *liberation*. People were poor, not because they needed development, but because they were oppressed and exploited. Thus what was needed was not a theology of development but a theology of liberation.[44]

At the same time, such critical periods in history were crucial for the church. In the second chapter I already mentioned the awakening that took place in Moldova after the collapse of the Soviet Union due to an adequately chosen missionary paradigm. The same thing happened in Romania. Brother Andrew testified: "In most countries where communism

---

42. D. J. Bosch, "In Search of a New Evangelical Understanding" in *In Word and Deed: Evangelism and Social Responsibility*, ed. B. Nicholls and Lausanne Committee for World Evangelization and the World Evangelical Fellowship (Grand Rapids: Eerdmans, 1985), 66.

43. S. Escobar, *A Time for Mission: The Challenge for Global Christianity* (Leicester: Inter-Varsity Press, 2003), 145.

44. Bosch, "In Search of a New Evangelical Understanding," 67.

is settled, the church now attracts millions. In the midst of persecution, people flock to the remaining churches or meet in the open. In Romania, one of the most oppressed countries in Eastern Europe, we find the largest evangelical gatherings in Europe."[45]

I have already pointed out that the church was always socially responsible, but in the first half of the twentieth century Evangelical missiologists did not formulate a theological basis for social responsibility. There were two reasons for this: (1) "social gospel," developed by liberal theologians; (2) dichotomy in thinking.[46] The first was outward, because the evangelical believers were afraid to be affiliated with liberals, and the second reason was inner. A dualistic, Gnostic worldview was (and is) so widespread in Christian circles, that it does not give freedom for understanding the Bible, for applying biblical principles, and for courage to proclaim one's own opinion. Anyway, in the second part of the 1960s the time for rethinking from a dualistic worldview to a holistic view came.

The Evangelical missiologists at that particular moment were not worried about the issue – whether or not the church should be involved in social service, but about what was more important – social responsibility or evangelism. They also examined the question of the relationship between evangelism and social ministry.

There were pronounced three kinds of relationships between social action and evangelism: "(1) that social action is *a result* or *consequence* of evangelism; (2) that social action is *a means (bridge)* to evangelism; (3) that social action is *a partner* of evangelism,"[47] though, not everyone agrees with these classifications. I would like to provide a more comprehensive classification system, which will allow us to see the issue from a different, broader perspective. Tokunboh Adeyemo saw nine different views among evangelicals on the topic of relations between evangelism and social responsibility.[48]

---

45. Brother Andrew, "The Church That Loves," in *Proclaim Christ until He Comes. Calling the Whole Church Take the Whole Gospel to the Whole World*, ed. J. D. Douglas (Minneapolis: World Wide Publications, 1990), 133.

46. Lausanne Committee for World Evangelism, *Evangelism and Social Responsibility. An Evangelical Commitment*, 4 (a), (Wheaton: Lausanne Committee for World Evangelism, World Evangelical Fellowship, 1982), 20.

47. Ibid., 21–23.

48. Adeyemo, "A Critical Evaluation," 48–56.

To make the comprehension easier, I have permitted myself to change their position in the author's list, creating a kind of palette of shades and colors, where number 1 is the most hardline approach, expressed by Peter Wagner, and number 9 is an approach similar to social gospel.

1) That social action is a betrayal of evangelism
2) That social action is a distraction from evangelism
3) That social action is a result or consequence of evangelism
4) That social action is a means (bridge) to evangelism
5) That social action is a manifestation of evangelism
6) That social action is a partner of evangelism
7) That social action and evangelism are equally important but genuinely aspects of the total mission of the church
8) That social action is part of the good news – evangelism
9) That social action is evangelism

In my opinion, these nine views can be divided into three large groups. The first group would include the first three approaches. They have in common the leveling of the social responsibility of the church. The difference between them consists only in the degree to which the social service is neglected. It is not right to say that they are against social ministry, but they take social action out of the church mission, and put it on the shoulders of the church members. Now it is their decision what they will do with all the needs which they see around themselves.

The second group, which is the largest one, includes point four to seven. These positions share the idea that social action is a part of the mission of the church, which should be actively promoted, and at the same time, continue to take evangelism very seriously. This group could be divided into two subgroups. The fourth, fifth and sixth approaches give priority to evangelism. As Christopher J. H. Wright said: "Within biblical holism the necessity of sensitive evangelism is clear and nonnegotiable."[49] Andrew Kirk believes that the Lausanne Movement and John Stott in particular, uses a wrong method. He says: "It is my conviction that evangelical and ecumenical appeal to a condensed view of scriptural teaching. Elements that do not fit into the traditional pattern are ignored or discarded. The

---

49. Chris J. H. Wright, *The Mission of God: Unlocking the Bible's Grand Narrative* (Nottingham: InterVarsity Press, 2006), 439.

result is a distortion on both sides of the task of evangelism."[50] Chongnahm Cho considers that, "The effectiveness of the church's mission will depend on how faithful that Christian is. This service cannot be expected, therefore, without the disciple-making ministry of the church. A disciple-making ministry will result in a remarkable social and political transformation. In this sense, the importance and primacy of evangelism cannot be over emphasized."[51]

Their opponents say that they consider the relationship between evangelism and social involvement from a dichotomous perspective. David Bosch assessed Stott's position critically, which is closer to the sixth point: "John Stott's suggestion is to regard evangelism and social action as both being components of mission. In other words: evangelism + social action = mission. The problem with describing evangelism and social action as two separate segments or components of mission is, however, that this still leaves us, at least potentially, with the battle of supremacy. Stott himself maintains the primacy of evangelism."[52]

The seventh position studies the issue integrally. It refers to holistic mission. Therefore it may be categorized in the third as well as in the second group as it does not reject the importance of the verbal proclamation of the gospel. Similar views are held by D. Bosch, J. Sider, and S. Escobar. Comparing his views with Stott's, Bosch wrote: "Unlike Stott, I would not call evangelism and social action separate components or parts of mission, but dimensions of the one, indivisible mission of the church."[53] V. Samuel and C. Sugden supported Bosch's opinion: "This view [Stott's] is closely allied with the view that men are distinct individuals and that society plays little part in their formation or identity. Society is but the aggregate of

---

50. J. A. Kirk, *Good News of the Kingdom Coming: the Marriage of Evangelism and Social Responsibility* (Downers Grove: InterVarsity, 1983), 97.

51. C. Cho, "The Mission of the Church: Theology and Practice" in *In Word and Deed. Evangelism and Social Responsibility*, ed. B. Nicholls, Lausanne Committee for World Evangelization and the World Evangelical Fellowship (Grand Rapids: Eerdmans, 1985), 229.

52. Bosch, "In Search of a New Evangelical Understanding," 79.

53. Ibid., 81.

individuals. Thus social change comes about if there are a significant number of transformed individuals to influence society."[54]

Further: "The Hebrew view of man is that man is a unity . . . Since the Old Testament prohibited images, we must gain our understanding of image from its use in the Ancient Near East. The king and the idol in the temple were representatives of the absentee god who dwelt on the mountains or elsewhere. They exercised stewardship or authority over the god's territory on his behalf . . . The doctrine of the image of God is about man's role as steward of God's creation."[55]

As Bill Prevette said, Samuel and Sugden initiated the Oxford Center for Mission Studies as a reaction from the mainstream of Lausanne.[56] Today OCMS is well known as one of the main developers of holistic mission.

It is worth mentioning that holistic mission is also a part of the *missio Dei* concept, and was developed in ecumenical circles. I will return to a more detailed analysis of holistic mission in chapters 6 and 7 of this book.

The third group is the closest to the social gospel approach, paying special attention to social service, often at the expense of evangelism, or providing social service as the most perceived means of evangelism. This wing is the most open to dialogue with the WCC. J. Andrew Kirk adduces proofs of why people oppose evangelism: "Firstly, it has been connected in many people's minds either with forced conversions imposed on people of other faiths by colonial authorities or with material inducements to join the missionaries' religion. Secondly, it implies that the beliefs of non-Christians are inferior, insufficient or perverse. Thirdly, it is associated with the supposed desire of some missionaries to promote a Western ideological agenda against the legitimate claims of non-Western nations for economic justice and political self-determination."[57]

I would particularly like to mention the third reason in the context of Eastern Europe. In countries where citizenship is associated with religious affiliation (and this is what happens in the Orthodox countries), where to

---

54. Samuel and Sugden, "Evangelism and Social Responsibility," 195.

55. Ibid., 198.

56. B. Prevette to the author, 22 September 2011.

57. J. A. Kirk, *Mission under Scrutiny: Confronting Current Challenges* (Darton, Longman & Todd, 2006), 92.

be Russian, Ukrainian and Moldavian means to be an Orthodox, in the region which has always been at the forefront of the battle between East and West (as shown in the first chapter) the issue of pro-Westernism of all the representatives of the Protestant and Evangelical worlds is extremely acute.

In conclusion I would like to emphasize the importance of the Lausanne Movement for the development of Evangelical missiology and for the relationship between evangelism and social action. It seems necessary to quote from the Declaration on the difference between the two most important concepts of social service: "Social service: relieving human need; philanthropic activity; seeking to minister to individuals and families; works of mercy. Social action: removing the causes of human need; political and economical activity; seeking to transform the structures of society; the quest for justice . . . And individuals and churches should be involved in both of them, according to their spiritual gifts."[58]

As Vinay Samuel and Chris Sugden mentioned: "God's covenant with the community is the basis for the identity of the individual, and a vital community life in obedience to God requires members who are personally loyal to the community's Lord and to one another. Thus the very basis for personal change is the establishment of a new society which is in itself an element of social change."[59]

In order to not lose its effectiveness, the church must remain relevant to the current period of time and be responsive to the changes it needs to make. As Bert Hoedemaker remarked: "Church is a community, traveling from context to context, emerging in different cultural spaces, putting up signs of the coming kingdom and providing safe environments for people who try to make sense of their world with the aid of the gospel. It lives on the basis of the pneumatological contextualization of Christ."[60]

Unlike the Church Growth Movement, we cannot identify any significant influence of the Lausanne Movement on the evangelical churches in Moldova. After examining the essence of the message of Lausanne, I did

---

58. Lausanne Committee for World Evangelism, "Evangelism and Social Responsibility," 43–44.

59. Samuel and Sugden, "Evangelism and Social Responsibility," 211.

60. B. Hoedemaker, "Toward an Epistemological Responsible Missiology," in *To Stake a Claim: Mission and the Western Crisis of Knowledge*, ed. J. A. Kirk and K. J. Vanhoozer (Maryknoll: Orbis Books, 1999), 225.

not see a close relationship between the findings obtained in the second chapter and the trends of the Lausanne Movement.

Now I will consider the influence of Anabaptist missiology on the Evangelical churches of Moldova.

An Anabaptist Missiology

I have just looked at two missiological schools which have made significant contributions to the development of missiology in the second half of the twentieth century. I consider it reasonable to include in this list one more trend in mission thinking – an Anabaptist one. This is not only because it is required by Samuel Escobar's classification with which I agree, but also because this school has had the greatest impact on the development of Evangelical churches in Moldova in the late nineteenth and early twentieth centuries. As mentioned in the first chapter, German Mennonites were one of the original sources of the evangelical movement in the territory of Bessarabia.

First of all, it seems worth pointing out that Anabaptists began to pay serious attention to the development of missiology only in the second half of the twentieth century, since "from 1525 The Anabaptist/Mennonite tradition developed a mistrust of academic theology."[61] This was the why in the twentieth century they had to largely borrow pre-existing concepts and join a dialogue that had existed for a long time. "Mennonites have also learned much from the modern missionary movement. Mennonites have been ecumenical borrowers."[62]

After all, it would not be right to state that Anabaptists did not do *missions*. *On the contrary*, in the sixteenth century, Anabaptists were known as the most zealous evangelists and missionaries. In their first communities in Europe,[63] Anabaptists succeeded in combining two approaches in the practice of mission. "On the one hand, leaders with apostolic gifts traveled far and wide preaching, baptizing, and organizing new congregations. On

---

61. W. Shenk, "Forging Theology of Mission from an Anabaptist Perspective," *Mission Insight* 13 (2000): 2.

62. W. Shenk, *By Faith They Went Out: Mennonite Missions 1850–1999* (Elkhart: Institute for Mennonite Studies, 2000), 116.

63. Ibid., 18.

the other hand, members of each congregation were actively engaged in witness in their community and region in the course of daily living."[64]

During the sixteenth century Anabaptists thought of the whole of Europe as their missionary field, since the main difference between Anabaptists on one side and Roman-Catholics and Magisterial Reformers on the other consisted in their view of the concept of being born again and belonging to the church, as well as on the issue of the so-called "canonical territory" (or church and state relationship). As a result, Anabaptists were heavily persecuted by both Roman Catholics and Protestants. Since then, persecutions became an integral part of their view of the genuine church. In just a few decades tens of thousands of people were baptized and hundreds of local congregations were started[65].

The seventeenth century was calmer, as most Anabaptist communities had changed direction. Menno Simons' adherence to the Anabaptist movement changed the direction of the Radical Reformation. "In contrast to their Anabaptist forebears who evangelized vigorously, Mennonites became known as 'the quiet in the land.'"[66] The main focus of their mission was on a life of witness. "The church is by nature called to struggle for justice, for the righteousness of God is to be expressed in the life of his people through just relationships. The world knows little of justice. The cries of the poor and the oppressed rise up continually before God. The church is called to demonstrate before the world the meaning of salvation, including the new order of relationship it brings."[67]

---

64. Ibid., 15.

65. For a detailed account on the paradigms of the early Anabaptist mission expansion, see Parush Parushev, "Knowing the Risen Christ: The Anabaptist Holistic Witness as Mission," a plenary paper for the *Mission and Evangelism* work group of the Baptist World Alliance, presented at the Jubilee Annual Gathering of the BWA celebrating 400 years of the Baptist movement in Ede, The Netherlands, 27 July – 1 August 2009. Cf. also Colin Robert Godwin, "Baptizing, Gathering, and Sending: the Significance of Anabaptist Approaches to Mission in the Sixteenth-Century Context" (A thesis submitted for the Degree of Doctor of Philosophy, University of Wales through International Baptist Theological Seminary, 2010).

66. Shenk, "Forging Theology of mission," 2.

67. W. Shenk, "Kingdom, Mission, and Church" in *Exploring Church Growth*, ed. W. Shenk (Grand Rapids: Eerdmans, 1983), 213.

In the second half of the twentieth century the Mennonite communities become more dynamic in their purposeful missionary activity, not to mention the opening of new churches and social involvement.

It is worth noting that the Mennonite way of life captured people's attention. An apparent lack of evangelistic vitality did not lead to a decrease in the number of converts or to the degradation of the church. On the contrary, Mennonite communities developed as more and more people were converted. It can be assumed that such an approach to evangelism strongly influenced their social and religious environment. Facing the pressure of being under constant stress, they were compelled to preach the Word of God only in churches. The same thing happened in Moldova. One of the conditions, which caused the resettlement of Germans to the Russian Empire was their commitment not to spread their faith among the Orthodox people. But their lifestyle caught the attention of ordinary people. They held devotional hours for Bible study and prayer, and later developed churches, as described in chapter 1.

The history of Anabaptists and Mennonites and their missionary work influenced the formation of Anabaptist missiological thinking. It would be worth mentioning some of the founding fathers of Anabaptist missiology: Wilbert Shenk, David Shenk, Walter Sawatsky, James Krabill and Peter Penner. There were a few theologians in the twentieth century whose baptistic theology[68] had a significant impact on Anabaptist (or baptistic) missiology: John Howard Yoder, James McClendon, and Parush Parushev – a person who has helped to develop and popularize their ideas in the modern European Anabaptist/Baptist context.

Speaking of the Anabaptist approach to mission, it must be said that mission and church are inseparable in their understanding. Each church

---

68. As Parush R. Parushev introduces it: "The term 'baptistic' is used as an umbrella term for a variety of believing communities practicing believers' baptism and demanding radical moral living such as Baptists or Pentecostals. This stream traces its roots to the sixteenth century radical reformation movements of the Anabaptists." See his "Baptistic Conventional Hermeneutics," in *The Plainly Revealed Word of God?*, ed. Helen Dare and Simon Woodman (Macon: Mercer University Press, 2011), 173; cf. Rollin Grams and Parush Parushev, "Towards a 'Baptistic' Contextual Theology," in *Towards an Understanding of European Baptist Identity: Listening to the Churches in Armenia, Bulgaria, Central Asia, Moldova, North Caucasus, Omsk and Poland: Mapping Baptist Identity*, ed. R. Grams and P. Parushev (Prague: International Baptist Theological Seminary, 2006), 175–181.

is in fact a missionary one, and every missionary activity is aimed at the community, although unlike McGavran's school, Anabaptists are less ecclesiocentric. "The missionary vision was thoroughly theocentric."[69] Because "the Old Testament portrays Israel as a people on the way of salvation, in moments of worship and through the voices of the great prophets a vision broke through that the *shalom* given to Israel was also for the whole world (Ps 67:1f; Isa 2:2f; 11:9; 42:6)."[70] Because of that, the growth of the local community is not an indicator of effectiveness. The number of church members does not constitute a criterion of church growth, since this entirely depends on God. "When Jesus dispatched his disciples on their first missionary journeys, he did not instruct them to preach the gospel of the church but the gospel of the kingdom."[71]

All the parables of the kingdom told by Jesus show the importance of growth, but all of them also underline that the growth is a prerogative of God. Wilbert Shenk addresses the kingdom parables, making the conclusion that growth is natural in the kingdom. We should wait for the growth of any healthy body, but the process and the result of this growth is not in our hands – only God knows what and when something will grow. The growth in the kingdom is a mystery and a secret.[72]

The starting point of the Anabaptist mission is not the local community, but the kingdom. The most prominent preacher and missiologist is not the apostle Paul, but Jesus Christ. "Jesus proceeded by bringing the messianic character of the kingdom into sharper focus. He not only proclaimed the kingdom; he was the kingdom. Social righteousness and personal wholeness were placed at the heart of his ministry (Matt 4:17, 23; Luke 4:18–19)."[73]

Yoder also concurs: "Jesus did in the world what we are supposed to be doing in the world. If we want to be his, we must be in him. That means

---

69. W. Shenk, "Which Paradigm for Mission?," in *Mission Focus*, ed. W. Shenk (Scottdale: Herald Press, 1980), 161.

70. Ibid.

71. Shenk, "Kingdom, Mission, and Church," 211.

72. W. Shenk, *Exploring Church Growth* (Grand Rapids: Eerdmans, 1983), 214–216.

73. Shenk, "Which Paradigm for Mission?," 164. Cf. W. Shenk, "An Anabaptist View of Mission" in *Anabaptism and Mission*, ed. W. Shenk and P. Penner (Schwarzenfeld: Neufeld Verlag, 2007), 42–58.

we must be with him. The way to be in and with him is to be the kind of person in our historic experience that he was when he was on the earth."[74]

The focus of mission is primarily eschatological, and thus, *parousia* is much closer than it seems. "The kingdom of God is to be understood eschatologically."[75] Further:

> The Christian interprets present experience and all history in view of *parousia*, Christ's return. The pull of the future – what we call hope – continually bears on what we are doing. This means that we must live in a tension between the "now" and the "not yet." Whenever the church becomes preoccupied with the "now" and loses touch with the "not yet," it loses power and a sense of direction. It identifies church with kingdom, and the church becomes the centre of its concern and action. If the church concentrates on the "not yet," it attempts to flee the world.[76]

Anabaptists have developed their own understanding of the Trinitarian foundation for mission. Wilbert Shenk gives his understanding of Trinitarian mission, and it is very important to emphasize that at the end of the twentieth century, practically all Christian circles were on the same Trinitarian platform. Each branch gives its own understanding and puts in this paradigm something different, but all of them use the same terminology (*missio Dei*, Trinitarian understanding, mission of Father, Son and Holy Spirit, kingdom, etc.).[77]

Allan H. Howe remarked that the churches of the Anabaptist tradition have proved generally unable or unwilling in the twentieth century to identify themselves with either of two major trans-denominational groupings within Protestantism: the ecumenical movement – most visible in the

---

74. J. Yoder, *Christian Attitudes to War, Peace and Revolution: A Companion to Bainton* (Elkhart, IN: Goshen Biblical Seminary, 1983), 186.

75. Shenk, "Kingdom, Mission, and Church," 208.

76. Ibid.

77. W. Shenk, *Changing Frontiers of Mission* (Maryknoll: Orbis Books, 1999), 9–14.

World Council of Churches and national councils – or the "Evangelicals" – most visible in the U.S. National Association of Evangelicals.[78]

The Anabaptist school, unlike previous schools, is not Calvinistic. Good deeds can play a significant role in the rescue process. Ethics is not the personal choice of the members of the community. Ethics is the responsibility of the entire community. Particularly in Anabaptism, ethics and mission are so closely interrelated with each other that it is difficult to distinguish where one ends and the other begins. It is difficult to find a dichotomy in Anabaptism because initially it was holistic. It would be acceptable to assert that the conclusions many of the missiologists came to only in the second half of the twentieth century were made by Anabaptists before the Enlightenment.

Contemporary Anabaptist missiology as well as McGavran's school proclaims the necessity of verbal evangelism and that of opening new churches. Their difference consists in the belief that no technology, or sociological or anthropological research will serve the purpose. "Modern missions have been marked by pragmatism. It is frequently observed that the missionary movement has been motivated more by how than why. Theology of mission, as a division of theology generally, did not emerge until late in the nineteenth century . . . during the past several decades the contribution of the social sciences to missiology has probably been more influential than that of theology."[79]

Describing followers of the CGM as he observed their attitude, Yoder made conclusions, putting his words in McGavran's mouth: "We do not really need any *more* theological clarification. What we need now is efficiency."[80]

Wilbert Shenk considered that "Allen's approach was biblical-theological. McGavran's is pragmatic and social science."[81] Only God is able to start a church, and *only he* makes the *church* grow. Despite all the criticism

---

78. A. Howe, "The Church: Its Growth and Mission" in *The Challenge of Church Growth: A Symposium*, ed. W. Shenk (Scottdale, PA: Herald Press, 1973), 49.

79. Shenk, "Which Paradigm for Mission?" 168.

80. J. Yoder, "Church Growth Issues in Theological Perspective" in *The Challenge of the Church Growth: A Symposium*, ed. W. Shenk (Scottdale, PA: Herald Press, 1973), 27.

81. W. Shenk, "Church Growth Studies: A Bibliography Review," in *The Challenge of the Church Growth: A Symposium*, ed. W. Shenk (Scottdale, PA: Herald Press, 1973), 21.

addressed to the Church Growth Movement, Yoder declared, "I am in favor of church growth."[82]

Contemporary Anabaptist missiology, as well as the Lausanne Movement, are both for social involvement and active participation in the life of needy people. They state: "Our 'word and deed' perspective continues to fail because it causes us to miss the sense of wholeness that for Jesus was foundational to all else."[83] Besides, Anabaptists do not want to do this together with the governmental structures, which are by definition corrupted by sin and Satan's influence. Joon-Sik Park considering Yoder's writing said: "Yoder without hesitation credits the Anabaptists with the discovery that the 'world' is not simply an amorphous conglomerate of evil impulses but a structured reality taking concrete in the demonic dimensions of economic and political life. He believes that the Anabaptists were able to have such a realistic view of the world because of their vision of the church as a new kind of social reality which is an alternative structure and power in society."[84]

Some scholars regard Yoder's approach and that of the Anabaptists as sectarian, but Yoder's affirmations are stronger than the sectarian ones: "The 'world' of politics, the 'world' of economics, the 'world' of the theater, the 'world' of sports, the under-'world', and a host of others – each is a demonic blend of order and revolt. The world 'as such' has no intrinsic ontological dignity."[85] Those words are not the words of a sectarian figure – only a prophet can make such hard statements.

The church should participate in the life of a society at that level on which one church or group of churches is capable. Yoder states, "The Christian church as a social reality is the needed corrective. The alternative to the focus on the redeemed individual is not to pay attention only to structures or to massive movements of the mob and the media, but rather to recognize that there is a particular point where the redeemed individual

---

82. Yoder, "Church Growth Issues," 31.

83. Shenk, *Changing Frontiers of Mission*, 29.

84. J. S. Park, *Missional Ecclesiologies in Creative Tension: H. Richard Niebuhr and John Howard Yoder* (New York: Peter Lang, 2007), 92.

85. J. Yoder, *The Royal priesthood: Essays Ecclesiological and Ecumenical* (Scottdale: Herald Press, 1998), First published 1994 by Eerdmans, 56.

and social structure are both present, namely, in the Christian community as a visible body within history."[86]

According to Anabaptist theologians and missiologists, the main problem of the church is:

> This should be sufficient to exemplify – though not to exhaust – my claim that many strands of Christian faith point us into responsible, distinctive social presence, and that we may find our way farther and faster if we begin – rather than starting "from scratch" or "ideally" – with what has obviously gone wrong: individualism in faith and ethics, the search of power, pragmatism as justification, provincialism, the abuse of communication . . . I have not itemized liberation, violence, peace, economic justice, productivity, ecology, gender equality, generational justice as value definitions. This is not because the Bible would not speak as well, or because we should not, to the matters of content signaled by these slogans: it certainly does. But what has been holding us apart from one another and holding us away from the task has been the debates about the whether rather than unclarity about the what, and the what will vary according to context. The why is the same hope as of old, but a hope whose fulfillment we claim Jesus began.[87]

Discussing the differences between the WCC and the Lausanne missiologies, Wilbert Shenk sees that both of them have wrong roots. There are some connections between the liberal theology of Rauschenbusch and Conciliar Missiology, especially between the 1950s and 1982, when they emphasized only the social responsibility of the church. He also supposed that the Enlightenment's individualism influenced the fundamentalistic approach "to save souls," not taking into consideration the social environment of these "souls."[88]

---

86. J. Yoder, *For the Nations: Essays Evangelical and Public* (Grand Rapids: Eerdmans, 1997), 185.
87. Ibid., 197–198.
88. Shenk, *Changing Frontiers of Mission*, 22–24.

Despite the fact that a small number of people in a community may reduce the extent of its influence, P. Parushev and L. Andronoviene identified three levels of involvement: "presence, assistance, and fellowship – define holistic social involvement,"[89] where "social involvement is not a goal of itself; it is natural expression of witness for the value of the kingdom for the world as it is now. As a result of its social involvement, the church could influence other groups."[90] "The defining mark of the church was most evident in the way the community of disciples conducted all human relationships: the love ethic was to be the basis for human interaction both within the church and in the world. This remains ever essential to authentic missionary witness and service, for it arises from the *missio Dei* (John 3:16–17)."[91]

Conclusions

In this chapter I investigated three approaches, which were developed and applied by Evangelicals in mission theory and practice. All of them are in constant dialogue with ecumenical missiology and all of them can give something important for defining the mission model for Moldova. There are a few similarities and differences between them, but I will evaluate those in chapter 8. Now I want to underline a few conclusions from my research, which could help us in the further reasoning.

1) The Church Growth Movement sees the goal of mission in church planting, evangelism and training of new leaders. They reject the holistic approach in mission, and see social responsibility as a personal reaction of converted individuals to revealed human needs. They see that the only direction in which churches should invest their money and people is church growth. They are not very active in ecumenical dialogue. They have the most significant influence in contemporary Moldova through the Southern Baptist Convention.

---

89. L. Androviene and P. Parushev, "McClendon's Concept of Mission as Witness," in *Anabaptism and Mission*, ed. W. Shenk and P. Penner (Schwarzenfeld: Neufeld Verlag, 2007), 262.

90. Yoder, *For the Nations*, 187.

91. Shenk, "Forging Theology of Mission," 28.

2) The Lausanne Movement was born among Evangelicals who saw a big lacuna between WCC and CGM. They were concerned with combining evangelism and social responsibility. Their voices did not sound in unison, a few different understandings developed, but the main victory was that they found a theological and biblical foundation for holistic mission, being in constant conversation with ecumenical missiologists who were developing a Trinitarian foundation for *missio Dei*. The Lausanne Movement has less influence and attention in contemporary Moldova.
3) The most significant influence on the Evangelical mission in Moldova in the past had an Anabaptist missiological paradigm – witness as life style. This mission model was the only one applied during the Soviet times. Anabaptists are active now in different dialogues with representatives from ecumenical and evangelical circles.

The next chapter will show how mission is seen among Orthodox theologians, how the Orthodox Church sees its calling, and which methods are used for implementation of their mission paradigm.

CHAPTER 5

How "Mission" is Perceived by Orthodox Theologians

In the previous chapter I observed the heterogeneity of the missiological concepts and approaches in evangelical circles. This heterogeneity on the one hand is the result of a deep theological understanding of the doctrine of the priesthood of all believers, and thus the formulation of theology is not the prerogative of those devoted to the church priesthood. On the other hand, Evangelical theology was born and developed mainly in countries which are called democratic where freedom of speech and expression is one of the highest achievements in the field of human rights.

Against this background it may seem that Orthodox missiology must be unambiguous and peremptory since Orthodoxy does not put emphasis on human rights. Vigen Guroian considers: "In modern liberalism and human rights theory, the good is autonomy. In Orthodoxy, the good is theonomy: the fulfillment of humankind is participation in and communion with the divine Life itself (2 Pet 1:4). No temporal human good exists apart from a movement either toward or away from holiness in the company of the saints."[1]

In addition, Orthodoxy is not accused of anarchist exegesis as Evangelical Christians are.[2] The mission of Orthodoxy derives from the conciliar understanding of the texts of the Scriptures, and is aimed at not only individuals, but entire peoples and communities.

---

1. Guroian, "Evangelism and Mission," 238.
2. V. F. Ciobanu, *Speech at the Round Table Meeting "Church and Aids,"* Chisinau, Moldova, November 2008 (available to the author).

However, the Orthodox environment is not as harmonized as it might seem at first glance. In Orthodox theology there is also an ambiguous understanding of the church's mission, its main goals and the methods that are considered necessary for achieving them. This chapter introduces Orthodox missiology, trends and movements. Special attention is paid to the approaches that have been developed in the territory of the Russian and Romanian Orthodox churches, and to scholars, whose influence in the twentieth century cannot be overestimated.

I give heed to the meaning and content of the Orthodox mission, and then consider two fundamental theological concepts, the development of which, in my opinion, played a crucial role in the understanding of the mission of the church in Orthodox theology. The interchangeability of such terms as Orthodox theology and Orthodox missiology as Orthodoxy does not separate the concept of "missiology" from theology, as it often can be found in the Protestant and Evangelical circles. "The essential connection must be maintained between ecclesiology and missiology, between the proclamation of *basilea* and the building up of the body of Christ in history as a sacrament of the kingdom."[3]

The Foundation and Content of Orthodox Mission

There is a prevailing opinion that the Orthodox Church is not active in mission. As Ion Bria stated: ". . . in the false, but unfortunately common stereotype among Christians of other traditions that the Orthodox churches are 'non-missionary' churches."[4] To be totally fair, I must agree with his opinion about the falsity of this assertion. This wrong impression could arise when using certain categories common to Evangelical circles to try to identify the contents of the Orthodox mission. Particularly, the study of Orthodox mission from the perspective of the Church Growth Movement would really give the impression that the Orthodox Church is not effective in starting new churches and evangelizing the unconverted. In the Orthodox community there are very few laymen attending conferences and seminars on evangelism, and the "dynamics of the church" is

---

3. Bria, *The Liturgy*, 26.
4. Ibid., 27.

not perceived as a category of statistical and anthropological measurement. This does not mean that the Orthodox Church does not keep records of its members or churches, but it means that there is no direct dependence on applied techniques and increasing numbers of attendants – "it is not the number of 'converts' or the statistical membership of the church that can point to the existence of mission; the holiness, unity and catholicity."[5]

Besides, it is necessary to draw attention to the context in which the Orthodox Church had to live and serve during the last hundred years. Before the Bolshevik Revolution, Orthodox theologians were concentrated mostly in Russia. The following persecutions of the 1920s exhausted the forces of Orthodoxy. The church received a blow from which it has still not recovered. At that time, unlike Western churches, the Orthodox Church did not have the opportunity to evangelize. Mitropolitan Kallistos of Diokleia, writing about this said, "Experience of persecution and martyrdom is surely the most important single element of the history of the Orthodox Church in the twentieth century, if not of the twentieth century world as a whole. Our Orthodox witness in this century has been rendered not primarily through the spoken word but through silence, through patient and voiceless *kenosis*."[6]

Nevertheless, the Orthodox Church has a clearly identified missionary task, which it promotes actively in the community. To better explain the purpose and content of the Orthodox mission, I would like to draw our attention to two aspects which are essential for Orthodoxy.

The Origin of the Mission of the Church

It is always difficult to emphasize only one feature as being at the origin of a mission and at the same time try to remain more or less objective. Nevertheless, pointing out the Orthodox mission, there is an almost perfect understanding between theologians concerning its theological origin. The rich patristic tradition of the Orthodox Church gives every reason to consider the theology and missiology of the Orthodox Church a Trinitarian

---

5. I. Bria. *Go Forth in Peace: Orthodox Perspective on Mission*, compiled and edited from several Orthodox consultations on mission (Geneva: World Council of Churches, 1986), 12.

6. Bishop of Diokleia, Kallistos, "The Witness of the Orthodox Church," *The Ecumenical Review* 52 (2000): 47–48.

and holistic one: "The source of the mission is the Holy Trinity, which expresses itself through God the Father who sent his Son on Earth and the Holy Spirit sent down upon the Apostles (John 20:21–22)."[7] The reason for this is rooted in the times of the Fathers of the church, when there were disputes about Christ's divinity, the three hypostasis of the Trinity, which continued at the turn of the first and second millennium with the debate about the nature and work of the Holy Spirit, and which in the twentieth century were developed in modern language by Vladimir Lossky and Dumitru Staniloae.

Ion Bria highlights the origin of the mission from a holistic point of view: "There are six important foundations for the mission: Trinitarian theology, the centrality of Christ, the incarnation, the cross, the resurrection, and the work of the Holy Spirit. Understanding all these foundations, The Church is called for synergetic work with God, but the church's response could be possible only after repentance, being in obedience to the will of God."[8]

Petros Vasiliadis, in his turn, sees that Orthodox theology is also determined by the following criteria: (1) the idea of living tradition, (2) the Trinitarian basis for all theology, (3) the pneumatological dimension, (4) the eschatological perspective and (5) the cosmic dimension of its identity,[9] where tradition is not a static entity but a dynamic reality, not a dead acceptance of the past but a living experience of the Holy Spirit in the present."[10]

One of the authors refers to five postulates, the other to six. Only one of the postulates is mentioned by both of them – Trinitarian theology. It seems that in the other cases there is no contradiction, as Bria would not disagree with the importance of tradition, and Vasiliadis with the significance of Christ's incarnation, death and resurrection. Thus, the differences do not lie in the nature of these criteria, but in their rank, position and degree of priority.

---

7. The concept of the missionary activities of the Russian Orthodox Church, Preamble http://www.mospat.ru/en/documents/social-concepts/i/ accessed 13 August 2011.

8. Bria, *Go Forth in Peace*, 3–9.

9. P. Vassiliadis, *Eucharist and Mission: Orthodox Perspective on the Unity and Mission of the Church* (Geneva: WCC publications; Brookline, MA: Holy Cross Orthodox Press, 1998), 11.

10. Ibid.

Trinitarian theology manifests itself in missionary postulates, in the liturgy, and even the structure of the Orthodox Church, which does not have one particular leader on earth. "The mission and witness of the Orthodox Church in the modern world have also been hampered by weakening of the sense of unity between the local autocephalous Orthodox churches."[11] Orthodoxy, despite the divergences arising among the autocephalous churches, continues to uphold the doctrine of the local church. Even taking into consideration these conflict situations, nobody talked about the merger of the churches in one structure, which could resolve conflicts and defuse tensions. The pleas of the Orthodox prophets are addressed to forgiveness and humility toward one another. There is also recognition of weaknesses, but these weaknesses are at the same time an evidence of power – consciousness of the unity of the Trinity, worship of the Triune God. Bria went even further, applying this principle not only to the Orthodox Church, but also to other denominations: "The one church cannot be created by putting all the local churches and individual denominations into the one worldwide structure. The unity of the church is the unity in Christ, by the Spirit, with the Triune God."[12]

In chapter 3 we turned our attention to the different views of Orthodox and Evangelical theologians on the teaching of canonical territory, which today present grounds for dispute in contention and in the third part of this work, I will examine in detail the ecumenical prospects in Eastern Europe (ch. 9). Nevertheless, the Orthodox Church nowadays (with the rare exception of Georgia and Bulgaria) is involved in the ecumenical movement, and therefore prepared to talk with other confessions, particularly if such dialogue occurs on neutral territory. Thus, the mission of the church should be carried out not only within the same denomination, and not only by the Orthodox Church. The task of the mission is of greater size and complexity, and this is exactly why "Christian mission can be justified only if we conceive our missionary task as the projection in human terms of the life of communion that exists within the Holy Trinity."[13]

---

11. Bria, *Go Forth in Peace*, 62.
12. Ibid., 69.
13. Vassiliadis, *Eucharist and Mission*, 34.

The whole life of the church should be built on the doctrine of the Trinity. This is one of the most significant differences between Orthodox theology and Protestant, Evangelical and even Catholic doctrines. The doctrine of the Trinity should enter into society, family and personal life where catholicity and communion in love become the foundations of all life processes. "All the prayers, rituals and symbols, which are taken from biblical texts, make christological affirmations which relate to the Trinity as a whole."[14] Further, "the christological and ecclesiological dimensions of the liturgy are in accord with the understanding of the one God as a communion of the Holy Trinity, which shapes every reality: prayer, ethics, mission, *diakonia*."[15]

It is also worth noting that the twentieth century was the century of early development of both Protestant and Evangelical Trinitarian theology. In chapter 6 I will examine in detail the very concept of *missio Dei*, which was developed in Protestant circles, and was later adopted in the discussion circles of Catholics and Evangelicals. The ecumenical movement itself was able to create the platform on the basis of which could be elaborated a common language between different traditions. Trinitarian theology is not only a basis for mission, but it is also a special language, *lingua franca*, uniting in dialogue the representatives of many confessions. If Protestants and evangelicals came first to the idea of missiology and then to Trinitarian theology, (as we shall see in ch. 6) the Orthodox Church came first to Trinitarian theology and then to missiology.

It has been mentioned that Orthodox theology is not only Trinitarian but is also holistic. The Trinity is the unity of Father, Son, and Holy Spirit and the church is united in the Holy Trinity, and mission is united through the church. The mission of the Orthodox Church does not consist only in the salvation of the human soul (though many may give this a priority). It concerns all humanity, society and state, all that was created by God, the entire universe as a whole. Later I will develop this idea while examining the *kenosis* as part of the mission of the church. Ion Bria, determining the relationship between a holistic understanding of God and a holistic

---

14. Bria, *The Liturgy*, 5.
15. Ibid., 6.

understanding of mission wrote: "The salvation of the world should be seen as a 'program' of the Holy Trinity for the whole of creation. The kingdom of God is the inner movement and the final goal not only of every human adventure, but of all the dynamic of the universe."[16]

Mission begins with communication between the Trinity and the redeemed people, gathered together in worship, in reading the Word and in prayers. "The Orthodox understanding of mission is inseparable from Christology and ecclesiology, so that *mission is unity enacted.*"[17] "Trinitarian theology best elucidates the Eucharist, which is not only the mystery of church but also is a projection of the inner dynamics (love, communion, equality, *diaconia*, sharing, etc.) of the Holy Trinity into the world and cosmic realities."[18] "The most significant characteristic of the liturgy is its Christocentric character as part of an explicitly Trinitarian theology."[19] Furthermore, we will take a closer look at the importance of the liturgy, its nature and its connection with the mission of the church.

The Content of the Church's Mission

Orthodox theology defines the nature of the church as being a missionary one. Orthodox theologians, in this case, share the same views as Evangelical missiologists. The difference consists in the connotation of the concept of "missionary nature." Nevertheless, both churches agree that the church does not exist for its own sake, in order to satisfy its needs and requirements. "Church is 'apostolic' insofar as she is sent and sending; sent by Christ and sending her apostles 'to all creation.' Her being sent (that is her mission) is not something additional to or beyond herself, but a constituent of herself, her own nature."[20]

At the same time "mission is not related exclusively to the 'apostolicity,' but to all the *notae* of the church, including unity, holiness and catholicity."[21]

---

16. Bria, *Go Forth in Peace*, 3.
17. Guroian, "Evangelism and Mission," 238.
18. Vassiliadis, *Eucharist and Mission*, 6.
19. Bria, *The Liturgy*, 5.
20. A. N. Papathanasiou, *Future and Background of History: Essays on Church Mission in an Age of Globalization* (Montreal: Alexander Press, 2005), 14.
21. Bria, *Go Forth in Peace*, 12.

Before determining what the target of the mission of the church is, it would be worth noting that, "mission does not aim primarily at the propagation or transmission of intellectual convictions, doctrines, moral commands etc., but at the transmission of the life of communion that exists in God."[22] The Orthodox Church does not involve itself in the scholastic disputes of the Western churches. Indoctrination is not one of its characteristics. Apophatic theology lies in the very foundation of Orthodoxy; understanding of the transcendent God is not a collection of doctrines, and the mission of the church is not the implementation of this collection.

Bulgarian researcher Valentin Kozhuharov writes: "In the Orthodox understanding, the purpose of the mission can be rightly grasped only if we consider the three important theological principles of being a Christian are: the soteriological, the ecclesiastical and the eschatological."[23]

The Patriarch of Moscow, Kirill says: "I would like to stress that the spiritual and moral rebirth of humanity should be a priority for the churches if they are to remain faithful to the spirit of the gospel of Christ. Therefore, mission as a witness to the spiritual and ethical heritage of Christianity becomes the number one task for the churches."[24]

Bria, in his turn, considered the final goal of mission from a more practical point of view: "The goal and aim of the proclamation of the gospel, and thus of mission, is the establishment of Eucharistic communities in every locality, within its own context and culture and in its own language."[25] It is interesting to note how skillfully Bria used ecumenical language to express traditional Orthodox concepts and beliefs. He is not trying to teach the international community the language of Orthodox theology, but translates his message into a more understandable language for the Protestant and Evangelical communities. We shall see this more than once.

Hieromonk Innokentiy (Pavlov) at a conference dedicated to the one thousandth anniversary of Christianity in Russia said: "The work of the

---

22. Vassiliadis, *Eucharist and Mission*, 12. The same idea is underlined by Bria, *Go Forth in Peace*, 3.

23. V. Kozhuharov, *Towards an Orthodox Christian Theology of Mission: An Interpretive Approach* (Veliko Tarnovo: Vesta Publishing House, 2006), 15.

24. Metropolitan Kirill of Smolensk and Kaliningrad, "Gospel and Culture," 68.

25. Bria, *Go Forth in Peace*, 12.

church of Christ on earth is called mission. The mission of the church is concentrated on individuals as well as on entire societies. It influences the spiritual, moral and cultural aspects of human life aiming for the salvation of the human soul. The term of missiology refers to a narrower, although very important area of primary familiarization of both individuals and entire nations with the teachings of Christ and the life in Christ."[26]

This statement highlights in the first place the soteriological perspective, not only the anthropological and social perspectives. The contemporary concept of social service of the ROC contains the following sections:

> Church and nation, church and state, Christian ethics and secular law, church and politics, labor and its fruits; property, war and peace, crime, punishment, correction, questions of personal, family and public morals, health of individuals and of the people as a whole, issues in bioethics (which include the church's attitude towards abortion, homosexuality, etc.), environmental issues, the church and science, culture and education, church and international relations, the challenges of globalization and secularism.
>
> The "Church and State" section specifies the following areas of cooperation between the church and the state: (a) peacemaking at the international, inter-ethnic and civic levels, promotion of mutual understanding and cooperation between people, nations and states; (b) concern for the preservation of morality in society; (c) spiritual, cultural, moral and patriotic education and training; (d) deeds of charity and philanthropy, the development of cooperative social programs; (e) the protection, restoration and development of historical and cultural heritage, including the preservation and protection of historical and cultural monuments; (f) dialogue with governmental authorities of all branches and at all levels on issues important to church and society, including those in connection with the

---

26. "The missionary activity of the Russian Orthodox Church," presented at the church-historical conference dedicated to the 1000th anniversary of Christianity in Russia (Kiev, 21st–28th July 1986), in *Theological Works*, the 28th edition of the Moscow Patriarchate (Moscow, 1987), 175.

formulation of relevant laws, regulations, orders and decisions; (g) the care of soldiers and law enforcement agencies, their spiritual and moral education; (h) works on crime prevention, the care of persons in custody; (i) science, including human studies, (j) healthcare; (k) culture and creative activity; (l) the work of church and secular media; (m) activities aiming at environmental conservation; (n) economic activity for the benefit of the church, state and society; (o) support of the family, motherhood and childhood; (p) resistance against the pseudo-religious structures that are dangerous to individuals and society.[27]

According to Androvene and Parushev, "the Orthodox Church has a catholic (i.e. universal) vision of the world. It assumes the pastoral care of humankind."[28] The extent and diversity of the interests of the ROC is undoubtedly astounding, the church being virtually involved in all spheres of life in modern society.

Orthodoxy in its very essence draws a close parallel between *eshaton* and the presence of the kingdom nowadays. "Our vocation is not to propagate religious ideas or to establish religious sects but to reveal Jesus Christ as the Lord and to introduce into the world the reality of his kingdom."[29] Later I will tackle the issue of the role of the liturgy and the Eucharist in the realization of the kingdom here and now. Orthodoxy, unlike Evangelical thinking, believes not only in the fact that the kingdom will come, and has not simply the belief that it has come, but also has materialized faith at the moment of communion. "The presence of Christ belongs to each sacramental, Eucharist-centered community."[30]

The model, which was explained by Bria in *The Liturgy after the Liturgy*, is not totally new for the Orthodox Church, but at the same time, not

---

27. "The basis of the social concept of the Russian Orthodox Church," http://www.mospat.ru/en/documents/social-concepts/i/ accessed 13August 2011.

28. L. Androviene and P. Parushev, "Tserkov', gosudarstvo I objestvo," 182–183.

29. Vassiliadis, *Eucharist and Mission*, 35.

30. P. Parushev, "On some developments in Russian Orthodox Theology and Tradition," in *Baptists and the Orthodox Church: On the Way to Understanding*, ed. I. Randall (Praha: International Baptist Theological Seminary, 2003), 88.

many Orthodox priests in Russia and Moldova are familiar with it and apply it in the life of the church. Sometimes, the impression is given that Bria's ideas were accepted more among Protestants in the WCC circles than among the Orthodox. But he continued the line, which was started in the 1940s when the Romanian Orthodox Church began ecumenical contacts, and later was continued by an extraordinary Orthodox theologian, Dumitru Staniloae. The profundity of Orthodox theology, confirmed by a long history combined with the freshness of ecumenical debates of the 1950s–1970s, gave them a new perspective for the life of the Orthodox Church in new realities.

In Bria's writings we see a great passion for people who do not know God, the very clear and open concept of evangelism, and at the same time a holistic approach, which is so widely known because of the theology of liberation and WCC debates. I will look at this in detail in the third part of this work. It is very hard to find more evangelical words than the following:

> The final goal of evangelistic witness is conversion and baptism. Conversion is a willful turning from sin, death and evil to true life in God. Baptism is the reception of a new member into the new life of the community of God's people, the church. There are also many intermediate goals: the increase of love and dialogue among Christians and non-Christians; the formation of the gospel message into the language and thought-forms of the non-Christian neighbor; the interpenetration of the structures of society; the promulgation of the will of God to the injustice among us; and the prophetic challenge to the world's values.[31]

Father Thomas Hopko develops these ideas in the concept which is well known to the Orthodox: "Christian evangelism is always accompanied by teaching (*didaskalia*) and confession (*homologia*) and defense (*apologia*) and witness (*martyria*). And it is accomplished in works of love for human beings performed in concrete acts of mercy without condition or discrimination. This is Christian philanthropy understood not merely as various forms of charitable actions and almsgiving, but as sacrificial service

---

31. Bria, *Go Forth in Peace*, 31.

(*diakonia*) and witness (*martyria*) in all areas of human existence that contribute to human dignity, freedom, justice, and peace on earth according to God's gospel in Jesus."[32]

"The *church of nations* is at the heart of the whole history of Orthodox mission."[33] "Evangelism demonstrates that what we are saying and doing is about *them*, not *us*."[34] These quotations of two Orthodox priests and theologians sound in unison. They feel the same passion, have the same thoughts, and share the same gospel.

For contemporary Orthodoxy, evangelism to non-Christians sounds more theoretical than practical point in mission. I have already mentioned Pavel Evdokimov (pg 94) and he lists countries where the Orthodox Church has been very active in sharing the gospel with non-Christians: peoples of Siberia, the Altai, the Far East, the Far North and Alaska, China, Korea, Japan and Finland. Evaluating the evangelism of the Orthodox Church, I can say, that in the past it was more effective in terms of witnessing to the nations. The Orthodox approach was changed in the last century from verbal proclamation to the nations towards educating its own flock. Bria saw the proclaiming of the kingdom not only verbally. For him proclaiming meant all that God is doing through his servants for the kingdom. "Every Christian is called to proclaim the kingdom and to demonstrate its power. Hence a manifold function: the exorcism of demons; the healing of the sick; voluntarily accepted poverty; fasting; identification with all those who go hungry; chastity; revaluation of humility; mutual submission; constant interior prayer."[35]

At the same time, Patriarch Kirill writes that for fifty years the WCC has been concerned about different social and political issues, such as sexism, oppression, poverty, etc. But he sees that all of these issues are the result of a deeper spiritual problem, and we need to put our common efforts to resolve this main problem.[36] He says that corrupted morality is the real

---

32. T. Hopko, *Speaking the Truth In Love: Education, Mission, and Witness in Contemporary Orthodoxy* (Crestwood: St Vladimir's Seminary Press, 2004), 70.

33. Bria, *The Liturgy*, 25.

34. Hopko, *Speaking the Truth in Love*, 70.

35. Bria, *Go Forth in Peace*, 39-40.

36. Metropolitan Kirill of Smolensk and Kaliningrad, "Gospel and Culture," 69.

root of all social and political issues, and church should direct her forces for propaganda of Christian morality.[37]

I will study this matter later in more detail, but now I would like to underline the different readings of church mission, and the common understanding of its final goal – the establishment of the kingdom of God. As Petros Vassiliadis mentioned: "Only when Satan and his concrete expressions in history does not rule on earth any more, giving place to the reign of the Lamb, will salvation be accomplished."[38]

History teaches an ancient Orthodox law – there is no church where there is no bishop. Bria added one more important principle: "Mission belongs to the very nature of the church, whatever the conditions of its life, for without mission there is no church."[39] The church is a church only when it achieves its missionary goals.

Kenosis as an Incarnated Method of Orthodox Mission

Having determined that Trinitarian theology is at the base of Orthodox mission, and that the purpose of that mission is to restore the kingdom of God in the soul of each individual believer as well as in the whole universe, it is necessary to define the method by which the mission is achieved.

Orthodoxy teaches *kenosis* as the principal method of achieving a mission. Orthodox Christology is kenotic. Christ descended to Earth, taking upon him the form of a servant (Phil 2:7), becoming one of us. "In all Gospel traditions Jesus is presented in the way he himself described his mission, namely as the one who came down to this world 'not to be served but to serve' (Mark 10:45)."[40] "As church life reflects the loving life of the Holy Trinity, she also reflects the constant pouring out of the divine love towards every creature, without discrimination."[41] Orthodox Christology relates God's saving action, as well as his own way of life. "Mission is the

---

37. Ibid.
38. Vassiliadis, *Eucharist and Mission*, 41.
39. Bria, *Go Forth in Peace*, 11.
40. Vassiliadis, *Eucharist and Mission*, 4.
41. Papathanasiou, *Future and Background*, 89–90.

application and reminder of a major doctrine: since Christ's incarnation was not virtual but real, it took place in the context of concrete people and culture."[42]

Dumitru Staniloae emphasized the importance of the soteriological aspect for the foundation of the mission of the church. He noted that Russian Orthodox theology of the nineteenth century gave rebirth for kenotical ministry. "Beginning with the Russian theology of the last century, Orthodox theology has returned almost completely to the broader understanding of salvation proper to the Greek Fathers, and, under the influence of the ministry of *diakonia* to the world which the church has assumed, Orthodox theology in recent years has been developing in a contemporary form those pan-human and cosmic dimensions of salvation which also form part of the patristic heritage."[43]

Mission begins with repentance. "The first step in effectively mediating the life of Christ to the world is to call ourselves to repentance and to a life of renewed faith and disciplined obedience to the will of God."[44]

Repentance is necessary not just to establish a closer relationship with Christ, as is commonly believed in evangelical circles. "There is no doubt that each man must personally accept salvation and make it his own, but cannot do so nor can he persevere and progress in the way of salvation unless he is helped by others and helps them himself in return, that is unless the manner of our salvation is communal."[45]

Besides, Christians themselves need to repent, as their focus on themselves cannot reflect the kenotic nature of the mission of Christ, and therefore that of his church. "Christ did not bring us salvation so that we might continue to live in isolation, but that we might strive towards a greater and ever more profound unity which has as its culmination the eternal kingdom of God."[46] "The Church is walking towards the End not only

---

42. Ibid., 17.

43. D. Staniloae, *Theology and the Church* (Crestwood: St. Vladimir's Seminary Press, 1980), 187.

44. Bria, *Go Forth in Peace*, 9.

45. Staniloae, *Theology and the Church*, 204.

46. Ibid.

having been incarnate, but also in the *process of becoming incarnate*."[47] "In his (Jesus') society the washing of a disciple's feet was more than an ultimate act of humble and kenotic *diakonia*; it was an act of radical social behavior, in fact a rite of inversion of roles within the society."[48]

As I have observed, evangelical circles engage in discussions about the roles played by witness, evangelism and social responsibility within the mission of the church. In this regard, Athanasios (Thanasis) N. Papathanasiou defines very clearly the position of the Orthodox Church. He draws an interesting parallel between social responsibility and witness, comparing them with the witness and witnessing of miracles. He said that many Christians believe in the reality of apostolic miracles and the miracles performed by saints. But nobody had the idea to separate miracles from the preaching of the gospel. All these were seen as part of a whole. So, what is the source of the idea of separating gospel preaching from social involvement, which has also been an integral part of the life of the church?[49] Earlier Staniloe emphatically stated that: "The incarnation is also a kenosis of the humanity in Christ which has its existence, not autonomously in its own hypostasis, but in the divine hypostasis, a kenosis which is wholly dedicated to God. The emptying out of self is so much the sign of love that without it love cannot be manifested. For in love a person forgets himself and gives himself to the other in a total self-surrender; yet it is precisely through this love that he reveals himself in his own fullness."[50]

The social aspect in Papathanasiou's Orthodox holistic witness resonates with Vassilisadi's understanding that, "In the earlier ecumenical period the churches were interested in charitable *diakonia*, with concrete expressions that were directed towards the results of social indifference and injustice. After some time, an interest in social *diakonia* began to develop within the WCC, and the concrete expressions of that interest likewise shifted towards the causes of social indifference and injustice. The change in concrete expression was a function of the change in context."[51]

---

47. Papathanasiou, *Future and Background*, 17.
48. Vassiliadis, *Eucharist and Mission*, 4.
49. Papathanasiou, *Future and Background*, 88.
50. Staniloae, *Theology and the Church*, 192.
51. Vassiliadis, *Eucharist and Mission*, 21.

The social dimension of the Orthodox witness expressed above is widely shared across the theological spectrum of the sisterhood of Orthodox churches. "Our efforts to overcome unjust social and political orders and to renew the creation, risk becoming negative and destructive if they are not grounded in the sanctification of the heart, where everyone has his or her own light."[52] The desire of the church to fulfill the kenotic part of the mission should not be separated from the second most important task – *theosis*. Below I will focus on the issue of deification. I would like to emphasize the inextricable link between these two processes. "There is no Christian evangelical or philanthropic activity without suffering and death; just as there is no consolation without crucifixion, no glorification without humiliation, and no *theosis* without *kenosis*."[53]

The integrity of the Orthodox mission is aimed at all the spheres of human life and society. The ROC states that the church must go through a process of historical *kenosis* while fulfilling its redemptive mission. Its purpose is not only to rescue the people of this world, but also to save and restore the world itself.[54] This view is shared by Greek Orthodox missiologists. According to Vassiliadis: "Redemption is not limited to liberation of individuals from sin, death and the satanic powers, but is extended even to liberation from alienation, oppression and injustice. It goes beyond, however, being expected to cover the restoration of the whole creation."[55] Similarly, Papathanasiou states: "Concern for social justice can function in a missionary manner in two ways: (1) it is a foretaste of the expected kingdom of the Triune God; (2) it reveals in deeds the marrow of the church within a religiously and ideologically pluralistic world and it usually becomes the measure by which the seriousness of the Christian message is judged."[56]

These views are in harmony with Staniloae's Romanian Orthodox social perception:

---

52. Bria, *The Liturgy*, 9.
53. Hopko, *Speaking the Truth In Love*, 77.
54. "Basis of the Social Concept of the Russian Orthodox Church," article I.2 http://www.mospat.ru/en/documents/social-concepts/i/ accessed 13 August 2011.
55. Vassiliadis, *Eucharist and Mission*, 42.
56. Papathanasiou, *Future and Background*, 91.

> If Christians in the past often limited their acts of service to needy individuals because social structures tended to remain static, today, when social structures are more elastic because of the powerful influence of those who are aware of their own solidarity as victims of injustice and who confidently believe that they can produce more satisfactory forms of social life, Christians must make the kind of contribution which will favor the continuous adaptation of these structures to meet contemporary aspirations for greater justice, equality, and fraternity in man's relation to man.[57]

Quoting these three appreciated Orthodox theologians, our attention has once again been attracted not just to the content of their messages, but to the language they use and some of the concepts which are close to those of the Theology of Liberation: justice, equality, liberation from alienation, oppression, social structures, solidarity, etc. Due to a common language, Orthodox theology is gaining in popularity and is now spreading to the West. The stereotypes, which give the impression that Orthodoxy is aimed only at preserving the ancient traditions, are being broken down. "An astonishingly large number of patristic texts throughout the centuries provide us with sample material which early shows that care for social justice has been of vital importance for genuine Christian consciousness."[58] It turns out that the concepts which Protestants, Catholics and Evangelicals believe to be their own, have had a very long history in the Orthodox environment, except that Orthodoxy used other terms to designate many of them. For example, solidarity with the poor was always called charity and brotherly love, social structures – the struggle for justice – was the search for the righteousness of God, and so on. Being heard in plain language, Orthodox theology has become accessible and interesting.

For us, this is a clear answer as to why the Evangelical voice has not yet been heard by society and the Orthodox Church of Moldova, as well as by other Eastern European countries. Evangelicals in Moldova speak an incomprehensible, often unfamiliar, and sometimes even hostile language.

---

57. Staniloae, *Theology and the Church*, 210.
58. Papathanasiou, *Future and Background*, 86.

They use suspicious terminology, which is aggressive in tone, and even contradictory. My attention has been captured by the resemblance between many missiological concepts employed by modern Orthodox theology (especially in the West) and the missiological concepts I utilized in the chapter on Evangelical missiological paradigms, and in the chapter on the *missio Dei*. Bria said: "One way to find the ground for the ecumenical community lies in an ecumenical hermeneutics which challenges false postulates and stereotypes, highlights common doctrines and recognizes superficial universality. But before they forge a new source of universality, the churches have much to learn about ecumenical receptivity."[59]

As we have seen, Orthodox mission is aimed at social responsibility – "social care is not an embellished and illusory shop-window, but an actual revelation of the mystical self of the church"[60] – as well as at verbal witness. "Evangelistic witness is here understood to be communication of Christ to those who do not consider themselves Christian, wherever these people may be found. This includes the need of the church to witness to some of its own nominal members."[61] Some modern Orthodox theologians believe that the most current sermon is a sermon through actions: "Missionary action means not so much preaching from the pulpit as preaching outside the church through words and actions. It means a truly Christian approach to contemporary problems."[62] "Christ draws the world towards himself in a state of continuous change. He reveals himself to the world at every new step of the way in some new perspectives even though for the world he mainly remains incognito. We Christians must move forward along this road together with the world, and tell the world, who this person is, who is attracting Him."[63]

"*Orthodoxia* leads to the maximum possible application in *orthopraxia* of charismatic life in the freedom of the Holy Spirit in all aspects of daily

---

59. Bria, "Looking Anew at Orthodox Theology: Three recent consultations," *The Ecumenical Review* 52 (2000): 258.

60. Papathanasiou, *Future and Background*, 95.

61. Bria, *Go Forth in Peace*, 30.

62. V. Fedorov, "Ecumenical Missionary Needs and Perspectives in Eastern and Central Europe Today: Theological Education with an Accent on Mission As a First Priority In Out Religious Rebirth," *International Review of Mission* 92, no. 364 (January 2003): 73.

63. Staniloae, *Theology and the Church*, 205.

life in society and the cosmos."⁶⁴ "Justice, equality, brotherhood and lasting peace cannot be realized if we have no interest in the material universe."⁶⁵ The Orthodox Church emphasizes the importance of "the appearance of Christ to the world" through actions, relationships, and self-sacrifice. "Any appeal, whether silent or voiced, addressed by one man to another on this earth, is also an appeal made in word or in silence by Christ himself. Any sacrifice, any act of service or love for others is a response prompted by the power of Christ's sacrifice to an appeal which also comes through us from Christ himself."⁶⁶

It is necessary to recognize that almost all of the quotations cited in this chapter are either by Orthodox theologians close to the ecumenical community, or by believers from the Orthodox Diaspora in Western countries. Moldavian Orthodox people with few exceptions do not hear these voices. But the voice that calls today's Orthodox believers to repent can be heard as their own voice: "The Lord can produce 'garlands in place of ashes' as he has done before (Isa 61:3); for with God all things are possible. For this miracle to happen, however, the Orthodox churches in all parts of the world, our 'global village', have to die to their present Byzantine/Ottoman and imperial Russian structures and human institutional forms and live as Christ's one holy Church."⁶⁷

After considering kenotic motives in Orthodox theology of mission, I will turn now to review *theosis* as a characteristic feature of Orthodox theological and missiological thinking.

Theosis as the Final Goal of Orthodox Mission

The coming of the Son of God on earth gives the sons of men a chance to gain access to heaven. *God became* man *so* that a human might become a god. This was not an instantaneous event. It was a long process necessitating not only faith, but also requiring collaboration between God and humanity, which is called synergism by Orthodoxy. This is a relationship

---

64. Vassiliadis, *Eucharist and Mission*, 9.
65. Stanilaoe, *Theology and the Church*, 211.
66. Ibid., 208–209.
67. Hopko, *Speaking the Truth In Love*, 76.

between the power of God and the power of human being so that a person could reach God as God has reached to human. The process of salvation is called deification or *theosis*. "Theosis is the movement from the divine image to the divine likeness."[68]

The concept of social involvement of the Russian Orthodox Church may be expressed by the following words: "by the power of the Holy Spirit the Church deifies the creation, performs the original plan of God for the world and man."[69] "The Orthodox Church understands *theosis* as a union with the energies of God and not with the essence of God which always remains hidden and unknown."[70]

The process of *theosis* applies not only to what a person does within the church, but to all aspects of human life and the whole creation. "Eucharist signals the centrality of Christ for the whole of creation and for all of humanity."[71]

At the same time, Orthodoxy criticizes the neglect of the process of deification and the means by which the church achieves this goal. "The Orthodox have often . . . ignored the social and political consequences of *theosis* (deification) and disregarded the historical concretization of Eucharistic spiritually. In so doing they interrupt the flow of the liturgical act, breaking off *diakonia* at the end of worship, at the door of the church."[72]

Valentin Kozhukharov stresses the fact that *theosis* plays a particular role in the Russian Orthodox Church, where it is seen as an inherent impulse and quality in faithful Christians lives.[73]

First of all, the church regards the participation of believers in the liturgy, where God is spiritually present in the Bread and Wine, as the primary means of deification. "Eucharist as the unique and primary sacrament of the church is a reflection of the communion that exists between the persons

---

68. D. B. Clendenin, *Eastern Orthodox Christianity: A Western Perspective* (Grand Rapids: Baker, 2003), 133.

69. "Basis of the Social Concept of the Russian Orthodox Church," http://www.mospat.ru/en/documents/social-concepts/i/ accessed 13August 2011.

70. Kozhuharov, *Towards an Orthodox Christian Theology*, 17.

71. Bria, *The Liturgy*, 15.

72. Ibid., 23.

73. Kozhuharov, *Towards an Orthodox Christian Theology*, 17.

of the Holy Trinity."[74] The liturgy, and the Eucharist which is an integral part of the liturgy, makes people stop thinking about themselves and partake of the divine nature.

Participation in the liturgy means participation in the mission of the church. "The Orthodox have chosen their way of understanding and undertaking mission. As they celebrate the liturgy, they are equipping, nourishing and sending missionaries outside. Tradition is also true mission, because it implies a creative encounter between gospel and culture."[75] "A Eucharist revival will help the church to move away from a certain christocentric universalism and towards a Trinitarian understanding of the divine reality and of the church's mission that embraces the entire *oikoumene* as the one household of life. Especially for mission, this means the abandonment of any effort of proselytism."[76]

The mission of the church begins with the Eucharist, and with the Eucharist it ends. "But the liturgy is not simply a tool for confessing Christ or an instrument of mission, rather it must be seen as the starting event of the Christian movement for mission, the point of departure given to the church for pursuing its location in the wider society, which is also a point of arrival."[77]

The Eucharist is not a "magical" ritual which gives people a supernatural force. "In sum, it is fair to argue that the gospel of John understands the Eucharist not as a mere cultic and sacramental act, but primarily as a diaconal act and alternative ways of life with clear social implications."[78] The entire liturgy is filled with special meaning, and those who see the otherworldly force in what is happening in the church are wrong. As metropolitan John D. Zizioulas notes: "All gestures, colors, and so on, employed in the liturgy are used typologically. Typological mysticism seeks to connect

---

74. Vassiliadis, *Eucharist and Mission*, 5.
75. Bria, *The Liturgy*, 27.
76. Vassiliadis, *Eucharist and Mission*, 61.
77. Bria, *The Liturgy*, 28.
78. Vassiliadis, *Eucharist and Mission*, 4.

past or present events with the *eschaton*; it does not include the mind to higher intelligible realities by means of the senses."[79]

We must understand the meaning the fathers of the church put into it. But at the same time some Orthodox theologians see a real problem in celebrating the Lord's Supper, because in most cases people do not understand the liturgy, which is in a way and language that is not easy to understand. "One of the blatant contradictions in the Orthodox churches is the celebration of the liturgy in ancient languages which are no longer spoken or written by the people."[80]

We should be grateful to Bria, not only for his excellent explanation of the meaning of the liturgy and the role of the Eucharist, but also for being fair in his treatment of Orthodoxy and his appeal to explain the liturgy to people. "If the language and vocabulary make the text impossible to understand, the people are bound to ignore it."[81] He urges the use of comprehensible modern languages, as he believes the impossibility to understand the Word is the main cause of Orthodox believers' passivity. "Many people are not committed to mission and evangelism because they do not understand the liturgical language, the depth and meaning of the rites, especially during the first part of liturgy."[82] Otherwise, it may happen as Vasiliadis writes: "Without the prophetic voice of theology, the *leitourgia*, the primary expression of the church, and the Eucharist as its centre and climax can easily become at best a useless typolatry . . . and this is something that eventually distances the members of the community from the 'other', leading them to death, to hell."[83]

This echoes Bria for whom the Eucharist is the message into the world and first of all for the *diakonia* service. "The dynamics of the liturgy go beyond the boundaries of the Eucharist assembly to serve the community at large. The Eucharistic liturgy is not an escape into an inner realm of prayer, a pious turning away from social realities; rather, it calls and sends

---

79. J. D. Zizioulas, *Communion and Otherness: Further Studies in Personhood and the Church* (New York: T & T Clark, 2006), 298.
80. Bria, *The Liturgy*, 23.
81. Ibid.
82. Ibid., 28.
83. Vassiliadis, *Eucharist and Mission*, 60.

the faithful to celebrate 'the sacrament of the brother' outside the temple in the public marketplace, where the cries of the poor and marginalized are heard."[84]

The modern Romanian theologian Mihai Sasaujan writes: "There must also be a new and dynamical liturgical renewal. The liturgical-doxological vocation of Orthodoxy bears the risk of a so-called 'liturgical ghetto', the risk of ritualism, of liturgical formalism, without essential effects in our social, cultural and political life."[85]

This statement is in line with Bria's understanding that, "above all, the Eucharistic liturgy is not terminated in the prayerful intimacy of the worship, but it continues with *diakonia*, apostolic mission, visible and public Christian witness."[86]

In the second place the Eucharist is a message for the witness. Therefore, "in terms of mission, this will also result in moving towards a common evangelistic witness. Beyond the biblical imperative, the Eucharistic perspective of mission points far beyond denominational boundaries, beyond Christian limitations, even beyond the religious sphere in the conventional sense, and towards the manifestation of the kingdom of God, the restoration of the 'household' (*oikos*) of God, in its majestic eschatological splendor."[87]

The church must find its identity, "the Eucharist/liturgical understanding of the early Christian community's identity, considering the church as an icon of the *eschaton*"[88] and understand its authenticity. Otherwise, the mission of the church becomes ineffective. "The efficacy of the church's missionary witness depends on the authenticity of our communion. Our ability to present the light of the kingdom to the world is proportionate to the degree in which we receive it in the Eucharistic mystery."[89] Furthermore,

---

84. Bria, *The Liturgy*, 20.

85. M. Sasaujan, "Romanian Orthodox Theologians as Pioneers of the Ecumenical Dialogue Between East and West: The Relevance and Topicality of Their Position in United Europe," in *Religion and The Conceptual Boundary in Central and Eastern Europe: Encounters of Faith*, ed. T. Bremer (New York: Palgrave MacMillan, 2008).

86. Bria, *The Liturgy*, 28.

87. Vassiliadis, *Eucharist and Mission*, 61.

88. Ibid., 54.

89. Bria, *Go Forth in Peace*, 19.

"as a place for gathering for praying and sharing the body and blood of Christ, every local parish is also a point of departure into the world to share the joy of resurrection."[90]

Within the concept of missionary activity, the ROC draws attention to the fact that the missionary task today is to reach bishops and priests as well as laity and active worshipers.[91] Mission should change not only people on the streets, but first of all, people who lead the parishes. In fact, mission includes five main forms of activity: educational mission (churching), apologetic mission, informational mission, external mission and mission of reconciliation.[92]

In the third place participation in the liturgy and Eucharist demonstrates the unity of Christians. The plea for unity is one of the fundamental components of the Orthodox mission. "The Orthodox have always been concerned about the unity of all churches and of the whole of humankind in the liturgical service."[93] The mission of a disintegrated church cannot be an effective one nor even conceived of as a mission itself. "In Orthodox theology the only true mission is a mission that serves unity. This is a truth that is eternally validated in the person of Christ, that is, through the incarnation of the Word and his unity with the Father in the triune Godhead."[94]

It is worth mentioning that in practice it turns out that the liturgical and Eucharistic controversy has served to cause disintegration of the church. To mention only a few well-known examples: the Old Believers split off from the main trunk of Orthodoxy after the liturgical practices had been modified; the pre-implementation issue has caused centuries-old disputes between Orthodoxy and Catholicism; the views of Lutherans, Calvinists, and radical reformers on the question of communion was a major dispute. Nowadays, the ecumenical movement can bring together representatives of many churches to solve theological and missiological issues, share social service, witness, but still cannot reconcile them on the issue of the Bread

---

90. Ibid., 31.

91. "The concept of the missionary activities of the Russian Orthodox Church," §2.1. http://www.mospat.ru/en/documents/social-concepts/ii/ accessed 13 August 2011.

92. Ibid .

93. Bria, *The Liturgy*, 42.

94. Guroian, "Evangelism and Mission," 239.

and Wine. The main consequence of religious divergences and disciplinary penalties is excommunication from partaking of communion.

Fourth, the Eucharist bears witness to the *eschaton*, the Second Coming of Christ.

> The liturgy begins and ends with the invocation of the kingdom. Here and now, on earth and in time, the liturgy inaugurates the eschatological community of the redeemed. As such it is also a moment of judgment for the Christian community – of how the kingdom of heaven is or is not present in the church as a sociological community, of how the church is or is not overcoming barriers to justice, freedom and solidarity, of how it is or is not an effective sign of something greater than the liturgical assembly.[95]

> It is this eschatological perspective which determines the proper relationship between the mission and the national culture, as the eternal purpose of the mission is the transformation of the whole cosmos – humanity and nature, in the words of the Apostle Paul, 'God may be all in all' (1 Cor 15:28). The mission is therefore to become closer to the world, to bless and renew it, put a new content into people's habitual lifestyle, accept the local culture (if it is not hostile to the Christian faith and the ways of its expression) and transforming them into means of salvation.[96]

It is difficult to overestimate the role of the Eucharist for an Orthodox believer. Petros Vasiliadis states categorically that Eucharist is considered as vitally crucial for the Orthodox, even more than the preaching of the Word.[97] The Evangelical churches of the former Soviet Union are unlikely to agree with the above statement, since for the vast majority of the Evangelical churches the preaching of the Word is the center of church

---

95. Bria, *The Liturgy*, 16.

96. "The concept of the missionary activities of the Russian Orthodox Church, Preamble." http://www.mospat.ru/en/documents/social-concepts/i/ accessed 13 August 2011.

97. Vassiliadis, *Eucharist and Mission*, 15.

worship (or liturgy). A proof is the location of the pulpit in the center of the houses of prayer. The pulpit is where God works with his people. The Orthodox liturgy attaches a particular importance to the altar, on which there are the Bread and Wine. In many Moldavian Orthodox churches, sermons are not practiced. The Evangelical churches practice communion once a month as a reminder of the death and suffering of the Lord, avoiding or even rejecting the term "sacrament," while the Orthodox celebrate the sacrament every Sunday, although, it is believed that communion is preceded by repentance. "In the Orthodox tradition, the spiritual requirements for the members are: an active participation in the liturgy in a spirit of prayer and *methanoia*."[98]

While Bria stated that where there is no mission there is no church, Vasiliadis adds: "It is only in the Eucharist that the church becomes church in its fullest sense."[99] Thus, deification is possible only through the liturgy, the Eucharistic unity with the community as well as with the Triune God. Participation in the liturgy does not bring a human being to God if there is no repentance, humility, understanding of what is happening and the desire to serve. A person is not blessed by only attending the liturgy. At the same time, it is difficult to talk about understanding the Divine Nature when there is only understanding, humility and service, but there is no Eucharistic communion. Only a synthesis of both makes a person become better and return to the blameless image of the Creator. These mutual efforts are called synergies.

Conclusions

Chapter 5 differs from previous chapters from a methodological point of view. The entire chapter is devoted to finding the foundation, content and goal of Orthodox missiology. I did not present different points of view on these questions and I did not push views of different theologians, but tried to find a common ground in some of them for defining the answers to our questions, connecting them with the actual situation in Eastern Europe. A few very important and beneficial points were realized during this research.

---

98. Bria, *The Liturgy*, 39.
99. Vassiliadis, *Eucharist and Mission*, 10.

1) Trinitarian theology lies at the foundation of Orthodox ecclesiology and missiology. Trinitarian teachings were developed by the church fathers, who have an outstanding authority in Orthodoxy, and became an essential part of all activities and ministries: liturgy, mission, Eucharist, leadership, Christian life.
2) Orthodox missiology is holistic, including soul and body, nature and universe. A holistic approach in mission flows from Trinitarian theology and touches all aspects of human life, society, state and ecology.
3) The content of Orthodox mission is witness to all nations and pastoral care for humankind.
4) *Kenosis* is the principal method of achieving mission. Every mission begins with the repentance of Christians. The Orthodox Church emphasizes the importance of the appearance of Christ to the world through actions, relationships, self-sacrifice.
5) The final goal of Orthodox mission is deification, *theosis*, which can be achieved only through Eucharist. The Lord's Supper is the center of Orthodox mission – internal and external. Every mission begins from Eucharist and finishes with Eucharist. Any activity of the church has eternal meaning only from the perspective of the unity of Christians, which could be showed in communion.

There are a lot of common points in foundations between Evangelical and Orthodox Churches, but at the same time there are a lot of differences in methods, theologies and mission practices. We are still in search of a *Lingua Franca*, which will help us to find something which will build a bridge between these two Churches in Moldova. The next chapter is a step towards this goal – studying the concept of *missio Dei* will show possible variations for dialogue and common understanding.

CHAPTER 6

How "Mission" is Perceived in Ecumenical Circles

I have looked at Evangelical and Orthodox missiologies, finding that there are a lot of misunderstandings between them, not only for parishioners and priests, but also for experts, theologians and denominational leaders. We see that there is a deficit of communication and acceptance. One of the reasons is the lack of a common language. A common language has already been articulated and shaped in the middle of the twentieth century in ecumenical circles where both Orthodox theologians and Evangelical missiologists were active participants. Therefore, the common language does exist, but the problem is that it has not been evaluated in CIS, and in Moldova particularly. The goal of chapter 6 is to explore what has been done in this area, and to suggest a neutral territory for further conversations. I propose that such a "territory" could be the *missio Dei* concept.

Missio Dei as an Ecumenical Paradigm

During the entire twentieth century, the church tried to understand her real calling and role in history, the contemporary world and the future. There were different approaches, perspectives and methods of understanding those issues, and a few of them were covered in the previous chapters. Mission was conceived in soteriological, ecclesiological, or cultural terms. In the age of the Enlightenment for the first time in history, mission was not regarded as God's very own work, but as a human effort. Mission was seen in anthropological terms.

So, as a result of such differences, various concepts of mission or missions came into being. One of the significant points of view was formed and developed in the second part of the twentieth century. It was the concept of *missio Dei*.

In the first half of the twentieth century theologians developed the obligation of the church before the world (the Conference of the IMC in Tambaram, 1938). The church was in the center of mission. The accent of all mission efforts was shifted to the local churches, which were full of contradictions and for this reason a lot of divisions were born in the body of Christ.[1] Then, in the middle of the twentieth century they understood that traditional approaches to missions were not far from death.[2] Church-centric missionary thinking is bound to go astray, because it revolves around an illegitimate center.[3] J. Hoekendijk considered that mission with the church in the center was a crowd of contradictions.[4] The Christian faith deals not only with the nature of God revealed in Christ. It centers upon the activity of God.[5]

At the missionary conference at Willingen (1952) a new concept for mission was founded, in which it was confirmed that, "the missionary movement of which we are a part has its source in the Triune God himself."[6] Mission is entirely based on God and, moreover, God is the content of the message.[7] It is important to mention that as early as 1934 German missiologist Karl Hartenstein was motivated by Karl Barth's emphasis on the

---

1. L. Newbigin, *The Relevance of Trinitarian Doctrine for Today's Mission* (London: Edinburgh House Press, WCC Commission on World Evangelism, 1963), 11–12.

2. T. Stransky, "Missio Dei," in *Dictionary of the Ecumenical Movement* (Geneva: WCC Publications; Grand Rapids: Eerdmans, 1991), also a very deep evaluation of the *Missio Dei* developed in E. W. Poitras, "St. Augustine and the Missio Dei: A Reflection on Mission at the Close of the Twentieth Century," *Mission Studies* 16, no. 32 (1999): 28–45.

3. J. C. Hoekendijk, "The Church in Missionary Thinking," *International Review of Missions* 41 (1952): 324–336.

4. Ibid.

5. E. L. Smith, *God's Mission – and Ours* (Nashville; Abingdon Press, 1961), 50.

6. International Missionary Council, *The Missionary Obligation of the Church, International Missionary Council, Willingen, Germany, 5–17 July 1952* (London: Edinburgh House Press, 1952), 1–5.

7. Later this concept was developed by G. F. Vicedom in his book *The Mission of God*, translated by A. Thiele and D. Hilgendorf (Saint Louis: Concordia Publishing House, 1965), 51.

actio Dei, over against the human-centered focus of liberal theology at that time.[8] Karl Barth rejected the liberal agenda in which mission was understood as a "civilizing" human activity of witness and service. Mission for Barth, began with the divine sending of God's self in the Holy Trinity.[9]

John Flett doesn't see any connections between Trinitarian foundation for mission and Barth's writings: "Not a single fragment of textual evidence supports the connection between Barth's 1932 lecture and Willingen's Trinitarian developments."[10] Later he said: "Barth's 1932 lecture does not ground missions in the doctrine of the Trinity. His emphasis on God's subjectivity is a direct consequence of his understanding of the doctrine, but he does not develop a positive account of the Trinity's missionary economy. He never articulates something similar to the central *missio Dei* affirmation that 'God is a missionary God' . . . Barth's attempt to dislocate mission from creation is precisely the approach against which *missio Dei* theology reacts."[11] At the same time he articulated that Barth's writings, Trinitarian foundation for mission, and the *missio Dei* concept is more an ontological question, than theological. "The problem of *missio Dei* [is that it] became identified with its key methodological move rather than with its deficient Trinitarianism."[12]

Although:

> One of the crucial missiological problems of the second half of the twentieth century has been how to accomplish a successful transition from an earlier church-centered theology of mission to a kingdom-oriented one without loss of missionary vision or betrayal of biblical content. It can scarcely be denied that we are in the midst of such a transition. It is equally clear that we have not yet fully grasped the meaning of a move toward the kingdom orientation, which closely correlates with

---

8. McIntosh, "Missio Dei," 632.

9. T. Norman, *Classic Texts in Mission and World Christianity* (Maryknoll: Orbis Books, 1995), 104.

10. J. G. Flett, *The Witness of God: The Trinity, Missio Dei, Karl Barth, and the Nature of Christian Community* (Grand Rapids: Eerdmans, 2010), 15.

11. Ibid, 122.

12. Ibid, 50.

the Trinitarian *missio Dei* viewpoint that gained currency in the 1950s.[13]

"The *missio Dei* is in some sense greater than the mission of the visible church."[14] After Willingen, a reaction within the ecumenical tradition accented the work of the Father and Spirit outside the church, identifying all dynamic movements in culture as the work of God. So, as a result of such a view, the church in many cases directed its attention from God to the world. There were a lot of presuppositions for that.

At the Willingen conference there were statements like the following: "God has sent forth one Savior, one Shepherd to seek and save all the lost, one Redeemer who by his death, resurrection and ascension has broken down the barrier between man and God, accomplished a full and perfect atonement, and created in himself one new humanity, the Body of which he is the exalted regnant Head."[15]

In the same place there are words that are even stronger:

> The church's words and works, its whole life of mission, are to be a witness to what God has done, is doing, and will do in Christ. But this word "witness" cannot possibly mean that the church stands over against the world, detached from it and regarding it from a position of superior righteousness or security. The church is in the world, and as the Lord of the church identified himself wholly with mankind, so must the church also do. The nearer the church draws to its Lord the nearer it draws to the world. Christians do not live in an enclave separated from the world. They are God's people in the world."[16]

In the Willingen statements, mission has its source in the nature and action of the Triune God. God is a missionary God and mission is the first

---

13. James A. Scherer, "Church, Kingdom, and Missio Dei Lutheran and Orthodox Correctives to Recent Ecumenical Mission Theology," in *The Good News of the Kingdom Mission Theology for the Third Millennium*, ed. C. Van Engen, D. S. Gilliland, and P. Pierson (Maryknoll: Orbis Books, 1993), 82.

14. W. F. Crum, "The Missio Dei and the Church: An Anglican Perspective," *St Vladimir's Theological Quarterly* 17, no. 4 (1973): 287.

15. International Missionary Council, *The Missionary Obligation*, 3.

16. Ibid., 5.

of all his actions. The missionary initiative flows from the love of God to reconcile his created yet alienated world.

There are two major points I want to emphasize in Willingen's declaration. First, mission is first and foremost God's mission. The church does not have its own mission. The primary emphasis is on what God is doing for the redemption of the world. Thereafter, consideration is given to how the church participates in God's redeeming mission. Second, God's mission is defined in terms of the Triune character and work of God.

It is significant that theologians talked about words and works. Yes, they imparted a new meaning to the word "words" in Tambaram, but also it was very important to be and to proclaim. The newness was that the church should not stay against the world,[17] but she ought to identify herself with the world, with the world's needs.

There is an abiding tension between two differing ecclesiologies in the ecumenical tradition.[18] The tension between these two competing ecclesiologies is the result of differing understandings of *missio Dei*. The term *missio Dei* was initially intended to move beyond an ecclesiocentric basis for mission by placing the church's calling within the context of the mission of the Triune God. Originally the *missio Dei* was interpreted christologically – the Father sends the Son who in turn sends the church in the power of the Spirit. The church participates in the mission of God by continuing the mission of Christ. However, after Willingen the *missio Dei* concept gradually underwent modification.[19] Because of the efforts of the Dutch missiologist Hoekendijk there was a great change in the understanding of the direction of mission and the role of the church in it. Until the 1960s the majority in missiological circles understood mission from God through the church to the world. In the 1960s the paradigm was changed to God – World – Church. The *missio Dei* is God's work that embraces both the church and the world.

These ideas dominated subsequent WCC reports: "Witness in Six Continents" (Mexico City, 1963), "World Conference on Church and

---

17. A quite popular overview of different positions between the church and the world can be found in the classical book of H. Richard Niebuhr, *Christ and Culture*, any edition.
18. D. Bosch, *Transforming Mission* (Maryknoll: Orbis Books, 1991), 368–389.
19. Ibid., 391–392.

Society" (Geneva, 1966), and especially the studies in evangelism report, "The Church for Others" (1967).[20]

The focus of the *missio Dei* moved from Christ to the Spirit: "This wider understanding of mission is expounded *pneumatologically* rather than christologically."[21] In this understanding, the church participates in God's mission by participating in what God is doing through the Spirit in the world. These different understandings of the *missio Dei* continue to inform the contrasting ecclesiologies of the ecumenical tradition. "And already in 1967 we can observe a shift of focus onto social work, it is not so important to proclaim by words, the most important thing is to proclaim by deeds. Participation in God's mission is therefore entering into partnership with God in history, because our knowledge of God in Christ compels us to affirm that God is working out his promise in the midst of the world and its historical processes."[22]

Then, later theologians specified the problem of what God is doing in the world, because this understanding can give them the way – what the church should do in the world. L. Newbigin proposed to pay attention to what God was doing in history and not only in the church.[23] So, the church turned her face to the world. The major task of the church – to be very attentive to the history of the world and to be a part of this history. Later Newbigin emphasized that the church should not go to the extremes of only social presence and evangelistic crusades. This idea was captured well in Janos Pasztor's phrase: "In the church tell the story, in the world live the story."[24] C. F. Cardoza-Orlandi further unpacks it: "The church that participates in God's mission in the world incarnates itself in the world to be a sign of the gospel of the kingdom (as an object of mission), to discern God's missionary activity outside its institutional reality, and to be

---

20. McIntosh, "Missio Dei," 632.

21. Bosch, *Transforming Mission*, 391.

22. World Council of Churches, *The Church for Others and The Church for the World: A Quest for Structures for Missionary Congregations. Final Report of the Western European Working Group and North American Working Group of the Department on Studies in Evangelism* (Geneva: WCC, 1967), 13.

23. Newbigin, *Relevance of Trinitarian Doctrine*, 20–24.

24. J. Pasztor, "God's Mission Taken Up as the Mission of the Church," in *Hope for the World: Mission in Global Context. Papers from Campbell Seminar*, ed. W. Brueggemann (Louisville: Westminster John Knox Press, 2001), 19.

transformed, together with the world, through participation in God's mission (as a subject of the mission of God)."[25]

Fifty years later in Willingen 2002, many theologians tried to evaluate the *missio Dei* concept. Tormod Engelsviken, from a Lutheran perspective, underlined that the real sense of the *missio Dei* had been lost because of the secularization of theology. He says: "Hoekendijk played a very important role in that. He underlined three major points in mission – *kerygma*, *koinonia* and *diakonia*, but sadly he forgot two also very important tasks – propaganda and church planting."[26] Charles Van Engen from his perspective went further and made his affirmation stronger. He considers that Hoekendijk's theology of mission essentially amounted to the euthanasia of the church.[27]

During the last few decades the church lost the real meaning of *missio Dei* and her participation in it. A. Kirk held that *missio Dei* has become more of a slogan than a defining phrase.[28] John Flett, quoting Wolfgang Gunther, said: "The resulting vacuity renders *missio Dei* an elastic concept capable of accommodating an ever-expanding range of meanings. For Wolfgang Gunther, *missio Dei* functions as a 'container term, which is filled differently depending upon each individual author.'"[29]

Wilhelm Richebacher critically evaluating the actual situation suggests:

> Evidence for the two effects can be found in the endless references to *missio Dei* made in mission theology statements of the final decades of the 20th century. Not for nothing was it called a "catch-all" term. The concept of *missio Dei* can be used by some to justify the Christocentric definition of all the mission of the church as distinct from religious propaganda,

---

25. C. F. Cardoza-Orlandi, *Mission: An Essential Guide* (Nashville: Abington Press, 2002), 47.

26. T. Engelsviken, "Missio Dei: The Understanding and Misunderstanding of a Theological Concept in European Churches and Missiology," *International Review of Mission* XCII, no. 367 (October 2003): 488.

27. C. Van Engen, *Mission on the Way: Issues in Mission Theology* (Grand Rapids: Baker, 1996), 154–156.

28. J. A. Kirk, *What Is Mission: Theological Explorations* (Minneapolis: Augsburg Fortress Press, 2000), 25.

29. Flett, *The Witness of God*, 5.

and by others to do just opposite, i.e. to propound a deity that bears witness to itself in other religions and thereby counter the absolute claims of Christianity.[30]

At the same time there are voices which insist that developing the concept of *missio Dei* makes the church lazy. Thinking that God will take the responsibility for mission, Christians became slow and lost their energy. "For too long Christians have believed that mission is God's mission and God will take care of bringing about a change to the world. The time has come for Christians to take responsibility for the world to be changed in accordance with God's intention in the incarnation of Jesus of Nazareth."[31]

It looks as if the church hid behind the concept of *missio Dei*. "The phrase '*missio Dei*' was sometimes used in such a way as to marginalize the role of the church."[32]

Charles Van Engen saw the reasons for such a situation: "(1) integration of the International Missionary Council into the World Council of Churches; (2) the birth of the Trinitarian concept of the *missio Dei*; (3) studies of the missionary nature of the church. All of them helped to shape a consensus that united church and mission in a way never before accomplished... In a such a situation both church and mission can get lost."[33] This is a crucial question, because some theologians see the Trinitarian foundation for mission as invigorating mission practices in the church, while others see it as potentially diluting the mission focus of the church.

Flett, referring to Dieter Manecke, wrote: "Mission becomes a hidden but controlling assumption, not only of the doctrine of Trinity, but also of the doctrine of reconciliation."[34] Kirsteen Kim in her turn said:

> Basing theology of mission on the Trinity had a number of profound theological effects. First, it shifted the ownership of

---

30. W. Richebacher, "Willingen 1952 – Willingen 2002," *International Review of Mission* XCII, no. 367 (October 2003): 465.

31. N. Smith, "From *Missio Dei* to *Missio Hominum*, *En Route* in Christian Mission and Missiology," *Missionalia* 30, no. 1 (April 2002): 19.

32. L. Newbigin, *The Open Secret: An Introduction to the Theology of Mission*. Revised edition (Grand Rapids: Eerdmans, 1995), 18.

33. Van Engen, *Mission on the Way*, 150–153.

34. Flett, *The Witness of God*, 43.

mission from the church to God (*missio Dei* approach) . . . Second, *missio Dei* put mission at the heart of God, the Trinity . . . Whereas in the West reflection on God as Trinity had tended to be on the nature of God as loving communion, the Willingen statement was closer to the view of the Orthodox churches, whose understanding of the Trinity had always emphasized what Irenaeus called 'the two hands of the Father,' that is the Trinity's engagement with the world through the dual economy of the Son and Spirit. *Missio Dei* thus encouraged a more dynamic understanding of God as outgoing and missionary. Third, the Church was also seen to be missionary by its very nature and its mission was seen as a participation in the greater mission of God."[35]

I don't see the reasons for escalating the debates in my dissertation, but at the same time I need to formulate more or less an objective view. I see Miroslav Volf's position as a balanced understanding in resolving this issue: "To think consistently in Trinitarian terms means to escape this dichotomy between universalization and pluralization. If the triune God is *unum multiplex in se ipso*, if unity and multiplicity are equiprimal in him, then God is the ground of both unity and multiplicity."[36]

So, today there is a misunderstanding of this concept, and not only of the concept, but also of God's mission itself. What is God doing today? What should the church do? Now it is time to rethink the *missio Dei* and the church's role in it. To achieve this goal we have to discover the content of *missio Dei* and its purpose.

The Content of *Missio Dei*

What is divine mission? What is the true meaning of God's mission? We observed the importance of the understanding of the *missio Dei* concept, but it is time to discover its meaning and content.

---

35. K. Kim, *Joining in with the Spirit: Connecting World Church and Local Mission* (London: Epworth press, 2009), 28–29.

36. M. Volf, *After Our Likeness: The Church as the Image of the Trinity* (Grand Rapids: Eerdmans, 1998), 194.

Many researchers of mission agree that the real meaning of *missio Dei* can be understood only in Trinitarian terms.[37] I will look later at the specific roles of God the Father, God the Son, and God the Holy Spirit, but now I want to emphasize that "the *missio Dei* concept has helped to articulate the conviction that neither the church nor other human agent can ever be considered the author or bearer of mission. Mission is, primarily and ultimately, the work of Triune God, Creator, Redeemer, and Sanctifier, for the sake of the world, a ministry in which the church is privileged to participate."[38]

The ground and fountain of *missio Dei* is the triune God of love.[39] L. Newbigin saw Trinitarian mission as Faith in Action, Love in Action, and Hope in Action.[40] His impact in developing mission as *missio Dei* is highly recognized. I will try to evaluate his understanding of the content of *missio Dei*, critically observing other sources.

Newbigin's understanding of the mission of the Triune God was fundamentally eschatological. The gospel is the announcement of the entrance into history of the end times of Jesus Christ. Newbigin understood *missio Dei* in terms of a movement in history toward a goal. Everything must be understood in terms of the *telos* of history.[41]

The good news is that in the life, death, and resurrection of Jesus, the end has been revealed in the middle. The Spirit is an end-time gift that witnesses to the kingdom revealed and accomplished in Jesus. Thus the main headings of the following sections on the mission of the Triune God all

---

37. Significant biblical and theological background has been given by Vicedom, *The Mission of God*, 45–92. Also see Newbigin, *Relevance of Trinitarian Doctrine*, and *The Open Secret*; Seng-Kong Tan, "A Trinitarian Ontology of Missions," *International Review of Mission* 93, no. 369 (April 2004), among others.

38. Bosch, *Transforming Mission*, 392.

39. S. K. George, *Called as Partners in Christ's Service: The Practice of God's Mission* (Louisville, KY: Geneva Press, 2004), 20.

40. Newbigin, *The Open Secret*, 33–63.

41. See the Theo Sundermeier's critical evaluation of the Western understanding of time and waiting the Kingdom of God "in time language." He ironically talks about the "shalomization" of Hoekendijk. Later I will talk about the "shalom" as a goal of kingdom. But I recommend reading Sundermeier's article "Missio Dei Today: On the Identity of Christian Mission," *International Review of Mission* XCII, no. 367 (October 2003): 569–571. He says that Western understanding of time and telos is founded in Greek worldview, while Jesus talked about the kingdom in Ancient Eastern understanding, where time is not a line, but a cycle. I can agree with him on some points, but we see it as too radical.

direct attention to the close link between the *missio Dei* and the kingdom of God: Jesus reveals and accomplishes the kingdom of the Father in his mission in the power of the Spirit. I will develop the kingdom understanding of *missio Dei* more deeply in the next part.

This research is founded on theistic but not deistic deductions, and for this reason I am sure that "God is indeed active in history. But his action is hidden within what seems to be the opposite – the suffering and tribulation of his people. The secret has been entrusted to those whom God chose."[42] The Bible is not merely concerned with one strand of cultural history but offers a story of universal history the beginning and end of all things and therefore provides a clue to the meaning of all that happens. Therefore, there cannot be a separation between world history and redemptive history. As Orlando Costas said: "We cannot separate God's redemptive activities in the evangelistic process from what Father, Son, and the Spirit are doing in the secular affairs of life."[43]

God is at work in history in some sense in movements of national liberation, of scientific discovery, of cultural renaissance, and reform in non-Christian religions. "Mission is not only about changing the church but also about changing the society. Without being dictated to by social pressure, churches and fresh expressions can serve diverse communities and at the same time exhibit the unity in the one Spirit . . ."[44] But it is essential to press further to learn in what sense God is at work in these movements.

Newbigin's dilemma was how to affirm the uniqueness of Christ without denying God's work in the world; to probe the relation between what God has done in Christ and what God is doing in the life of humankind as a whole. Only a proper understanding of this relationship will "enable Christians to communicate the gospel in words and patterns of living which are in accordance with what God is doing."[45]

The missionary conferences from Tambaram (1938) to Willingen (1952) placed God's work in the church at the center of its theological

---

42. Newbigin, *The Open Secret*, 55.

43. O. Costas, *Liberating News: A Theology of Contextual Evangelization* (Grand Rapids: Eerdmans, 1989), 84.

44. Kim, *Joining in with the Spirit*, 66.

45. Newbigin, *Relevance of Trinitarian Doctrine*, 28.

reflection. However, in Willingen this church-centric view of mission was challenged and the question posed about the relation of God's work in his church and his work in world history. This question was posed with new urgency at New Delhi (1961) but there was no agreement. There were two answers: on the one side, there were those who stressed that God was at work in the events of the day and mission meant discerning his work and engaging the world in dialogue and not monologue. On the other side, there were those who believed this would lead to a syncretism in which the distinctive claims of the gospel were compromised. The question as to whether and how God was at work in world history was an urgent one for the mission of the church.

It was determined above that the first foundation would be a Trinitarian understanding of God's mission. It is readily apparent from this insight that God's mission is holistic. P. Orjala saw holism in a comprehensive mission to the whole human being.[46] G. Gutierrez from his point of view looks further – God's activity extends in human history and throughout the whole universe,[47] a position, which is very close to Orthodox theology.

The Trinitarian and holistic mission of God includes the Three Persons of the Trinity, the whole universe, humankind, and the whole person including the person's needs, as God has created him. I would like to look at human beings from the ancient Hebrew point of view, where a person is not partitioned into two or three parts, "clearly, in the Old Testament a mortal is a living soul, rather than having a soul."[48] Greek philosophy divided a person into two or three parts (flesh, soul and spirit), and it had a great influence on the early interpretations of the New Testament. In the missiology of the nineteenth and twentieth centuries the church had a problem with understanding her mission. The dualistic point of view divided the church's mission into two parts – spiritual (care for soul and spirit) and social (care for flesh and universe). Controversies on this point

---

46. P. R. Orjala, *God's Mission is my Mission* (Kansas City, MO: Nazarene Publishing House, 1985), 58.

47. G. Gutiérrez, *The God of Life* (Maryknoll, NY: Orbis Books, 1998), 2.

48. C. Schultz, "Soul," in *Evangelical Dictionary of Biblical Theology*, ed. W. A. Elwell (Grand Rapids: Baker; Carlisle, Cumbria: Paternoster, 1996), 743.

continue to the present day. "*Missio Dei* converts and transforms individuals, churches, communities, structures, the world, and all creation."[49]

I should quote here two luminaries of missiology of the twentieth century. J. C. Hoekendijk wrote: "With regard to the relation of church and mission this title can be said, that the church can never be 'more' than the mission."[50] But S. Neil argued: "If everything is mission, nothing is mission. If everything that the church does is to be classed as 'mission,' we shall have to find another term for the church's particular responsibility for 'the heathen,' those who have never yet heard the name of Christ."[51]

C. Van Engen strongly supported S. Neil, many times repeating his assertion: "If everything is mission, nothing is mission."[52] He stated: "Given Hoekendijk's perspective, the sociopolitical usefulness of the church overshadows any biblical concept of mission. Subsumed under the church, mission becomes equated with the church's usefulness in producing social revolution. The church gets lost in the jungle of sociopolitical and economic agendas."[53]

I suggest that when we talk about the church, we should imply the image of God's people, their position, as proposed by E. Roels.[54] When we talk about mission, we should intend and mean the functions of God's people. Why should we divide one from another?[55] The Western European Working Group in its Final Report "The Church for Others and the Church for the World," said: "The mission of God (*missio Dei*) is to be distinguished from missions. As our present missions have sprung up as historically determined answers of the churches to challenges in the past, they may be understood as transitory forms of obedience to the *missio Dei*."[56]

---

49. George, *Called as Partners*, 86.
50. Hoekendijk, "The Church," 335.
51. S. Neill, *Creative Tension* (London: Edinburgh House Press, 1959), 81.
52. Van Engen, *Mission on the Way*, 150–156.
53. Ibid., 155.
54. E. D. Roels, *God's Mission: The Epistle to the Ephesians in Mission Perspective* (Franeker: T. Wever, 1964), 15–79. Author talks about Church in terms of prototypes, of her position in God; and he sees that all prototypes of the Church are static, fixed, and this is the reason why we should not talk so much about her functions. The Church is not a dynamic constitution; functions are in God's hands but not the Church's responsibility.
55. World Council of Churches, *The Church for others*, 13.
56. Ibid.

Historic, those words were justified, because the church at that time was divided in her understanding of mission (and till now the church is not united). But we think that now is a time for rethinking of such division in understanding of the mission and as the result of such a kind of rethinking, should be followed by rethinking of unity and common witness.

They appear to be one indivisible whole. This is the third understanding of holistic mission: to be and to do (*missio Dei* and *imago Dei*).[57] D. T. Niles considered that "the *imago Dei* is God's foundation-covenant with man."[58] "The *missio Dei* is said to spring from God's boundless and matchless love for the universe he has created, and particularly for the beings within it that bear his image."[59]

J. Matthey, one of the leading missiologists of contemporary Europe, describing the misunderstanding of the *missio Dei* concept, says:

> *Missio Dei* has helped to overcome the ecclesiocentric approach which had been highlighted since the 1930s (Tambaram). *Missio Dei* has been and can be a constant reminder that the church is not the ultimate goal of mission . . . *Missio Dei* also helped to open up the realms of politics and economics so that they became an integral part of the mission agenda . . . *Missio Dei* helped to change the post-Tambaram paradigm used in relation with people of other religions, and enabled Christians to have a more positive approach . . . As a result, we came to see that God is also active in mission outside the church . . . *Missio Dei* theology was linked with secularism, and, as a result, evangelism practically disappeared from the mission agenda of mainline churches in the West and North."[60]

A split appeared in ecumenical missiology because of the pneumatological understanding of God's mission as was mentioned early. The role of evangelism should be revised if God is active outside the church. As

---

57. Tan, "A Trinitarian Ontology," 279.

58. D. T. Niles, *Upon the Earth: The Mission of God and the Missionary Enterprise of the Churches* (New York: McGraw-Hill Book Company, 1962), 45.

59. Kirk, *What is Mission*, 28.

60. J. Matthey, "God's Mission Today: Summary and Conclusions," *International Review of Mission* XCII, no. 367 (October 2003): 580.

Kirsteen Kim says: "The Athens conference in 2005 [WCC] was the first mission conference since 1910 to look at mission from the perspective of theology of the Holy Spirit (pneumatology). This was particularly appropriate not only because of Pentecostal participation but also because the event was hosted by the Greek Orthodox Church, in which pneumatology as a discipline has traditionally attracted greater attention than in Western theology."[61] Petros Vassiliadis, addressing Bishop John Zizioulas, explains this division in the following way:

> Bishop John Zizioulas (of Pergamon) has convincingly argued that from the time of the New Testament and early patristic writings there are two types of pneumatology. One is "historical" and one "eschatological." One is familiar in the West to the present day and understands the Holy Spirit as fully dependent on Christ, as being the agent of Christ to fulfill the task of mission (cf also the filioque). The other, which was more consistently developed in the East, understands the Holy Spirit as the source of Christ, and also understands the church in terms more of "coming together" (i.e. as the eschatological synaxis of the people of God in his kingdom) than of "going forth" for mission.[62]

What are the practical outputs from such an understanding? Kim continues:

> The Holy Spirit does not just affirm and encourage what is good in human culture; the Spirit also transforms culture and liberates it from what is bad . . . From the perspective of pneumatology, the expression of the gospel in different cultures begins with discerning the Spirit, or finding out where the Spirit is at work according to the criterion set by Jesus Christ.[63]

---

61. Kim, *Joining in with the Spirit*, 27.

62. P. Vassiliadis, "Reconciliation as a Pneumatological Mission Paradigm: Some Preliminary Reflections by an Orthodox," *International Review of Mission* 94, no. 372 (January 2005): 38.

63. Kim, *Joining in with the Spirit*, 45.

J. Matthey, in his turn, suggests an idea, which contradicts the main stream of conciliar missiology of the 1960s and 1970s and to the pneumatological emphasis in God's mission: "A renewed *missio Dei* theology needs to give space at its core to the concern of evangelism, i.e. the sharing of the gospel with people. A really holistic understanding of mission includes a clear commitment to evangelism."[64]

It seems that the pneumatological and christological approach in Trinitarian missiology leads to very different mission practices. A christological emphasis uses contextualization as a mission method being sensitive to the local culture, but also remaining on the paternal position of "knowing the Truth." A pneumatological paradigm will lead to a more learning than teaching position of a missionary (inculturation model)[65]. Kim gives an example from Liberation theology:

> Liberation theology's intention is not only to interpret the text but also to change society, and its concern is not with academics but with social transformation. Praxis is not merely practice but action informed by reflection. Liberation theology suggested a new pattern of doing theology that combined action with theological reflection. It began with identifying with the poor, listening to them, rereading the Bible in the light of their experience, raising questions of theology and other structures of authority, and joining with people's movements to bring about change from the grassroots. This involvement in turn led to further reinterpretation of the Bible.[66]

The mission agency, or sending church, should evaluate the cultures and find the signs of God's presence among them. "The world is the realm of God's acting in which he establishes signs of the kingdom."[67] The goal of my dissertation is not to find a solution for resolving this issue, but rather to show the existing tension. Costas' opinion is very close to mine in this

---

64. Matthey, "God's Mission Today," 582.

65. K. Kim talks about that in her article "The Potential of Pneumatology for Mission in Contemporary Europe," *International Review of Mission* 95, no. 378–379, July/October (2006): 336.

66. Kim, *Joining in with the Spirit*, 115.

67. Flett, *The Witness of God*, 53.

sense: "We cannot separate God's redemptive activities in the evangelistic process from what Father, Son, and the Spirit are doing in the secular affairs of life."[68]

God's mission results from "who God is"[69] in the same way the church's mission results from "who the church is." At the same time we should not narrow her functions only to her image, because it is impossible to describe God's functions in the world only in terms of his image. Functions follow from his essence, but who can say that he has perceived God's essence? At the same time, who can say that he has recognized the church's image? The church is the bride of Christ and the house of the living God at the same time. How can we interrelate those two images? God is much wider than his image, but his mission results from his known and unknown being. The church is much wider than her images, but her mission results from her known and unknown essence. There are no contradictions between being and doing; there are few lacunas in our understanding. To resolve this issue the church should be wise in order to understand what God is doing in the world. L. Newbigin said that God's mission should not be examined only in terms of church history, because in that case medics who saved human lives were not a part of God's mission, therefore, God's servants are only clergy in the churches.[70] Talking on the same topic John Taylor said: "The missionaries of the Holy Spirit include the probation officer and the literacy worker, the researcher chemist and the worn-out school teacher in a remote village, the psychiatrist and the designer, the famine-relief worker and the computer operator, the pastor and the astronaut."[71]

Newbigin introduced a new term – ghettoism. The church lives in a ghetto, which she invented for herself.[72] The reason to create such a ghetto was a fear of syncretism. There were fears that the fallen world could destroy the church. We are so afraid of syncretism, that we have to keep quiet, for fear the world will change the church. But the task for this generation is to

---

68. Costas, *Liberating News*, 84.
69. Kirk, *What is Mission*, 28.
70. Newbigin, *Relevance of Trinitarian Doctrine*, 24–26.
71. J. V. Taylor, *The Go-Between God: The Holy Spirit and the Christian Mission* (Philadelphia: Fortress Press, 1972), 38.
72. Newbigin, *Relevance of Trinitarian Doctrine*, 26–27.

change the world, although those changes can only be a reality through suffering, and not through ruling.[73] *Missio Dei* is experienced in both the Old and the New Testament as the *epiphany* of God.[74] The beginning point of the mission of God for us is his self-disclosure. He reveals himself through the Spirit and through the Word.[75]

Theo Sundermeier, quoting Proverbs 25:2 compares the mission of God with a mystery, where the priests' work is to open this mystery and to make it open for the people of God. In Israel priests made this mystery a secret, but secret and mystery are not the same. God raised a new counter-tradition movement – a prophetic movement. Their deal was to make open God's mystery – his mission. Priests kept the mystery in their hands with the help of different rites; the prophets gave the mystery to Israel through texts.[76]

At the same time he declares that God's mission is a mystery, and also it includes freedom, pluralism and dense hope.[77]

To understand what God has in mind, Newbigin suggested three questions: (1) Does God work in post-Christendom countries? (2) Does God work in areas which traditionally were considered "Christian ministries" (counseling, orphanages and so on) and now in many cases they are under the state's care? (3) Does God work in the countries where till now there have been no Christian churches? Or does God work in the countries where Christian churches do not reveal unity?[78]

Mission is self-emptying, self-giving, and other-receiving.[79] *Missio Dei* is God's movement toward the world.[80] "The *missio Dei* is the work of God through which everything that he has in mind for man's salvation – the complete fullness of his kingdom of redemption – is offered to men through those whom he has sent, so that men, freed from sin and removed

---

73. Ibid., 41–44, also Vicedom, *Mission of God*, 132–142.

74. Western European Working Group, "Mission is God's Mission," in *Planning for Mission: Working Papers on the New Quest for Missionary Communities*, ed. T. Wieser (London: Epworth Press, 1966), 49.

75. Orjala, *God's Mission*, 19.

76. T. Sundermeier, "*Missio Dei* Today: On the Identity on Christian Mission," *International Review of Mission* XCII, no. 367 (October 2003): 562.

77. Ibid., 561–568.

78. Newbigin, *Relevance of Trinitarian Doctrine*, 28–30.

79. George, *Called as Partners*, 13.

80. Ibid., 2.

from the other kingdom, can again fully come into his fellowship. Thus the sending becomes an act of the love of God to lost men. It is an expression of his mercy."[81]

If the church wants to understand God's purpose, and his mission, she should try to discover the real meaning of *missio Dei* for herself, because "the mission is not ours, but God's."[82]

So, from the meaning of *missio Dei*, we now move to its goal.

The Goal of *Missio Dei*

God has his own goal in his mission. Is his mission goal the same as the goal he has for the church? When will his goal be fulfilled? Does it have a temporary or an eternal destination? What are the tasks he accomplishes to reach his goal?

Vicedom saw that "the goal of the mission is the proclamation of the message to all mankind and gathering them into the church. However, Scripture does not say that this goal will be reached . . . but the church has the responsibility for all of humanity."[83]

The purpose of the church is to proclaim redemption.[84] But what is the role of God here? Vicedom was categorical in his answer: "The Bible in its totality ascribes only one intention to God: to save mankind. Therefore, the service of the mission cannot be derived from the task of the church. Every task of the church makes sense and has a purpose only as it leads to the mission."[85] He says further: "The church herself is only the outcome of the activity of God who sends and saves. Mission is work that belongs to God. This is the first implication of *missio Dei*."[86] The final goal of the *missio Dei* is to incorporate mankind in the *basileia tou Teou*, and to convey

---

81. Vicedom, *The Mission of God*, 45.
82. Ibid., 78.
83. Ibid., 103.
84. Ibid., 97–102.
85. Ibid., 4.
86. Ibid., 5.

to mankind the gifts thereof.[87] The calling of the church to the world is *metanoia*.[88]

Vicedom supposed that the kingdom is the final goal of the *missio Dei*, and when this goal will be reached, the *missio Dei* will be finished. Not all scholars agree with him in this point. Moltmann, for example, cites Joachim and sees four kingdoms: the kingdom of the Father, the Son, the Holy Spirit, and fourth – the kingdom of the Triune God's kingdom of glory.[89] So, in that case, mission could have a continuation – eternal glory and eternal worship of the Triune God. But, in this context I should clarify the connection between *missio Dei* and the kingdom. Many scholars are in agreement that the final goal (in terms of time, I do not mean of eternity) of missio is the kingdom (Verkuyl, Scherer, Newbigin and others).[90]

Vicedom sees that repentance is closely related with the kingdom. Without repentance there is no forgiveness, and without forgiveness there is no way to the kingdom. If the goal of *missio Dei* is the kingdom,[91] therefore, repentance and forgiveness are the methods to achieve this goal.

It is very important to mention that the Orthodox Church, long before the Evangelicals and Protestants, declared the kingdom of God as its eschatological goal.

> The Orthodox vision of God's mission sees the salvation of the world as the "program" of the Holy Trinity for creation. The kingdom of God is the eschatological goal. Attention always focused on the central act of confessing the incarnate, crucified and risen Christ as the one who restores our broken communion with God. Such Orthodox perspectives can be enormously enriching for evangelical mission. The contention of this essay is that the special Orthodox contribution to ecumenical mission theology, at a decisive moment in the

---

87. Ibid., 14.
88. Ibid., 33.
89. J. Moltmann, *The Trinity and the Kingdom: The Doctrine of God* (San Francisco: Harper & Row, 1981), 207.
90. Vicedom, *The Mission of God*, 132–142.
91. J. Verkuyl, *Contemporary Missiology: An Introduction* (Grand Rapids: Eerdmans, 1978, reprinted 1987), 197.

history of the ecumenical missionary movement, has helped to save ecumenical mission theology from serious aberration by bringing it back to solid moorings in Scripture and apostolic tradition."[92]

It was assumed that the purpose of mission was Christianization – bringing human beings to God through Christ and his church. "Today the fundamental question is much more that of true man and the dominant concern of the missionary congregation must therefore be to point to the humanity in Christ as the goal of mission."[93]

From temporal and particular tasks the church redefines her goal and tasks to the global and eternal goal. It is very significant that in this redefinition theologians are involved from the main branches of Christianity. Evangelicals and Protestants, the Lausanne Movement and the World Council of Churches, have all tried to rethink how the church can understand that her goal is accessible, and what the signs are of the right way towards the goal. In the first half of the twentieth century, theologians and practitioners saw "three-self"[94] churches as a sign of performed mission. But after 1952 the process of redefinition was started by the WCC. The planting of the church cannot be an adequate definition of the goal of missionary work: beyond the churches the mission is directed towards the end of the earth (the region beyon') and the end of the time.[95] "The church cannot be the final goal of God's purpose. It is rather the instrument and the sacrament of God in his dealing with the whole of creation. The church, which has the promise but is not itself God's kingdom, has to live in the historic and social course of events because the kingdom of God is the goal of the whole world."[96]

We can observe how the sense and goal of *missio Dei* have changed extremely during these ten years. I mentioned above the reasons and the main figures of such changes, but now I will try to determine the historical movement of understanding of the goal of the *missio Dei*.

---

92. Scherer, "Church, Kingdom, and *Missio Dei*," 87.
93. World Council of Churches, *The Church for Others*, 78.
94. Self-propagating, self-governing and self-supporting.
95. Hoekendijk, "The Church," 336.
96. World Council of Churches, *The Church for Others*, 38.

Roels saw that the glory of God is the final purpose of the original creation.[97] "The mission, that has been repeatedly emphasized, is God's from beginning to end: he is its author, he is its goal. All the power of the mission is found in him, all that is accomplished is wrought by him."[98] Roels saw that God himself takes care of his mission; the church should think about sanctification.

The kingdom to which the Bible testifies, involves proclamation and realization of a total salvation, one which covers the whole range of human needs and destroys every pocket of evil and grief affecting mankind.[99] At the same time, "By the announcement (of the reign of God) there is also a call to a radical reversal of normal attitudes. The announcement is therefore at the same time a call to turn around and look the other way – to repent. Only as part of such a radical turnabout can Israel receive the gift of faith – faith to believe that the reign of God is indeed present, faith to know the secret of the kingdom of God (Acts 4:11)."[100]

This is fundamentally important, for confessing Jesus without following him as his disciple makes no sense at all. The kingdom of God concerns every side of human and universal being if we talk in terms of the holistic mission. If the mission is holistic, so the kingdom is "much more holistic." The purpose of God's creation and of God's saving mission is to give fullness of life to all.[101]

In seeking to define the purpose of the *missio Dei*, we are helped by the biblical term *shalom*.[102] "He is our peace. We understand our missions to be movements that participate in the *missio Dei*, which is to sum up all things

---

97. Roels, *God's Mission*, 15.
98. Ibid., 82.
99. Verkuyl, *Contemporary Missiology*, 197.
100. Newbigin, *The Open Secret*, 22.
101. George, *Called as Partners*, 4.
102. World Council of Churches, *The Church for Others*, 13. Also, see N. Kassab, "Partnership in God's Mission: Community of Women and Men in Church Today," in *Partnership in God's Mission in the Middle East. The Papers and Report of the Consultation of Women and Men of Reformed Tradition in the Middle East, Ayia Napa, Cyprus, 2-8 June 1996*, eds. J. D. Douglass and P. Réamonn (Geneva: World Alliance of Reformed Churches, 1998), 20.

in Christ, – and are therefore led to set up many signs of God's *shalom* in the world. *Shalom* is salvation, peace."[103]

Now it is very important to mention the signs of God's kingdom, the signs of *shalom*. D. Burnett conducted research on the signs of the kingdom in the New Testament, and all of them are very significant: "(1) Jesus in the midst of his people (Luke 17:21; Matt 18:20). (2) The preaching of the gospel of the kingdom (Luke 17:21). (3) Exorcism (Matt 12:29; Mark 3:27). (4) Healing and nature miracles (Luke 22; John 14:12). (5) Miracles of conversion and new birth (1 Thess 1:9, 10). (6) Manifestation of a Christlike character (Gal 5:22, 23). (7) Suffering (1 Pet 2:21)."[104]

All those signs are confirmation of God's presence among his people; they confirm that the kingdom of God has appeared; it is not far from us. If churches know God, they will go and expand the kingdom of God in the world. *Shalom* is a social happening, an event in interpersonal relations. It can therefore never be reduced to a simple formula; it has to be discovered as God's gift in actual situations.[105]

Finally, the kingdom of glory must be understood as the consummation of the Father's creation, as the universal establishment of the Son's liberation, and as fulfillment of the Spirit's indwelling.[106]

This change was seen in understanding the goal of God's mission – from Vicedom (salvation and redemption through repentance and forgiveness) to the WCC's understanding in the second part of the twentieth century (*shalom* in society, justice between rich and poor, and tolerance). The beginning of the twenty-first century showed that many churches (especially in Europe) lived with utopian ideas. One hundred years ago the same was true with post-millennium theology, when the first and then the second world wars showed that humankind will not build the kingdom with their own forces. The attacks on 9/11 again showed the lack of *shalom*. Now even from WCC circles we can hear the voices: "The terms *missio Dei* and kingdom of God are used in imperialistic ways when we include in them almost

---

103. Western European Working Group, "Mission is God's Mission," 51.
104. D. Burnett, *God's Mission: Healing the Nations* (Bromley: MARC Europe, 1986), 128.
105. World Council of Churches, *The Church for Others*, 13.
106. Moltmann, *The Trinity and the Kingdom*, 212.

everything the church is supposed to do, or even more, what God is doing, particularly with regard to the contemporary world and its many needs."[107] "The goal of *missio Dei* is friendship with God,"[108] because "it is not we who build the kingdom; it builds us."[109] "We should understand the kingdom of God primarily not in socio-political terms, but in soteriological terms, otherwise how we can explain Jesus' proclamation that the kingdom of God is near (Mark 1:15). If we are talking about the kingdom, where God rules over the whole world, then we are so far from that kingdom."[110]

Conclusions

During the discussions in chapter 6 I showed that the concept *missio Dei* is very controversial and polysemantic. There is not an easy answer of how to find a common language for Evangelicals and the Orthodox. Nevertheless, I see something which can help us in that process and I will illuminate some of these ideas in the following points.

1) The *missio Dei* concept is very Trinitarian and has a lot in common with Orthodox theology. The Lausanne Movement and Anabaptists can find the tools for designing a foundation for collaboration with Orthodox in Eastern Europe.

2) The Trinitarian foundation for *missio Dei* directs the holistic approach in mission, which is very close to the Orthodox understanding of the church's mission. The conversation is about a holistic approach to human beings and a holistic approach to the universe. The church, which is involved in the *missio Dei*, should have an adequate response for all challenges from the world. God is active not only in the church, but also from outside the church, and this means that the church should be very attentive to historic, political and economic processes in the contemporary world. God can use the church to change the world and can use the world to change the church.

---

107. Engelsviken, "Missio Dei," 484–485.
108. Sundermeier, "Missio Dei Today," 572.
109. Ibid.
110. Engelsviken, "Missio Dei," 483–484.

3) The final goal of *missio Dei* is the full glory of God and presence of the kingdom of God, but there are a few intermediate objectives, such as proclamation of the gospel of the kingdom of God, death and resurrection of Jesus Christ and repentance. Also there is a sign of achieving the final goal – *shalom* – which should be established in human hearts and on the earth. We see that God's mission can become the church's mission only if the church obeys the King and follows him in his mission.

I have finished with the descriptive and analytical parts of this book. The next step will be constructing a synthetic methodology, which will shape a new paradigm for Evangelicals in Moldova. In the next chapter I will discover the deeper understanding of a Trinitarian mission, talking about the mission of the Father, Son and Holy Spirit.

Part 3

Perspectives for the Mission of Evangelical Churches in Moldova

Part 1 of this dissertation showed the actual situation in Moldova in the Evangelical movement, comparing it with the neighboring countries in terms of mission and dialogue with the Orthodox Church. The situation was shown from a historic and missiological prospect. Part 2 gave a critical evaluation of the existing missiological paradigms, comparing them with each other. The most important point is the connection between them and the current situation in Moldova, seeking the roots of the contemporary missiological approach in Evangelical Baptist churches. During the Soviet era an Anabaptist paradigm of silent witness was the most useful. After the collapse of the USSR, the church growth movement paradigm came to Moldova through a strong partnership with the Southern Baptist Convention, and it gave very positive results in the 1990s. At the same time Evangelicals in Moldova faced a crisis of self-identification in their approach to missions at the beginning of the twenty-first century. Old methods did not give expected results, but new methods were not suggested. In addition, tensions between the Orthodox Church and Evangelicals did not become softer. I can define today's situation as critical. Because of that I investigated the situation in the country and tried to suggest a possible escape from the current crisis.

Part 3 will show the reality of a Trinitarian foundation for mission, then will give an analytical and synthetic evaluation of the missiological paradigms. It will propose a new paradigm as a result of rethinking the *missio Dei* as a proposal for the future.

CHAPTER 7

The Trinitarian Foundation for Mission

Chapter 7 is focused on a detailed explanation of the Trinitarian foundation for the mission of the church. It will show the meaning and role of each person in the Holy Trinity in mission, talking about the separate roles mostly from an epistemological and functional prospect, and not dividing the natural relations in the Trinity. I will examine the mission of God the Father, God the Son and God the Holy Spirit.

As a methodological approach I will use exegetical studies, looking through some passages from the Old and New Testaments, comparing opinions of commentators and theologians with missiological understandings. The Trinitarian foundation will lie at the very basic level of shaping a new paradigm for Moldavian Evangelicals.

Mission of the Father

It is impossible to undertake studies in contemporary mission without studying the relationships between the Holy Trinity, because this is the foundation for all kinds of church missions. "To speak about the *missio Dei* is to indicate, without any qualification, the *missio Trinitatis*."[1]

The church's mission (or missions) reflects the relationships between God the Father, God the Son, and God the Holy Spirit. God becomes not only the Sender, but simultaneously the One who is sent.[2] The Blessed Trinity constitutes the first ultimate foundation of the missionary nature

---

1. Kirk, *What Is Mission*, 27.
2. Vicedom, *The Mission of God*, 7.

of the church.³ As we reflect the relations in the Trinity, we are involved in God's mission. God is the founder of his mission.

God created all things, he sustains all things, he rules over history and is directing all events according to his purpose. God in his mercy holds off the end, sustaining and maintaining the world, so that there may be time for repentance. As the obedient Son, Jesus submits himself wholly to the Father's ordering of events. He does not seek to take control of the reins of history.

Seng-Kong Tan notes that the Father is the only person of the Trinity who revealed himself to the world but who was not sent.⁴ We have looked at the Father as the One who sends both the Son and the Spirit,⁵ adds David Bjork.

The relations within the Holy Trinity are the greatest mystery in Christian beliefs. We are not ready today to find the complete answer to all questions.

Who we are is entirely dependent upon our own cultural and theological background. We can evaluate our dependence only in a retrospective way. T. Sundermeier is one of the contemporary theologians who prefer to talk not only about knowing God, but also about the mystery of God. "When we say that mission has its roots in the Triune God, we should understand the results of such affirmations. *Missio Dei* has its roots only in God and this is a mystery. Because of that we cannot find any other motives or explanations for mission. We cannot explain mission from our denominational, social-political or cultural points of view, we cannot explain the real source of missio, because we cannot explain the real sense of Trinity."⁶

But, perhaps, it is not necessary to find an answer. J. Matthey seconds this opinion: "I would personally hesitate to go deeper into any analytical description of inner-Trinitarian processions. Who are we to know the inner

---

3. A. Wolanin, "Trinitarian Foundation of Mission in Following Christ in Mission," in *Following Christ in Mission: A Foundational Course in Missiology*, ed. S. Karotemprel (Boston: Pauline Books & Media, 1996), 49.

4. Tan, "A Trinitarian Ontology," 280.

5. D. E. Bjork, "Toward a Trinitarian Understanding of Mission in Post-Christendom Lands," *Missiology* 27, no. 2 (1999): 233.

6. Sundermeier, "Missio Dei Today," 572–573.

life of God? We could easily fall into the temptation of transferring to God our vision of the ideal community or society."[7]

One of the statements by J. Moltmann is of much interest: "The Trinity means: The Father sends the Son through the Spirit, the Son comes from the Father in the power of the Spirit. The Spirit brings people into the fellowship of the Son with the Father."[8] For our discussion it is not so important to find a resolution of the division of the Catholic and Orthodox churches. I want to focus our attention on the relations between Evangelical churches and the Orthodox Church. However, in this sense many Evangelical and Orthodox theologians do not have contradictions according to the Sender and the Messenger (or Messengers). "What, then, is a divine mission? Logically, it would seem possible that there could be six possibilities of divine missions, since there are three persons of the Trinity and a distinction between visible and invisible missions. Augustine eliminates two of these possibilities from the outset. There can be missions, or sendings, of the Son and the Holy Spirit, but never of the Father."[9]

I can agree with this opinion if we will talk about missio only in passive way – in other words, somebody was sent by somebody. In this case we cannot talk about sending (or mission) of the Father. But, if we talk about missio in active terms, we can (or must) talk about the mission of the Father, because the Father has sent his beloved Son (John 17:21).[10] The Sender is the same missionary as the Messenger. "God's entrance into history is a double entrance. He becomes part of it in Jesus Christ. He makes this part embrace the whole through the Holy Spirit. Jesus Christ is the content of the gospel – the good news of what God has done. The Holy Spirit is the missionary of the gospel. It is he who makes the gospel explosive in men's lives and in human affairs."[11]

"His [Father's] activity is the central source of power of the Christian mission. God the Father is a missionary God. His decisive missionary

---

7. Matthey, "God's Mission Today," 582.

8. Moltmann, *The Trinity and the Kingdom*, 75.

9. Poitras, "St. Augustine and the Missio Dei," *Mission Studies* 16, no. 32 (1999): 32.

10. D. Bjork considers that those words are the missionary mandate of Jesus Christ and for this reason should be the missionary mandate of the church. See Bjork, "Toward a Trinitarian Understanding," 231.

11. Niles, *Upon the Earth*, 67.

activity was the sending of his Son, Jesus Christ."[12] God is always present in his sending. The Sender is also a missionary, not only the Messenger. Furthermore, we can suppose that God the Father sent himself to create the universe, where the Son and Holy Spirit joined the Father's mission.

This broader context of the Father's rule over history and meta-history opens up a deeper understanding of the church's mission. God is not concerned simply with what is going on in the historical community that arose in the ministry of Jesus. God's rule is over all and he is the sovereign Lord of history. The events of world history are not mere props for a play in which the church is the only actor. The church's mission, following Jesus, is to witness to the rule of God.

The history of the nations and the history of nature can only be understood in the larger framework of God's history narrated in Scripture. This redemptive history proceeds by way of election, issues from the love of the Father, and has as its central theme the kingdom of God. While it is in the form of cosmic and universal history, the story proceeds by a process of narrowing. God chooses people to be the bearers of the true end of history for the sake of all. The central theme of history is the reign of God over all things. His elective purposes are integral in moving history to its conclusion.

Sending is, therefore, an expression of his presence at work in judgment and grace. Thus the missio becomes the testimony of his deity.[13] Further, "God reveals himself in that he performs the sending himself. If there were no *missio Dei*, then we would also have no revelation. He sends his Word to man and reveals himself in such a way that, in his Son, he himself comes to them through the Holy Ghost (John 3:16; Rom 1:16)."[14]

When we think of God the Father and mission, the theme that emerges is that he is the source, the originator, and the end of all things, including mission.[15] A. Fernando assumes that the model of the Father is a

---

12. Smith, *God's Mission*, 49.
13. Vicedom, *The Mission of God*, 10.
14. Ibid., 45.
15. A. Fernando, "God: the Source, the Originator, and the End of Mission," in *Global Missiology for the 21st Century: The Iguassu Dialogue*, ed. W. D. Taylor (Grand Rapids, MI: Baker, 2000), 192.

participation in all the processes of the world.¹⁶ God's redemptive activity or the *missio Dei* does not begin with Jesus. Rather the Bible tells a story that finds its unity in the mighty acts of God that culminate in the sending of Jesus Christ. God's love for the world is demonstrated in the long road of redemption that he walks with Israel. Jesus is conscious of being the one sent to complete and make known the purposes of the Father.

The Father sent the Son to make visible the kingdom. This kingdom mission of Jesus was unfolded in communion with the Father. His life was that of an obedient and loving Son. The work of the Father was the pervasive atmosphere for the mission of the Son.

Today several different ideas have been developed according to the roles of the three persons of the Holy Trinity in mission. I present a few of them, which are very useful for resolving our main issue – to rethink *missio Dei* among Evangelical churches in an Eastern European Orthodox context. But rethinking *missio Dei* without rethinking the role of the Father is impossible. Moltmann developed the very interesting idea of the "bisexuality or transexuality" of God. He says:

> But if the Son proceeded from the Father alone, then this has to be conceived of both as a begetting and as a birth. And this means a radical transformation of the Father image; a father who both begets and bears his son is not merely a father in the male sense. He is a motherly father too. He is no longer defined in unisexual, patriarchal terms but – if we allow for the metaphor of language – bisexually or transexually. He has to be understood as the motherly Father of the only Son he has brought forth, and at the same time as the fatherly Mother of his only begotten Son.¹⁷

The concept of "bisexuality of God" shows a very intimate side of God's nature and the relations in Trinity. I know that this idea will not be accepted in the near future – not only by Orthodoxy, but even Evangelicals are very suspicious of it – especially Eastern European Evangelicals. We cannot, however, ignore the fact that the word *ruah* in Hebrew is feminine, and

---

16. Ibid.
17. Moltmann, *The Trinity and the Kingdom*, 164.

not masculine as *spiritus* in Latin or neutral as *pneuma* in Greek. Having in mind this idea, Genesis 1–2 appears in a very different way, especially when the author talks about creating human beings in the image of God. This understanding can bring a new light to the *imago hominum* and women's role in mission. However, I think that for this dissertation these thoughts could create additional tensions. It could be a topic for further research. Coming back to the main area of studies, I will remain in the traditional understanding of Trinitarian theology.

J. Pasztor wrote a paper for the Campbell Seminar in 2000 at the Columbia Theological Seminary. He presumed that a Trinitarian understanding of the *missio Dei* includes four aspects.

> (1) God the Trinity has been present in the world since creation and has not abandoned his handiwork. (2) The central event of God's dealing with creation is the Christ-event, with its bearing upon the whole universe (Col 1:15–17). (3) The work of the Holy Spirit makes human agency possible. (4) The Trinitarian emphasis will guard against separating the Father, the Son, and the Holy Spirit from each other . . . the church will be the new form of existence of Christ, witnessing to the presence of God in his creation.[18]

So, he talks about the mission of the Trinity, the mission of the Son and the Holy Spirit, but he does not emphasize the special role of the Father. It is very interesting that the Source of all kinds of missions is not underlined as a separate[19] mission.

L. Newbigin sees three different tasks in the Trinity: faith in action, love in action and hope in action (as it was mentioned above). The Father proclaimed his kingdom in the Old Testament, the Son presented it in himself, but the Holy Spirit confirmed it.[20] "I shall therefore begin by looking at the Christian mission in three ways – as proclaiming the kingdom of the Father, as sharing the life of the Son, and as bearing the witness of

---

18. Pasztor, "God's Mission Taken Up," 149.

19. I talk about separation only in epistemological terms, or sometimes in functional. But I do not divide the Trinity in essential terms.

20. Newbigin, *The Open Secret*, 33–65.

the Spirit."²¹ The beloved Son was sent by the Father to make known and accomplish the purposes of God for universal history. This understanding of the Father's work forms the context for the mission of Jesus. He is sent to a world created and loved by the Father, a world upheld by God in which no one is ultimately a stranger to God, and a world in which all the events of history are under the sovereign control of the Father.

Moltmann sums up "the works of the Trinity" as creation for the Father, liberation for the Son and glorification for the Holy Spirit.²²

Kane says that the sovereignty of God is seen in all three of his divine activities: creation (Rev 4:11), redemption (Eph 1:5–9), and judgment (Rev 15:3–4; 16:5–7; Rom 9:18–3).²³ Furthermore, the Christian mission is a part of God's sovereign activity in the realm of redemption. From first to last the Christian mission is God's mission, not of humans.²⁴

There are several other opinions: J. Pasztor confirms that God's mission consists of three parts: (1) creation of the world; (2) God sent his Son into the world; (3) the Holy Spirit was sent to the world with the goal of identifying himself with the world.²⁵ Cardoza-Orlandi sees the Triune God

---

21. Ibid., 29.

22. Moltmann, *The Trinity and the Kingdom*, 212. In this fundamental book J. Moltmann describes three forms of the kingdom, which will be very helpful for our understanding of the *missio Trinitatis*. The first form of the kingdom is *the kingdom of the Father*. This is the creation and preservation of the world. In this kingdom God rules over all things through his power and providence. His lordship over men and women is determined by his law and the fear it evokes. The second form of the kingdom is *the kingdom of the Son*. It is the redemption from sin through the servitude of the Son. In this kingdom God rules through the proclamation of the gospel and the administration of the sacraments of the church. Through their fellowship with the Son, people become the children of God instead of slaves under the Law. Their fear of God is transformed into trust in God. The third form of the kingdom is *the kingdom of the Spirit*. It is the rebirth of men and women through the energies of the Spirit. It brings the *intelligentia spiritualis*. In this kingdom God rules through direct revelation and knowledge. Through the experience of the indwelling Spirit people turn from being God's children into his friends. The form of life lived in the kingdom of the Spirit is a charismatic one. "According to Joachim, the times and forms of the kingdom are so entwined with one another that the one is already pregnant with the next, and presses forward towards it. The kingdom of the Spirit is already implicit in the kingdom of the Son, just as the kingdom of the Son was already prepared for in the kingdom of the Father" (Ibid., 205).

23. J. H. Kane, "Role of God in Mission," in *Christian Missions in Biblical Perspective* (Grand Rapids, MI: Baker, 1976), 98.

24. Ibid.

25. Pasztor, "God's Mission Taken Up," 137–150.

in a following way: God the Creator, God the Redeemer, and God the Sustainer. Since God is the primordial agent of mission, mission is thus an event in and of community. God's mission is a participatory and communal activity among the Godself.[26] "God's action in the world includes much more than what happens in the church."[27]

We see that very often theologians talk about the Father's mission in terms of creation and sending. But it is important to note that the Son also was involved in the process of creation (Col 1:9–20). But much more important to underline here, that God-Father was very active after creation, during the history of the nations and also during the history of his nation – Israel. The concept of the kingdom of God did not begin with Jesus. It had developed over a long period of Israel's history.[28] In biblical theology there is the very famous Theology of the Covenants.[29] God the Father enacted several covenants with humankind. So, God works with humankind, and people wanted to meet God, to be a part of his kingdom. R. Williamson says that in the Old Testament the coming of the kingdom was synonymous with the coming of God. It was God's presence for which the people looked and longed.[30]

The International Missionary Counsel at Willingen proposed looking on the mission of the Triune God in a more practical way:

> Nevertheless, we are convinced that it is not only possible but also necessary to discern by faith the ways in which God is exercising his sovereignty in our time: – in personal life, where he takes hold of deeds performed faithfully amidst tragedy and frustration and weaves them into his on-going purpose; – in the movements of political and social life, where he both shows his judgment and also confronts whole societies with new opportunities of living; – in the process of scientific

---

26. Cardoza-Orlandi, *Mission*, 45.

27. Ibid.

28. R. Williamson, *For Such as Time as This: Sharing in the Mission of God Today* (London: Darton, Longman & Todd, 1996), 51.

29. See R. Zuck, *A Biblical Theology of the Old Testament* (Chicago, IL: Moody Press, 1991).

30. Williamson, *For Such as Time as This*, 54.

discovery, where he opens up new ranges of creation, with their promises of hope and possibilities of disaster. In such and other ways of his action God is carrying out his judgment and redemption in the revolutionary movements of our time. It is only possible to say these things in faith, but it is also necessary to say them, for two reasons: (a) because God speaks to us through the events of our time by revealing the depth and opportunities of the church's task, and expects us to discern his stimulus and respond to it; (b) because this conviction is given to us in order that the thrust of the mission may be maintained against ineffectiveness and disappointment. This is the dynamic (as distinct from the authority) of the missionary commission.[31]

Many theories and suggestions about God's mission have been proposed. Seng-Kong Tan outlines four popular models:

(1) The Processional model portrayals God the Father as the source of divinity, while at the same time affirming the involvement of all three members of the Trinity in both the creation and redemption of man. The Father is the generative source of all things. At the same time, the Father, Son and Holy Spirit share a single monarchy, such that within the economy of God, the glory of the Father is a participation through the Spirit in the mission of the anointed Christ. In simple words, it could be summarized as "Divine Sovereignty."

(2) The Linguistic model emphasizes that Jesus Christ is the medium of salvific revelation. As the medium he is himself the message; and as the message he is the medium to both the origin and the end. Without the Son, the Father would be eternally silent and historically hidden, and the Spirit would be ontologically "unspirated" and temporally "unemployed." The eternal, perfect divine image of God is translated into humanity in Jesus. As a result of this our theologies of mission must be local, contextual "translations" of the great translation. Likewise, Christians also feel the

---

31. N. Goodall and International Missionary Council, *Missions Under the Cross Addresses delivered at the Enlarged Meeting of the Committee of the International missionary Council at Willingen, in Germany, 1952* (London: Edinburgh House Press, 1953), 240.

need to be good listeners to the genuine cries of the world of God. This approach could be referred to as "human participation."

(3) Within the Dispositional model, the Holy Spirit of the Father and the Son is the dynamic completion of love. Trinity is essential love, which is described as the "I," "Thou" and "We" in God. The mysterious work of the Holy Spirit liberates us from programmatic fixation and achievement orientation, which so easily beset our missionary activity. The Holy Spirit, as the "go-between" God, is self-effacing in nature for he attests to and glorifies the Son and the Father. The unitive nature and function of the Holy Spirit brings us into a vertical oneness with God, and into a horizontal communion with other believers. As a result of this, Christian mission is seen as a common witness mirroring the nature of the church, which is One. This concept is very close to *missio Dei*.

(4) The Social model is based on the doctrine of *Perichoresis* and pictured as a "divine dance." The being of the eternal three, therefore, includes eternal rest and action, residence and journey, *hypostasis* and *ekstasis*. Such an understanding of God brings about a radical critique to our activism to cause a better understanding of who we are. Our movement away from ourselves to the world is but an expression of our identity as God-related, Christ-like and Spirit-filled. We participate in God's mission through the energies of the Spirit. This mission could be defined as prayer and spirituality.[32]

However we can only conclude that the Trinity is a mystery and as D. Bjork mentioned: "My belief is that reflection on the mystery of the Godhead – Trinity in Unity and Unity in Trinity – can lead us to a fuller comprehension of the missionary's role in these lands."[33]

So, what is the sense, the theological and practical value of a rethinking of *missio Dei*? Newbigin in an excellent paper "The Relevance of Trinitarian Doctrine for Today's Mission" observes that during the history of the Christian church there has been a very interesting impact of the Trinitarian doctrine on mission and vice versa, the role of the mission of the church in the development of Trinitarian doctrine. A very brilliant example is the

---

32. Tan, "A Trinitarian Ontology," 280–294.
33. Bjork, "Toward a Trinitarian Understanding," 232.

dispute about this doctrine in early church history and also in the ninteenth and twentieth centuries. Why are those periods well known as periods of missionary activities of the church? However, the period of Reformation (an epoch of great theological discussions) disregarded this doctrine. Why? I suppose because the church was very passive in mission in those times.[34] Trinitarian doctrine was always on the edge of mission, because the nations asked the church questions about God, about the role of Jesus in salvation, about the role of the Holy Spirit, and about relations between the Father and Son.[35]

So, I can agree that God's mission can no longer be perceived as a one-way path. It is an encounter with people, where change takes place. Mission cannot fulfill God's will unless it is open to the work of the Holy Spirit and the challenge of mutual change.[36] God works through his church, through his faithful people in mission, and much more than that – he works with them in their mission. Sometimes, missionaries cannot say where the results are better – in them or outside of them.[37] One of the ways God works with his people is that sometimes he closes the doors for mission in concrete places, regions well defined by him for an interval of time.[38] The *missio Dei*, embracing the entire activity of God, can therefore also be equated with the lordship of God.[39] Christian mission is not first *Christian* mission, but God's mission (*missio Dei*).[40] Only the Triune God can finish God's mission and fully establish God's realm.[41]

I agree with J. Verkuyl that the goal of God the Father's mission is the words from the Lord's Prayer: "Hallowed be your name, your kingdom

---

34. When we talk about mission in this context, we have in mind mission as sending, including evangelism and social actions.
35. Newbigin, *Relevance of the Trinitarian Doctrine*, 32–34.
36. Kassab, "Partnership in God's Mission," 18.
37. F. Raytchinets, Unpublished sermon, Sarka-Valey Community Church, Prague, January 30, 2006.
38. Kane, "Role of God in Mission," 104.
39. Vicedom, *The Mission of God*, 11.
40. Pasztor, "God's Mission Taken Up," 17.
41. George, *Called as Partners*, 64.

come, your will be done on earth as it is in heaven" (Matt 6:9–10)."[42] It includes *shalom* in the terms which I explained in the previous chapter.

Mission of the Son

I have defined *missio Dei* as the mission of the Trinity, which is indissolubly interrelated and existing in her completeness, but at the same time, I supposed that there are functional and epistemological distinctions. Thus I will consider the Son's mission or *missio Christi*.

The mission of the Son began at the time of the incarnation. "The visible mission of the Son, the incarnation, is the focus of all the divine missions. The birth of Jesus from a woman is the actual coming of the Son in his visible mission. It is the making visible of that which was already present in the world but in an invisible form. The invisible becoming visible, the eternal becoming temporal, the unknowable becoming known – these are the descriptions of the Son's being sent."[43]

G. Vicedom agrees that the highest mystery of the mission out of which it grows and lives is: God sends his Son.[44] The early Orthodox tradition introduced the term *kenosis*, which I explained in chapter 5 and it has the meaning of "to empty." J. Moltmann described this concept in following words: "The traditional doctrine about God's *kenosis* has always looked at just the one aspect of God's self-limitation, self-emptying, and self-humiliation. It has overlooked the other side: God's limitations inwardly are delimitations outwards. God is nowhere greater than in his humiliation. God is nowhere more glorious than in his impotence. God is nowhere more divine than when he becomes man."[45]

The famous hymn concerning Christ's *kenosis* is written in Philippians 2:5–7. Jesus confined himself; put himself within human limitations. This is where the *kenosis* theory comes from, which states that Jesus gave up some of his divine attributes while he was on earth. These attributes were

---

42. J. Verkuyl, "The Kingdom of God as the Goal of the Missio Dei," *International Review of Mission* 270 (April 1969): 169.
43. Poitras, "St. Augustine and the Missio Dei," 35.
44. Vicedom, *The Mission of God*, 8.
45. Moltmann, *The Trinity and the Kingdom*, 119.

omniscience, omnipresence, and omnipotence.[46] In the mission of Jesus we recognize God as a sending God. God's people experience God's Lordship in being sent. The witness and obedience of the church are determined by this experience.[47]

The *kenosis* of Jesus Christ is the eternal example for his followers, "reading the *missio Christi* in terms of kenotic action, we will have to apply the same category to the church."[48]

> In Jesus, fully God and fully human, we have the model which bears the tension between bringing the good news that is divine, and the act of emptying ourselves to know anew the real meaning of God's love for the people. In Jesus' model of mission, we are asked to live the paradox of knowing the truth and still learning what it really means. It is presenting the good news to others, yet at the same time learning what the good news means to us. It is experiencing the paradox of the already and the not-yet.[49]

E. Poitras adds: "To see the divine missions in full perspective, it is necessary to understand them *as* both sendings and returnings to the Father."[50] For sure, the kenotic Jesus proclaimed his mission but only the glorified Jesus accomplished it.

Above it has been said that sometimes theologians see the Son's mission as redemption. Though there is a maxima, that Jesus Christ is *missio Dei*. I will observe a few important texts in the New Testament where Jesus himself proclaimed what his mission is about.

The opening words of Jesus' ministry are: "The time has come. The kingdom of God is at hand. Repent and believe the good news" (Mark 1:15). Jesus announces the arrival and presence of the kingdom of God in history. It is an announcement that God's reign is now confronting all people as a present reality. Another time Jesus said that the kingdom is

---

46. J. Reimer, "Mission as Kenotic Action: Understanding Orthodox Theology of Mission," *Missionalia* 32, no. 1 (April 2004): 69.
47. Western European Working Group, "Mission in God's Mission," 49.
48. Reimer, "Mission as Kenotic Action," 72.
49. Kassab, "Partnership in God's Mission," 19.
50. Poitras, "St. Augustine and the Missio Dei," 40.

"among you" (Luke 17:21). New Testament scholar Craig Keener said, "By teaching that the kingdom as God's reign is somehow presented, Jesus implies that something of the kingdom – such as the messianic king – is already among them."[51] The power of that reign is at work in the midst of history. "If I drive out demons by the Spirit of God, then the kingdom of God has come upon you" (Matt 12:28). The signs of his power were visible and touchable. Of course person and power cannot be separated. It is very important to mention that the presence of the kingdom is hidden and not obvious to all people. If God were to reveal fully the end-time kingdom of God, then history would have reached its end. Since the kingdom has not been fully manifested, many cannot see the kingdom of God because they are facing the wrong way.

Another sign of power and kingdom is conflict. The parable of the tares makes clear that the presence of the kingdom of God precipitates an encounter with the power of darkness (Luke 22:53). The powers that be, both in their outward forms as the established religious, cultural and political structures, and in their inward reality as the principalities and powers of this age, are challenged and fight back. This brings suffering. The antithetical encounter intensifies until it reaches its climax on the cross. Thus the cross casts its shadow over this entire historical time period. The kingdom is not a smooth, continuous movement of progress toward a final realization of God's purposes. History "between the times" is characterized by conflict, struggle, and suffering.

I want to concentrate on a very important text in theological and sociological discussions, which takes place in the heart of the different theological schools, on the topic "what is the mission of the Son, based on Luke 4?" During the last thirty years Liberation theology has offered answers to this question.

This text is interesting due to one main reason – the reminder that Jesus was with the poor to whom he came to preach the good news. What kind of poor are we talking about? Are "the poor in spirit" (Matt 5:3) and "the poor" (Luke 4:18) equivalent? Answering these questions, we can define *missio Christi*, because Jesus himself said that he came for this reason.

---

51. Keener, *The IVP Bible Background Commentary: New Testament* (Downers Grove: InterVarsity, 1993), 237.

In all the countries of Eastern Europe, society is now divided into rich and poor. It is necessary to note that among the Evangelical churches there are currently more wealthy people than formerly. Still the majority of the inhabitants of these countries are miserable and poor.

I would especially like to mention the situation in Moldova. It is important to pay attention to a dual phenomenon of this country. First, as mentioned in chapter 2, the number of members of Evangelical churches doubled in the 1990s. Second, during these years Moldova became the poorest country in Europe. Thus, the Evangelical churches are facing an urgent need to formulate a response to the poverty issue in this country, but sadly it has not yet been done.

Thus, Jesus begins to cite the prophet Isaiah (61:1). The words "the Spirit of the Lord is upon me," emphasizes not just the special importance of the words that follow (similar to the words "the word of the Lord that came to the prophet" [Mic 1:1; Hos 1:1; Joel 1:1]), but also talks about an undeniable authority.

In the last thirty years these specific words of Jesus ("because he has anointed me to preach the gospel to the poor") became the object of the most heated discussions among theologians. What kind of poor people does Jesus refer to? Depending on the answer, the term "to preach the gospel" also gets a specific meaning. For one group of poor people the good news consists in one thing and for the other, something else. Some missiologists of the twentieth century thought that the good news of the kingdom is that the whole of Christ's work is a work of liberation from the rule of sin, Satan, and death. Hence, the church must reflect liberation from the influence of the "dominion of darkness."[52]

There is an opinion that preaching to the poor is separate from everything else in this passage. This is not mixed in with all the other tasks of Jesus, his anointing having been given to him for this specific reason. It is hard to answer the question of who is "poor" with the words, "they are the lowest economic class of the society." "In the Old Testament the poor are not the ones who are economically poor people, but the ones who have

---

52. A. F. Glasser, C. E. Van Engen, D. S. Gilliland, and S. B. Redford, *Announcing the Kingdom: The Story of God's Mission in the Bible* (Grand Rapids: Baker, 2003), 339.

lived in a complete dependence upon God."[53] D. Dorr, in his turn, also with references to the Old Testament, comes to the following conclusion: "The term refers to those groups of people who are economically deprived, who have no social status, and who are treated unjustly by foreign rulers or by the authorities in their own land."[54]

Tom Houston, one of the primary leaders of the Lausanne Movement, pays attention not to the Old Testament understanding of the concept "poor or needy" but addresses the study of the Old Greek language: "The two words used for 'the poor' in the New Testament are *penes* and *ptochos*. *Penes* refers to the person who is oppressed, underpaid, and the working poor. *Ptochos* refers to the person who has no work to do and has to beg."[55]

In order to generalize the above-mentioned topic, I would like to quote D. Bosch's words: "*Ptochos* – is moreover often a collective term for all the disadvantaged."[56] D. Burnett considers that neither Jesus nor the apostles differentiated evangelism from social action as two different responses to two different sets of human needs.[57]

Luke, as no other evangelist, spends a lot of time on the issue of the poor and the rich (1:53; 3:12–14; 7:11–17; 18:2–5; Acts 11:27–30). Agreeing with Bosch, a question still remains: "What kind of good news did these poor people need?" We can answer this question with Houston's words: "It was the kind of good news that brought a prostitute to wash Jesus' feet with her tears and wipe them with her hair, and then to Jesus saying, 'Your sins are forgiven' (Luke 7:36–50, TEV)."[58] Further, "the good news of the kingdom of God is that sin, disease, and oppression are never the last word. Where Jesus is King, he brings forgiveness, healing, and liberation."[59]

---

53. H. Peskett and V. Ramachandra, *The Message of Mission* (Downers Grove: InterVarsity, 2003), 159.

54. D. Dorr, *Mission in Today's World* (Maryknoll, NY: Orbis Books, 2000), 151.

55. T. Houston, "Good News for the Poor," in *Proclaim Christ until He Comes: Calling the Whole Church to Take the Whole Gospel to the Whole World, International Congress on World Evangelization 1989* (Lausanne Committee, 1989), 155.

56. Bosch, *Transforming Mission*, 99, 435.

57. Burnett, *God's Mission*, 137.

58. Houston, "Good News for the Poor," 155.

59. Ibid., 156.

Jesus separates all the following phrases from the previous one. The Spirit of the Lord has anointed him to preach the gospel to the poor. In the Old Testament, anointing was used in order to separate one for a special mission. All the other components of Jesus' mission are accompanied by the verb "sent." "He sent me to heal the broken-hearted." It is interesting to mention that the commentators refer the least to the phrase "the broken-hearted." That is most likely because this phrase cannot be understood in a polysemantic way. The broken-hearted are the ones who, due to different reasons, have an emotional, psychological (or as people call it "heart") wound. This can be due to poverty as well as various other reasons (loss of close ones, war, famine, natural disasters, unshared love, poverty, etc.). All these categories of people need healing of their hearts, settling of peace in their hearts.

Some theologians see a parallel between the phrases "to preach deliverance to the captives" and "to set at liberty them that are bruised." The discussion again develops around the issue of whether these words had a physical or spiritual meaning. What kind of captives and bruised people are we talking about? D. Bosch writes that the "oppressed" or "bruised" in Isaiah 58:6 are the needy people from a material point of view, who fell into slavery and who do not have hope to get out of the choking bondage of poverty. Only the Jubilee year, "the acceptable year of the Lord," can give them the opportunity to come out of this situation.[60]

W. Larkin considers that there is no special basis to affirm that:

> To release the oppressed and to free the captives has a political or spiritual meaning. From one point of view there is proof that Jesus was driving out demons (4:33–37; 6:18, 19; 7:21; 8:2, 26–39; 9:37–43; 11:14–23; 13:10–17, 32). From another point of view there are passages that talk about Jesus bringing salvation and forgiveness of sin (1:77; 5:21–24; 7:47–49). Besides this, we see John the Baptist in prison and Jesus doesn't save him out of there. It means that we can doubt the political interpretation of this text. It rather has to deal with

---

60. Bosch, *Transforming Mission*, 101.

the heaviness of the burden of sin laying on people's shoulders and their demonic dependence."[61]

Then Jesus announces that he came to preach the acceptable year of the Lord. This is the year that according to Moses' law was celebrated only once every fifty years, a year in which all debts were forgiven, slaves were set free, and the land taken under guarantee was returned back to the owners (Lev 25). There has been serious discussion of the Jubilee year, as serious as on the issues of the "poor" and the "captives." The whole interpretation of the above-mentioned depends on understanding of the meaning of the words uttered here. Thus, if the Jubilee is an allegory, then all Jesus' words need to be understood only in a spiritual context. If he has literally proclaimed the Jubilee, then all the above-mentioned words should have become real for the synagogue listeners.

The acceptable year of the Lord is first of all the Jubilee year of Jesus' ethics. "The kingdom of God is that new order of affairs begun in Christ which, when finally completed by him, will involve a proper restoration not only of man's relationship to God but also of those between sexes, generations, races, and even between man and nature."[62] But at that time Israel was under the Roman Empire and thus it was impossible to talk about a literal proclamation of the Jubilee in Moses' terms, which was foreseen for independent Israel. Jesus announces the Jubilee year in old terms, but with a new meaning; like Old Testament prophets often did, so he did himself.

I would like to mention the omitted passage from Isaiah 61:1, 2. "To proclaim the day of vengeance of our God" – this is a second modification that Jesus includes in his reading. The foundation of this change becomes clearer especially after the second part of Jesus' sermon, where he talks about the Gentiles who received the word of the ancient prophets. Jesus' contemporaries obviously waited for God's vengeance onto the heads of his political enemies.

Jesus does not give his listeners what they wait for and it brings something that causes them to reject him – give up the idea of vengeance and

---

61. W. J. Larkin and J. F. Williams, *Mission in New Testament* (Maryknoll, NY: Orbis Books, 2002), 162.

62. Verkuyl, "The Kingdom of God," 168.

even more than that, go and preach to the Gentiles. God's vengeance will come but today is the day of peacemaking.

Jesus said "this day is the Scriptures fulfilled in your ears," after the people were already looking at him in surprise. The fulfillment of the Scriptures talked about the fact that liberation will come, but the confusion arose because they were waiting to see it in a different form. This one-way declaration of Jesus does not leave any doubt that he was the long-awaited Messiah of Israel.

Jesus brings two examples from the Old Testament regarding two respected prophets who had contact with the Gentiles, leading them to salvation. I can say that in the case of Elijah salvation had a dual character. The widow saved Elijah from a starving death and God through Elijah saved her house. J. Dupont saw the episode in Nazareth as a prelude to what will happen in Pisidian Antioch and in Rome, as well as to Paul's behavior.[63] D. Senior said that Jesus is open for official outsiders.[64] P. Hertig saw this in a more radical light: "Jesus restructured the traditional value systems according to God's mercy, which for first-century Jews turned their world upside down and their worldview inside out."[65] Jesus' project included radical forgiveness and this was revolutionary, since the main topic in Luke is salvation and forgiveness of sin.[66] "Jesus does a deed and gives a command that will bind them to him in a continually renewed and deepened participation in the mystery of his own being. His life, his cruel death, his resurrection will not only be a story to be proclaimed, recorded, studied: they will be something to be lived. The disciples will thus themselves become part of the revealed secret of the presence of the kingdom."[67]

At the same time we cannot talk about the fuller *missio Cristi*, without talking about the death and resurrection of the Lord Jesus Christ. On the one hand, the death and resurrection of Jesus are the culmination of Jesus'

---

63. J. Dupont, *The Salvation of the Gentiles: Essays on the Acts of the Apostles* (New York: Paulist Press, 1979), 22.

64. D. Senior and C. Stuhlmueller, *The Biblical Foundations for Missions* (Maryknoll, NY: Orbis Books, 1983), 261.

65. P. Hertig, "The Jubilee Mission of Jesus in the Gospel of Luke: Reversals of Fortunes in Missiology," *International Review* XXVI, no. 2 (1998): 174.

66. Peskett and Ramachandra, *The Message of Mission*, 165.

67. Newbigin, *The Open Secret*, 46.

kingdom mission. On the other, the kingdom mission of the church could not begin until Jesus had defeated the powers that opposed the reign of God. Together, the death and resurrection of Jesus stand at the center of redemptive history, a crucial point of cosmic history, and the turning point in history. "Mission does not come to an end with the death of the Son but takes on a new quality through the resurrection."[68] While Christ's death reveals God's judgment on the entire sinful creation, Christ's resurrection reveals God's love and intention to renew the entire creation.

In the death and resurrection of Jesus Christ, God has acted to reveal and accomplish his end-time purposes for all of history. In the cross and resurrection God has revealed the end of history. God has made his purposes known in many different events. The Christ event is the central place where his purposes for history have been revealed. In the death of Christ, God's judgment on sin has been made known.

This identification and separation at the cross actually accomplishs the redemption of the world, because at the cross Jesus exposes and destroys the world's sin. The cross reveals God's rejection of the world as corrupted and polluted by sin; but the cross is also an act that accomplishes God's judgment on sin.

Finally, I can make a few conclusions. First, the mission of Jesus was carried out in the power of the Holy Spirit. The Spirit was a gift promised by the prophets for the last days. The intertestamental period was a long period of waiting and hoping when the Spirit was not yet given. John appeared in this context of expectation announcing that the kingdom of God was at hand. This announcement was accompanied by a vivid and expressive prophetic action – baptism. Jesus identified himself with the people who came as sinners to receive the baptism of repentance and forgiveness. "That is the way of the *missio Dei*. Jesus, the first missionary, came to people like that. The way of the *missio Jesu* is also the way of the *missio hominum*. Their characteristics are the sensitivity of a lover, inwardly preparing to meet the other, and seeking and accompanying this special person with loving eyes."[69]

---

68. Sundermeier, "Missio Dei Today," 562.
69. Ibid., 563.

As for the second aspect of Jesus' ministry, Jesus made the kingdom of God known in his *life, words*, and *deeds*. He embodied the life of the kingdom in his entire existence; he displayed the power of the kingdom with his deeds; he announced the presence of the kingdom with his words.

Third, Jesus' kingdom mission was carried out in weakness and suffering. He served the weak and suffering people, who recognized their need in him. He is close to the poor, not separating spiritual poverty from material. The Old Testament pictured the Messiah with a number of images: military hero, wise ruler, son of David. But it also pictured the Messiah with the mysterious image of a suffering servant. Jesus ushers in the kingdom by way of the cross. People, similarly, are not forced to recognize the kingdom, because "Jesus said that his disciples are not his slaves, but his friends. So, his mission is to be a Friend to people, to make them friends with God, as it was with Moses (Exod 33:11). Friendship implies freedom."[70]

So, Jesus Christ is with his followers now. "Jesus accomplished his unique part in *missio Dei*, but God's mission is not yet completed. God is still at work in every nation of the world as initiator and perpetrator of God's mission of salvation, healing, liberation, and reconciliation."[71] The Holy Spirit was sent to the earth, and then the church was sent to the world.

Mission of the Spirit

In trying to determine God's continuing mission on earth it is important to pay attention to the third Person of the Trinity – the Holy Spirit. What is the mission of the Spirit? How can the definition of the Spirit's mission help us to understand the holistic concept of the mission of God? After the birth of the Son, the coming of the Spirit is second in importance to the acts of God in his descent to earth. "In their different ways, Christmas and Pentecost both celebrate the coming of God to become part of human history; to be involved in it."[72]

I can say with confidence that on the one hand, the work of the Holy Spirit is much talked about in the New Testament, yet on the other hand,

---

70. Ibid., 564.
71. George, *Called as Partners*, 6.
72. Niles, *Upon the Earth*, 66.

the Holy Spirit remains one of the most mysterious Persons of the Divine Trinity. At the same time I agree with A. Glasser, when he said: "We do not want to limit the Holy Spirit only to the work of awakening faith (justification) and to the work of perfecting faith (sanctification). The Spirit must primarily be seen as the driving force behind any and all movements of the people of God outward, beyond the frontiers of faith, to share the gospel with those who had not yet heard it. Mission means movement from Christ by his Spirit to the world he reconciled."[73]

"It is thus by an action of the sovereign Spirit of God that the church is launched on its mission. It remains the mission of the Spirit. He is central."[74] I agree with the centrality of the Holy Spirit in the epoch after the day of Pentecost. It is a great privilege, joy and hope that the Triune God presents among believers today, because the Holy Spirit was given to the believers as a deposit. Newbigin wrote: "(2 Cor 1:22; Eph 1:14) – the word used in these two passages, *arrabon*, is a commercial word denoting a cash deposit paid as a pledge of the full amount to be paid later. The disciples are not promised the full victory of God's kingdom now; they are promised immediately the *arrabon* – the advance installment that will make them the living evidences of the reality that is promised. The real presence of God's own life lived in their common life will be the evidence, the witness to all the nations, that the full reality of God's victorious reign is on the way. What is given here is not a command, but a promise. The presence of the Spirit will make them witnesses."[75]

In our search to define the mission of the Spirit let us look at A. Fernando's classification determining the sources of information on the work of the Spirit: "We could say that the Gospels focus on the promise of the Spirit, Acts on the power of the Spirit in mission, and the Epistles of Paul on the life in the Spirit."[76] S. Escobar thinks that theologians and Bible

---

73. Glasser et al., *Announcing the Kingdom*, 263.
74. Newbigin, *The Open Secret*, 58.
75. Ibid.
76. A. Fernando, "The Holy Spirit: the Divine Implementer of Mission," in *Global Missiology for the 21st Century: The Iguassu Dialogue*, ed. W. D. Taylor (Grand Rapids: Baker, 2000), 223.

scholars have rediscovered the important role the Holy Spirit plays in not only the Pauline epistles but also the Gospels, especially Luke and Acts.[77]

According to my readings of the Bible I see four aspects of mission of the Holy Spirit:

First of all, it is important to mention his work in the Old Testament. The Holy Spirit was very active in creation: "The Creator Spirit works from the inside of the processes not only by startling his creatures into awareness and recognition and luring them towards ever higher degrees of consciousness and personhood, but also by creating the necessity for choice in one situation after another. And the choice arises always from the contrast between the actual and the potential."[78] The Holy Spirit worked through the judges (Judg 3:10; 6:34; 11:29; 14:19), prophets (1 Sam 10:10; 2 Sam 23:2; Ezek 3:27; 11:5), priests (Num 11:17; Mic 3:8). It is interesting that we find term the "Holy" applied to the Spirit only in New Testament. The Old Testament named him the Spirit of God, or the Lord's Spirit. Even in Genesis we read that "the Spirit of God was hovering over the waters" (Gen 1:2). We cannot be sure of the Holy Spirit's ministry in the redemptive work of God in the Old Testament, but work in creation of the universe and God's nation is very clear. Again we see the holistic concept, but this time in the Spirit's mission. "It is in keeping with classic Trinitarian theology to say that the works of the Trinity towards the outside, ad extra, cannot be divided. It is therefore not correct to say that God the Father is at work in the whole of creation, while the work of the Son and the Spirit are limited to the church. Both the Son and the Spirit are also active in creation and in the world."[79]

Second, the Holy Spirit was very active in Jesus' ministry. From the very beginning we read that Mary "was found to be with child thorough the Holy Spirit" (Matt 1:18), that "Elizabeth was filled with the Holy Spirit" (Luke 1:41), that "Jesus was led by the Spirit into the desert to be tempted by the devil" (Matt 4:1), and so on. "Beginning with the birth of Jesus, his life and ministry are possible only by a creative and powerful action of the Spirit (Luke 1:35). Luke emphasizes that the Holy Spirit was working in

---

77. Escobar, *A Time for Mission*, 113.
78. Taylor, *The Go-Between God*, 33.
79. Engelsviken, "Missio Dei," 491.

the midst of history, through the ministry of Jesus, in order to accomplish God's purpose."[80]

I mentioned that even in Luke 4 Jesus "returned to Galilee in the power of the Spirit" (Luke 4:14), and he announced, "the Spirit of the Lord is on me" (Luke 4:18).

> Where Jesus Christ is, the year of jubilee, of grace, has become reality. This corresponds to my reading of Luke 4. However, I would develop this idea by asking whether in Lukan theology we should not say that the Spirit is the jubilee power. It is the Spirit who inspires Jesus in his sermon in Nazareth, and also the Spirit who at Pentecost enables the ideal community of Acts 2 and 4 to share all resources. This could lead us toward a renewed missiological pneumatology, according to which the following consequences of the Spirit's presence could be listed: * the experience of God's presence and the joy of salvation; * the capacity to discern Christ in the Bible, church tradition and the world; * the power to heal physical, psychological or spiritual wounds; * the courage to share resources."[81]

It is a very daring but challenging suggestion to proclaim the jubilee as an epoch of the Holy Spirit in the context of Luke 4. It will be a real "renewed missiological pneumatology," and it may be that Pentecostal and Charismatic movements try to rethink their missiology in that way, but for Protestants and many Baptists it is a real challenge.

Third, the birth of the church on the great day of Pentecost was the result of the Holy Spirit's mission. Much more, the Holy Spirit remains the Sustainer of the church, distributing the spiritual gifts (1 Cor 12:11), causing spiritual fruit (Gal 5:22–23); the Spirit is responsible for the application of divine truths (John 16:12–13), communicating to human hearts the divine truths in a way that humans will understand (John 14:17; 15:26; 17:17).

The Spirit is called the Advocate and the Comforter, which means he gets to know the needs of God's children; he knows what has to be taught

---

80. Escobar, *A Time for Mission*, 121.
81. Matthey, "God's Mission Today," 585–586.

to each and every human being at each time. "The Holy Spirit directs the campaign in which the Christian is a participant, so that without him the Christian life simply becomes a religious exercise."[82] God does not cease to participate in the missionary enterprise with the sending of Jesus. He does not initiate mission with the sending of Jesus and then leave the missionary work to be carried on by a human institution that followed the pattern of Christ with the help of the Spirit.

The Holy Spirit gives the teachers gifts to explain the truths written down in the Bible. He makes believers, who have basic knowledge of Jesus Christ, to be able to stand against false teachings. He motivates people to study the Scriptures in order to draw the truths from them and to communicate these truths to other people.

Fourth, the Holy Spirit is very active in the world. John wrote: "When he comes, he will convict the world of guilt in regard to sin and righteousness and judgment: in regard to sin, because men do not believe in me; in regard to righteousness, because I am going to the Father, where you can see me no longer; and in regard to judgment, because the prince of this world now stands condemned" (John 16:8–11). So, the Holy Spirit works among nations, using sometimes unknowing and unintelligible methods for people. "First, the Spirit is active in the whole created world . . . Second, the Spirit is experienced in human cultures . . . Third, the Spirit is at work in social movements. Fourth, the Spirit may be recognized in a world of many faiths. Fifth, the Spirit is present in reconciled diversity."[83]

Somehow, he bears the truth until the end of the earth, through cultural symbols, ancient stories, hope and so on. There are many stories in mission history, when missionaries were faced with very interesting phenomena – people were ready to hear the gospel, and nobody could explain how they had received readiness. It has something in common with the Conciliar Mission Theology of the 1970s, but the difference is very important. His part of *missio Dei* is to convict the world of guilt in regard to sin, because men do not believe in Christ. He prepares nations for acceptance of the good news. "The Holy Spirit is the invisible third party who stands

---

82. Niles, *Upon the Earth*, 64.
83. Kim, "The Potential of Pneumatology," 336–337.

between me and the other, making us mutually aware. Supremely and primarily he opens my eyes to Christ. But he also opens my eyes to the brother in Christ, or the fellow-man, or the point of need . . . He is the giver of that vision."[84] He convicts human beings of their sin. He gives the second birth. He causes new believers to grow and gives them spiritual gifts.

Conclusions

I have been defining the *missio Dei* concept that could be the *lingua franca* for Evangelicals and Orthodox in Moldova for their search for common mission, and I talked especially about the Trinitarian foundation for mission. I think that Evangelicals can be taught by Orthodox theologians in that area. Orthodoxy has much more to say about the energies of God, which from their perspective show the inner life of God, which flows outside from God. At the same time I explained that WCC missiologists and theologians were very active in formulating functional explanations for God's mission, based on the biblical texts.

I would like to mention a few important conclusions from this chapter:

1) *Missio Dei* can be defined only in Trinitarian terms.
2) God the Father is constantly active in mission, sending his Son and the Holy Spirit to achieve his purposes with humankind and the whole universe.
3) God the Son came not only to proclaim that the kingdom has come. His mission was holistic: he brought redemption and salvation from eternal death and at the same time he came to the poor and oppressed to liberate them from all kinds of oppression and injustice. The culmination of his mission was his death and resurrection, but he was always among people, answering their daily needs as well as their deeper emotional, social, spiritual and existential needs.
4) God the Holy Spirit continues the mission of God the Father and God the Son, being very active in the ministry of prophets of the Old Testament, in the life of Jesus, in church activity and in the world, where he is present in a mysterious way.

---

84. Taylor, *The Go-Between God*, 19.

5) The church should be very attentive to what she sees in the world and in the midst of herself, discovering the signs of the Holy Spirit.

A Trinitarian foundation lies at the very basic level of shaping and articulating a new paradigm for Moldavian churches. For many years the doctrine of Trinity was used by Christian ministers in Moldova only in a scholastic way with an apologetics goal, as a field for conversation and debates with other religious groups (such as Jehovah's Witnesses), but it was not put as a foundation for mission or daily Christian life. The mission of Moldavian Evangelicals in the past was very Christocentric in terms of proclamation of his death and resurrection, and it brought some tension with Orthodoxy.

Having in mind that God is not only God the Son in daily mission and in shaping of missiology, I hope that this new outlook will bring some positive results for possible dialogue and common witness.

CHAPTER 8

Analytical and Synthetic Evaluation of the Missiological Paradigms

In chapters 4, 5 and 6 I have examined different missiological paradigms, which in practice have been reflected in particular missionary approaches. The seventh chapter revealed the meaning and content of Trinitarian theology, which lays at the base of many missiological concepts, and in particular the *missio Dei*.

The eighth chapter aims to conduct a comparative analysis of the above mentioned approaches of the Evangelical and Protestant churches identifying them with the mission of the Orthodox Church. On these grounds, I will emphasize effective methods of missionary work. The ninth chapter will focus on a particular missionary paradigm.

First of all, I am going to pay attention to the differences existing between Evangelical and Orthodox missiology. Second, I am trying to find the similarities between them and at the end of the chapter, on a theological basis, I will formulate a coherent, synthetic missiology of the church as the body of Christ located in a predominantly Orthodox country. The comparative analysis is to be carried out methodologically on the basis of the Orthodox understanding of mission compared to the managerial, post-imperial, Anabaptist and ecumenical missiologies.

Distinctions and Similarities in Different Missiologies

From the first view it looks as if there are more distinctions than similarities in these two understands of missiology, but this is not true. It will be shown that there are a lot of common points which could play a key role for further conversation. At the same time we do not want to close our eyes to the reality of tensions and I will analyze the reasons for them. Every time we compare Orthodox missiology with one from the studied missiological schools, we will invite other partners to this dialogue, critically evaluating our remarks and conclusions from different perspectives.

Orthodox Missiology *vis-à-vis* the Church Growth Movement

The Church Growth Movement was one of those movements launched in a country with so-called liberal-democratic values – the USA. The freedoms of speech and religion have been highly appreciated there since the founding day of that country. The United States was populated by immigrants representing different religious groups and confessions (beginning with the seventeenth century up to the 1980s those were mostly Christians). The CGM was born in the very depths of American individualism and was immediately accepted by much of the middle class. As a result, the emphasis was put on individual decisions, as outlined in chapter 4. Every person decides on their religious beliefs and the denomination or the church which could satisfy their spiritual hunger. Quite differently, the Orthodox Church, which has been for centuries shaping the world outlook of the majority of Eastern European inhabitants, places emphases on community.

The CGM especially emphasizes the salvation of the human soul, and for this reason, all good works of charity, and even more social projects are related to an individual decision. A person may carry out charity work or may not, but this does not define the degree of his spirituality or maturity. Money is required not for charity in the first place but for the achievement of evangelistic projects, short- and long-term missionary trips and foundation of new churches. The Orthodox Church cannot accept such an approach, since there is salvation not only of the human soul, but of the human being as a whole, of mankind, of all creation. The charity works are an indication of spiritual maturity and sincere faith.

The purpose of the CGM mission is the enrollment of followers ready to plant new churches, which will become independent and self-governed. In contrast to the Orthodox Church, the unity issue is discussed only at the level of individual congregations. In all other aspects each individual community has every right to self-determination and to choose its own path of development. Most churches and denominations that follow this missionary paradigm are not part of the ecumenical movement, do not consider it necessary to participate in joint projects, and regard cautiously (and sometimes aggressively) people of other faiths.

The indicator of a mission's effectiveness is the number of new communities and followers. The Orthodox Church does not count the people coming to worship, and the ultimate goal of its mission is the *theosis*, deification of human beings, when people can become as God. As Valentin Kozhuharov states: "The ultimate goal of mission is again formulated thus: mission aims at fulfilling God's primordial provision – *theosis* of man and of all creation."[1] Such a mission starts during the life of a single person as well as of a people in general, and continues after people's death through the prayers of the people remaining on earth.

The starting point of the missionary activity of the church from the point of view of the CGM is the spiritual gifts and the apostolic example of St Paul, while the Orthodox Church has been viewing for many centuries God the Father as leading Sender, and the Son and the Spirit as envoys. Based on the foregoing, it may give the impression that they do not have any common ground. In fact, there are a few things that can be defined in both positions.

The first, as well as the second, concept accentuate the central role of Jesus Christ in the church's activity, the salvation of human beings and mission. In addition, in both cases there may be noted the role of the local community. People are invited to attend the church and from there they are sent into the world to serve. Serving refers to different concepts, as already mentioned, but the role of community involvement is extremely high in the formation of a Christian.

Orthodox Missiology *vis-à-vis* the Lausanne Movement

The so-called post-imperial paradigm took shape at the time when many former colonies had recently obtained their independence (the 1960s and

---

1. V. Kozhuharov, "Developments in the Mission of the Russian Orthodox Church," *Acta Missiologiae, Journal for reflection on missiological issues and mission practices in Central and Eastern Europe* 2 (2009): 21.

1970s). Accordingly, this had a big impact not only on the political world, but also on the religious world. The voice of the Third World countries (as they used to be called) began to be heard. It was speaking about the poverty and injustice prevailing there, the oppression and famine, war and disease. It was saying that the church should not engage in evangelism while nearby thousands of children were dying and their deaths could be prevented. Nevertheless, one of the Lausanne Movement's goals was the evangelization of the whole world (see ch. 4). Unlike the CGM, the social responsibility not only of individual Christians, but also of the local communities, denominations and interdenominational organizations began to play an important role in the mission of the church. "Evangelical theology of mission today encompasses more than just evangelistic proclamation, but includes also much of what traditionally would have been called 'good works' or the 'social gospel.' This touches on what is perhaps the most difficult topic to work through, the relationship between mission and evangelism."[2]

The Evangelical missiologists themselves, echoing the World Council of Churches, called their own approach holistic, which largely overlapped with the standpoint of Orthodoxy. Though Lausanne was not talking about the salvation of the whole creation, the dualistic worldview was receding into the past. People were spoken of as holistic personalities without functionally separating the body, mind and soul. Despite the use of similar terminology, Orthodoxy means something different when speaking about the integrity of salvation. As mentioned above, integrity means continuity of people concerning their culture, land, and ancestral heritage. A person is seen as an indivisible part of an indivisible whole. On the other hand, the Lausanne Movement, speaking of integrity, called the church to pay attention not only to the spiritual, but also to the physical needs of people in this case, increasingly giving preference to the spiritual needs and namely to the need of hearing the good news. As mentioned at the ACUTE meeting in 2001: "Evangelicals see themselves as people with good news for the world."[3]

---

2. D. Hilborn, *Evangelicalism and the Orthodox Church. A Report by the Evangelical Alliance (UK) Commission on the Unity and Truth among Evangelicals (ACUTE)*, ed. Tim Grass (London: ACUTE, 2001), 136.

3. Ibid., 7.

In addition, it should be noted that one of the main features of this approach is individualism. The attention paid to a single person exceeds the attention paid to the people and society as a whole. The difference in the degree of attention does not mean its absence. The Lausanne Movement began paying attention increasingly to the restoration of justice in those countries where human rights were violated, corruption flourished and the government was dealing openly with the underworld. Given the degree of influence and the large number of partisans of this movement, some successful results have been achieved in recent years.[4] Its impact on the world community is quite comparable with that of the Orthodox Church on the modern Russian leadership or the Bulgarian authorities. The European Union should also listen to the voice of the Orthodox Church: "It is important that the Orthodox actively participate now in the dialogue with European political structures, at a time when the identity of the New Europe is still in the process of formation and when legislation which will define the face of the European Union is being created. It is also important to prevent the monopoly of one worldview which might dictate its conditions to all residents of the EU, including those belonging to traditional religious confessions."[5]

Even if this involvement has different theological backgrounds, it should be emphasized that there is a certain similarity between the Lausanne Movement and the Orthodox Church. Almost from the very beginning the missiologists and theologians participating in the Lausanne dialogue were developing Trinitarian theology as the foundation for the church's mission. Although the Orthodox understanding of *periehoresis* uses a completely different methodology to explain the relationship within the Trinity, the similarity lies in the fact that the doctrine of the Trinity is not valuable just from the apologetic point of view, but serves as real basis for the life and the ministry of the church.

---

4. I am acquainted with Jennifer Roemhildt-Tunehag, who is an international consultant on human trafficking within the Lausanne Movement and the World Evangelical Alliance, and one of the coordinators of the European Freedom Network. The activists of this network are lobbying laws with the Euro Parliament to represent the interests of victims of trafficking in international courts. They also conduct active awareness campaigns.

5. Hilarion, Bishop of Vienna and Austria, "Orthodoxy in a New Europe: Problems and Perspectives," *Religion in Eastern Europe* XXIV, no. 3 (June 2004): 24.

Another distinctive feature is the ability to dialogue with the representatives of other denominations and churches. The Lausanne Movement itself is a movement, where participants represent many evangelical traditions. As stated in the Manila Manifesto in 1989:

> Our reference to "the whole church" is not a presumptuous claim. The universal church and the evangelical community are synonymous. For we recognize, that there are many churches which are not part of the evangelical movement. Evangelical attitude to the Roman Catholic and Orthodox Churches differ widely. Some evangelicals are praying, talking, studying Scripture and working with these churches. Others are strongly opposed to any form of dialogue or cooperation with them. All are aware that serious theological differences between us remain. Where appropriate, and so long as biblical truth is not compromised, cooperation may be possible in such areas as Bible translation, the study of contemporary theological and ethics issues, social work and political action, we wish to make it clear, however, that common evangelism demands a common commitment to the biblical gospel.[6]
>
> Evangelicals value unity and fellowship among Christians for more effective witness of the gospel and to foster interpersonal relationships of common faith, trust, and prayer, rather, than relying on organizational or hierarchical structures.[7]

At the same time, open theological discussions are held with Orthodox theologians in order to carry out joint evangelistic work. Some churches, supporting the Lausanne Movement, are at the same time part of the World Council of Churches and of other ecumenical organizations.

Although it looks like there are more differences than similarities, it does not mean that further dialogue is impossible. Conversation should go forward, but taking in consideration that the Lausanne Movement is not

---

6. F. A. Oborji, *Concepts of Mission: The Evolution of the Contemporary Missiology* (Maryknoll, NY: Orbis Books, 2006), 170.

7. F. A. Oborji, "Mission as Ecumenical Dialogue," in *Concepts of Mission: The Evolution of the Contemporary Missiology*, ed. F. A. Oborji (Maryknoll, NY: Orbis Books, 2006), 168.

well known in Moldova, it might be that Moldavian Evangelicals can find another platform for fruitful discussion with the Orthodox.

Orthodox Missiology *vis-à-vis* the Anabaptist Movement

In comparison with the previous two approaches, that of the Anabaptists is seen favorably in the eyes of the Orthodox, as strange as it may seem. Modern Anabaptism, as well as Orthodoxy, does not use the term "evangelism," or the meaning behind it. Both prefer to use the word witness, speaking of the spread of the good news to the world. Both of them pay special attention to witness by their way of life, as opposed to active evangelism, which follows the two previous approaches. Witness as a daily living example, as mentioned in chapters 1 and 4. As a result, the churches adhering to the Anabaptist approaches to mission are not growing as fast as the churches adhering to the CGM. Although it is interesting to mention that Anabaptists do not try to determine the degree of their effectiveness by quantitative growth. In this they are also similar to the Orthodox. Efficiency is determined by the degree of people's obedience to God (for both of them).

Mission is based on Trinitarian theology, and the vision is theocentric, while not all contemporary theologians are investing the same meaning into this concept. Anabaptist theologians do not aim to describe the ontological relationship between the three persons of the Trinity, as did the church fathers and the Orthodox theologians of the nineteenth and twentieth centuries. Anabaptists, as mentioned above, stepped into the existing dialogue on this subject enriching it with good deeds and charity. Most Anabaptists believe in the significant role of good works in the rescue process. This is their particular resemblance to Orthodoxy, which has a similar concept about synergetic work with God. Despite the fact that repentance has a beginning, it does not end in this life on earth. The whole of human life is a process of rethinking the relationship with God and with people. This does not diminish or depreciate the role of Jesus Christ and that of his sacrifice on Calvary. Both Anabaptists and Orthodox argue that salvation is possible only through faith, and faith is the starting point of Christian life. But the future life consolidates and confirms the chosen path.

It is also necessary to note the role of the community and the church. For Anabaptists ethics ("spirituality" in Orthodox language) is not the personal choice of every individual, but is the responsibility of the entire community.

Anabaptist communities, unlike all of the above mentioned, pay special attention to the role of the community in the education of each believer. It may seem that in Eastern Europe this is the consequence of the Soviet era when people were also educated collectively. But the Mennonites in Germany, the USA, and Canada still use the same methods. "The aim of the meeting of the church members, for instance, is to find together the mind of Christ who is present in the midst of his church, and to use the Scriptures to help us in this search for his purpose in our world today."[8] People in the community have a relatively close relationship, and collectively help each other in following Christ and in compliance with the rules of conduct and the standards of the church. "From their earliest days, Baptists did not insist on the 'independence' of the local church, but rather the direct dependence of the local church on the authority of Christ . . . But on the other hand, because the aim of the local church members was to discover Christ's purpose for them, they gladly affirmed that they needed the counsel and insight of other Christian congregations who made up the one Body of Christ, and with whom they lived in covenant relationship."[9]

Though the majority of Orthodox parishes in Eastern Europe rarely practice the same forms of education and discipline as Anabaptists, group thinking clearly dominates individual choice (which was emphasized in chapter 3 about proselytism and canonical territory). Anabaptists also have their own vision of the concept of *missio Dei*. Shenk supposes that Jesus' self-understanding issued directly from the *missio Dei*.[10]

When thinking about the differences, one of the most difficult issues is to understand the unity of the church. Anabaptists, as well as representatives of the Church Growth Movement, stress the unity of Christians of one and the same community and faith although they are making their first steps in theological debates, initiating dialogues with the ecumenical community, the Lausanne Movement, and the Orthodox Church. The

---

8. Ibid., 16.

9. Ibid., 17.

10. W. Shenk, "Crossing Frontiers," in *Anabaptism and Mission*, eds. W. Shenk and P. Penner (Schwarzenfeld: Neufeld Verlag, 2007), 26.

issue of the unity of the church is not key in the mission of these groups as it is for the Orthodox Church. Nevertheless, in recent times, believers deny "aggressive evangelism" and proselytism. "If Baptist evangelists try to proselytise among active members of other Christian churches for the purpose of increasing the numbers of the Baptist denomination, they fail to fulfill their calling."[11]

Orthodox Missiology *vis-à-vis* the Ecumenical Movement

Naturally, speaking about the development of the ecumenical missiological paradigm, the development of the concept of *missio Dei* should be noted first of all, which appeared and developed mainly within WCC circles.

Briefly I am going to summarize the main points.

Missio Dei means a Trinitarian basis for mission. The Trinitarian understanding, as well as the mission of Orthodoxy, is not just a scholastic exercise. The Trinity is the initiator of the mission, embodies the mission, and supports the mission.

> A Trinitarian approach to the *missio Dei* is therefore important. On the one hand, this promotes a more inclusive understanding of God's presence and work in the whole world and among all people, implying that signs of God's presence can and should be identified, affirmed and worked with even in the most unexpected places. On the other hand, by clearly affirming that the Father and the Spirit are always and in all circumstances present and working together with the Word, the temptation to separate the presence of God or the Spirit from the Son of God, Jesus Christ, will be avoided.[12]

It is very difficult to talk uniquely about the development of the ecumenical missionary paradigm in comparison with the Orthodox missionary

---

11. E. Geldbach, "Religious Liberty, Proselytism, Evangelism: Some Baptists Considerations," in *Baptist Faith & Witness. Book Two. The papers of the Study and Research Division of the Baptist World Alliance 1995-2000*, ed. T. Cupit (McLean: Baptist World Alliance, 1999), 28.

12. World Council of Churches, "Mission and Evangelism in Unity Today" (2000), point 12, in *"You are the Light of the World" (Matthew 5:14): Statements on Mission by the World Council of Churches 1980-2005* (Geneva, Switzerland: WCC Publications, 2005). World Council of Churches, *Mission and Evangelism: An Ecumenical Affirmation* (Geneva, Switzerland: WCC, 1982), 65.

paradigm, since the Orthodox Church almost from the very beginning has been actively involved in the World Council of Churches and other ecumenical organizations. Indisputably, Orthodox theology influenced the formation of the Trinitarian foundation of the WCC mission. Therefore, in this regard, the ecumenical paradigm is most similar to Orthodoxy in comparison with the approaches studied above. As a result of the Trinitarian theology and holistic approach, service to the poor is widely practiced as one of the fundamental principles of the kingdom: "To believe in Jesus the King is to accept his undeserved grace and enter with him into the kingdom, taking sides with the poor struggling to overcome poverty. Both those who announce Jesus as the servant king and those who accept this announcement and respond to it are invited to enter with him daily in identification and participation with the poor of the earth."[13] Further, "the evangelistic witness will also speak to the structures of this world; its economic, political and societal institutions . . . We must re-learn the patristic lesson that the church is the mouth and voice of the poor and the oppressed in the presence of the powers that be."[14]

Based on Trinitarian theology, the ecumenical paradigm is also holistic. "Mission carries a holistic understanding: the proclamation and sharing of the good news of the gospel by word (*kerygma*), deed (*diakonia*), prayer and worship (*leiturgia*) and the everyday witness of the Christian life (*martyria*); teaching as building up and strengthening people in their relationship with God and each other; and healing as wholeness and reconciliation into *koinonia* – communion with God, communion with people, and communion with creation as a whole."[15]

The emphasis is laid on the principles of the kingdom, rather than on the values of specific local communities. The ecumenical movement inspires local communities to consider not only their own interests, but also primarily those of the whole church and those of their partners. In this regard, we see that the ecumenical paradigm is more kenotic, than others. As Cathy Ross says: "It is difficult to have a truly mutual relationship when the two parties possess unequal power. But that is the reality of our

---

13. World Council of Churches, *Mission and Evangelism*, point 7, 9.
14. Ibid., 14.
15. Ibid., 63–64.

world today... The model of the incarnation can help us. We can let go of our pride and power, our privilege and sense of entitlement, insofar as we empty ourselves following Christ's way depicted in Philippians 2."[16]

The unity issue is significant for the ecumenical movement. As written in the 1982 document, article 1: "The present ecumenical movement came into being out of the conviction of the churches that the division of Christians is a scandal and an impediment to the witness of the church."[17] It compels attention. Unity, in this case, is viewed from the Orthodox perspective, which means unity in receiving the Eucharist. "On the one hand, the Eastern tradition has stated clearly that the broken unity in faith is not a simple matter of theological diversity but something that touches the common confession of faith. On the other hand, the common reception of the apostolic faith is fundamental in relation to the sacramental and Eucharistic communion."[18] Further, "the 'undivided church' is sometimes affirmed in a way that suggests that it is a peculiar model which never existed in history. But the position is stated clearly: unity means the overcoming and the realization of communion in the unique church of Christ, which is not an abstract reality."[19]

At the same time, the WCC and the CEC are directing their efforts at softening the attitude of the Orthodox Church towards Evangelical and Protestant churches, calling first of all, to joint missions and after that to full unity with regards to Eucharist. "Authentic common witness presupposes respect and understanding for other traditions and confessions."[20]

This is the significant difference between most of the participants of the ecumenical movement and the Orthodox Church. Orthodoxy sees the achievement of unity as a starting point for mission. Unity, in this case,

---

16. C. Ross, "The Theology of Partnership," *International Bulletin of Missionary Research* 34, no. 3 (July 2010): 148.

17. World Council of Churches, *Mission and Evangelism*, 5.

18. I. Bria, *The Sense of Ecumenical Tradition: The Ecumenical Witness and Vision of the Orthodox* (Geneva: WCC Publications, 1991), 37.

19. Ibid., 50.

20. World Council of Churches, "Towards Common Witness: A Call to Adopt Responsible Relationships in Mission and to Renounce Proselytism (September 1997)," point 2, in *"You are the Light of the World" (Matthew 5:14). Statements on Mission by the World Council of Churches 1980-2005* (Geneva: WCC Publications, 2005), 47.

means unity of teachings. "Full Eucharistic communion will not be possible until full unity of faith is achieved."[21] Further:

> In terms of the prerequisites for Eucharistic communion, the practical principles are these: (1) Unity of faith, unity in the doctrine of the undivided church, does not prevent the diversity of legitimate liturgical traditions and Eucharistic rites according to churches, cultures and places. Dogmatic imprecisions and canonical disputes which obstruct reciprocal recognition must be the focus for theological dialogue before a unanimous consensus can be reached. (2) Where there is disagreement of the essentials of the faith, there can be no communion in sacraments. The faithful must confess the same faith before sharing the same table and cup. This point can be traced back to the apostolic church, in which fraternal reconciliation was indispensable before bringing gifts to the altar. (3) Ecclesial *oikonomia* intervenes where the church sees its mission and action for the salvation of persons as requiring an immediate entry point.[22]

Moreover, the Orthodox representatives have reiterated on many occasions that Orthodoxy is not ready to make concessions regarding its doctrine[23] as it was inherited from the church fathers and for this reason it is expected that other churches will compromise, or in other words, those fallen away from the truth will return to the bosom of mother church. With regard to the ecumenical movement, the starting point is joint participation in the mission of the church, and in the process of joint serving believers are invited to continue theological discussions. "The unity we look for is not uniformity but the multiple expression of a common faith and a common mission."[24] "The Trinity, the source and image of our existence,

---

21. Bria, *Sense of Ecumenical Tradition*, 56–58.
22. Ibid.
23. "The Orthodox are confronted with the dominant Reformation understanding that the New Testament itself witnesses to a great variety of apostolic responses to the gospel, so that many different points of view can claim biblical sanction", said Bria in *Sense of Ecumenical Tradition*, 53.
24. World Council of Churches, *Mission and Evangelism*, point 27, 19.

shows the importance of diversity, otherness and intrinsic relationships in constituting communities."[25]

Orthodox missiologists are also members of the WCC work groups. They agree that, "Unity in plurality or diversity is nothing new, from the Orthodox viewpoint. The church has existed legitimately and meaningfully in this way since early in its first millennium – in diversity amongst local churches and diversity in the autonomous administration of the regional churches, as affirmed by the ecumenical councils in which all churches took part; hence the later eastern and western patriarchates."[26]

Even from the context of this statement it is clear that one and the same concepts are interpreted differently, and that in this case, the Orthodox mean the differences existing for centuries between the autocephalous Orthodox churches. The ecumenical circles believe that proselytizing obviously harms the witness and proclamation of the good news. "Christian witness is constructive: it enriches, challenges, strengthens and builds up solid Christian relationships and fellowship . . . Proselytism is a perversion of authentic Christian witness and thus a counter witness."[27]

I will make an attempt to summarize this in the following words: for Orthodoxy, unity is ontological tending to functional unity while for the ecumenical movement the functional unity may lead to the ontological.

In this sense, the results of Stefan Tolber's research carried out in the "Ecumenism" course taught in the theological schools of Romania are of great interest: "All Orthodox theological faculties (in Romania) have 'Missiology and Ecumenism' among the compulsory subjects."[28] Further, "the Baptists in Oradea and Bucharest have no subject named 'Ecumenism.'"[29]

---

25. Ibid., 75.

26. G. Larentzakis, "We believe in 'One Holy Catholic and Apostolic Church'," in *Charta Oecumenica: A Text, a Process and a Dream of the Churches in Europe*, eds. V. Ionita and S. Numico (Geneva: WCC Publications, 2003), 54.

27. World Council of Churches, "Towards Common Witness," point 2, 50–51.

28. S. Tobler, "The Ecumenical Situation in Romania and the Ecumenical Research Institute in Sibiu," in *The Future of Ecumenical Theological Education in Eastern and Central Europe: Full report of the International Seminar for young lectures and professors of theology, Sambata de Sus, Romania, 24-28 September 2008*, eds. V. Ionita and D. Werner (Geneva: Conference of European Churches, World Council of Churches, 2009), 44.

29. Ibid., 45.

Regarding the community's role in individual decision making, in ecumenical circles it is very difficult to draw an unambiguous conclusion on this issue because of the diversity of churches and their constituents. Nevertheless, the WCC notes that people have the right to make their own deliberate choice: "Some people may move from one church to another out of true and genuine conviction, without any proselytistic pressure or manipulation, as a free decision in response to their experience of the life and witness of another church."[30]

In 1997 the following practical recommendations were given:
- make greater efforts to educate their own faithful in local congregations, Sunday schools, training centers and seminaries to respect and love members of other churches as sisters and brothers in Christ;
- actively promote knowledge of the heritage and contributions of other churches that, despite differences, confess the same Jesus Christ as God and Savior, worship the same triune God and are engaged in the same witness in the world;
- promote efforts towards reconciliation by addressing historical wounds and bitter memories;
- initiate (with the assistance of the WCC when necessary) encounter and dialogue at the local, national and regional levels with those engaging in mission work that is perceived as proselytism . . . ;
- seek opportunities for working together with other churches on pastoral and social issues that affect local communities and countries as a whole, and be open to authentic cooperation with others in addressing the needs of the people being served;
- together renounce proselytism as a denial of authentic witness and an obstruction to the unity of the church, and urge support for common witness, unity and understanding among the churches proclaiming the gospel;

---

30. World Council of Churches, "Towards Common Witness," point 2, 50–51.

- continue to pray together for Christian unity, allowing God's Spirit to lead the churches into fuller truth and faithfulness.[31]

Comparative Analysis of All Paradigms

Having studied all the missiological paradigms and compared them to the paradigm of the Orthodox mission, I am going to present the results schematically to make them easier to understand. This data will serve as bases for the ninth chapter in which I will suggest a better approach for the Evangelical churches in Moldova.

---

31. Ibid., 49–50.

	Church Growth Movement	**Lausanne Movement**	**Anabaptist Movement**	**Ecumenical Movement**	**Orthodox Church**
Worldview	Individualistic	Individualistic	Corporate	Divergent	Corporate
Foundation for Mission	Theology of apostle Paul	Trinitarian	Trinitarian	Trinitarian	Trinitarian
Goal of Mission	New disciples and churches	Evangelization of the whole world	Preaching the gospel	Shalom	Theosis
Mission's Approach	Evangelism	Holistic	Witness	Holistic	Holistic, witness
Unity	In particular congregation	Among all Evangelicals	Congregation, confession	Among all Christians	Among all Christians in Orthodox church
Participation in Social Ministry	No	Yes, partly	Yes	Yes	Yes
View on Proselytism	Not important	Sensitive	Sensitive	Very sensitive	Painful
View on Canonical Territory	Absence of this concept	Absence of this concept	Absence of this concept	Dialoguing with Orthodoxy	Strict
Presence of *Missio Dei* Concept	No	Yes	Yes	Yes	Yes, implicitly

It should be noted that all the items were worked out based on the study of biblical texts with the use of various hermeneutical keys. They are all biblical. This is, in my view, a very important observation, since it can prevent attacks against the suggestion of developing a new relevant approach to the missionary work of Evangelical churches in Moldova. None of these paradigms is contrary to the teachings of the gospel. The only issue is their adequacy in modern Moldova. Thus, it is obvious that the CGM approach is the most inadequate in the Orthodox context. It causes the greatest number of controversial issues, conflicts with the Orthodox Church, and creates contentious comments. It has nothing in common with Orthodoxy and on many issues is opposed to the representatives of other evangelical paradigms. The only issue on which the CGM, Lausanne and Anabaptists agree is the issue of canonical territory. All of them reject this idea, and most of the ecumenical missiologists think that this teaching is not relevant in a contemporary, globalized post-modern world. I will talk about that on a deeper level in the last chapter.

Concerning the rest of the approaches, three paradigms have three points out of ten in common with the Orthodox Church: presence of the *missio Dei* concept, participation in social ministry and foundation for mission. They also refer with consideration to the pain the Orthodox Church feels with regard to proselytism. Speaking about the world vision, Anabaptists are closer to the Orthodox than anyone else. As for the goal of mission and the issue of unity, then, the ecumenical paradigm has more in common with the Orthodox Church than all the rest.

The results of this research allow me to offer a new missiological paradigm for the Evangelical churches in Moldova, which will lead to the elaboration of new missionary methods and approaches. To do this I need to generalize the results of the study performed in chapters 1, 2 and 3.

Mission of the Orthodox Church *vis-à-vis* the Mission of ECB in Moldova

First, I would like to highlight the items that are most similar between the Evangelical Church of Moldova and the Orthodox Church in Moldova. In the first place, both of them are followers of theological and ethical conservatism. The ACUTE reports states the common grounds between Evangelicalism and the Orthodox Church:

(i) Doctrinal conservatism. Both Orthodoxy and Evangelicalism are conservative in holding to the apostolic presentation of Jesus Christ and the giving of the Spirit and the birth of the Church in the New Testament. Both hold to the historicity of the apostolic record – to the virginal conception of Jesus in Mary, to his ministry and healings and other miracles, to his bodily resurrection and exaltation and awaited reappearing from heaven at the last day. (ii) Scripture. Understanding this shared set of convictions is a shared high view of Scripture as inspired by God (2 Tim 3:14–17; 2 Pet 1:20–21; see ch. 8). Orthodox do not think in terms of sola Scriptura (which in any case came to sharp expression in the sixteenth-century divide, in which the Eastern churches were not involved), but they regard Scripture as given by inspiration of God. (iii) God. (iv) Eschatology. (v) The Church and its mission. (vi) Christian experience. (vii) Ethics."[32]

They actively oppose the legalization of gay marriage, and try to minimize the number of divorces and abortions piously respecting the texts of the Old and New Testaments. The role of the community is significant in vital decision making, especially in the case of repentance. The Christocentric character of salvation is obvious, although often Evangelical Christians believe that Orthodoxy compromises in this matter. As said in "Orthodox language," "the Orthodox also closely links the universality of the church with the image of Christ as *Pantokrator*, the one who brings eschatology and glorification – *basilea* – into history."[33]

At the same time, an Orthodox theologian, Bradley Nassif, sees four areas, where Evangelicals and Orthodoxy can start their dialogue, because they can find common language:

> **Crucicentrism** – through the life, death, and resurrection of Jesus, God provided a way for the forgiveness of my sins. He shows the following segments from that context: (a) Atonement and justification, where he says that *theosis* and

---

32. Hilborn, *Evangelicalism and the Orthodox Church*, 28–36.
33. Bria, *Sense of Ecumenical Tradition*, 90.

justification by faith (in the evangelical understanding) have the same theological foundation in their roots. (b) Orthodox Trinitarianism. (c) Orthodox Christology. He says that the sacraments of baptism and the Eucharist are ways in which the incarnate Christ communicates his divine life to believers in the church. Cyril's theology of the presence of Christ in the bread and wine is representative of contemporary Orthodox understandings of the Eucharist and takes on significant implications for ecclesiology. It was not a memorial meal in the sense in which most evangelicals today view the Lord's Supper, but an eschatological presence in time and space of the risen, now present, and returning Lord. (d) Christological Maximalism.

Biblicism – the Bible is the inspired Word of God and is to be taken literally, word for word. He sees a very interesting difference between Evangelicals and Orthodox. Orthodox read the Bible, beginning with a personal encounter with Trinity. Evangelicals begin their encounter with the text, where they find information about Christ and Trinity.

Conversionism – I have committed my life to Christ and consider myself to be a converted Christian." He talks about (a) baptism and faith, even if this area is most disputable for both sides, but both see (b) the necessity of baptism in the name of Holy Trinity.

Activism – it is important to encourage non-Christians to become Christians. He concludes his message with a calling to Orthodoxy to learn from Evangelicals how to live the Christian life, but Evangelicals can learn from Orthodoxy not only about salvation of individuals, but to think about corporative soteriology.[34]

---

34. B. Nassif, "Are Eastern Orthodoxy and Evangelicalism Compatible? Yes. The Evangelical Theology of the Eastern Orthodox Church," In *Three Views on Eastern Orthodoxy and Evangelicalism*, eds. Stanley N. Gundry and James J. Stamoolis (Grand Rapids: Zondervan, 2004), 37–81.

The fact that both are concerned about the ecumenical movement is also of great interest. Both are very wary of each other as well as of other Christian churches from the country.

As for their differences, there is a different understanding of grace and mercy and of the role of the church and priesthood in this. But it is likely that the most controversial point still remains the human right to move from church to church and the interpretation of canonical territory and proselytism. If in the case of proselytism it is still possible to find a mutually acceptable consensus (such a possible consensus will be offered in ch. 9), then concerning canonical territory, there has not yet been found a common ground (the last point of ch. 9 will tackle this issue).

With regards to the Orthodox mission in Moldova, it is primarily associated with the restoration of the lost unity within a country where there are still two patriarchates. At least until the second half of 2011 this conflict had not been solved, and in some cases even worsened due to the arrival in power of liberal-democratic parties. One example of this is the declaration of 25 December as a bank holiday related to the Christmas celebration, while the Russian Orthodox Church celebrates Christmas on January 7. This action of the new liberal-democratic party caused a lot of protests by Russian Orthodox priests and believers.[35] Bishop Hilarion (Alfayev) of Vienna and Austria noted that in modern European history there have been cases of direct support of schisms by secular authorities. For example, the schism of Philaret in the Ukraine was supported by former president L. Kravchuk. Bulgarian schisms in the early 1990s were also supported by authorities at the time.[36]

Taking into consideration conclusions from chapter 2, and the observations from above, I can confirm that the contemporary Evangelical-Baptist mission approach in Moldova is not adequate, not only because it has a lot of contradictions in itself, but also because it has much more contradictions with the dominant Christian group in the country – Orthodoxy. Evangelical Baptists do their mission in a way like they live in a pagan country, they not only neglect Orthodox traditions, but it looks as though

---

35. http://terra.md/ru/news/moldova/hjgiuhgju/page_1/default.aspx#ancCom
36. Hilarion, "Orthodoxy in a New Europe," 22.

they do not even pay attention to them. And one more very important point – mission approaches, which are applied by Evangelicals in Moldova, are very different from church to church and from pastor to pastor. It is not an easy task to identify the ECB position towards Orthodoxy, because there is nothing written on this topic.

Because of these reasons I see growing importance of the results, which will flow from this dissertation. I would like to mention just two of them right now. First, the *missio Dei* concept gives a holistic understanding for the church's mission. As it was mentioned in the introduction to this dissertation, Moldova has faced a lot of different social problems. The Church Growth Movement doesn't give an answer as to how to resolve them. The *missio Dei* approach has such an answer. I will give a detailed explanation how it could be applied in chapter 9. Second, relations with the Orthodox Church. Baptists in Moldova are so concerned about unity among themselves that they often forget about unity with other Christian groups. *Missio Dei* suggests such a perspective, because it was developed and grown in ecumenical circles. In some points I can say that *missio Dei* is more an inclusive than exclusive concept. Twenty years of Moldavian independency has shown that exclusive model didn't bring positive results and created more tensions than unity. Because of that we need to look at the church's mission as at synthetic dynamics of (and for) the whole church.

Mission of the Church – Synthetic Dynamics for the Whole Church

The mission of God is many-sided: it has its purpose – the kingdom – and to carry out this mission God has a certain plan and instruments. The idea of the church's role in the divine plan of salvation has been changing throughout history. The church structures, forms and tasks have changed accordingly. Nowadays, the range of opinions about the nature of the church's mission is so wide that it is practically impossible to make any statements that would have certainty. However, there have been a number of attempts to achieve this purpose within the last few decades.

So, what is the mission of the church? How is it related to the mission of God and what role does it have in the development of the *missio Dei* concept? It can be stated with certainty that the mission of the church is directly related to the mission of God. A. Fernando said, "Jesus makes a connection between the nature of the church and the nature of the Trinity, even describing the church as a mirror of the Trinity."[37] Thus, by reflecting God, the church fulfills the mission of God; and in order to do this the church has to know what God is doing. "Every disciple must become a son who knows what his Father is doing; must become a slave who awaits the return of his Lord, alert, expectant, patient, confident; must learn to interpret the Law and the prophets as Jesus did; to interpret the tradition of Jesus' words in the light of that truth that was in Jesus; must have his mind shaped by that covenant of life that was made available to all men in his death."[38]

The main question in this area deals with how to determine what the Father is doing. History has proven that quite often churches have had a wrong understanding of the mission of God; his purposes, methods and tasks set before the church. S. K. George considers that all that the church calls "mission" may not be God's work. It is easy to have mixed motivations and to present one's own personal and cultural projects and advancement as though they were God's.[39]

It seems to me that the most correct understanding of what God wants from the church can be inferred from what God values. The values marked by the Triune God must serve as our guiding lines in defining the mission of the church.

"If the world is so much the arena of God's activity, then Christians must think of the world as a key arena of their service. Trinitarian mission would include involvement in the world, whereby Christians seek to uphold God's values (some would say 'kingdom values')."[40] The following continues the thought: "In a world where so many people are 'blind' to the

---

37. A. Fernando, "The Church: The Mirror of the Trinity," in *Global Missiology for the 21ˢᵗ Century: The Iguassu Dialogue*, ed. W. D. Taylor (Grand Rapids: Baker, 2000), 241.

38. P. S. Minear, "The Covenant and the Great Commission," in *Missions Under the Cross, Addresses Delivered at the Enlarged Meeting of the Committee of the International missionary Council at Willingen, in Germany, 1952; with Statements Issued by the Meeting*, ed. International Missionary Council (London: Edinburgh House Press, 1953), 77.

39. George, *Called as Partners*, 7.

40. Fernando, "God," 198.

values of God's reign of peace and justice, where the forces of death and violence seem to prevail over life, we must seek, recognize, and join 'God's works.'"[41] "Wherever injustice is opposed, racism is rebuked, ignorance is dispelled, healing is experienced, and reconciliation takes place, there the frontiers of evil are driven back, the kingdom comes and the transforming mission of God proceeds on its way."[42]

The World Council of Churches in its "Final Report of the Western European Working Group and North American Working Group of the Department on Studies in Evangelism" in 1967 defined the nature of the church's mission:

> (1) The Church must not think it can separate itself from the world nor must it segregate itself within a position of spiritual pride. The Church can only be the true Church when it knows that it is a part of the world which God loves and to which he reveals his love. (2) The Church lives in order that the world may recognize its true nature. Hence the Church's most important duty is to be present in the world in the knowledge that any loss of contact with it is disobedience to God's will for the world and leads to the destruction of the Church itself. (3) When the Church is aware that the presence and activity of God are not only manifest in itself, it will be constantly vigilant to discern any signs whereby God makes himself known to the world. There is no true Church without a humble dialogue with non-Christians or without fellowship with them. In this dialogue the role of the Church is that of a partner ready to listen and receive.[43]

Traces of those statements are still seen in missions research papers. Comparing these two lists we see that in the wide church and missions circles for over half a century the same issues have been treated and the same topics discussed. S. K. George summarized this in her book with the following statement: "The church's mission is everything. God sends

---

41. George, *Called as Partners*, 10.
42. Williamson, *For Such as Time as This*, 62.
43. World Council of Churches, *The Church for Others*, 12.

the church into the world to do, say, and be in response to and participation in God's mission. It includes evangelism, compassionate service, and social justice."[44] Discussing the subject of God's values, the kingdom and the church, it is impossible not to pay attention to the contribution that the representatives of Liberation theology have made to modern theology. As Gustavo Gutiérrez said: "It is the task of the church to bear witness to this dwelling and this new world (Rev 21:1–4); in this way it proclaims the kingdom in which the Lord makes himself present in human history."[45]

On his part J. Verkuyl makes the following statement: "The call to mission includes an appeal to engage in social and medical work . . . Mission includes: – church's response to physical and psychical distress of people; – the burden of ignorance; – the burden of poverty and hunger; – the burden of racial discrimination; – the struggle for cultural identity; – the threat of approaching death."[46]

D. Burnett gives a brief overview of the discussions that are going on between :the Social Gospel" and evangelical missiologists. He says, "With the rise of liberal scholarship, emphasis was placed upon social action as part of what came to be known as 'the social gospel'. In reaction to this, many evangelicals swung to the position of rejecting all social action, apart from medical work and education. They considered their mission was evangelism alone."[47]

Throughout many years similar discussions have been going on, and they continue today. It is encouraging that within the last twenty years theologians and missiologists have begun to listen to each other more than in the middle of the 1960s. There are clear signs of dialogue. However I have to note here that today's trends among Evangelicals are drastically different from those of the previous generation. The works written by the Evangelical missiologists during the last decade have been putting more and more emphasis on the social ministry of the church, on getting involved with the needs of the community.

---

44. George, *Called as Partners*, 2.
45. Gutiérrez, *The God of Life*, 106.
46. Verkuyl, "The Kingdom of God," 173–174.
47. Burnett, *God's Mission*, 136.

At the same time the majority still criticize the statement that "the world dictates the agenda for the church," and in their criticism, they say that the church has to react to the needs of the society. In my understanding, reaction to needs is quite similar to the adoption of a plan. If the needs of the world determine the areas of church ministry, then consequently, the world determines these areas, at least those that have to do with the social ministry of the church. I cannot state that there are certain "worldly" structures that are working to make a "plan" for the church; rather this is the answer to certain historical processes. Talking about this, we recognize that behind the history of the world there is God – the Lord of the entire universe. From this it follows that at least part of these processes are initiated by God himself, and consequently, he dictates the "agenda for the World." God draws the attention of the church to the world through his plan.

Thus, by reacting to the historical situation, to the needs of the society in which the church is located, the church follows God's plan if, of course, it uses God's methods in doing this.

Besides the debate regarding the "plan" there are talks about the "center of the mission." Various models are offered here: Christ-centered, Theo-centered, Church-centered, etc. Kirk observes:

> During the last half century, a vigorous debate has been joined within the Church on the relationship between the *missio Dei*, the Church and the world. There have been times in the past when Christians assumed that all God's purposes would be fulfilled exclusively through the Church. There have been theologies which have either identified the kingdom completely with the Church or which have regarded the kingdom as a purely future event. A Church-centered missiology undergirded the extraordinary missionary thrust of the last two centuries, with its emphasis on the planting of self-supporting, self-governing and self-propagating churches, although perhaps the "civilising" aspect of the mission reflected some kind of (distorted) reference to the kingdom.[48]

---

48. Kirk, *What is Mission?*, 33.

Many people today are talking about the need for radical changes in the church, about a "radical mission." "Being a prophetic presence through a radical biblical community life may be one of the biggest challenges facing the church in the 21st century."[49] "On the practical level this means that the church is to be a radical presence in society. It is always putting itself in true repentance wholly into God's hands, submitting to God's revealed will in Scripture and trusting in his mercy."[50] "If the church is to pursue and maintain an effective and radical mission towards the nation, seeking the nation's true health and wholeness through a prophetic ministry of the Word of God, it must also open itself to the necessity for radical repentance, reform and renewal."[51] "A church under the cross should be the exact opposite of an introverted and contemplative company. It should be a church *for* the world."[52] "The essential church is never the same during any two days, because it is constantly becoming, developing, and 'emerging'. Yet in another sense the church is already by nature what it is becoming and simply must continually change, improve, reform and emerge."[53]

Van Engen explains what he means by an emerging church. "The concept of emerging . . . provides a clue to the interaction of missiology and ecclesiology as we apply our understanding of the dialectical tension between present reality and future hope."[54] And, "mission calls us to a radical reexamination. If mission is a part of the essence of the church's nature as the body of Christ and the people of God, then it ought to be at the top of the list."[55]

As Yoder mentioned, "Our fundamental observation was that through most of the history of the Christian church, the geographical and numeral expansion of Christianity was the result not of separately organized,

---

49. Fernando, "The Church," 255.

50. Glasser et al., *Announcing the Kingdom*, 340.

51. Williamson, *For Such as Time as This*, 66.

52. R. Thadden, "The Church Under the Cross," in *Missions Under the Cross: Addresses Delivered at the Enlarged Meeting of the Committee of the International Missionary Council at Willingen, in Germany, 1952*, ed. N. Goodall and International Missionary Council (London: Edinburgh House Press, 1953), 62.

53. C. Van Engen, *God's Missionary People: Rethinking the Purpose of the Local Church* (Grand Rapids: Baker, 2001), 41.

54. Ibid., 44.

55. Ibid., 80.

centrally administered, and externally financed missionary specialists. It came through normal, often unplanned, usually self-supporting movements of Christians who took their living faith with them as they moved with their sources of livelihood."[56]

Talking about the purpose of the church, Kirk explained it well using the following words. "To clarify the nature of mission is to answer the question, what is the church for? It is entirely for the purposes for which God called it into being. It was a community in response to the *missio Dei*, bearing witness to God's activity in the world by its communication of the good news of Jesus Christ in word and deed."[57]

"One may say that we are in danger of perpetuating 'come-structures' instead of replacing them by 'go-structures.'"[58] The replacement of structures throughout history has been accompanied by pain and loss. But today, the church has practically no choice. In face of the many challenges the church faces in the world today, the church has indeed to reconsider its tasks and structures.

It is impossible to reconsider the structures without a deep re-thinking of its mission, its role in the divine plan and its purpose. Jesus Christ said, "As the Father has sent me, I am sending you." The church has been sent in the same way as the Son was sent. The sending model of the Son was discussed above. First, the Son was sent into the world; second, the Son was sent to preach the approaching kingdom; third, the Son was sent to be the approaching of the kingdom. Thus, the church is sent into the world, the church is sent to preach the values of the kingdom, the church is sent to be the sign of the kingdom. "God so loved the world that he gave his one and only Son, that whoever believes in him shall not perish but have eternal life" (John 3:16). The Father gave away his dearest. The Son, in his turn, loved this world so much, that he gave away the dearest thing he had – his 'Body' (his church) – to testify about him. God the Father gives away his possession for the sake of the world; God the Son gives away what he has. The church is given to the world for the sake of the world's salvation. "The

---

56. J. H. Yoder, *As You Go: The Old Mission in a New Day* (Scottdale, PA: Herald Press, 1961), 17.

57. Kirk, *What is Mission?*, 31.

58. World Council of Churches, *The Church for Others*, 19.

church, in the power of the Spirit, is also God's gift to the world because the church is the body of Christ, of whom Christ himself is head. The church embraces its identity and pursues the *missio Dei* in as much as and precisely to the extent that the church bears witness in its life to the grace of God in Christ and lives."[59]

"*Missio Dei* pushes us beyond ourselves and our familiar routines. The church exists toward and for the world."[60] As L. Newbigin has said, "Mission changes not only the world but also the church."[61] "The *missio Dei* is *missio ecclesiae* . . . the *missio ecclesiae* is not the *missio Dei*. Mission cannot be something the community possesses, for it is not the community in isolation. It is this living fellowship in which the divine retains the initiative and the community lives in response. This ordered identity means that the community must be active by the Spirit in following her Lord into the world."[62]

In the context of this dissertation it is necessary to note that it is impossible to speak about *missio Dei* in the context of one local church or even one denomination. The mission of God involves a certain ecumenical dialogue and recognizing "Christian neighbours." "Not only does Christian unity reflect the unity of the Trinity, but it also is part of our essential tie with God. So if we do not relate properly with other Christians, we do not relate properly with God."[63]

Church unity is also part of the mission of God. In other words, the mission of God can be carried out only when there is unity. "The concept of *missio Dei* might in future become a point of convergence, after having contributed to past divisions."[64] Further: "We should develop the *missio Dei* concept, even if we use it only as a metaphor for God's love and presence, unconditional availability, as well as God's unknown aspects . . . . It makes sense to begin any reflection on the matter with those aspects

---

59. M. Jinkins, "The Gift of the Church: *Ecclesia Crucis, Peccatrix Maxima*, and the *Missio Dei*," In *Evangelical Ecclesiology: Reality or Illusion?*, ed. J. Stackhouse (Grand Rapids: Baker, 2003), 206.

60. George, *Called as Partners*, 92.

61. Newbigin, *The Open Secret*, 59.

62. Flett, *The Witness of God*, 291.

63. Fernando, "The Church," 241.

64. Matthey, "God's Mission Today," 581.

of God's mission which we do know, i.e. with *missio Christi*, mission in Christ's way."[65]

We should try to find common points in God's mission, even if we have had failures in the past. The comparison between business and mission, which was made by Theo Sundermeier, is very interesting:

> Cultural, economic and social differences are rarely enough taken seriously in business life. Because they are played down or ignored, 70% of joint ventures fail. Ecumenical relations also often fail because cultural, social and spiritual differences are under-estimated. That is why the idea of partnership has to be enriched by that of friendship. Partners must become friends. Only where true friendships arise through and from congregational partnership, be they between single persons, a few families or special church groups, will such partnerships succeed and survive through the years even in spite of difficulties and tensions. Partners seek equality, and depend on the same interests and tasks, but friends enjoy differences and preserve the distance that is the space of freedom.[66]

Further:

> Anyone who does not change is dominant and only tries to change the others they meet, that has nothing to do with mission.[67]

Holistic and dynamic approaches in mission mean openness of the churches to listen to each other, and altogether listening to the world. If we say that God speaks to the world not just through the church, it means that it is possible to hear his voice through the world. From my understanding this is the only way today to be heard by the world, because listening to the world, the church will be allowed to speak to the world.

---

65. Ibid.
66. Sundermeier, "Missio Dei Today," 564.
67. Ibid., 566.

Conclusions

A comprehensive comparative analysis of four missiological paradigms developed among Evangelical and ecumenical circles has been made and they have been compared with Orthodox missiology. We found that there is no one ideal model for Evangelicals, which could be applied and which will have success in contemporary Moldova. As a result of that we can make the following conclusions:

1) The Church Growth Movement approach is the most ineffective in contemporary Orthodox countries, because it sees Orthodoxy as the mission field, does not recognize Orthodox traditions and uses methodology and language that confronts mainstream Christianity and creates additional tensions.
2) Lausanne's synthetic approach of a combination of evangelism and social responsibility, the WCC holistic approach and Anabaptist witness can give Moldavian Evangelicals a foundation for shaping a new paradigm.
3) Evangelicals from Moldova should take into consideration Orthodox theology in constructing their own missionary vision. To build one's own church while destroying others has nothing in common with God's mission and call to unity.
4) Evangelicals from Moldova are responsible for articulating their own missiology, which should be done in Moldova, and should not be exported from other countries.

Finally, the responsibility of any local church is to try to find its part in the universal church, in her mission, in *missio Dei*, to spread the gospel of the Lord Jesus Christ in the power of the Holy Spirit with the goal that all people will subordinate themselves to the will of God in his kingdom, which is among them, with shalom in their hearts. Every local church is responsible for finding her mission in unity with the other Christian traditions and local churches with the hope that one day all Christians from the all nations and generations will praise the Triune God in the eternal kingdom of God.

CHAPTER 9

Holistic and Cooperative Approach in Mission

In the previous chapter we saw distinctions and similarities among all researched missiological paradigms. I defined the most controversial points between contemporary Evangelicals and Orthodox in Moldova and observed their roots. The second section of chapter 8 was written as a call to Moldavian Evangelicals to rethink their mission approach, as preparation for chapter 9, where I will discuss holistic and cooperative approaches in mission, talking about biblical, theological and practical aspects for holistic mission and also suggest a new missionary paradigm as the result of this research.

Chapter 9 is written as a final chapter for the entire dissertation and it is offered as a possible theologically rooted, practical guide for Evangelicals in Moldova, if they wish to find themselves as a part of *missio Dei* and would be interested to begin a long-term conversation with the Orthodox Church. This guide is offered while not claiming it to be the final answer. It will take a lot of effort; the process of rethinking is a very hard and long process, but from my perspective there is no way to continue to use the current ineffective mission approach, which demands a lot of spiritual, financial and emotional effort, but does not bring the expected results, such as continuation of church growth and new planted churches in every settlement of Moldova.

I believe that conversation in this dissertation is only one step in the process of rethinking and evaluating a Moldavian missionary paradigm. Given also the great importance that Evangelical Christian Baptists give to the texts of the Bible, the first section of this chapter is dedicated to an analysis of some passages taken from the Old and New Testaments reflecting the relationship between social ministry, prophetic presence and evangelism.

Biblical, Theological and Practical Aspects for Holistic Mission in Moldova

This section is a continuation of the study of the concept of *missio Dei* and a rethinking of the boundaries imposed on Evangelical churches in an Orthodox country. It is carried out on the basis of the materials coming out of the conference on mission of the European Baptist Federation, which took place in 2010.[1] Based on earlier research, I will try to trace the relationship of theological and practical aspects between evangelism and the social responsibility of the church and in this chapter I would like to add one more point – the prophetic presence of the church. I will look for examples of this relationship in the Bible, as well as find its role in the modern Evangelical church in Moldova. One of the reasons I have chosen these particular three aspects is that they perfectly match the findings of earlier studies presented in chapters 7 and 8 of this work, which were centered on the practical application of Trinitarian missiology.

Social Responsibility and Social Action

I have already written a lot about the social responsibility of the church. When speaking of the church some mean "Church" as the institution as a whole, while some understand it as denomination and others as a local group of worshiping believers. Some authors prefer to use the phrase "social responsibility" while others talk about "social action" and I defined the concept of social participation in chapter 2. From my point of view, social responsibility seems to be an ideological component of social action. Although practically, there are communities which are involved actively in the social sphere, at the same time they are not aware of the responsibility that lies on them.[2] As well, there are churches which understand their

---

1. Documents of the conference can be found at http://ebf.org/resources

2. Some representatives of Liberation theology say that "the action itself is the truth." Newbigin, *The Open Secret*, 97.

responsibilities, but in exchange, do nothing.³ The ideal variant would be responsibility based on theological and ideological concepts reflected in concrete social projects. Summarizing much of what has been written in the previous chapters, I will give my own definition of social action. Thus, social action is the result of a deep analysis of Scripture and the surrounding context, and as a result of this, the answer to the needs of the modern society based on the ethics of the kingdom.

Also, I should point out such a concept as social service. John Stott, referring to the report on the Lausanne Covenant after a meeting in Grand Rapids, Michigan, makes the following distinction between social service and social action:⁴

Social service	Social action
Relief of people's needs	Elimination of people's needs
Philanthropy	Political and economic activity
Attempts to serve people and families	Attempts to change the structure of the society
Charity	Demand for justice

There is an increasing polarization of opinions in Moldova on the issue of the appropriateness of social responsibility within Evangelical churches. Voices are heard saying more loudly and strongly that social responsibility is the concern of the state and the church has nothing to do with it. Stott, echoing many other authors, calls the first half of the twentieth century the "great fall"⁵ referring to Evangelical Christians rejecting social responsibility. Lesslie Newbigin writes, "Again and again voices are heard insisting on the fact that 'social service' diverts the attention of the missions from their primary objective – evangelism. New missionary institutions were founded which vowed to avoid any involvement in social affairs and concentrate entirely on the proclamation of the Gospel. However, again and again, even

---

3. L. Newbigin considers those to be idealists who think that it is possible to separate beliefs from practical action. Newbigin, *The Open Secret*, 97.

4. J. Stott, *Issues Facing Christians Today* (Grand Rapids: Zondervan, 2006), 33.

5. Ibid., 25.

the very logic of the Gospel was pushing them relentlessly to such matters as schooling and education, treatment of patients, distribution of food to starving people, help for the needy ones."[6]

In Moldova, a similar "fall" occurred in the first decade of the twenty-first century, as demonstrated in the second chapter of this dissertation. Stott gives five reasons why, at the beginning of the twentieth century in the West, Evangelical Christians did not want to be involved in social activities: First, the fight against theological liberalism; second, rejection of the social gospel; third, pessimism with regard to the increasing human evil during and after World War I; fourth, the influence of pre-millenialism; fifth, the spread of Christianity "among middle-class people, who tended to dilute it by identifying it with their own culture."[7]

Parushev and Andronoviene add one more point. "Such relegation has its roots in the dichotomy of evangelism versus social responsibility, which in its turn is connected to the dichotomy of soul versus body."[8]

In the US the most ardent follower of the "great fall" was the Southern Baptist Convention. The agreement on division of responsibility for various countries signed in 1920 in London[9] (mentioned in ch. 1) determined the way of development of churches in Moldova for almost a century. At that time, Moldova was part of Romania and the pastors from the Moldavian Baptist churches were studying at the Bucharest seminary, which was not only receiving financial support from the Southern Baptist Convention, but also ideological perspectives – SBC representatives were teaching at the seminary in Bucharest.

After that, followed the adherence of Moldova to the Soviet Union and almost total isolation from the rest of the Christian world. The government did not allow churches to engage in charity work or any other social service. The church could continue its activity only in houses of worship and at the homes of active members of local congregations. Almost half

---

6. Newbigin, *The Open Secret*, 100.

7. Stott, *Issues Facing Christians Today*, 25–28.

8. L. Androviene and P. Parushev, "McClendon's Concept of Mission as Witness," in *Anabaptism and Mission*, eds. W. Shenk and P. Penner (Schwarzenfeld: Neufeld Verlag, 2007), 258.

9. Minutes of Executive Committee and Other Representative Baptists, held at the Baptist Church House, Southhampton Row, London, from 19th to 23rd July, 1920, 18–19.

a century of such life had an impact on the practice and theology of the church. When in the late twentieth and early twenty-first centuries the call was heard to pay attention to social and community problems, most of the pastors ignored them, even though the background had changed. I agree with Parushev and Andronoviene, that the later passion for holiness became the main understanding of evangelical mission in post-Soviet countries. "Ironically, fighting 'the world' had been so much of an agenda for these churches during the Soviet time, yet they have failed to see how much of this 'world' easily, naturally, and, in fact, necessarily made its way into the corporate life of the church and the private lives of its members."[10] Further, "if the church avoids social involvement because it values holiness more than compassion, it is on a straight road to legalism and formalism. But if the social politics of the upside-down kingdom of the Sermon on the Mount first of all in practices of the gathering community, then even the small projects it will attempt for society will have a serious impact."[11]

Nevertheless, the call to free those suffering was heard as an order. As Stott said, "Social responsibility becomes an aspect not of Christian mission only, but also of Christian conversion."[12] "Participation or non-participation in social ministry it is not more a question of ethics, this question is about obedience to Christ's commandments, who served in deed as well as in word, and it would be impossible in the ministry of Jesus to separate his works from his words . . . therefore our mission, like his, is to be one of service."[13]

Arthur McPhee adds that "the real challenge – and touchstone of authentic evangelism – is the Lord's own ministry, which integrated the verbal proclamation of the gospel with a ministry of healing and deliverance."[14] Further, I am going to tackle the issue of the prophetic presence, which has

---

10. Androviene and Parushev, "McClendon's Concept of Mission," 260.

11. Ibid., 263.

12. J. Stott, *Christian Mission in the Modern World* (Downers Grove: InterVarsity, 1975), 53.

13. Ibid., 24.

14. A. McPhee, "Authentic Witness, Authentic Evangelism, Authentic Church," in *Evangelical, Ecumenical, and Anabaptist Missiologies in Conversation: Essays in Honor of Wilbert R. Shenk*, eds. J. R. Krabill, W. Sawatsky, and C. Van Engen (Maryknoll, NY: Orbis Books, 2006), 134.

not been studied yet, and will give some additional details on the social responsibility of churches and their evangelistic activity.

Prophetic Presence

In the case of social activity, the situation is clear though debatable, while the prophetic presence is not even discussed so much, and very little has been written about it from a Baptist perspective. Speaking of the biblical meaning of the word "prophet," we should recall that one of the basic meanings is "a person who speaks by divine inspiration." We deliberately ignore the speculation over this term of some religious (and other) groups that emphasize the notion of "prophecy" only as a prediction of the future. Considering the meaning of the prophecy from a biblical perspective, there is no doubt that the prophet of God is the one who "speaks in the name of God," on his behalf, with his authority.

At some point this may be a prediction of the future without any apparent reason in the present (supernatural revelation) such as prophecies about the signs of the end of the world, famines, floods, etc. At the same time, there are prophecies predicting the future only as a consequence of disobedience to God's commandments (natural prophecy). Such prophecies are based on the text of the Law, which prescribes certain consequences for certain sins. Kirk, for example, considers that the root of all the sins of the peoples of biblical times is idolatry.[15]

But it was not a purely religious message. He mentions all that the prophets were speaking to the leaders of nations concerned all aspects of life. They were letting people know God's thoughts about people's religious life, economic relations, moral beliefs and foreign policy.[16] Weak people were exploited by powerful ones, debts were not forgiven (as was spelled out in the Law), the parcels of land of vulnerable groups were expropriated and violence was flourishing. For all these the Lord should punish people. At the same time, as I understand Kirk's idea, that every prophecy unavoidably contained the promise of a new beginning.[17] The punishment was al-

---

15. Kirk, *Mission under Scrutiny*, 158.
16. Ibid.
17. Ibid., 160.

ways associated with the recovery, or rather with the possibility of recovery (subject to certain conditions).

Denouncing others, "the prophet runs the risk of self-righteousness as he or she turns the warning of judgment on others, by definition the unrighteous."[18] The purpose of the prophet is to show the releasing God. God offered not only religious and moral norms, but also was that One who had power and authority to give freedom from the yoke of the idols, the burden of sin and violence. G. Gutierrez wrote that "the liberation must be carried out at three different levels: the liberation from the social situations of oppression and marginalization, from any kind of personal slavery and from the sin which is the rupture of friendly relations with God and with other people."[19]

Reading the Old Testament attentively, we notice that the prophecies were addressed to the pagans, to the kings of Israel and Judah, the priesthood, God's people and individuals; that is, to all. The message of the prophet was not selective and did not depend on convenience or inconvenience. The prophet was risking his reputation, influence, public opinion and, often, life. The message of the prophet was inflexible. As Kirk writes, "The prophetic message was tinged with great sorrow and compassion (Isa 1:18; Mic 6:3), yet it was quite uncompromising."[20]

Though sometimes people asked the prophets to persuade God to fulfill their wishes, to turn a blind eye to lawlessness and take a step forward (as in the case of Jeremiah described in Jer 42–43), God was uncompromising. In this case, there was always a way out.

> When you spread out your hands in prayer, I hide my eyes from you; even when you offer many prayers, I am not listening. Your hands are full of blood! Wash and make yourselves clean. Take your evil deeds out of my sight; stop doing wrong. Learn to do right; seek justice. Defend the oppressed. Take up the cause of the fatherless; plead the case of the widow. Come now, let us settle the matter, says the LORD. Though your

---

18. Ibid., 157.
19. Guttiérrez, *A Theology of Liberation* (Maryknoll, NY: Orbis Books, 1988), xix.
20. Kirk, *Mission under Scrutiny*, 159.

sins are like scarlet, they shall be as white as snow; though they are red as crimson, they shall be like wool. (Isa 1:16–18)

The Relationship between the Prophet and Social Problems in the Bible

The prophets in the Old Testament were repeatedly drawing the people's attention to social issues. D. York sees in this the achieving of *missio Dei* of the Old Testament.[21] It is difficult to calculate the number of prophecies on social problems in relation to so-called spiritual issues. As usual, prophets were speaking about both of them in one and the same message. One of the most striking examples is the prophecy of Micah 6:8: "He has shown you, O mortal, what is good. And what does the LORD require of you? To act justly, and to love mercy, and to walk humbly with your God." As we see, two of the three behests refer to social issues. These are a few more examples: Isaiah 3:14; Ezekiel 16:49, 22:7; Amos 2:6–8, 5:11; Zechariah 7:9–10; Malachi 3:5.

The Lord is calling his prophets to stand up for the poor, strangers, widows and orphans. The outcasts of those ages were under the special protection of prophets. The prophets' message was addressed to the whole society, but especially to those who kept power in their hands, who broke the balanced social policy, which was conceived by God and outlined in the Torah. The powerful people were kings distorting the Law, priests fawning before the rich and oppressing the poor, traders cheating while selling goods, employers not paying salaries on time, officials taking bribes, judges distorting the Law in favor of the rich, and landowners not donating a part of the harvest to the immigrants. It is difficult to recall even one serious prophetic denunciation aimed specifically at the poor for theft, burglary or robbery. It seems that even the sin of stealing becomes merely a result of oppression by the rich. According to the words of Agur, "Keep falsehood and lies far from me; give me neither poverty nor riches, but give me only my daily bread. Otherwise, I may have too much and disown you and say, 'Who is the LORD?' Or I may become poor and steal, and so dishonor the name of my God." (Prov 30:8–9).

---

21. J. York, *Missions in the Age of the Spirit* (Springfield, MO: Logion Press, 2000), 48.

It is obvious that the presence of the prophet is active. "Presence" means "active existence" rather than "passive observation." "Presence" is the opposite of "absence." It is possible to be absent even being physically there where criminal actions are carried out. The presence is manifested in active protest against the occurring processes, which are contrary not only to personal ethics and the Ten Commandments, but especially to the social justice which was originally conceived by God for his people.

God warns people about the coming judgment through his prophets. Kings and princes will lose their territories, will be captured, and the capital of their country will be destroyed. Priests will lose their temple, which was not only a source of income for them (which was meant by God) but also a source of unjust enrichment. The merchants and landowners will not enjoy the fruits of their trade and land; their enemies will get everything and jackals will live on their lands. Every person will be judged except the oppressed and the disadvantaged who have already suffered a lot in their life.

Prophets and Social Activity Nowadays

What is the role of a prophet nowadays? What is the relationship between the prophetic presence and social service? How does this relate to evangelism? What can and should the church do to remain faithful to its vocation?

There are too many questions, and they are too serious to be able to provide a definitive answer in a concise manner. Nevertheless, I believe that it is inadmissible to keep silent on this subject.

It is necessary to notice that it would be hermeneutically incorrect to project blindly the model of the Old Testament prophets, belonging to a theocratic society, on the modern church, which is separated from the state. The modern institution of the priesthood accomplishes completely different functions from that of Jerusalem two to three thousand years ago. Strangers do not go into villages and fields, but huddle in cities. The status of widows in many countries has changed. However, I am going to formulate some values on the bases of biblical examples.

Value one. In the Scriptures, God reveals himself as the God of social justice. The Old as well as the New Testament show that both the state and the church should pay attention to those who cannot take care of themselves and ensure themselves a decent life. The principles of "wild capitalism" or liberal democracy have nothing in common with the biblical view on the relationship of rich people towards the poor. As Reinhard Frieling says, "It is part of the church's message to tell the politicians and entrepreneurs in no uncertain terms that a Common Market which is ruled only by so-called laissez-faire capitalism has to be corrected, because in the long run it accepts mass poverty in human society."[22]

In this regard, I may give the example of Valery Ghiletchi who was twice a member of the Commission on Human Rights, which is not contradictory to Christian norms. On the other hand, in Moldova there is a lack of evangelical presence in the social sector where social justice is forgotten. In Eastern European countries, this topic still remains unpopular. The socially oriented platform of the Scriptures became unpopular because of the distortions of history by some socialist parties and states, and because of that "the history of Soviet evangelicals is a good illustration of the danger of self-serving seclusion which seriously damages the efforts to fulfill the prophetic task . . . In order to have any social involvement, the church must be present in the immediate culture."[23]

Kirk says the following:

> One way of thinking of the church, in the light of the prophetic message about idolatry, justice and a future hope, is as a people collectively aware of and resistant to the destructive forces of our times. These include the kind of economic and social fatalisms that give the impression that only one kind of economic system and one kind of society is feasible in the twenty-first century. This kind of church seeks to overcome everything that militates against the gift of life and well-being, such as child-labour, boy soldiers, debt insolvency, absence of clean water, preventable diseases, domestic violence, trafficking of prostitutes, alcohol and drug dependency, abortion and euthanasia.[24]

---

22. R. Frieling, "Our Common Responsibility in Europe," in *Charta Oecumenica: A Text, a Process and a Dream of the Churches in Europe*, eds. V. Ionita and S. Numico (Geneva: WCC Publications, 2003), 64.

23. Parushev and Andronoviene, "McClendon's Concept of Mission," 261.

24. Kirk, *Mission under Scrutiny*, 169.

Being silent we are absent where the so-called laws of the "liberal democracy" flourish. The church, which does not promote social justice and adopts economic liberal values, risks standing in a row with exploiters and aggressors. As John Chryssavgis, an Orthodox theologian from Australia, said, "A true person cannot tolerate creating miserable poverty for the sake of accumulating exorbitant wealth. The moral crisis of our global economic injustice is integrally spiritual; it signals something terribly amiss in our relationship with God, with people, and with things."[25]

This kind of thing has happened repeatedly in history. The reason for this is the wrong interpretation of the sacred texts of the Bible read from the perspective of rich people. "The poor are the most authentic interpreters of the text," – as Kirk writes, – "in many ways, the poor have a more profound understanding of the text than many people who have dedicated their lives to its study."[26] He also says, "Experience seems to show that those who handle the Scriptures with respect and expectation, including the willingness to be challenged by the hard sayings, are more likely to discover its practical, liberating power than those whose hermeneutic obliges them to stand in judgement on the text."[27] Are Western democracies nowadays able to let the text criticize them instead of being in the role of critics? The struggle for human rights fascinated many Western (particularly European) churches, so that they have often ignored God's rights through the process of democratization.

Today's church (as always) needs repentance. According to Bosch:

> The church is itself an object of the *missio Dei*, in constant need of repentance and conversion; indeed, all traditions today subscribe to the adage *ecclesia semper reformanda est*. The cross which the church proclaims also judges the church and censures every manifestation of complacency about its "achievements." A church that pats itself on the shoulder frustrates

---

25. J. Chryssavgis, "Orthodox Spirituality and Social Activism. Reclaiming Our Vocabulary – Refocusing Our Vision," in *The Orthodox Churches in a Pluralistic World: An Ecumenical Conversation*, ed. E. Clapsis (Geneva: WCC Publications; Brookline, MA: Holy Cross Orthodox Press, 2004), 136.

26. Kirk, *Mission under Scrutiny*, 161.

27. Ibid., 162–163.

the power of the cross in its life and ministry. Still, the cross conveys a message not only of judgment but of forgiveness and hope as well, also for the church.[28]

The prophets of the church should first of all denounce the church itself because of its "prophetic absence," concealment of the sins of powerful people and of those of their own leaders. If local churches neglect the weak and defenseless people, and millionaires become more and more influential, then these churches have forgotten about the existence of the God of justice, of the impartial God, of the God of the poor.

Value two. In the Scriptures God calls people who are loyal to him to participate actively in the life of the weak.

Dietrich Bonhoeffer wrote: "The church is the church only when it exists for others . . . The church must share in the secular problems of ordinary human life, not dominating, but helping and serving."[29] The image of the church as servant is not popular. Few speak of the church as a servant. Even the word "ministry" has acquired the meaning of honor, status or rank. "Minister" often means not ministering or serving but ruling. "The church had a secure place in society and assisted the government in such matters as maintaining the civil register and the collection of taxes. The Anabaptists confronted and contested this system"[30]. "The greatest challenge before the contemporary church is to repossess the prophetic notion of evangelization as both a joyful announcement to Christians and people of other faiths as well as a contextualized witness in secular society. For it seems that there are more *practical* atheists (that is, people who confess God with their lips but deny God with their deeds) inside communities of faith than there are active atheists (who deny the existence of God's being) outside of them."[31] Further, "they denounced the state-church system because it corrupted the church. They asserted that the church is truly the church only if it is answerable to Jesus Christ alone."[32]

---

28. Bosch, *Transforming Mission*, 387.
29. D. Bonhoeffer, *Letters and Papers from Prison* (London: SCM Press, 1971), 382.
30. Shenk, "An Anabaptist View of Mission," 51-52.
31. Costas, *Liberating News*, 47.
32. Ibid.

Christians are called not only to denounce the sins of powerful people but also to help those who have been oppressed by them. James wrote: "Pure and undefiled religion in the sight of [our] God and Father is this: to visit orphans and widows in their distress [and] to keep oneself unstained by the world." (Jas 1:27).

Many churches got so involved in respecting the second part of this passage that they completely forgot about the first part. Some understand it in its literal sense. They help only the orphans and widows. It is obvious that in James' time, which was a time of political instability, wars and rebellions, these two groups were the most socially vulnerable. In the times of hope for a developing theocratic state, there were many more such groups: hired workers, poor, beggars, and strangers (Deut 24:14); and also orphans and widows (Exod 22:22).

The budget of the church is largely used to meet the needs and interests of people donating this money, forgetting about the needy. Bosch, referring to Hoekendijk, stated (may be a little harshly): "If the church attempts to sever itself from involvement in the world and if its structures are such that they thwart any possibility of rendering a relevant service to the world, such structures have to be recognised as heretical."[33] Heresy is not only a lack of orthodoxy, but also a lack of orthopraxy. The lack of orthopraxy means not only violation of ecclesiastical ethics but primarily the lack of social activity and passivity in matters of assistance to the pariahs of these days.

Snyder wrote, "Church people think about how to get people into the church; kingdom people think about how to get the church into the world. Church people worry that the world might change the church; kingdom people work to see the church change the world."[34]

I do not call for the rejection of traditional evangelism as proclamation. I mean that only proclaiming, and forgetting the rest, we destroy the balance of the church's mission conceived by God. As Charles West said, "The church exists to take up the deepest conflicts of the world into itself and to confront both sides there with the forgiving, transforming power which

---

33. Bosch, *Transforming Mission*, 378.
34. H. Snyder, *Liberating the Church* (Downers Grove: InterVarsity, 1983), 11.

breaks and remakes them into a new community, with a new hope and a new calling."³⁵

Talking about prophetic presence and its connection to evangelism, I need to refer to Orlando Costas: "The prophetic perspective is foundational for a theology of contextual evangelization. For, on the one hand, the roots of evangelization in the New Testament are found in the prophetic literature that originates in the Diaspora [in Exile]. And, on the other hand, evangelization is not a mechanical practice unrelated to specific situations; it is an announcement clearly linked to God's liberating action in a specific social and historical moment."³⁶

Evangelism or Witness?

As mentioned above, at an EBF conference, along with social participation and prophetic presence, evangelism was declared as one of the components of the holistic mission of the church. Nevertheless, the very title of subchapter 1.5 shows that I aim to find the answer to the difficult question that is the title of this chapter. Is it appropriate that Evangelical churches use the term "evangelism" in an Orthodox context? In addition, I will consider the appropriateness of the approach itself, which stands behind this term.

This idea sprang to mind after listening to discussions on evangelization held within the WCC. The fact that the Orthodox understand "evangelism" to mean proselytism also made me think of a solution. While writing this dissertation, I had to pay greater attention than ever before to the writings of the church fathers, as well as to the studies of modern Orthodox theologians at a deeper level than before. In addition, in chapter 3, I have described the history of the emergence of the WCC in Moldova, and its actual activities in which I am also directly involved along with Orthodox colleagues. The joint work also showed that in Evangelical circles there are many myths about Orthodoxy, most of which are unjustified.

Therefore, one of the questions I asked myself while thinking about practical suggestions about the attitude Evangelical Christians should have towards Orthodox, has been answered. The question was as follows: "What

---

35. C. West, *The Power to Be Human: Toward a Secular Theology* (New York: Macmillan, 1971), 270.

36. Costas, *Liberating News*, 46.

kind of attitude should Evangelical Christians have towards the Orthodox? Should they be considered brothers in Christ, nominal believers, or non-believers?" In the process of this study, the third version was recognized as invalid. I am more and more inclined to think that Evangelical believers should treat the Orthodox as brothers in faith belonging to a more ancient tradition. It remains to identify the number of nominal believers in comparison to true believers in Orthodoxy. It is obvious that within the Orthodox Church there are a certain percentage of people baptized in childhood who as adults have nothing in common with God or the church. Among Evangelical Christians there also exist nominal Christians, so that such kind of accusations against Orthodoxy become irrelevant – namely the presence of nominal Christians within the Orthodox Church as well as within Evangelical churches offers opportunities for cooperation between churches in Moldova.

Thus, admitting the possibility of building fraternal relations between Evangelical and Orthodox believers, concrete actions should be undertaken in this direction. As a first step I suggest identifying the tense moments and find out what makes the Orthodox distant from Evangelicals. First of all, there is proselytism, which is linked in their minds with evangelism and especially with aggressive evangelism. This serves as a good reason to ask ourselves about the appropriateness of using this concept in Moldova.

I agree with W. Shenk: "We are all grateful for the important work that has been done over the past several decades by the restorative justice movement, conflict transformation and witness against violence. But our witness will only achieve coherence and integrity when these dimensions are integrated with evangelization and building of the body of Christ. There is only one gospel."[37] In another article he explains: "Kingdom and peace are linked in Luke 4:43; 8:1; 16:16; Acts 8:12. We are not being faithful to the mandate of Jesus the Messiah if we reduce the gospel to personal salvation or if we turn peace into a program for social action or the special vocation of a new people."[38]

---

37. Shenk, "An Anabaptist View of Mission," 40.
38. Ibid., 53.

In my view, neither social action, nor prophetic presence can really substitute for the proclamation of the good news. We have no doubts about proclaiming or not proclaiming. The process, as well as the methodology of the proclamation of the good news, should be studied in detail. First, it must be aimed at those who are not familiar with the gospel, as John Stott correctly noted: "Evangelism must not be defined in terms of the recipients of the gospel, although it is of course assumed that they will be sufficiently 'non-Christian' to need to hear it."[39] Vinay Samuel compares happily the mission to spread the message of the gospel with a journey:

> Mission is not itself an act of judgment. So, much mission gives the impression of being an act of judgment rather than a journey with people and communities towards God's intention. Mission is more of a journey than an event. Mission is mission on the way – inviting people to take part in a journey. An event on the other hand is a critical judgment.[40]

> It is inviting people to join a journey with you during which you witness to them of your Lord. You are not there to bring transformation yourself. You are on a journey yourself of self transformation, of community transformation, and you are inviting the people to join a journey, and witness to them of your Lord and your experience.[41]

The traditional way of the evangelism's goal is to make people know Christ and become Christians, but Costas saw the wider perspective: "The goal of evangelization is not only to promote the growth of the church or merely to help individuals come to salvation. Rather, the all-encompassing goal of evangelization is to make known God's kingdom as embodied in Jesus Christ and made present by the Holy Spirit."[42]

"Evangelization is the process by which the gospel takes hold of an individual or group and brings that person or group into relationship with

---

39. Stott, *Christian Mission*, 37.
40. V. Samuel, "Mission as Transformation," in *Mission as Transformation: A Theology of the Whole Gospel*, eds. V. Samuel and C. Sugden (Oxford: Regnum Books International, 1999), 229.
41. Ibid.
42. Costas, *Liberating News*, 82.

Jesus the Messiah, so that they, too, become Christ-like."[43] Stott says that "evangelism must not be defined in terms of results . . . 'To evangelise' in New Testament usage does not mean to win converts."[44] "If evangelism is to take place, there must be communication – a true communication between ancient revelation and modern culture. This means that our message must be at the same time, faithful and contemporary."[45]

The church should always be in search of relevant methods to proclaim the good news. Obviously, it should not forget about the experience of the previous generations, contemporaries or representatives of other cultures acquired. But data collected in one context may be inadequate and even detrimental to another one. It is for this reason I propose in the context of an East-European, predominantly Orthodox country, to back away from the concept of "evangelism" and replace it with the notion of "witness." Anticipating the criticisms, it is important to indicate that this is not an alien concept to Eastern European Evangelical believers. To be exact, this very concept was used by Anabaptist and Mennonite predecessors. "The German Mennonites and Slavic renewal groups understood the gospel primarily as God's holistic peace that effects the inner and outer person and leads to witness to others. The good news, in their understanding, including peace with God inside and nonviolence and active pacifism outside, acts in the life of a renewed person who belongs to the kingdom of God."[46]

As mentioned in chapter 1, the Mennonites were among those who contributed to the emergence and spread of Evangelical churches not only in Slavic lands, but also in the territory of Bessarabia of those times. Witness, from the Anabaptist point of view, does not bring conflict as it is by nature peacemaking. Witness produces changes not only in people's hearts, conciliates them not only with God but also with each other, incites them to changes not only in personal and church ethics, but also leads to active social participation.

---

43. Shenk, "Three Studies in Mission Strategy," in *Anabaptism and Mission*, eds. W. Shenk and P. Penner (Schwarzenfeld: Neufeld Verlag, 2007), 21.

44. Stott, *Christian Mission*, 38.

45. Ibid., 42.

46. P. Penner, "Peace Identity – Peace Witness? A Case Study from East European Context," in *Anabaptism and Mission*, eds. W. Shenk and P. Penner (Schwarzenfeld: Neufeld Verlag, 2007), 194.

Yet presence is the minimalist social involvement of the church. As a minimum, it is reductionist. The natural extension of presence, therefore, is social assistance, or involvement in practical terms, with some (not all) aspects of the culture. Social involvement is not a goal of itself; it is a natural expression of witness for the value of the kingdom for the world as it is now. Well-measured involvement of the church with acute social problems, and a possible remedy from them, is a very sound way of the church doing mission. It might look to be a very ambitious project for minority communities, but here is where the ecumenical extension of the world-wide evangelical community comes into focus.[47]

Social help is exactly that: assistance, not a Constantinian attempt for forced evangelism or control over needy church members. Being a witness, there is a natural evangelistic side to social assistance, which brings us to the third part of social involvement: fellowship.[48]

Such an approach can be called holistic and this is how Evangelical churches can join the *missio Dei*, become part of it, become a catalyst for positive change in society, establish peaceful relations with the Orthodox Church and find a way out of the crisis which was described in chapter 2. Such churches mirror the best the spirit of the New Testament at this time and in this context. "The New Testament was not written by scholars working quietly in monasteries. It was written on the frontier where faith was being tested by strong challenges . . . The only kind of theology Paul knows is mission theology. The only kind of church he recognized is what today we are calling missional churches."[49]

---

47. Parushev and Andronoviene, "McClendon's Concept of Mission," 262.
48. Ibid.
49. Shenk, "An Anabaptist View of Mission," 43.

Mission as Dialogue and Common Witness

I concluded earlier that the best approach in the mission of the Evangelical churches is witness in cooperation with the Orthodox Church. The main question that should be answered is about the possibility of such witness. Inevitably, it should be recognized that the aspiration of the Evangelical churches in this direction is not enough. Orthodoxy should prove readiness too. I am trying to analyze this possibility based on the documents of ecumenical organizations, declarations of the Orthodox Church, as well as the experience of such cooperation in Russia and Romania. I am suggesting an approach which hopefully will make the mission of Evangelical churches more efficient.

Common Witness in Soviet Time

First, I must note that there were such suggestions in the history of Evangelical Christian Baptists in the times of the USSR. As mentioned in chapter 1, the only official publication of the Baptist churches in the USSR was the magazine "Fraternal Herald" [Bratskij Vestnik]. In 1959 an article on the history of the ecumenical movement was published, in which the author concludes that most Baptists do not want to participate in ecumenical efforts.[50] In 1960, the representative of the AUECB, M. Y. Jidcov, participated as observer at the International Ecumenical Youth Congress. On the final day of the conference the service was held by Baptists, and he was the one who pronounced the main sermon.[51] In 1961, the second Conference of European Churches was held, at which nine delegates from the Soviet Union participated including a representative of the Orthodox Church as well as A. I. Mickevich from the AUECB. It is noteworthy that Mickevich said that "his heart was filled with joy due to the ecumenical meeting and that it was from God."[52]

---

50. A. V. Karev "Kak vozniklo i razvivalosi jekumenicheskoe dvijenie" [Origin and development of the ecumenical movement], *Bratskij Vestnik* 2 (1959): 65–74.

51. M. I. Jidcov, "Evropejskaja molodezhnaja jekumenicheskaja assambleja v Lozanne" [European Youth Ecumenical Assembly in Lausanne (Switzerland) from 13 to 24 July 1960], *Bratskij Vestnik* 5–6 (1960): 27–29.

52. A. Mickievich, "Vtoraja konferencija evropejskih cerkvej" [Second Conference of European Churches], *Bratskij Vestnik* 1 (1961): 17.

Also in 1961, during June, there was the All-Christian Peace Assembly, which culminated with an ecumenical worship that was attended by the representative of the AUECB leadership, M. I. Jidcov. In an article dedicated to this event, he wrote: "This service has brought to the hearts of the participants a bright ray of hope that instead of all the differences in the understanding and forms of worship, sacred unity and mutual acceptance between Christians of different confessions are still possible."[53]

In 1962, the editors of the magazine published the documents of the Third Assembly of the World Council of Churches without comments.[54] In June 1962, I. M. Orlov, the representative of the AUECB, took part in the WCC consultative meeting on the subject of peace and disarmament.[55]

On 18 September 1962, a truly historic event happened. The ECB Moscow community held an ecumenical church service which was attended by representatives of various faiths, but in addition, the first sermon was delivered by the representative of the Orthodox Church, the Archpriest Sokolowsky and the concluding speech was made by M. I. Jidcov from the AUECB.[56] In a three-year period, the dynamics of the relationship had changed significantly from skeptical and critical to an Orthodox preaching in a Baptist church. In addition, in the same issue, there were two more articles on ecumenism.[57]

Beginning with the second issue, in 1965, the magazine editors were publishing a permanent rubric on "Christian unity," as a result of which Evangelical believers from the Soviet Union were aware of all significant events taking place within the WCC and the CEC. What is more, the tone of the articles also changed. From year to year it became more and more positive. The rubric existed until 1990. Another rubric was called

---

53. M. I. Jidcov, "Jekumenicheskoe bogosluzhenie" [Ecumenical service at Bethlehem Chapel in Prague], *Bratskij Vestnik* 4 (1961): 12.

54. "Dokumenty tret'ej assamblei vsemirnogo soveta cerkvej" [Documents of the Third Assembly of the World Council of Churches held in New Delhi (India) from November 18 to December 6, 1961], *Bratskij Vestnik* 3 (1962): 6–9.

55. I. M. Orlov, "Vstrecha hristian Vostoka i Zapada v Zheneve" [Encounter between East and West Christians], *Bratskij Vestnik* 4 (1962): 22.

56. V. Trubin, "Jekumenicheskoe bogosluzhenie v MOEHB" [Ecumenical church service in the Moscow community of Evangelical Christian Baptists], *Bratskij Vestnik* 5–6 (1962): 12–17.

57. Ibid., 18, 21.

"Fraternal Communications," in which the emphasis was put not on the ecumenical movement but on unity among Evangelical believers. It is difficult nowadays to give reasons for the appearance of this column and its disappearance in 1990. It is more likely that the USSR peacekeeping image, which Leonid Brezhnev was trying to maintain, affected the situation in churches. Perhaps there were attempts by the authorities to put pressure on the church leadership. Unfortunately, access to KGB files is not allowed and members of the AUECB leadership of those days are not alive anymore.

In this case, we are more concerned about the reason the rubric was later excluded from the magazine content. It is even more interesting that, in 1990, starting with the fourth issue, articles on evangelism and mission were published for the first time in "*Bratskij Vestnik*." There were two long articles on this topic: "Conference on Evangelism and Missions"[58] and "Biblical Foundations of Evangelism."[59] An interesting fact is that the words of gratitude for the help in the organization of the missionary work was addressed to the representatives of such organizations as Slavic Gospel Association, Light to the East, as well as personally to Bill Brait.[60] These organizations in those years were known for their conservative theology, commitment to evangelism, lack of a holistic approach to mission and for almost nonexistent ecumenical relations. I have already mentioned in chapter 8, the accusations addressed to the Slavic Gospel Association by the Orthodox Church. There is insufficient data to prove that the AUECB ecumenical relationships of the Soviet era were the result of pressures from the authorities. But we have strong arguments to demonstrate that their absence was due to new relationships created in the era of Perestroika and developed in the 1990s.

Maybe today, thinking once again about the past experience, it is necessary to pay attention not only to the last twenty years, but also to an earlier stage in the development of Evangelical churches. In Moldova, there is a

---

58. E. Sokolov, "Konferencija po evangelizacii i missii" [Conference on evangelism and missions], *Bratskij Vestnik* 4 (1990): 63–72.

59. B. Ryaguzov, "Biblejskie osnovy blagovestija" [Biblical basis of evangelism], *Bratskij Vestnik* 4 (1990): 73–83.

60. Ibid., 64.

perception that the ecumenical movement is the result of liberalism. But obviously the AUECB union cannot be accused of liberalism. Nevertheless, it was previously actively developing relationships at the international level as well as bilateral relationships within the Russian Orthodox Church.

Common Witness in Contemporary Neighboring Countries

To be relevant in their own context, Moldavian Evangelical churches should pay attention not only to past experience but also to the experience of neighboring countries that have similar cultural values and spiritual heritage. Huub Vogelaar, referring to Radio Vatican, said that from the ecumenical point of view, Romania is the most open country.[61] He shares his impressions about ecumenical activity in Sibiu.

> In Sibiu, for example, I observed in 2003 five challenging ecumenical activities: praying together (The Week of Prayer and the World Day of Prayer are joined together and celebrated in March), interconfessional actions of the team of city pastors, the training courses of the Transylvanian Evangelic Academy, co-operative actions of the Orthodox and Lutheran Theological Faculties and the ecumenical student association Corpus Christi in which students of six denominations in Transylvania are working together in various activities including issuing a biannual ecumenical magazine.[62]

This happened despite the fact that these groups may cause potential conflicts. According to Stefan Tobler, "In the Romanian context, there are three matters with strong potential for conflict: – the tension between the Orthodox Church and Greek Catholic Church; – the blending of ecumenical matters with ethnic tensions between Hungarians and Romanians; – the increasing number of Neoprotestant Churches and groups: Baptists, Pentecostals, Adventists."[63]

---

61. H. Vogelaar, "An Ecumenical Journey in Romania: Orthodox – Protestant Relationships Since1989," *Exchange* 33, no. 3 (2006): 293.

62. Ibid., 286.

63. Tobler, "The Ecumenical Situation," 44.

To be correct, it should be noted that Baptists did not participate in this event. It is probably easier to hold such a dialogue in Transylvania than anywhere else, as Orthodox Romanians, as well as Reformed, Lutherans and Hungarian Evangelicals, have been living there historically. Faith, in this case, is not just individual choice, but part of the culture. As Reinhard Frieting mentioned: "Everywhere in Europe, churches have been closely connected with national cultures. The churches became 'cultural factors' through their influence . . . At the same time the churches became themselves 'products of culture', since for example French Catholicism, Greek Orthodoxy and German Protestantism are today each still characterized by a certain mentality and spirituality."[64]

Differences exist because one and the same concepts are often interpreted differently. On the one hand, this can serve as a breeding ground for conflicts, while on the other hand this is an additional reason to find common grounds. Let us take as an example the concept of "church." Romanian Baptists and Romanian Orthodox believers understand this concept completely differently. Bria considers that "congregationalist" ecclesiology can bring more confrontation in the ecumenical movement.[65] This is in spite of the fact that "ecclesiology should help people to understand anew the meaning of religion, humanity, salvation, culture and values, issues on which the traditional language of the church has become largely relevant."[66]

I think that a lot, in this case, depends on the goodwill of a particular leader or of a group of leaders. Vogetaar cites the example of a Romanian Baptist pastor: "Paul Botica, a Romanian Baptist minister, refers to common enterprises like working together in prisons, hospitals, orphanages, helping the poor, homeless and street children as proper opportunities to know one another better and initiate a relevant dialogue."[67]

In this case, there will hardly be accusations of proselytism. As Erich Geldbach writes: "The charge of 'sheep stealing' must be closely examined. Is another religious group really intruding into the life of a 'national' or 'territorial' church or is that group trying to reach the unchurched or those

---

64. Frieling, "Our Common Responsibility," 63.
65. Bria, *Sense of Ecumenical Tradition*, 104.
66. Ibid., 91.
67. Vogelaar, "An Ecumenical Journey in Romania," 290.

that behave like unchurched?"⁶⁸ "The Orthodox have also discovered in the ecumenical community a witnessing awareness, a spirit of sharing faith, a recognition of others and of the church for others. These experiences have been tremendously enriching for the Orthodox in terms of the personal, existential commitment of Christians to the wider fellowship of the community."⁶⁹

The words written by Bria are also very encouraging: "The existence of other Christians and churches is not a threat for the Orthodox. The Orthodox must recognize the distinct realities and signs of the Holy Spirit in the life and mission of other confessions. Moreover, the church cannot separate what God has put together: unity in the communion of the church and the renewal of human community."⁷⁰

If the Romanian Orthodox do not see a threat, why should Moldavian Orthodox or Evangelical Christians in Moldova see this as a threat? The issue of proselytism is particularly acute, namely in the countries and churches where there is a lack of dialogue and mutual fear and apprehension exist.

At the same time, the relations between the Russian Orthodox Church and the Evangelical Christian Baptist Union of Russia remain relatively tense. "Both denominations thereby distance themselves from newer religious movements which entered the country following the collapse of communism in 1990."⁷¹ It should be noted that both groups have distanced themselves not only from new religious movements, but also from each other: "In private conversations both sides lamented the persistence of lower-level disputes. Baptist mission efforts are often combated by the Orthodox and Baptists on their part seriously question the faith of Orthodox believers."⁷²

As Michael J. Christensen wrote, "I have been frustrated at times in my attempts to get Orthodox and Protestant leaders into the same room

---

68. Geldbach, "Religious liberty, proselytism, evangelism," 27.
69. Bria, "Sense of Ecumenical Tradition," 86.
70. Ibid.
71. K. Rösler, "Hearty Atmosphere among Church Leaders at the Top, Disputes Below: Second Moscow Summit between Orthodox and Baptists," 22 January 2007, http://www.ebf.org/hearty-atmosphere-among-church-leaders-at-the-top-disputes-below.
72. Ibid.

together for religious dialogue, let alone to propose collaborative projects. Mutual misunderstanding and suspicion persists."[73] But there are a few examples of very successful collaboration between Evangelicals and Orthodox Christians.[74]

Thus, neither the relationship in Romania nor in Russia can be called satisfactory. Nevertheless there is a certain positive dynamic between the Orthodox Church and some Evangelical and Protestant denominations. Baptists, to a greater extent, also stand apart from the ecumenical dialogue. Further, I will try to analyze whether there is hope for improvement from a global perspective.

General Situation in Ecumenical Circles

I have repeatedly tackled the issue of ecumenical cooperation in various chapters of this work. Trying not to repeat the same information, I will turn attention to the possibility of dialogue and cooperation in terms of a globalized world, the era of postmodernism, and compare this with the situation in Moldova.

Thus, in spite of the willingness or unwillingness of church ministers, theologians, and parishioners, the twenty-first century is marked by an entirely new form of thinking, which was not characteristic of previous generations. The shift of the ideological paradigm from the Middle Ages to the Renaissance was related to the Reformation. The transition of society from the Renaissance to the Enlightenment was accompanied by the emergence of liberal theology. The newest era brought with it the Emergent Church. The study of this phenomenon is not one of the objectives set for this research work. I just want to note that theological thought is developing in step with the times – responding to new challenges. As a result of certain reactions to theological thought, church forms, approaches and missionary paradigms also change.

In an era of globalization, the issue of "canonical territory" has taken a sharp turn. Countries split and merge, borders appear and disappear, peoples migrate from one continent to another. In addition, within the

---

73. M. J. Christensen, "Evangelical-Orthodox Dialogue in Russia on the Eve of the Tenth Anniversary of Chernobyl, 1994," (unpublished document, available from the author).

74. Ibid.

boundaries of a large city representatives of dozens or even hundreds of nationalities and religious faiths can live together.

Globalization and postmodernism are "walking" together. Globalization erases the geographical and geo-political boundaries, while postmodernism does the same in the mindset of a younger generation. One of the reasons for the appearance of postmodernity, some researchers see, is the bankruptcy of modernity, which could not give the final answers on the main questions, even if it uses scientific apparatus.[75]

Based on these observations and research, the teaching of the Orthodox Church on canonical territory is an archaism which has lost not only its relevance, but also become inconsistent with the existing reality. It is more likely that this is the reason why some in the hierarchy see a threat to Orthodoxy in the postmodern worldview.

> Four possible responses to post-modern pluralism seem to me to be unacceptable for Orthodox Christians. The first is to deny that "post-modern pluralism" exists and is rapidly growing throughout the world . . . Second, it would be a fatal mistake for Orthodox Christians to think that they and their churches are somehow immune to post-modernism and untouched by its influence and power . . . Third, Orthodox Christians must not respond to post-modern pluralism by imagining that we can reject the contemporary world by taking refuge in a world of our own making . . . Fourth, Orthodox Christians must not fall prey to the idea that the post-modern pluralistic worldview is a great new opportunity for humankind, inherently consistent with traditional Orthodox views of freedom, personal dignity, cultural diversity, incarnational theology and apophatic mystical theology.[76]

At first glance, it may indeed seem that the postmodern denial of the existence of absolute truth and mysticism are close to the apophatism of Orthodoxy and aimed at the sensuousness of the worship. "There is a great

---

75. M. Pocock, G. van Pheenen, and D. McConnell, *The Changing Face of World Missions: Engaging Contemporary Issues and Trends* (Grand Rapids: Baker, 2005), 107.

76. T. Hopko, "Orthodoxy in Post-Modern Pluralist Societies," *The Ecumenical Review* 51, no. 4 (October 1999): 367.

deal of affinity between Eastern Christian notions of apophatism and the doctrine of the Trinity and postmodern notions of language and difference, the temptation would be great to use postmodern thought as a means for validating Christian thought."[77] There are similar opinions among Evangelical theologians:

> Postmodernism is the greatest threat to theology, and it is on this subject that we must stand most firm. Postmodernism seeks to eliminate any construct of the quest for all-encompassing, objective truth, turning instead to a pragmatic and relative view of truth. This must be outrightly rejected, not simply because it is a threat to the discipline of theology, but because it is a denial of the Christian story. Along with this rejection of meta-narratives comes the threat of relativism and relativistic pluralism, both of which are undeniably set against the story of God as seen in Christian Scripture.[78]

I will not enter into debate with those who see in postmodernism only a threat, although I am inclined to seek dialogue with the modern worldview, and not just criticize it. These examples were given only to show that Evangelical as well as Orthodox Christians should really assess the situation and understand the era in which they live. There is no other solution and nobody can hide behind the walls of the church. I suggest learning to live in the new reality. One of the important points that can be learned in the era of postmodernism is the ability to listen and to build dialogue. In this case, listening involves risk. Aristotle Papanikolaou wrote on this subject: "Ecumenical gatherings presuppose conversation, which presupposes listening, which presupposes risk of a realized experience of recognition that leads to such statements as 'I never thought of that' or 'that seems right.' To recognize that a particular prohibition or practice within a tradition needs change is not to surrender to an incommensurable language game; instead,

---

77. A. Papanikolaou, "Orthodoxy, Postmodernity, and Ecumenism: the Difference that Divine-Human Communion Makes," *Journal of Ecumenical Studies* 42, no. 4 (Fall 2007): 544.

78. J. Hiebert, "Shaping Evangelical Theology in the Postmodern Turn," *Didaskalia* 13 (Spring 2002): 12.

it is a form of prophetic self-critique that allows a community to examine whether it is being faithful to its own central principles."[79]

Yet in 1997, the WCC drew the attention of the churches to this in one of their documents: "Christian fellowship and partnership will not be possible unless Christians and churches:

- Listen to one another in genuine dialogue aimed at overcoming ignorance, prejudices or misunderstandings . . .;
- Ensure greater sharing of information and accountability in mission at all levels, including prior discussion before launching programs for evangelism;
- Encourage, strengthen and complement one another in missionary activity in an ecumenical spirit;
- Demonstrate willingness to learn from others;
- Make greater efforts for inner renewal in their own traditions and cultural contexts."[80]

This research led me to conclude that both groups need change, but they also need to be listened to, because both of them have a lot to say. Orthodoxy needs rethinking – interpretation into modern language of the notional and actual works of the church fathers and the teachings and traditions of their church. Evangelicals need to understand their mission, to move from a managerial approach to a relevant approach for the Moldavian context. After all, the first as well as the second group of Christians face a crisis. The crisis of the Evangelical churches in Moldova has been studied in detail in chapter 2. In my view, the crisis of the Orthodox Church was very well described by Valentin Kozhuharov: "After 1994–1995 in almost all 'Orthodox' countries in Eastern Europe (to mention some of them: Russia, Ukraine, Belarus, Moldavia, Romania, Serbia, Bulgaria, Georgia, etc.), the churches became filled with people and the church as a whole grew rapidly. Then in the next several years the enthusiasm diminished and in the church remained mostly the believers who were strengthened in their faith and their Christian life."[81]

---

79. Papanikolaou, "Orthodoxy, Postmodernity, and Ecumenism," 545.
80. World Council of Churches, "Towards Common Witness," 54–55.
81. Kozhuharov, "Developments in the mission," 8.

People do not remain in churches. Despite the fact that I have reiterated on many occasions that the quantitative growth of the church is not included in the concept of *missio Dei*, and does not fit in the Theocentric vision of the kingdom, the leaving of church by those who have already entered into it is also a violation of the missionary assignment of Christ about making disciples (Matt 28:19–20). Thus, "the objective of ecumenical dialogue (in the sense of 'worldwide' and 'missionary') is to bring churches into closer contact with one another for the sake of mission and its credibility."[82]

New Paradigm for Evangelical Churches in Moldova from a *Missio Dei* Perspective

In talking about the link between missiology and ecclesiology, I would like to turn now to Avery Dulles and his models of the church. Dulles presented five models of the church: the Church as Institution, the Church as Mystical Communion, the Church as Sacrament, the Church as Herald and the Church as Servant.[83] He saw that "the institutional vision of the church defines the church primarily in terms of its visible structures, especially the rights and powers of its officers."[84] "In the institutionalist ecclesiology the powers and functions of the church are generally divided into three: teaching, sanctifying, and governing. This division of powers leads to further distinctions between the church teaching and the church taught, the church sanctifying and the church sanctified, the church governing and the church governed."[85] This model is closer to the historical churches, in the case of Moldova – to the Orthodox Church.

At the same time, the Orthodox Church is very close to its understanding the Church as Sacrament. "The model 'the Church as a mystical community' emphasizes the immediate relationship of all believers to the Holy Spirit, who directs the whole Church."[86] This model is closer to the Pentecostal and Neo-Pentecostal churches, while Baptists talk more about obeying to the Bible, but not the Holy Spirit. In many cases obeying the

---

82. Oborji, "Mission as Ecumenical Dialogue," 157.

83. A. Dulles, *Models of the Church* (Garden City, New York: Doubleday, 1974), 31–96.

84. Ibid., 31.

85. Ibid., 34.

86. Ibid., 49.

Bible, rather than the Holy Spirit. In many cases obeying the Bible is for Baptists a synonym to obeying the Holy Spirit. Thus Moldavian Baptists are closer to the fourth model from Dulles' list – the Church as Herald – which "makes the 'word' primary and the 'sacrament' secondary . . . The mission of the Church is to proclaim that which it has heard, believed, and been commissioned to proclaim."[87] From my perspective the fifth model could serve as better type of church for Evangelicals in Eastern Europe. "The 'Church as Servant' model may be called 'secular-dialogic': secular, because the church takes the world as a properly theological locus, and seeks to discern the signs of the times: dialogic, because it seeks to operate on the frontier between the contemporary world and the Christian tradition (including the Bible)."[88]

As a result of the study of the forms and methods of missionary activity in Moldova, a brand new paradigm springs inevitably to mind that I believe corresponds to the present context. Namely, the contextual missiology that is the area of study of the present research work.

Before suggesting a new paradigm for the Evangelical churches, it is necessary to make some preliminary remarks based on the conducted research:

- The concept of *missio Dei* is present in Moldova implicitly only within a small number of local congregations. With regard to the Union of Evangelical Christian Baptists it is present neither in documents, statements, nor in its activity.
- The Union of Evangelical Christian Baptists largely conducts its activities based on the paradigm of the Church Growth Movement, and at the same time, I can assertively state that this approach does not work.
- The proclamation of the gospel is made through new churches and "aggressive" evangelism.
- The Union of Evangelical Christian Baptists of Moldova does not even consider the possibility of dialogue with the Orthodox Church though on a private level the Union is flattered by any contact with it.

---

87. Ibid., 71.
88. Ibid., 86.

- Social ministry is not part of the strategy of the Union, although it is often carried out in local communities as part of evangelistic projects or as private forms of charity.
- The salvation of souls is the main purpose of mission.
- The worldview of the Union's leadership is collective.

Based on these conclusions, I will take as a basis for the formation of a new paradigm the Theology of Partnership, which was suggested by Ross. "Partnership is constituted of three factors. First, there must be the acceptance by each one concerned of genuine involvement, a committal of oneself to the other partner in trust . . . Second, partnership involves a ready acceptance of responsibility, a readiness to serve the purpose of the common enterprise. Finally, involvement must carry with it a readiness to pay the price of partnership, to accept all the liabilities and limitations that arise."[89]

Speaking about the Moldavian context, first of all, the Evangelical churches should formally recognize the Orthodox Church as a Christian church, rather than a semi-pagan, wrongheaded or corrupt one. Accordingly, it is expected that the Orthodox Church stop perceiving the Evangelical community as a sect that came to destroy the national culture, discredit the history and destroy the identity.

Regarding joint activities and collective participation in projects, I analyzed several studies carried out earlier in the search for such proposals.

The Manila Manifesto makes the following statements about ecumenical collaboration:

1) On the social level, Catholics, Orthodox, and Protestants can and must act together in the name of Christ and in the name of the gospel they proclaim. They must be the interpreters, defenders, and promoters of human dignity.
2) In working for peace and reconciliation – the application of the gospel in zones of conflict.
3) Collaboration in the arts and sciences and in human promotion.
4) Collaboration at religious and pastoral levels.[90]

---

89. Ross, "The Theology of Partnership," 145.

90. "1989 Manila Manifesto," in *Concepts of Mission: The Evolution of the Contemporary Missiology*, ed. F. A. Oborji (Maryknoll, NY: Orbis Books, 2006), 173–175.

Anastasios (Yannoulatos) offers his own view of cooperation:

1) "The most practical issues for a creative inter-religious dialogue are those unique themes that humanity confronts with such intensity today due to globalization (for example ecological issues, poverty) . . .
2) 'Dialogue of life' based on the acceptance of and respect for the religious freedom of others and their right to decide what their ultimate visions and goals are . . .
3) One of the first practical priorities of inter-religious dialogue must be to offer, as much as possible, as an objective of the doctrines, history and worship of the other religions in education text books, the press and the electronic media all over the world . . .
4) To abandon inter-religious dialogue is to give new impetus to the formation of ghettos, to ethnic or religious 'cleansing', and to the development of various new expressions of religious fanaticism . . .
5) Each religion is called upon to develop what is most genuine, deep and beautiful in what it possesses, and with these gifts to address the civil society in a peaceful and edifying manner.[91]

I will make an attempt to respond to all recommendations, generalizing the ones that echo each other:

- First, the existence in Moldova of Moldavian Christian AID is only the first step to collaboration. Joint projects are rarely carried out. There is rather an exchange of experience and views about the projects each group has launched independently. I hope that this experience will not only develop within the existing organization, but also multiply within many others at the community level as well as at the national level.
- Second, the resolution of the Transdniestrian conflict could become one of the first items on the agenda of the Union of Evangelical Christian Baptists and that of the Orthodox churches.

---

91. Anastasios (Yannoulatos), "Problems and Prospects of Inter-religious Dialogue: an Eastern Orthodox Perspective," *The Ecumenical Review* 52 (2000): 355.

- Third, the value of human life in Moldova is very low. This statement can be understood both in literal and in figurative sense. Corruption, human trafficking, total migration, poverty and environmental issues are just some of the issues people face in Moldova.
- Fourth, it is worth noting the necessity of joint scientific research work in the areas of missiology, sociology, ethnology, and culture. Joint pastoral conferences on ethical issues, religious teaching in schools, counseling of mental patients as well as joint publication of books and booklets that promote religious tolerance among the people must be undertaken.

The existence of so many problems in the country cannot wait until the church can find complete unity in matters of doctrine and practices of church worship. Otherwise, the church will not fulfill its calling while acting in accordance with its agenda rather than with the Scriptures.

Returning to the third point designated by Ross, the cost of the partnership, in this case, will be the humility of both partners. Perhaps it is appropriate to ask why the church artificially limits its possibilities and then looks for solutions to the created problems. Ross gives the answer to this question: "Our ego is broken open by encountering the Thou in the other, and through the Thou of other people we can meet the transcendent Thou, God."[92] Further, "partners share the sufferings of one another."[93] To be humble is a kind of suffering. To be partners today in Moldova, Orthodox and Evangelicals should humble themselves, which will cause some suffering. A partnership of this kind will create a new atmosphere of "suffering together" in the name of Jesus and for the kingdom.

The Triune God, creating human beings, made himself vulnerable to additional suffering. The involvement in the mission of the Son made Christ suffer as well as his Father and the Holy Spirit who intercedes for us through wordless groans (Rom 8:26).[94] Suffering for someone else has

---

92. Ross, "The Theology of Partnership," 147.

93. Ibid., 148.

94. It is interesting to note that in the 22nd and 26th verses of chapter 8 of Romans one and the same word – *stenagmois* (26) and *sustenazei* (22) is used, which conveys the inexpressible grief experienced by the Spirit, in situations where Christians are weak and do not know what to pray about.

a biblical and theological basis. Artificially moving over the suffering, Christians and churches do not follow the path of Trinitarian theology. Partnership implies self-restraint and self-emptying – kenosis.

With regard to the Orthodox Church, its self-restraint can be manifested in a moratorium on the teaching on canonical territory. Even John Meyendorf in 1978 said that new canonical legislation is desirable.[95] After all, in fact, to a greater extent, the Orthodox Church has the greatest influence in Moldova as mentioned in chapter 5. "An evangelistic church should also be an ecumenical community, and an ecumenical church should always be an evangelizing community."[96] As for the rest, the present research work does not assume the responsibility to recommend anything to the Orthodox Church. This is because the focus of this book, the purpose, the theme is: *Rethinking Missio Dei among Evangelical Churches in an Eastern European Orthodox Context*. Therefore, my further recommendations will address only Evangelical churches.

I will base my recommendations on the summary table, which was given in chapter 8:

- As mentioned above, the Evangelical churches favor collective thinking and decision making. In this case, it is not important whether it is inherited from the Anabaptist/Mennonite, or is dominant in the Orthodox context. It is important that this image of church leadership, disciplinary decisions, and approach to the mission of the church, are well suited for efficient activities in Moldova.
- Trinitarian theology should remain the core of the theological foundation of mission. Thus, the teaching about the Trinity will become reality in churches and people will see its value and practicality. In addition, it will enhance both vision and activities.
- In the case of the goal of mission, it is difficult in my opinion, to emphasize something in particular since each missiological paradigm has its own vision. Nevertheless, the concept of the Orthodox theosis does not contradict the Baptist doctrine of

---

95. J. Meyndorf, *Living Tradition: Orthodox Witness in the Contemporary World* (Crestwood, NY: St. Vladimir's Seminary Press, 1978), 105–110.

96. Costas, *Liberating News*, 86.

transformation into the image of Christ. The concept of theosis, of course, is much broader than the concept of "transformation," but it is justified by the Scriptures, which are very much appreciated by the Evangelical churches. Also, it is worth remembering the Anabaptist roots and that the gospel resides not only in words but in deeds.

- "Witness" is a concept which was very widely used by Evangelical churches in Moldova until 1990. We suggest making use of it instead of the concept of "evangelism" and "evangelization" which in the past twenty years are intertwined so closely with the aggressive forms of proclamation of the good news that they can bring more harm than good. The concept of "witness" is historically close to Evangelical believers in Moldova, and besides, it is also used by the Orthodox Church.
- The understanding of the concept of "witness" should lead to joint witness. Evangelical churches should reject narrowly confessional representation of unity. Unity refers not only to the representatives of the local community, not only to churches which are members of one and the same association or union, not even to Evangelical believers. The high-priestly prayer of Christ mentioned in chapter 6, refers to all those who believe in the words of the apostles. Evangelical churches should cease all attacks against the Orthodox Church in sermons and in private conversations. It is necessary to establish fraternal and partner relationships instead of competitive ones. In addition, such unity can be expressed in regular prayers at Evangelical meetings for the Orthodox Church, the restoration of unity and understanding.
- Evangelicals should pay particular attention to social responsibility. It should be excluded from the list of marginal tasks and be included in that of extremely importance objectives. It should be part of the strategic plans of the Union of Churches as well as of individual communities. It is recommended to allocate for this purpose appropriate amounts of the church budget, the preparation of human resources, the establishment of cooperative relationships with both international partners

and with other churches, and especially with the Orthodox. We suggest abandoning the dualistic worldview, which constantly raises the question of the primacy of evangelism and social service. We should perceive witness and social involvement as indivisible parts of the mission of the undivided church.

- Regarding proselytizing, I suggest abandoning the attempts to proclaim the good news to actively practicing Orthodox Christians. It is necessary to focus the witness on atheists, representatives of non-Christian religious groups, un-churched "cultural Orthodox," and to offer the possibility of choosing a church mentioning the Evangelical church as well as the Orthodox Church. In the case of a voluntary transfer from Orthodoxy to Evangelicalism, adult believers who were baptized earlier based on their faith, must not be baptized repeatedly.

- Referring to canonical territory I suggest reserving the right not to recognize this segment of the teachings of the Orthodox Church because of its non-compliance with modernity and because of the presence of many internal contradictions within Orthodoxy on this issue.

- The acceptance of the above paradigm will be the recognition of the fact that the mission of the church comes from God in three Persons, who is the initiator of salvation, which essentially is the missio Dei. The church following this path will truly be a missional church. The rethinking of mission will thus have an impact on the theory and practice of the mission in Moldova as well as on the following areas:
    - National level: Adopting this approach as a strategic one, the Evangelical Christian Baptist Union of Moldova can have access to public television, radio, print and electronic media and make known its decision, which in my opinion, will have a very positive impact on the image of the churches which will no longer be categorized as "sect" but will become a full-fledged part of society.
    - Interchurch level: The Orthodox Church in Moldova should be the first to learn about the decisions which are made in

this regard. This can be achieved through meetings of the leadership of the churches as well as through print media.
- UECB level: Pastoral conferences, a revised curriculum of the College of Theology and Education, and the print media are those tools through which it will be possible to make all the churches within the Union acquainted with the change.
- Local community level: Each member of the local community can learn about the rethinking during sermons, seminars and by reading the local newspapers.

Thus, the biblical and theological grounds of the *missio Dei* will become known to the greater part of Evangelical believers in the country, which will lead to practical changes in the life of churches.

A final remark: it is understood that the Orthodox Church, seeing the goodwill of the Evangelical churches will also compromise and propose an appropriate approach. But even if this does not happen, the Evangelical churches have to accept it as from the Lord, and bear with patience their cross till the end. Only in this way can the kenotic mission of God be realized in this country. The Light of Christ will be seen and the Living Word of God will produce real changes through the Evangelical churches in the country of Moldova.

Conclusions

It is very important to mention that I did not produce just a practical guide for how to be a more effective church in Moldova. I did not pursue pragmatic goals by this research. I do not believe that reading this last chapter without reading the previous eight chapters will help someone to understand what mission in Moldova means. I am sure that only deep and patient research of Orthodox theology, understanding the roots for our own mission and studying international experiences in the field could give some fresh insights and lead to a better understanding of the calling of the church in general and the understanding of the role of Evangelicals in Moldova in particular.

I would like to mention the main results and conclusions from chapter 9.
1) Evangelicals are responsible for developing a holistic approach in their mission, including social responsibility, prophetic presence

and proclamation of the good news, because all these things have biblical foundations and are relevant to the contemporary Moldavian situation.

2) Evangelicals need to rethink the concept of "evangelism," its meaning, methods and tools. My suggestion is to use the term "witness," which has more peaceful content, does not create tensions with Orthodoxy and has historical precedents on the Moldavian territory.

3) Evangelicals had much experience in dialogue with the Orthodox Church during the Soviet times. This experience should be raised again, revised and used in a new realm.

4) Evangelicals and Orthodox in Romania and Russia are involved at least in a kind of dialogue, and their cases could be good examples for Moldavian Evangelicals.

5) *Missio Dei* is very relevant for Moldavian society, which suffers from many social, political, economical and religious struggles. A holistic, Trinitarian mission of partnership could be a good sign for the whole population of Moldova.

I do not pretend that these suggested results could be applied without any changes or rethinking. I would like to influence church leaders to do their own research and to shape their own understanding of the church's mission as the result of *missio Dei*.

Conclusion

From the very beginning of this last section, it is necessary to mention that during the time this research was conducted many things have happened, both in Moldova and in my personal life. There was a change of political regime in Moldova (instead of communists, liberals came to power), but these changes brought nothing good to the economy – Moldova is still the poorest country in Europe. I have changed some emphases in my ministry – from an almost exclusively church-oriented ministry I have become more oriented to serving both the spiritual and the social needs of the community. I am more oriented toward society as a whole.

The following is an overview the entire paper which emphasizes some main and important conclusions.

The first chapter showed us the birth and development of the Evangelical churches in Moldova. We saw that for most of the last two hundred years, Moldova was a part of Russia and Romania. Because of that, the Church in Moldova was under the influence of the Russian Orthodox Church and Romanian Orthodox Church, and until today these tensions have not been resolved. The Orthodox Church has always had the most important impact on shaping the culture, worldview and practical behavior of Moldavians. We saw that the appearance of Evangelicals in Moldavian territory was conditioned by a few factors: the crisis inside of the Orthodox Church in the nineteenth century, spiritual hunger in the hearts of people, appearance of German migrants in Moldova, etc. During the first period of their existence, Evangelicals were not touched by the government, but very soon they were persecuted by the Orthodox Church and by the state. However, they have been very active in mission, which in the initial stage had a more Anabaptist face – witness by lifestyle. Evangelicals in Moldova united in one church and later in one union painlessly and were united regardless of their ethnic or cultural differences. It is important to indicate that the Pashkov movement was not very active in Moldova, and because of that, churches were not involved in social activities as part of their mission. They did a lot of charity work as part of their lifestyle. Persecution continued during the Soviet times, and witness by lifestyle was the only possibility to preach the gospel outside of the church walls. After Stalin's death, Evangelical Baptists became a part of many ecumenical forums and platforms and began a dialogue with the Russian Orthodox Church.

Chapter 2 talked about the mission of Evangelical churches in contemporary Moldova. It spoke about changes that happened right after the collapse of the Soviet Union. Many foreign agencies came to Moldova beginning in 1990. Most of them did not coordinate their activities with each other, and the Evangelical Baptist Union did not have enough capacity to do so. Agencies linked with local churches, and just few years later the Evangelical churches in Moldova lost their identity, which had been formed during the Soviet times, and did not create one common identity. At this time they lost their contacts with Orthodoxy. From 1990, Evangelical Baptists stopped talking about ecumenical contacts and began to talk about mission as evangelism, which later was seen as "aggressive evangelism." The main goal for the UCECBM, according to official declarations, is proclaiming the gospel; but according to my studies, it actually is the spiritual growth of church members. At the same time a holistic approach in the life of the Union and its theological reflections cannot be seen. I defined the mission of the UCECBM as ecclesiocentric.

Chapter 3 viewed contemporary relations between Evangelicals and the Orthodox Church. I looked at the reasons and foundations for the split within the Orthodox Church in Moldova, which was divided in two parts. This division created additional tensions in the country among Orthodox believers. This situation showed that the teaching about canonical territory does not work even within Orthodoxy. At the same time, tensions between the Orthodox and Evangelical believers decreased. We see that Evangelicals can raise their voices, inviting and calling Orthodoxy to unity. Such an attitude will be more beneficial if Evangelicals will refuse to practice the "aggressive evangelism" approach and will take some responsibilities in society on themselves. My suggestion, addressed to the Orthodox Church, was for it to freeze the attack against Evangelicals regarding proselytizing and breaching the Orthodox right in Moldavian territory. We saw that a platform for cooperation and possible future dialogue has already been established and it is important to work towards this direction. Sadly many pastors do not want to continue the dialogue with Orthodoxy and their desire to maintain peace within the Evangelical Baptist union is greater than their desire to find common ground with the Orthodox Church. At the same time on a personal and communitarian level, joint projects and dialogue are carried out, and new relationships are built. It is necessary to support such initiatives at all levels.

Chapter 4 tried to find connections and roots for such attitudes towards Orthodoxy in missiological paradigms. I investigated three missiological approaches: the Church Growth Movement, Lausanne Movement and Anabaptist approach. We realized the Church Growth Movement sees the goal of mission in church planting, evangelism and training of new leaders. They have rejected the holistic approach in mission, and see social responsibility as a personal reaction of converted individuals on revealed human needs. They are very suspicious about ecumenical dialogue, and have the most significant influence in contemporary Moldova through the Southern Baptist Convention. In their turn, representatives of the Lausanne Movement are concerned with a combination of evangelism and social responsibility. They have not shaped a common position on these issues, but most of them agreed that mission should be done from a *missio Dei* perspective and should have as its ground Trinitarian theology. We saw that the Lausanne Movement has little influence and attention in contemporary Moldova. The Anabaptist missiological approach is witness as lifestyle, and it was accepted in Moldova from the German predecessors and was the only possibility for mission during the Soviet times. I stated that the current most influential missiological paradigm in Moldova is the approach of the Church Growth Movement.

Chapter 5 was dedicated to Orthodox missiology, which is also very complicated and has many faces. I concentrated on Russian and Romanian Orthodox thinkers and missiologists such as Ion Bria, Dumitru Staniloae, Patriarch Kirill, Thomas Hopko and a few others. We saw that Trinitarian theology lies at the foundation of Orthodox ecclesiology and missiology.

Orthodox missiology is holistic, including soul and body, nature and universe. Their holistic approach in mission flows from a Trinitarian theology and touches all aspects of human life, society, state and ecology. Orthodoxy believes in holistic salvation and uses the concept of witnessing to the nations, and taking care of humankind. The Orthodox Church has proclaimed that the only method for mission is kenotic, which begins from repentance of Christians and self-sacrifice. The final goal for mission is *theosis* – deification of every human being and the Eucharist is one of the main tools of achieving this goal, because only in unity can and does the church fulfill its mission.

Chapters 4 and 5 showed that there are a lot of misunderstandings between Evangelicals and Orthodoxy and that there is currently no common ground for their dialogue, because both start from their own perspective and are not ready to hear each other. One of the reasons is they use different "languages," their critical and content apparatus are very different. The same words often carry different meanings. Both bodies need a *lingua franca*, which could give a common platform. For this purpose I addressed the work of the World Council of Churches, where the concept of *missio Dei* has been shaped, which can work as a *lingua franca* in general, and in Moldova between Evangelicals and Orthodox in particular.

Chapter 6 sought to understand how mission has been perceived in ecumenical circles. The *missio Dei* concept was developed in the middle of the twentieth century, experienced a conceptual crisis at the end of the twentieth century and received its "second birth" at the beginning of the twenty-first century. This concept is Trinitarian and has a lot in common with Orthodox theology. The Lausanne Movement and Anabaptist tradition can be used to find the tools for designing a foundation for collaboration with Orthodoxy in Eastern Europe. The Trinitarian foundation for *missio Dei* is directed to the holistic approach in mission, which is very close to the Orthodox understanding of the church's mission. Ecumenicals agree that God is active not only in the church but also is directed outwardly from the church: in culture, in history, in political and economic processes. The church, which is involved in *missio Dei*, should have an adequate response for all challenges from the world. God can use the church to change the world, and can use the world to change the church. The final goal of *missio Dei* is the full glory of God and presence of the kingdom of God. There is also a sign of achieving the final goal – *shalom* – which should be established in human hearts and on the earth.

If we talk about the church's mission in Trinitarian terms, we need to address the meaning of Trinitarian mission, going to the real roots of it. Chapter 7 does this, addressing the different sources, trying to identify the role of God the Father, God the Son and God the Holy Spirit in the mission of the church. I tried to find an answer not only in theological and missiological discussions, but also in the biblical texts, which talk about different aspects of the mission of each Person in Trinity. God the Father is constantly active in mission, sending his Son, the Holy Spirit and himself to achieve his purposes with humankind and the whole universe. God the Son came not only to proclaim that the kingdom has come. His mission was holistic: he brought redemption and salvation from eternal death and at the same time he came to the poor and oppressed to liberate them from any kind of oppression and injustice. The culmination of his mission was his death and resurrection. He was always among people, answering their daily needs as well as their deeper emotional, social, spiritual and existential needs. God the Holy Spirit continues the mission of God the Father and God the Son, being very active in the ministry of prophets of the Old Testament, in the life of Jesus, in church activity and in the world, where he is present in a mysterious way. If Jesus has sent the church in the same way as the Father sent him, it means that the mission of the church should reflect all aspects of God's mission or *missio Dei*. It should be holistic, it should have eternal goals and the church should be attentive to what God is doing from outside the church "walls."

With these results, chapter 8 was ready to present a comparative study concerning distinctions and similarities in different missiological approaches. In talking about the Orthodox context, we allowed Orthodox missiology to be a referee, which investigated Evangelical approaches on their relevancy to the language, culture and worldview of people who live in an Orthodox country. We discovered that the Church Growth Movement approach is the most ineffective in a contemporary Orthodox country, because it sees Orthodoxy as the mission field; does not recognize Orthodox traditions and uses methodology and language which confronts main stream Christianity and creates additional tensions. When we saw the discussion among Evangelical missiologists in Lausanne group, we saw that their concern about a combination of evangelism and social responsibility can give Moldavian Evangelicals a foundation for shaping their new paradigm. At the same time Moldavian Evangelicals should not forget about witness by lifestyle, which they took from Mennonites and which is very close to the Orthodox understanding of proclamation of the gospel. Evangelicals should take into consideration Orthodox theology, constructing their own missionary vision, because God's call to unity is still relevant. Finally, Evangelicals from Moldova are responsible for articulating their own missiology, which should be done in Moldova, and should not be imported from other countries.

Chapter 9 serves this goal. There was an attempt to shape a new missiological paradigm for Moldavian Evangelicals, which should be holistic and cooperative. We studied biblical, theological and practical aspects for holistic mission in Moldova and mission as dialogue and common witness. The results showed that Evangelicals are responsible for developing a holistic approach in their mission, including social responsibility, prophetic presence and proclamation of the good news. My suggestion for Evangelicals in an Orthodox country would be to rethink the concept of "evangelism" and to use the term "witness," which has a more peaceful content and does not create tensions with Orthodoxy. Because Evangelicals have had enough experience in dialogue with the Orthodox Church during the Soviet times, this experience should not be forgotten and should be taken up again. The *missio Dei* concept is very relevant for Moldavian society, which suffers from many social, political, economical and religious struggles. A holistic, Trinitarian mission of partnership could be a good sign for the whole population of Moldova.

To rethink *missio Dei* among Evangelicals in an Orthodox context means to be open to new insights, collaboration, partnership and much more – to be open to change.

Doing this research has helped me change many things in both my worldview and my own life. I was inspired to organize several seminars and conferences in Moldova as a result. These were on the topic of the responsibility of the church and those at the edge of the church. I was a part of a group that has written a pamphlet entitled "The Concept of Social Ministry of the Evangelical Churches."

I do not pretend that this research covered all lacunas in Evangelical mission in Moldova and that the proposed approach can be applied in its full content. I am faced with a lot of new challenges, which could be investigated in further research. I would like to mention just few of them:

1) The conflicts in vision between Orthodox theology, which was formed in the pre-modern era, and Evangelical theology, which was shaped in the modern era, and the contemporary situation in the world in which Christians live in post-modern and after-post-modern contexts. We see that many concepts which were effective for churches in the past are not relevant for the contemporary world now. The combination of individualism and communitarian accountability which proclaims the post-modern world is something different from Orthodox communion and Evangelical individualism. The roles of principles, tradition, and church decisions, which were made 50 or 1,500 years ago, sometimes sound very strange to the contemporary world. We did not pay a lot of attention in this research to such issues, but we see that this question is very important, and there is not an easy answer for such contemporary complexities.

2) The appearance of the Emergent Movement and the Post-Church Movement is also very significant. They have not proclaimed themselves officially in Moldova, but their approaches become more and more popular, especially among young and educated Baptists. We are aware that this question is very connected with postmodernist worldviews. It is interesting that the Emergent movement addresses the *missio Dei* concept very actively, and because of that we have one more reason to investigate the relevancy of their approach to an Orthodox context.

3) Social and economic problems in Moldova have given us a lot of insights to connect this situation with the context where Liberation theology was born. I used some Liberation theology materials and realized some similarities between Latin America and Moldova, but I think that this question is worth being

studied on a deeper level. The majority of the population in Moldova has a socialistic mindset; many people were raised during the Communist times in the past. Currently the Moldavian Communist party is still one of the biggest and most influential in Europe and the FSU.

4) Theological education in Moldova drew our attention. We see that there is big lacuna in ecumenical and Orthodox studies. While forming a new generation of ministers, the leadership team of the Baptist Union has not even been talking about the relevancy of our academic program to the actual situation in Moldova. We think that further research could be done in comparative studies for the curriculum of the College of Theology and Education, in the values of actual pastors and challenges which Evangelicals face from Orthodoxy and society.

Summarizing all the conclusions, I can say that if Evangelical Baptists would like to be light and salt, they should be servants for the sake of victims of social injustice, prophets for social justice, witnesses of the good news and peacemakers among all groups, which suffered from different conflicts (such as ethnical, religious and political).

Concluding this study, I would like to quote David Bosch:

> We may never limit mission exclusively to an empirical project; it has always been greater than the observable missionary enterprise. Neither, to be sure, should it be completely divorced from it. Rather, mission is *missio Dei*, which seeks to subsume into itself the *missiones ecclesiae*, the missionary programs of the church. It is not the church which "undertakes" mission; it is the *missio Dei* which continues the church. The mission of the church needs constantly to be renewed and re-conceived . . . The *missio Dei* purifies the church. It sets it under the cross – the only place where it is ever safe . . . As a community of the cross the church then constitutes the fellowship of the kingdom, not just "church members"; as a community of the exodus, not as a "religious institution," it invites people to the feast without end.[1]

---

1. Bosch, *Transforming Mission*, 519.

Bibliography

Primary Sources

"1989 Manila Manifesto," in *Concepts of Mission: The Evolution of the Contemporary Missiology*, edited by F. A. Oborji. Maryknoll: Orbis Books, 2006.

Christensen, M. J. "Evangelical-Orthodox Dialogue in Russia on the Eve of the Tenth Anniversary of Chernobyl, 1994." Unpublished document, available from the author.

Ciobanu, V. F. *Speech at the Round Table Meeting "Church and Aids."* Chisinau, Moldova, November 2008.

Elliot, M. "Orthodox Relations in the Post-Soviet Era." Presentation at a conference on Evangelicals in Mission within CIS. Prague: IBTS, February 2003.

Ghiletchi, V. *Annual Report of the Bishop of the UECBCM*. Chisinau, March 2008.

———. *Report of the Bishop of the UECBCM at the Annual Pastoral Conference*. March 2003.

Hamm, V. *Speech at the Missionary Conference*. Chisinau, Moldova, 2006.

Hilborn, D., ed. *Evangelicalism and the Orthodox Church: A Report by the Evangelical Alliance (UK) Commission on the Unity and Truth among Evangelicals (ACUTE)*. London: ACUTE, 2001.

International Missionary Council. *The Missionary Obligation of the Church: Willingen, Germany, July 5–17, 1952*. London: Edinburgh House Press, 1952.

International Missionary Council. *Missions under the Cross: Addresses Delivered at the Enlarged Meeting of the Committee of the International Missionary Council at Willingen, in Germany, 1952*. London: Edinburgh House Press, 1953.

Karev, A. V. "Otchet general'nogo sekretarja VSEHB Vsesojuznomu s#ezdu evangel'skih hristian baptistov" [Report of the AUCECB General Secretary to the All-Union Congress of Evangelical Christians-Baptists, 1969], in *Proceedings of the All-Union Congress of Evangelical Christians-Baptists.* 1969.

Lausanne Committee for World Evangelism. *Evangelism and Social Responsibility: An Evangelical Commitment, 2 (c).* Wheaton: Lausanne Committee for World Evangelism, World Evangelical Fellowship, 1982.

Lausanne Committee for World Evangelization. *The Lausanne Story.*

Matrenczyk, M. "WCC Moldova Partnership Program, Report on Activities for 2003–2004." Chisinau, 2005.

Minear, P. S. "The Covenant and the Great Commission" in *Missions under the Cross: Addresses Delivered at the Enlarged Meeting of the Committee of the International Missionary Council at Willingen, in Germany, 1952*, edited by International Missionary Council. London: Edinburgh House Press, 1953.

Minutes of Executive Committee and Other Representative Baptists, held at the Baptist Church House, Southampton Row, London, from 19 to 23 July 1920.

Parushev, P. "Knowing the Risen Christ: The Anabaptist Holistic Witness as Mission." A plenary paper for the Mission and Evangelism Work Group of the Baptist World Alliance, presented at the Jubilee Annual Gathering of the BWA celebrating 400 years of the Baptist movement in Ede, The Netherlands, 27 July – 1 August 2009.

Popovici, V. *Report at the ECBM Congress.* Chisinau, Moldova, July 1998.

———. *Report at the ECBM Congress.* Chisinau, Moldova, August 2002.

Raytchinets, F. Unpublished sermon. Sarka-Valley Community Church, Prague, January 30, 2006.

Rösler, K. "Hearty Atmosphere among Church Leaders at the Top, Disputes below Second Moscow Summit between Orthodox and Baptists." Moscow, 22 January 2007. http://www.ebf.org/hearty-atmosphere-among-church-leaders-at-the-top-disputes-below.

"Strategy of the Union of Churches of Evangelical Christian Baptist from Moldova for 2008 – 2012," presented by General secretary Ion Miron at the UCECBM Congress, March 2008.

Thadden, R. "The Church under the Cross." In *Missions under the Cross: Addresses Delivered at the Enlarged Meeting of the Committee of the International Missionary Council at Willingen, in Germany, 1952,* edited by N. Goodall, International Missionary Council. London: Edinburgh House Press, 1953.

Western European Working Group. "Mission in God's Mission." In *Planning Mission. Working Papers on the New Quest for Missionary Communities*, edited by Th. Wieser. London: Epworth Press, 1966.

World Council of Churches. *The Church for Others and the Church for the World: A Quest for Structures for Missionary Congregations. Final Report of the*

Western European Working Group and North American Working Group of the Department on Studies in Evangelism. Geneva: WCC, 1967.

———. *Mission and Evangelism: An Ecumenical Affirmation.* Geneva: WCC, 1982.

———. "Mission and Evangelism in Unity Today." In *"You are the Light of the World" (Matthew 5:14): Statements on Mission by the World Council of Churches 1980–2005.* Geneva: WCC Publications, 2005.

———. "Towards Common Witness: A Call to Adopt Responsible Relationships in Mission and to Renounce Proselytism (September 1997)." In *"You are the Light of the World" (Matthew 5:14): Statements on Mission by the World Council of Churches 1980–2005.* Geneva: WCC Publications, 2005.

Books and Monographs

Beeson, Tr. *Discretion and Valour: Religious Conditions in Russia and Eastern Europe.* Collins: Fontana Books, 1974.

Bonhoeffer, D. *Letters and Papers from Prison.* London: SCM Press, 1971.

Bosch, D. *Transforming Mission.* Maryknoll: Orbis Books, 1991.

Bria, I. *Go Forth in Peace: Orthodox Perspective on Mission.* Geneva: World Council of Churches, 1986.

———. *The Liturgy after the Liturgy: Mission and Witness from an Orthodox Perspective.* Geneva: WCC Publications, 1996.

———. *The Sense of Ecumenical Tradition: The Ecumenical Witness and Vision of the Orthodox.* Geneva: WCC Publications, 1991.

Burnett, D. *God's Mission: Healing the Nations.* Bromley: MARC Europe, 1986.

Cardoza-Orlandi, C. F. *Mission: An Essential Guide.* Nashville: Abington Press, 2002.

Clendenin, D. B. *Eastern Orthodox Christianity: A Western Perspective.* Grand Rapids: Baker, 2003.

Costas, O. *Liberating News: A Theology of Contextual Evangelization.* Grand Rapids: Eerdmans, 1989.

Dorr, D. *Mission in Today's World.* Maryknoll: Orbis Books, 2000.

Dulles, A. *Models of the Church.* Garden City, NY: Doubleday, 1974.

Dupont, J. *The Salvation of the Gentiles: Essays on the Acts of the Apostles.* New York: Paulist Press, 1979.

Escobar, S. A. *The New Global Mission: The Gospel from Everywhere to Everyone.* Downers Grove: InterVarsity, 2003.

———. *A Time for Mission: The Challenge for Global Christianity.* Leicester: Inter-Varsity, 2003.

Evdokimov, P. *Pravoslavie* [Orthodoxy]. Moscow: Biblical Theological Institute of St Apostle Andrew, 2002.
Flett, J. G. *The Witness of God: The Trinity, Missio Dei, Karl Barth, and the Nature of Christian Community.* Grand Rapids: Eerdmans, 2010.
George, S. K. *Called as Partners in Christ's Service: The Practice of God's Mission.* Louisville: Geneva Press, 2004.
Glasser, A. F., and D. A. McGavran. *Contemporary Theologies of Mission.* Grand Rapids: Baker, 1983.
Glasser, A. F., C. E. Van Engen, D. S. Gilliland, and S. B. Redford. *Announcing the Kingdom: The Story of God's Mission in the Bible.* Grand Rapids: Baker, 2003.
Goodall, N. and International Missionary Council. *Missions Under the Cross Addresses Delivered at the Enlarged Meeting of the Committee of the International Missionary Council at Willingen, in Germany, 1952.* London: Edinburgh House Press, 1953.
Gutiérrez, G. *The God of Life.* Translated from Spanish. Maryknoll: Orbis Books, 1991.
———. *A Theology of Liberation.* Maryknoll: Orbis Books, 1988.
Guy, R. C. *Theological Foundations in Church Growth and Christian Mission.* New York: Harper & Row, 1965.
Hopko, T. *Speaking the Truth in Love: Education, Mission, and Witness in Contemporary Orthodoxy.* Crestwood: St Vladimir's Seminary Press, 2004.
Kane, J. H. "Role of God in Mission." In *Christian Missions in Biblical Perspective,* edited by J. H. Kane. Grand Rapids: Baker, 1976.
Keener, C. *The IVP Bible Background Commentary: New Testament.* Downers Grove: InterVarsity, 1993.
Kim, K. *Joining in with the Spirit: Connecting World Church and Local Mission.* London: Epworth Press, 2009.
King, C. *The Moldovans: Romania, Russia, and the Politics of Culture.* Stanford: Hoover Institution Press, Stanford University, 2000.
Kirk, J. A. *The Good News of the Kingdom Coming: The Marriage of Evangelism and Social Responsibility.* Downers Grove: InterVarsity, 1983.
———. *Mission under Scrutiny: Confronting Current Challenges.* London: Darton Longman & Todd, 2006.
———. *What is Mission: Theological Explorations.* Minneapolis: Augsburg Fortress Press, 2000.
Kozhuharov, V. *Misionerskata dejnost na Ruskata pravoslavna c#rkva dnes: dokumenti i analizi* [Missionary Activity of the Russian Orthodox Church Today: Documents and Analysis]. Veliko Trnovo: Vesta, 2008.
———. *Towards an Orthodox Christian Theology of Mission: An Interpretive Approach.* Veliko Trnovo: Vesta, 2006.

Larkin, W. J., and J. F. Williams, eds. *Mission in New Testament*. Maryknoll: Orbis Books, 2002.

Lieven, S. *Duhovnoe probuzhdenie v Rossii* [Spiritual Awakening in Russia]. Light in the East, 1990.

Lubachshenco, V. *Istoria Protestantismu v Ukraine* [The History of Protestantism in Ukraine]. L'viv: Prosvita, 1995.

McClendon, J. Wm. *Biography as Theology: How Life Stories Can Remake Today's Theology*. Eugene: Wipf and Stock Publishers, 2002.

McGavran, D. *The Bridges of God: A Study in the Strategy of Missions*. New York: Friendship Press, 1955.

———., ed. *Church Growth and Christian Mission*. New York: Harper & Row Publishers, 1965.

———. *Effective Evangelism: A Theology Mandate*. Phillipsburg: P & R, 1988.

———. *Momentous Decisions in Missions Today*. Grand Rapids: Baker, 1984.

Meyndorf, J. *Living Tradition: Orthodox Witness in the Contemporary World*. Crestwood: St. Vladimir's Seminary Press, 1978.

Moltmann, J. *The Trinity and the Kingdom: The Doctrine of God*. Translated from German. San Francisco: Harper & Row, 1981.

Neill, S. *Creative Tension*. London: Edinburgh House Press, 1959.

Newbigin, L. *The Open Secret: An Introduction to the Theology of Mission,* revised edition. Grand Rapids: Eerdmans, 1995.

———. *The Relevance of Trinitarian Doctrine for Today's Mission*. London: Edinburgh House Press, WCC Commission on World Evangelism, 1963.

Niles, D. T. *Upon the Earth: The Mission of God and the Missionary Enterprise of the Churches*. New York: McGraw-Hill Book Company, 1962.

Norman, T. *Classic Texts in Mission and World Christianity*. Maryknoll: Orbis Books, 1995.

Oborji, F. A. *Concepts of Mission: The Evolution of the Contemporary Missiology*. Maryknoll: Orbis Books, 2006.

Orjala, P. R. *God's Mission is my Mission*. Kansas City: Nazarene Publishing House, 1985.

Papathanasiou, A. N. *Future and Background of History: Essays on Church Mission in an Age of Globalization*. Montreal: Alexander Press, 2005.

Park, J. S. *Missional Ecclesiologies in Creative Tension: H. Richard Niebuhr and John Howard Yoder*. New York: Peter Lang Publishing, 2007.

Parushev, P., and T. Pilli. "Protestantism in Eastern Europe to the Present Day." In *The Blackwell's Companion to Protestantism*, edited by Alister E. McGrath and Darren C. Marks, 155–160. Oxford: Blackwell, 2004.

Peskett, H., and V. Ramachandra. *The Message of Mission*. Downers Grove: InterVarsity, 2003.

Pocock, M., G. van Reenen, D. McConnell. *The Changing Face of World Missions: Engaging Contemporary Issues and Trends*. Grand Rapids: Baker, 2005.

Pollock, J. C. *The Faith of the Russian Evangelicals*. New York, Toronto: McGraw-Hill, 1964.

Popov, V. *I. S. Prohanov: stranicy zhizni* [I. S. Prokhanov: Pages of Life]. St Petersburg: Biblija dlja vseh, 1996.

———. *Stopy blagovestnika: zhizn' i trudy V. G. Pavlova* [The Footprints of an Evangelist: The Life and Works of V. G. Pavlov]. St Petersburg: Biblija dlja vseh, 1996.

Prokhanov, I. *V kotle Rossii. Avtobiografija Ivana Stepanovicha Prohanova s izlozheniem glavnyh faktov dvizhenija Evangel'skih hristian v Rossii* [In the copper of Russia. Autobiography of Ivan Stepanovich Prokhanov outlining the main facts of the movement of the Evangelical Christians in Russia]. Chicago: World Fellowship of Slavic Evangelical Christians, 1992.

Ramet, S. P. *Nihil Obstat: Religion, Politics, and Social Change in East-Central Europe and Russia*. Durham: Duke University Press, 1998.

Roels, E. D. *God's Mission: The Epistle to the Ephesians in Mission Perspective*. Fraeneker: T. Wever, 1964.

Sawatsky, W. *Evangelicheskoe dvizhenie v SSSR posle Vtoroj mirovoj vojny* [Evangelical Movement in the Soviet Union after the Second World War]. Moscow: ITS-Garant, 1995.

Schmemann, A. *The Eucharist: Sacrament of the Kingdom*. Translated from Russian by Paul Kachur. Crestwood: St Vladimir's Seminary Press, 2003.

Senior, D., and C. Stuhlmueller. *The Biblical Foundations for Missions*. Maryknoll: Orbis Books, 1983.

Shenk, W. *By Faith They Went Out: Mennonite Missions 1850–1999*. Elkhart: Institute for Mennonite Studies, 2000.

———. *Changing Frontiers of Mission*. Maryknoll: Orbis Books, 1999.

———. *Exploring Church Growth*. Grand Rapids: Eerdmans, 1983.

———. "Kingdom, Mission, and Church," in *Exploring Church Growth*. Grand Rapids: Eerdmans, 1983.

Smith, E. L. *God's Mission – and Ours*. Nashville: Abingdon, 1961.

Snyder, H. *Liberating the Church*. Downers Grove: InterVarsity, 1983.

Stamoolis, J. J. *Eastern Orthodox Mission Theology Today*. Maryknoll: Orbis Books, 1986.

Staniloae, D. *Theology and the Church*. Translated from Romanian. Crestwood: St. Vladimir's Seminary Press, 1980.

Stott, J. *Christian Mission in the Modern World*. Downers Grove: InterVarsity, 1975.

———. *Evangelical Truth: A Personal Plea for Unity, Integrity and Faithfulness*. Carlisle: Langham, 2013.

———. *Issues Facing Christians Today*, 4th edition. Grand Rapids: Zondervan, 2006.
Taylor, J. V. *The Go-Between God: The Holy Spirit and the Christian Mission.* Philadelphia: Fortress, 1972.
Van Engen, C. *God's Missionary People: Rethinking the Purpose of the Local Church.* Grand Rapids: Baker, 2001.
———. *Mission on the Way: Issues in Mission Theology.* Grand Rapids: Baker, 1996.
Vassiliadis, P. *Eucharist and Mission: Orthodox Perspective on the Unity and Mission of the Church.* Geneva: WCC publications; Brookline: Holy Cross Orthodox Press, 1998.
Verkuyl, J. *Contemporary Missiology: An Introduction.* Grand Rapids: Eerdmans, 1978, reprinted 1987.
Vicedom, G. F. *The Mission of God.* Translated by A. Thiele and D. Hilgendorf. St Louis: Concordia Publishing, 1965.
Volf, M. *After Our Likeness: The Church as the Image of the Trinity.* Grand Rapids: Eerdmans, 1998.
Wagner, C. P. *Frontiers in Missionary Strategy.* Chicago: Moody Press, 1971.
Walters, P., ed. *World Christianity: Eastern Europe.* Monrovia: MARC, 1988.
Wardin, A.W., ed. *Baptists around the World: A Comprehensive Handbook.* Nashville: Broadman & Holman, 1995.
Warren, R. *The Purpose Driven Church: Growth without Compromising Your Message & Vision.* Grand Rapids: Zondervan, 1995.
West, C. *The Power to be Human: Toward a Secular Theology.* New York: Macmillan, 1971.
Williamson, R. *For Such a Time as This: Sharing in the Mission of God Today.* London: Darton Longman & Todd, 1996.
Wright, C. J. H. *The Mission of God: Unlocking the Bible's Grand Narrative.* Nottingham: IVP, 2006.
Yoder, J. H. *As You Go: The Old Mission in a New Day.* Scottdale: Herald Press, 1961.
Yoder, J. *Christian Attitudes to War, Peace and Revolution: A Companion to Bainton.* Elkhart: Goshen Biblical Seminary, 1983.
———. *For the Nations: Essays Evangelical and Public.* Grand Rapids: Eerdmans, 1997.
———. *The Royal Priesthood: Essays Ecclesiological and Ecumenical.* Scottdale: Herald Press, 1998.
York, J. *Missions in the Age of the Spirit.* Springfield: Gospel Publishing House, 2002.
Zizioulas, J. D. *Communion and Otherness: Further Studies in Personhood and the Church.* New York: T & T Clark, 2006.

Zhuk, S. *Russia's Lost Reformation: Peasants, Millennialism, and Radical Sects in Southern Russia and Ukraine, 1830–1917.* Washington, DC: Woodrow Wilson Center Press; Baltimore and London: The John Hopkins University Press, 2004.

Zuck, R. *A Biblical Theology of the Old Testament.* Chicago: Moody Press, 1991.

Articles, Essays and Component Parts within Books

Adeyemo, T. "A Critical Evaluation of Contemporary Perspectives." In *In Word and Deed: Evangelism and Social Responsibility*, edited by B. Nicholls and Lausanne Committee for World Evangelization and the World Evangelical Fellowship, 41–62. Grand Rapids: Eerdmans, 1985.

Anastasios (Yannoulatos). "Problems and Prospects of Inter-Religious Dialogue: An Eastern Orthodox Perspective." *The Ecumenical Review* 52 (2000): 351–357.

Androviene, L., and P. Parushev. "McClendon's Concept of Mission as Witness." In *Anabaptism and Mission*, edited by W. Shenk and P. Penner, 247–264. Schwarzenfeld: Neufeld Verlag, 2007.

———. "'Tserkov', gosudarstvo I objestvo: o slojnosti uchastia postsovetskih evangeliskih hristian v jizni obshchestva" [Church, State and Culture: On the Complexities of Post-Soviet Evangelical Social Involvement], *Bogoslovskie razmishlenia* [Theological Reflections] 3 (2004): 194–212.

Berman, H. J. "Freedom of Religion in Russia: An Amicus Brief for the Defendant." In *Proselytism and Orthodoxy in Russia: The New War for Souls,* edited by J. Witte and M. Bourdeaux, 265–283. Maryknoll: Orbis Books, 1999.

Bjork, D. E. "Toward a Trinitarian Understanding of Mission in Post-Christendom Lands." *Missiology* 27 (1999): 231–244.

Bondareva-Zuehlke, I. "Separation or Co-operation? Moldavian Baptists (1940–1965)." In *Counter-Cultural Communities: Baptistic Life in Twentieth-Century Europe,* edited by K. G. Jones and I. M. Randall, 63–114. Milton Keynes; Colorado Springs: Paternoster, 2008.

Bosch, D. J. "In Search of a New Evangelical Understanding." In *In Word and Deed: Evangelism and Social Responsibility*, edited by B. Nicholls and Lausanne Committee for World Evangelization and the World Evangelical Fellowship, 63–84. Grand Rapids: Eerdmans, 1985.

Bourdeaux, M. "Religious Liberty in Soviet Union: Baptists in the Early Days of Protest (1960–1966)." In *Eastern European Baptist History: New Perspectives,* edited by Sh. Corrado and T. Pilli, 119–132. Prague: International Baptist Theological Seminary, 2007.

Bratskii Vestnik 4 (1957).

Bratskii Vestnik 5–6 (1958).

Bratskii Vestnik 2 (1959).

Bria, I. "Evangelism, Proselytism and Religious Freedom in Romania: An Orthodox Point of View," *Journal of Ecumenical Studies* 36, no. 1–2 (1999): 163–183.

———. "Looking Anew at Orthodox Theology: Three Recent Consultations," *The Ecumenical Review* 52 (2000): 255–260.

Brother Andrew. "The Church that Loves." In *Proclaim Christ until He Comes: Calling the Whole Church to Take the Whole Gospel to the Whole World*, edited by J. D. Douglas, 132–135. Minneapolis: World Wide Publications, 1990.

Brown, W., R. Grams, and P. Parushev. "Baptists in Moldova." In *Mapping Baptist Identity: Towards an Understanding of European Baptist Identity: Listening to the Churches in Armenia, Bulgaria, Central Asia, Moldova, North Caucasus, Omsk and Poland*, edited by R. Grams and P. Parushev, 113–133. Prague: International Baptist Theological Seminary, 2006.

Bulgac, V. "Apariția mișcării Baptiste în Besarabia (1812–1890)" [The appearance in Bessarabia of the Baptist Movement (1812–1890)]. *Pulse of Ministry* 5 (2002).

Bunaciu, O. "Romanian Baptists and Mission in the Twentieth Century." In *Baptists and Mission: Papers from the Fourth International Conference on Baptist Studies*, edited by I. M. Randall and A. R. Cross, 90–108. Milton Keynes: Paternoster, 2007.

Byford, C. T. "The Movement in Russia: Appendix: Baptist Work among Non-Russian Slavonic Peoples and the Balkan Races Generally." In *The Baptist Movement in the Continent of Europe: A Contribution to Modern History*, edited by J. H. Rushbrooke, 69–86. London: The Carrey Press; The Kingsgate Press, 1915.

Cho, Ch. "The Mission of the Church: Theology and Practice." In *In Word and Deed: Evangelism and Social Responsibility*, edited by B. Nicholls and Lausanne Committee for World Evangelization and the World Evangelical Fellowship, 215–237. Grand Rapids: Eerdmans, 1985.

Chryssavgis, J. "Orthodox Spirituality and Social Activism: Reclaiming Our Vocabulary – Refocusing Our Vision." In *The Orthodox Churches in a Pluralistic World: An Ecumenical Conversation*, edited by E. Clapsis, 130–138. Geneva: WCC Publications; Brookline: Holy Cross Orthodox Press, 2004.

"Communicating the Message: Common Witness/Evangelism/Proselytism (point I. Common Witness), a Group Report." *International Review of Mission* 90, no. 358 (July 2001): 354–357.

Corrado, Sh. "The Gospel in Society: Pashkovite Social Outreach in Late Imperial Russia." In *Eastern European Baptist History: New Perspectives*, edited by Sh. Corrado and T. Pilli, 52–70. Prague: International Baptist Theological Seminary, 2007.

Crum, W. F. "The *Missio Dei* and the Church: An Anglican Perspective." *St Vladimir's Theological Quarterly* 17, no. 4 (1973): 285–289.

Dima N. "Politics and Religion in Moldova." *The Mankind Quarterly* XXXIV, # 3 (Spring 1994): 175–194.

"Dokumenty tret'ej assamblei vsemirnogo soveta cerkvej" [Documents of the Third Assembly of the World Council of Churches held in New Delhi (India) from November 18 to December 6, 1961]. *Bratskij Vestnik* 3 (1962): 6–9.

Elliot, M. "Evangelism and Proselytism in Russia: Synonyms or Antonyms?" *International Bulletin of Missionary Research* 25, no. 2 (April 2001): 72–75.

Elliott M., and A. Deyneka. "Protestant Missionaries in the Former Soviet Union." In *Proselytism and Orthodoxy in Russia: The New War for Souls*, edited by J. Witte and M. Bourdeaux, 197–226. Maryknoll: Orbis Books, 1999.

Engelsviken, T. "Missio Dei: The Understanding and Misunderstanding of a Theological Concept in European Churches and Missiology." *International Review of Mission* XCII, no. 367 (October 2003): 481–497.

Fedorov, V. "Ecumenical Missionary Needs and Perspectives in Eastern and Central Europe Today: Theological Education with an Accent on Mission as a First Priority in Our Religious Rebirth." *International Review of Mission* 92, no. 364 (2003): 66–83.

Fernando, A. "The Church: The Mirror of the Trinity." In *Global Missiology for the 21st Century: The Iguassu Dialogue*, edited by W. D. Taylor, 239–256. Grand Rapids: Baker, 2000.

———. "God: The Source, the Originator, and the End of Mission." In *Global Missiology for the 21st Century: The Iguassu Dialogue*, edited by W. D. Taylor, 191–206. Grand Rapids: Baker, 2000.

———. "The Holy Spirit: the Divine Implementer of Mission." in *Global Missiology for the 21st Century: The Iguassu Dialogue*, edited by W. D. Taylor, 223–238. Grand Rapids: Baker, 2000.

Fiddes, P. S. "Towards a New Millennium: Doctrinal Themes of Strategic Significance for Baptists." In *Baptist Faith and Witness, Book Two: The Papers of the Study and Research Division of the Baptist World Alliance 1995–2000*, edited by T. Cupit, 13–22. McLean: Baptist World Alliance, 1999.

Frieling, R. "Our Common Responsibility in Europe." in *Charta Oecumenica: A Text, a Process and a Dream of the Churches in Europe*, edited by V. Ionita and S. Numico, 60–68. Geneva: WCC Publications, 2003.

Gavrish, O. "Ukrainskoe hristianstvo: bol'she obwego, chem razlichnogo" [Ukrainian Christianity: more alike than different]. *Zerkalo nedeli* [The Mirror of the week] 32, 24 August 2002.

Geldbach, E. "Religious Liberty, Proselytism, Evangelism: Some Baptists Considerations." In *Baptist Faith and Witness, Book Two: The Papers of the Study and Research Division of the Baptist World Alliance 1995-2000*, edited by T. Cupit, 23–28. McLean, VA: Baptist World Alliance, 1999.

Grams, R., and P. Parushev. "Baptists in Moldova," in *Towards an Understanding of European Baptist Identity: Listening to the Churches in Armenia, Bulgaria, Central Asia, Moldova, North Caucasus, Omsk and Poland: Mapping Baptistic Identity*, edited by R. Grams and P. Parushev, 113–133. Prague: International Baptist Theological Seminary, 2006.

———. "Towards a 'Baptistic' Contextual Theology." In *Towards an Understanding of European Baptist Identity: Listening to the Churches in Armenia, Bulgaria, Central Asia, Moldova, North Caucasus, Omsk and Poland: Mapping Baptistic Identity*, edited by R. Grams and P. Parushev, 175–181. Prague: International Baptist Theological Seminary, 2006.

Guroain, V. "Evangelism and Mission in the Orthodox Tradition." In *Sharing the Book: Religious Perspectives on the Rights and Wrongs of Proselytism*, edited by J. Witte and R. C. Martin, 231–246. New York: Orbis Books, 1999.

Hainsworth, D. K. "Deciding for God: The Right to Convert in Protestant Perspectives." In *Sharing the Book: Religious Perspectives on the Rights and Wrongs of Proselytism*, edited by J. Witte and R. C. Martin, 201–230. New York: Orbis Books, 1999.

Hertig, P. "The Jubilee Mission of Jesus in the Gospel of Luke: Reversals of Fortunes." *Missiology* XXVI, no. 2 (1998): 167–180.

Hiebert, J. "Shaping Evangelical Theology in the Postmodern Turn." *Didaskalia* 13 (Spring 2002): 7–23.

Hilarion, Bishop of Vienna and Austria. "Orthodoxy in a New Europe: Problems and Perspectives." *Religion in Eastern Europe* XXIV (June 2004): 18–26.

Hoedemaker, B. "Toward an Epistemological Responsible Missiology." In *To Stake a Claim: Mission and the Western Crisis of Knowledge*, edited by J. A. Kirk, K. J. Vanhoozer, 217–234. Maryknoll: Orbis Books, 1999.

Hoekendijk, J. C. "The Church in Missionary Thinking." *International Review of Missions* 41 (1952): 324–336.

Hopko, Th. "Orthodoxy in Post-Modern Pluralist Societies." *The Ecumenical Review* 51, no. 4 (October 1999): 364–371.

Houston, T. "Good News for the Poor." In *Proclaim Christ until He comes: Calling the Whole Church to Take the Whole Gospel to the Whole World. International Congress on World Evangelization 1989*, 153–154. Lausanne Committee, 1989.

Howe, A. "The Church: Its Growth and Mission." In *The Challenge of Church Growth: A Symposium,* edited by W. Shenk, 49–64. Scottdale: Herald Press, 1973.

Ioann, Archbishop of Belgorod and Stariy Oskol. "Ecclesiological and Canonical Foundations of Orthodox Mission." Translated from Russian, *International Review of Mission* 90, no. 358 (2001): 270–279.

Ivanov, I. "Po obshchinam Moldavii" [On the Moldavian Congregations]. *Bratskii Vestnik* 5 (1946): 35–38.

———. "Iz istorii evangel'sko-baptistskogo dvijenia. Vospominania o vozniknovenii dela Gospodnego v Moldavii" [From the history of Evangelical-Baptist movement. Memoirs about birth of Lord's deeds in Moldavia]. *Bratskii Vestnik* 2 (1955): 53–62.

Jackson, D. "Proselytism in a Central and Eastern European Perspective." *Journal of European Baptist Studies* 8, no. 2 (January 2008): 18–36.

Jidcov, M. I. "Evropejskaja molodezhnaja jekumenicheskaja assambleja v Lozanne" [European Youth Ecumenical Assembly in Lausanne (Switzerland) from 13 to 24 July 1960]. *Bratskij Vestnik* 5-6 (1960): 27–29.

———. "Jekumenicheskoe bogosluzhenie" [Ecumenical Service at Bethlehem Chapel in Prague] *Bratskij Vestnik* 4 (1961): 11–12.

Jinkins, M. "The Gift of the Church: *Ecclesia Crucis, Peccatrix Maxima*, and the *Missio Dei.*" In *Evangelical Ecclesiology: Reality or Illusion?,* edited by J. Stackhouse, 179–209. Grand Rapids: Baker, 2003.

Kallistos, Bishop of Diokleia. "The Witness of the Orthodox Church." *The Ecumenical Review* 52 (2000): 46–56.

Karev, A. V. "Kak zarodilos' i razvivalos' jekumenicheskoe dvizhenie." [Origin and Development of the Ecumenical Movement]. *Bratskij Vestnik* 2 (1959): 65–74.

Kassab, N. "Partnership in God's Mission: Community of Women and Men in Church Today." In *Partnership in God's Mission in the Middle East: The Papers and Report of the Consultation of Women and Men of Reformed Tradition in the Middle East, Ayia Napa, Cyprus, 2-8 June 1996*, edited by J. D. Douglass and P. Réamonn. Geneva: World Alliance of Reformed Churches, 1998.

Kim, K. "The Potential of Pneumatology for Mission in Contemporary Europe." *International Review of Mission* 95, no. 378–379, July/October (2006): 334–340.

Kozhuharov, V. "Developments in the Mission of the Russian Orthodox Church." *Acta Missiologiae, Journal for Reflection on Missiological Issues and Mission Practices in Central and Eastern Europe* 2 (2009): 7–26.

Larentzakis, G. "We Believe in 'One Holy Catholic and Apostolic Church'." In *Charta Oecumenica: A Text, a Process and a Dream of the Churches in Europe*, edited by V. Ionita and S. Numico, 49–55. Geneva: WCC Publications, 2003.

The Light of Life 5 (1929).

The Light of Life 6–7 (1930).

The Light of Life 11 (1931).

The Light of Life 1 (1995).

The Light of Life 1 (1996).

The Light of Life 1 (1997).

Malancea, M. "From the Editor." *Pulse of ministry* 1 (April 2000).

Matthey, J. "Evangelism, Still the Enduring Test of Our Ecumenical – and Missionary Calling." *International Review of Mission* 96, no. 382 (July/October 2007): 355–367.

———. "God's Mission Today: Summary and Conclusions." *International Review of Mission* XCII, no. 367 (October 2003): 579–587.

McIntosh, J. "Missio Dei." In *Evangelical Dictionary of World Mission*, edited by A. S. Moreau, H. A. Netland, C. E. van Engen and D. Burnett, 631–633. Grand Rapids: Baker; Carlisle: Paternoster, 2000.

McPhee, A. "Authentic Witness, Authentic Evangelism, Authentic Church." In *Evangelical, Ecumenical, and Anabaptist Missiologies in Conversation: Essays in Honour of Wilbert R. Shenk*, edited by J. R. Krabill, W. Sawatsky, and C. Van Engen, 130–139. Maryknoll: Orbis Books, 2006.

Metropolitan Kirill of Smolensk and Kaliningrad. "Gospel and Culture" (text speech presented at World Council of Churches Conference on World Mission and Evangelism, November 1996, Bahia, Brazil). In *Proselytism and Orthodoxy in Russia: The New War for Souls*, edited by J. Witte and M. Bourdeaux, 66–76. Maryknoll: Orbis Books, 1999.

Mikhalchuk, P. "Aggravation of Relations." *The Light of Life* 3, 25 (2000).

Mickievich, A. "Iz istorii evangel'sko-baptistskogo dvijenia. Vospominania o vozniknovenii dela Gospodnego v Moldavii" [From the history of evangelical-baptist movement. Memoirs about birth of Lord's deeds in Moldavia]. *Bratskii Vestnik* 2 (1955): 53–62.

———. "Vtoraja konferencija evropejskih cerkvej" [Second Conference of European Churches]. *Bratskij Vestnik* 1 (1961): 16–17.

Nassif, B. "Are Eastern Orthodoxy and Evangelicalism compatible? Yes. The Evangelical theology of the Eastern Orthodox Church." In *Three Views on*

Eastern Orthodoxy and Evangelicalism, edited by S. N. Gundry and J. J. Stamoolis. Grand Rapids: Zondervan, 2004.

Negrov, A., and T. Nikol'skaia. "Baptists as a Symbol of Sectarianism in Soviet and Post-Soviet Russia." In *Eastern European Baptist History: New Perspectives*, edited by S. Corrado and T. Pilli, 133–142. Prague: International Baptist Theological Seminary, 2007.

Nichols, G. L. "Ivan Kargel and the Pietistic Community of the Late Imperial Russia." In *Eastern European Baptist History: New Perspectives*, edited by S. Corrado and T. Pilli, 71–87. Prague: International Baptist Theological Seminary, 2007.

Oborji, F. A. "Mission as Ecumenical Dialogue." In *Concepts of Mission: The Evolution of the Contemporary Missiology*, edited by F. A. Oborji, 153–180. Maryknoll: Orbis Books, 2006.

Oeldemann, J. "The Concept of Canonical Territory in the Russian Orthodox Church." In *Religion and the Conceptual Boundary in Central and Eastern Europe: Encounters of Faith*, edited by T. S. Bremer, 229–236. New York: Palgrave Macmillan, 2008.

Orlov, I. M. "Otchiot Starshego Presvitera I.T. Slobodchikova" [Report of the Senior Presbyter I.T. Slobodchikov]. *Bratskii Vestnik* 3 (1948): 66–67.

———. "Vstrecha hristian Vostoka i Zapada v Zheneve" [Encounter Between East and West Christians]. *Bratskij Vestnik* 4 (1962): 22.

Papanikolaou, A. "Orthodoxy, Postmodernity, and Ecumenism: The Difference that Divine-Human Communion Makes." *Journal of Ecumenical Studies* 42, no. 4 (Fall 2007): 527–546.

Parushev, P. "Baptistic Conventional Hermeneutics." In *The "Plainly Revealed" Word of God?*, edited by H. Dare and S. Woodman. Macon: Mercer University Press, 2011.

———. "On Some Developments in Russian Orthodox Theology and Tradition." In *Baptists and the Orthodox Church: On the Way to Understanding*, edited by I. Randall, 81–97. Praha: International Baptist Theological Seminary, 2003.

Pasztor, J. "God's Mission Taken Up as the Mission of the Church." In *Hope for the World: Mission in Global Context. Papers from Campbell Seminar*, edited by W. Brueggemann, 137–150. Louisville: Westminster John Knox Press, 2001.

Penner, P. "Peace Identity – Peace Witness? A Case Study From East European Context." In *Anabaptism and Mission*, edited by W. Shenk and P. Penner, 185–207. Schwarzenfeld: Neufeld Verlag, 2007.

Pilli, T. "Baptist History in Moldova." In *A Dictionary of European Baptist Life and Thought*, edited by J. H. Briggs, 335–337. Milton Keynes; Colorado Springs: Paternoster, 2009.

———. "Baptist Identities in Eastern Europe." In *Baptist Identities: International Studies From Seventeenth to the Twentieth Century*, edited by I. M. Randall, T. Pilli, and A. Cross. Milton Keynes: Paternoster, 2006.

Poitras, E. W. "St. Augustine and the *Missio Dei*: A Reflection on Mission at the Close of the Twentieth Century." *Mission Studies* 16, no. 32 (1999): 28–46.

Ponomarchiuk, D. I. "Starshii presviter VSEHB po Moldavskoi SSR brat D.I. Ponomarchiuk soobshchaet" [Senior Presbyter AUCECB in Moldavian SSR brother D.I. Ponomarchiuk reports]. *Bratskii Vestnik* 4 (1957): 77–78.

Pope, E. A. "Ecumenism, Religious Freedom, and the 'National Church' Controversy in Romania." *Journal of Ecumenical Studies* 36, no. 1–2 (Winter-Spring, 1999): 184–201.

Popov, V. "Evangel'skie hristiane-pashkovcy. Voznikonovenie i duhovno-prosvetitel'skoe sluzhenie" [*Evangelical Christians-Pashkovtsy*. The emergence and the spiritual and educational ministry]. *Bogomyslie* [Theological thinking] 7 (1998).

"Poseshchenie obshchin Moldavskoi SSR starshim presviterom bratom F.R. Astahovim" [Senior Presbyter F.R. Astahov visits congregations in Moldavian SSR]. *Bratskii Vestnik* 6 (1956): 51–55.

Prokhorov, C. "The State and the Baptist Churches in the USSR (1960–1980)." In *Counter-Cultural Communities: Baptistic Life in Twentieth-Century Europe*, edited by I. M. Randall and K. G. Jones, 1–54. Milton Keynes; Colorado Springs: Paternoster, 2008.

Reshetnikov, Y. "Istorija Evangel'sko-baptistskogo dvizhenija v Ukraine" [History of the Evangelical Baptist movement in Ukraine]. *Bogomyslie* 6 (1997).

Reimer, J. "Mission as Kenotic Action: Understanding Orthodox Theology of Mission." *Missionalia* 32, no. 1 (April 2004): 68–83.

Richebacher, W. "Willingen 1952 – Willingen 2002." *International Review of Mission* XCII, no. 367 (October 2003): 463–468.

Ross, C. "The Theology of Partnership." *International Bulletin of Missionary Research* 34, no. 3 (July 2010): 145–148.

Ryaguzov, B. "Biblejskie osnovy blagovestija" [Biblical basis of evangelism]. *Bratskij Vestnik* 4 (1990): 73–83.

Samuel, V. "Mission as Transformation." In *Mission as Transformation: A Theology of the Whole Gospel*, edited by V. Samuel and C. Sugden. Oxford: Regnum Books International, 1999.

Samuel, V., and C. Sugden. "Evangelism and Social Responsibility: A Biblical Study on Priorities." In *In Word and Deed: Evangelism and Social Responsibility*, edited by B. Nicholls and Lausanne Committee for World Evangelization and the World Evangelical Fellowship, 189–214. Grand Rapids: Eerdmans, 1985.

Sasaujan, M. "Romanian Orthodox Theologians as Pioneers of the Ecumenical Dialogue Between East and West: The relevance and Topicality of Their Position in United Europe." In *Religion and the Conceptual Boundary in Central and Eastern Europe: Encounters of Faith*, edited by T. Bremer, 146–165. New York: Palgrave MacMillan, 2008.

Sawatsky, W. "The Re-positioning of Evangelical Christians-Baptists and Sister Church Union Between 1980 and 2005." In *Eastern European Baptist History: New Perspectives*, edited by S. Corrado and T. Pilli, 187–209. Prague: International Baptist Theological Seminary, 2007.

Scherer, J. A. "Church, Kingdom, and *Missio Dei*: Lutheran and Orthodox Correctives to Recent Ecumenical Mission Theology." In *The Good News of the Kingdom Mission Theology for the Third Millennium*, edited by C. Van Engen, D. S. Gilliland, and P. Pierson, 82–88. Maryknoll: Orbis Books, 1993.

Schultz, C. "Soul." In *Evangelical Dictionary of Biblical Theology*, edited by W. A. Elwell, 743–744. Grand Rapids: Baker; Carlisle: Paternoster, 1996.

Sedletski K. S. "Otchiotnii doklad episkopa soiuza tserkvei evangeliskih khristian-baptistov Moldovi 26-mu siezdu moldavskogo bratstva" [Final Report of the Bishop of the Union of the Evangelical Christian Baptist Churches to the 26 Congress of Moldavian Brotherhood]. *Bratskii Vestnik* 4 (1992): 87–88.

Shenk, W. "An Anabaptist View of Mission." In *Anabaptism and Mission*, edited by W. Shenk and P. Penner. Schwarzenfeld: Neufeld Verlag, 2007.

———. "Crossing Frontiers." In *Anabaptism and Mission*, edited by W. Shenk and P. Penner. Schwarzenfeld: Neufeld Verlag, 2007.

———. "Church Growth Studies: A Bibliography Review." In *The Challenge of the Church Growth: A Symposium*, edited by W. Shenk, 7–24. Scottdale: Herald Press, 1973.

———. "Forging Theology of Mission from an Anabaptist Perspective." *Mission Insight* 13 (2000).

———. "Three Studies in Mission Strategy." In *Anabaptism and Mission*, edited by W. R. Shenk and P. F. Penner, 8–58. Schwarzenfeld: Neufeld Verlag, 2007.

———. "Which Paradigm for Mission?" In *Mission Focus*, edited by W. Shenk, 159–168. Scottdale: Herald Press 1980.

Sinichkin, A. "I oni poshli . . ." [And they went . . .]. *Missioner* [The Missionary] 1 (2004).

Smith, N. "From *Missio Dei* to *Missio Hominum*, En Route in Christian Mission and Missiology." *Missionalia* 30, no. 1 (April 2002): 4–21.

Sokolov, E. "Konferencija po evangelizacii i missii" [Conference on evangelism and missions]. *Bratskij Vestnik* 4 (1990): 63–72.

Stalnaker, C. "Proselytism or Evangelism?" *ERT* 26, no. 4 (2002): 337–353.
Stransky, T. "Missio Dei." In *Dictionary of the Ecumenical Movement*, edited by Nicolas Lossky, 687–689. Geneva: WCC Publications; Grand Rapids: Eerdmans, 1991
Sundermeier, T. "*Missio Dei* Today: On the Identity on Christian Mission." *International Review of Mission* XCII, no. 367 (October 2003): 260–278.
Tan Seng-Kong. "A Trinitarian Ontology of Missions." *International Review of Mission* 93, 369 (April 2004): 279–296.
Teplitskaya, N. "Istorija teologo-pedagogicheskogo kolledzha" [History of the college of Theology and Education]. *Pulse of Ministry* 7 (2003).
Thangaraj, M. T. "Evangelism *sans* Proselytism: A Possibility?" In *Sharing the Book: Religious Perspectives on the Rights and Wrongs of Proselytism*, edited by J. Witte and R. C. Martin, 335–352. New York: Orbis Books, 1999.
Tobler, S. "The Ecumenical Situation in Romania and the Ecumenical Research Institute in Sibiu." In *The Future of Ecumenical Theological Education in Eastern and Central Europe. Full Report of the International Seminar for Young Lectures and Professors of Theology, Sambata de Sus, Romania, 24-28 September 2008*, edited by V. Ionita and D. Werner, 43–48. Geneva: Conference of European Churches, World Council of Churches, 2009.
Torfs, R. "Experiences of Western Democracies in Dealing with the Legal Position of Churches and Religious Communities." In *Legal Position of Churches and Religious Communities in South-Eastern Europe*, edited by S. Devetak, L. Kalcina, and M. Polzer, 19–25. Maribor: ISCOMET; Ljubljana: IDSE; Vienna: OSI, 2004.
Trubin, V. "Jekumenicheskoe bogosluzhenie v MOEHB" [Ecumenical Church Service in the Moscow Community of Evangelical Christian Baptists]. *Bratskij Vestnik* 5-6 (1962): 12–16.
Uzzell, L. A. "Don't call It Proselytism." *First Things* (October 2004): 14–16.
Vassiliadis, P. "Mission and Proselytism: An Orthodox Understanding." *International Review of Mission* 85, no. 337 (1996): 257–275.
———. "Reconciliation as a Pneumatological Mission Paradigm: Some Preliminary Reflections by an Orthodox." *International Review of Mission* 94, no. 372 (January 2005): 30–42.
Verkuyl, J. "The Kingdom of God as the Goal of the *Missio Dei*." *International Review of Mission* 270 (1969): 168–175.
Vogelaar, H. "An Ecumenical Journey in Romania: Orthodox – Protestant Relationships Since 1989." *Exchange* 33, no. 3 (2006): 269–295.
Webster, A. F. C. "Evangelicals vs. Orthodox in Romania." *The Christian Century* (May 30–June 6, 1990): 560–561.

Western European Working Group. "Mission in God's Mission." in *Planning for Mission: Working Papers on the New Quest for Missionary Communities*, edited by T. Wieser, 48–52. London: Epworth Press, 1966.

Wolanin, A. "Trinitarian Foundation of Mission in Following Christ in Mission." In *Following Christ in Mission,* edited by S. Karotemprel, 47–64. Boston: Pauline Books & Media, 1996.

Yoder, J. "Church Growth Issues in Theological Perspective." In *The Challenge of the Church Growth: A Symposium*, edited by W. Shenk, 25–48. Scottdale: Herald Press.

Theses and Dissertations

Godwin, C. R. "Baptising, Gathering, and Sending: The Significance of Anabaptist Approaches to Mission in the Sixteenth-century Context." (A thesis submitted for the Degree of Doctor of Philosophy, University of Wales through International Baptist Theological Seminary, 2010).

Jones, K. G. "The European Baptist Federation: A Case Study in European Baptist Interdependency 1950-2006." (Thesis submitted for the degree of Doctor of Philosophy, University of Wales, 2007). Published as a book *European Baptist Federation: A Case Study in European Baptist Interdependency 1950-2006,* foreword by Ian M. Randall. Milton Keynes, Colorado Springs, Hyderabad: Paternoster, 2009.

McConnell, R. T. "Indigenous Baptists and Foreign Missionaries: Baptist Communities in Romania, Hungary, and Yugoslavia 1872-1980." (A dissertation submitted as partial fulfillment of the requirements for the degree of Doctor of Philosophy in the Department of History, University of South California, 1996).

Nichols, G. L. "Ivan V. Kargel (1849-1937) and the Development of Russian Evangelical Spirituality." (A thesis submitted for the Degree of Doctor of Philosophy, University of Wales through International Baptist Theological Seminary, 2009).

Parushev, P. "Walking in the Dawn of the Light: On the Salvation Ethics of the Ecclesial Communities in the Orthodox Tradition from a Radical Reformation Perspective." (PhD dissertation, Schools of Theology, Fuller Theological Seminary, 2006).

Popov, A. "The Evangelical Christian Baptists in the Soviet Union as a Hermeneutical Community: Examining the Identity of the All-Union Council of the ECB (AUCECB) Through the Way the Bible Was Used in Its Publications." (A thesis submitted for the Degree of Doctor of

Philosophy, University of Wales through International Baptist Theological Seminary, 2010).

Shemchishin, V. "History of Evangelical Christian Baptists in the Southern Bessarabia." (A thesis for the Doctor of Ministry Degree).

Electronic Sources

CGIAU of the Kamenetz-Podolsk office, *Podolsk* Spiritual *Consistory.* Fund 315, inv. I Volume I; units. 9808, l.52. [CD-ROM]. *History of the Evangelical movement in Eurasia, 3.0.* Odessa: Euro-Asian Accrediting Association.

Istorija EHB v SSSR [History of Evangelical Christians Baptists in the USSR]. Moscow, AUCECB publishing house, 1989. [CD-ROM]. *Evangelical movement in Eurasia, 2.0.* Odessa: Euro-Asian Accrediting Association.

Regional State Archive of Zhytomyr region. F.1 inv. 22 E 1336, sheet 40, the first letter. *Evangelical Movement in Russia, 3.0.* [CD-ROM]. Odessa: Euro-Asian Accrediting Association.

State Archive of Odesa Oblast. F.37 inv.1 D 3797, pp. 2–3. *History of the Evangelical movement in Eurasia, 3.0.* [CD-ROM]. Odessa: Euro-Asian Accrediting Association.

Interviews
(in chronological order)

Interview with Olga Mocan, October 2002.
Interview with Irina Bondareva, September 2005.
Alexandr Girbu to author, November 2005.
Ghenadie Russu to the author, February 2006.
Valeriu Ghiletchi to the author, December, 2006.
Interview with Vadim Bulgac, May 2007.
Lilia Bulat to the author, May 2007.
Natasha Affermann to the author, December 2007.
Miroslav Matrenczyk to the author, June 2010.
Interview with Fiodor Mocan, August 2010.
Interview with Alla Alexeeva, September 2010.
Group Discussion with Sergey Namesnic, December 14, 2010.
Bill Prevette to the author, September 2011.

Web Sources

"Basic principles related to the attitude of the Russian Orthodox Church towards Non-Orthodox." Article 1.16, http://www.patriarchia.ru/db/text/418840.html, accessed 26.08.2010.

"The Basis of the Social Concept of the Russian Orthodox Church." http://www.mospat.ru/en/documents/social-concepts/i.

"The concept of the missionary activities of the Russian Orthodox Church," §2.1. http://www.mospat.ru/en/documents/social-concepts/ii/ accessed 13 August 2011.

Ghiletchi, V. Interview with the Bishop of the Union of Evangelical Christian Baptist Churches of Moldova, http://mdn.md/ru/index.php?view=viewarticle&articleid=944, accessed 25 November 2004.

Nazarkina, E. "The Social Image of the Protestant Communities in Modern Ukraine," http://www.religio.ru/relisoc/97.phpl.

Nevolin, M. "The Theological, Structural and Social Self-identification of Russian Protestants," http://www.kbogu.ru/?3-5-21.

Maximilian, A. "Causes of the Conflict Between the Metropolitan of Moldova and the Metropolitan of Bessarabia" at http://www.mitropoliabasarabiei.ro/cauzele_conflictului.html accessed 02 February 2008.

Pavlov, I. "Missionerskaja dejatel'nost' Russkoj Pravoslavnoj Cerkvi" [The missionary activity of the Russian Orthodox Church], http://www.portal-credo.ru/site/index.php?act=lib&id=1536 accessed 06 September 2011.

"Proselytizing and Religious Freedom in Moldova" Article 4, paragraph 4, http://kultam.net/rus/Ukraine/Science/ExpertOpinions/article-28 of 2009.03.16

Venediktov, I. "The Reunification of the Russian Orthodox Church and the Moldovan Christians" at http://www.mdn.md/ru/ortodoxal.php?rubr=3144 accessed 22 July 2007.

Langham Literature and its imprints are a ministry of Langham Partnership.

Langham Partnership is a global fellowship working in pursuit of the vision God entrusted to its founder John Stott –

to facilitate the growth of the church in maturity and Christ-likeness through raising the standards of biblical preaching and teaching.

Our vision is to see churches in the majority world equipped for mission and growing to maturity in Christ through the ministry of pastors and leaders who believe, teach and live by the Word of God.

Our mission is to strengthen the ministry of the Word of God through:
- nurturing national movements for biblical preaching
- fostering the creation and distribution of evangelical literature
- enhancing evangelical theological education

especially in countries where churches are under-resourced.

Our ministry

Langham Preaching partners with national leaders to nurture indigenous biblical preaching movements for pastors and lay preachers all around the world. With the support of a team of trainers from many countries, a multi-level programme of seminars provides practical training, and is followed by a programme for training local facilitators. Local preachers' groups and national and regional networks ensure continuity and ongoing development, seeking to build vigorous movements committed to Bible exposition.

Langham Literature provides majority world preachers, scholars and seminary libraries with evangelical books and electronic resources through publishing and distribution, grants and discounts. The programme also fosters the creation of indigenous evangelical books in many languages, through writer's grants, strengthening local evangelical publishing houses, and investment in major regional literature projects, such as one volume Bible commentaries like *The Africa Bible Commentary* and *The South Asia Bible Commentary*.

Langham Scholars provides financial support for evangelical doctoral students from the majority world so that, when they return home, they may train pastors and other Christian leaders with sound, biblical and theological teaching. This programme equips those who equip others. Langham Scholars also works in partnership with majority world seminaries in strengthening evangelical theological education. A growing number of Langham Scholars study in high quality doctoral programmes in the majority world itself. As well as teaching the next generation of pastors, graduated Langham Scholars exercise significant influence through their writing and leadership.

To learn more about Langham Partnership and the work we do visit **langham.org**

www.ingramcontent.com/pod-product-compliance
Lightning Source LLC
Chambersburg PA
CBHW070233240426
43673CB00044B/1773